ture Notes in Computer Science

d by G. Goos, J. Hartmanis and J. van Leeuwen

T0238016

pringer

erlin
eidelberg
ew York
arcelona
ong Kong
ondon
ilan
aris
ngapore
okyo

ard Heys Carlisle Adams (Eds.)

elected Areas
Cryptography

Annual International Workshop, SAC'99
gston, Ontario, Canada, August 9-10, 1999
eedings

 Springer

Series Editors

Gerhard Goos, Karlsruhe University, Germany
Juris Hartmanis, Cornell University, NY, USA
Jan van Leeuwen, Utrecht University, The Netherlands

Volume Editors

Howard Heys
Faculty of Engineering and Applied Science
Memorial University of Newfoundland
St. John's, Newfoundland, Canada A1B 3X5
E-mail: howard@engr.mun.ca

Carlisle Adams
Entrust Technologies
50 Heron Road, Suite E08
Ottawa, Ontario, Canada K1V 1A7
E-mail: cadams@entrust.com

Cataloging-in-Publication Data applied for

Die Deutsche Bibliothek - CIP-Einheitsaufnahme

Selected areas in cryptography : 6th annual international workshop ;
proceedings / SAC '99, Kingston, Ontario, Canada, August 9 - 11,
1999. Howard Heys ; Carlisle Adams (ed.). - Berlin ; Heidelberg ; New
York ; Barcelona ; Hong Kong ; London ; Milan ; Paris ; Singapore ;
Tokyo : Springer, 2000
(Lecture notes in computer science ; Vol. 1758)
ISBN 3-540-67185-4

CR Subject Classification (1991): E.3, C.2, D.4.6, K.6.5, F.2.1-2, H.4.3

ISSN 0302-9743
ISBN 3-540-67185-4 Springer-Verlag Berlin Heidelberg New York

Springer-Verlag is a company in the specialist publishing group BertelsmannSpringer
© Springer-Verlag Berlin Heidelberg 2000
Printed in Germany

Typesetting: Camera-ready by author
Printed on acid-free paper   SPIN 10719627   57/3144   5 4 3 2 1 0

Preface

SAC'99 was the sixth in a series of annual workshops on Selected Areas in Cryptography. Previous workshops were held at Carleton University in Ottawa (1995 and 1997) and at Queen's University in Kingston (1994, 1996, and 1998). The intent of the annual workshop is to provide a relaxed atmosphere in which researchers in cryptography can present and discuss new work on selected areas of current interest. The themes for the SAC'99 workshop were:

- Design and Analysis of Symmetric Key Cryptosystems
- Efficient Implementations of Cryptographic Systems
- Cryptographic Solutions for Web/Internet Security

The timing of the workshop was particularly fortuitous as the announcement by NIST of the five finalists for AES coincided with the first morning of the workshop, precipitating lively discussion on the merits of the selection!

A total of 29 papers were submitted to SAC'99 and, after a review process that had all papers reviewed by at least 3 referees, 17 were accepted and presented. As well, two invited presentations were given: one by Miles Smid from NIST entitled "From DES to AES: Twenty Years of Government Initiatives in Cryptography" and the other by Mike Reiter from Bell Labs entitled "Password Hardening with Applications to VPN Security".

The program committee for SAC'99 consisted of the following members: Carlisle Adams, Tom Cusick, Howard Heys, Lars Knudsen, Henk Meijer, Luke O'Connor, Doug Stinson, Stafford Tavares, and Serge Vaudenay. As well, additional reviewers were: Christian Cachin, Louis Granboulan, Helena Handschuh, Julio Lopez Hernandez, Mike Just, Alfred Menezes, Serge Mister, Guillaume Poupard, Victor Shoup, Michael Wiener, and Robert Zuccherato.

The organizers are very grateful for the financial support for the workshop received from Entrust Technologies, the Department of Electrical and Computer Engineering at Queen's University, and Communications and Information Technology Ontario (CITO). Special thanks to Stafford and Henk must be given for, once again, hosting SAC and being responsible for all the local arrangement details. The organizers would also like to thank Sheila Hutchison of the Department of Electrical and Computer Engineering at Queen's University for administrative and secretarial help and Yaser El-Sayed from the Faculty of Engineering at Memorial University of Newfoundland for help in preparing the workshop proceedings.

On behalf of the SAC'99 organizing committee, we thank all the workshop participants for making SAC'99 a success!

November 1999   Howard Heys and Carlisle Adams

Organization

Program Committee

Howard Heys (co-chair)	Memorial University of Newfoundland
Carlisle Adams (co-chair)	Entrust Technologies, Ottawa
Tom Cusick	SUNY, Buffalo
Lars Knudsen	University of Bergen
Henk Meijer	Queen's University at Kingston
Luke O'Connor	IBM, Zurich
Doug Stinson	University of Waterloo
Stafford Tavares	Queen's University at Kingston
Serge Vaudenay	Ecole Normale Supérieure, Paris

Local Organizing Committee

Stafford Tavares	Queen's University at Kingston
Henk Meijer	Queen's University at Kingston

Table of Contents

Cryptography for Network Applications

A Universal Encryption Standard

Helena Handschuh[1] and Serge Vaudenay[2]

[1] Gemplus – ENST
handschuh@gemplus.com
[2] Ecole Normale Supérieure – CNRS
Serge.Vaudenay@dmi.ens.fr

Abstract. DES and triple-DES are two well-known and popular encryption algorithms, but they both have the same drawback: their block size is limited to 64 bits. While the cryptographic community is working hard to select and evaluate candidates and finalists for the AES (Advanced Encryption Standard) contest launched by NIST in 1997, it might be of interest to propose a secure and simple double block-length encryption algorithm. More than in terms of key length and block size, our Universal Encryption Standard is a new construction that remains totally compliant with DES and triple-DES specifications as well as with AES requirements.

1 Introduction

For many years, DES [9] has been used as a worldwide encryption standard. But as technology improved for specialized key-search machines [26,8], its 56-bit key size became too short, and a replacement was needed. 2-key triple-DES has since become the traditional block cipher used both by the cryptographic community as well as industry. However, there is a second drawback to DES which is also the case for triple-DES: its 64-bit block size. Therefore NIST launched a contest to select and evaluate candidates for a new encryption standard, the AES, in late 1997 [1]. The basic requirements for this new algorithm were that it be at least as secure and fast as triple-DES, but that its block size be of 128 bits instead of 64, and that its key size take possible values of 128, 192 and 256 bits.

Meanwhile, people are still using DES and triple-DES, and may want to start developping applications where these two as well as the new AES may independently be used as the encryption components. In order to be compliant with DES and triple-DES, we propose a new construction which is based on these building blocks, but which can take AES specifications as a requirement for its key and block sizes. Therefore, when AES is finally selected, it will come as a natural plug-in replacement of the actual structure whithout anybody being forced to change input and output interfaces.

We notice that double block-length encryption primitives based on DES already exist: as an example, take DEAL, which uses DES as the round function in a traditional 6-round Feistel scheme [16]. One can also think of multiple modes

Howard Heys and Carlisle Adams (Eds.): SAC'99, LNCS 1758, pp. 1–12, 2000.

with two blocks, where DES is the underlying cipher [10], but except for two-key triple DES in outer CBC mode which is vulnerable to dictionary and matching ciphertext attacks, none of these constructions are backward compliant with DES and triple-DES, nore do they make use of the full strength of a 128-bit block size (the second half of the plaintext never influences the first half of the ciphertext). Furthermore, multiple modes are either insecure [3,4,5,6] or require confidentiality or integrity protected initial values [25,11]. We are also aware of the attacks by Lucks on 3-key triple DES [18] and DEAL [19].

The rest of the paper is organized as follows: section 2 presents our new encryption standard. Sections 3 and 4 provide details on collision attacks when some of the components of our UES are cut out. Section 5 provides additional security arguments on our construction and evaluates its strength based on the FX construction. Finally, we argue why we believe our construction is sound.

2 A Universal Encryption Standard

In this section we give the specifications of our new double block-length encryption algorithm. It basically runs two triple-DES encryptions in parallel and exchanges some of the bits of both halves inbetween each of the three encryption layers. Note that Outerbridge proposed a similar idea [21]. We investigated several related constructions and decided to add pre and post-whitening with extra keys, as well as an additional layer where bits of the left and the right half of the scheme are swapped under control of the extended secret key. Justification for these final choices will be given throughout this paper. The key schedule is considered to be the same as DEAL's.

2.1 Notations

We use the following notations for our scheme as well as for the attacks presented in the next sections (all operations are on bitstrings):

$a|b$: concatenation of a and b
$a \oplus b$: bitwise "exclusive or" of a and b
$a \wedge b$: bitwise "and" of a and b
$\bar{a}$: bitwise 1-complement of a
001110100111_b : bitstring in binary notation
$3a7_x$: bitstring in hexadecimal notation with implicit length (multiple of four)

In addition we let $\text{DES}_k(x)$ denote the DES encryption of a 64-bit block x by using a 56-bit key k, and we let $3\text{DES}_{k_1,k_2}(x)$ denote the 2-key triple-DES encryption of x in EDE mode (Encryption followed by Decryption followed by Encryption), $i.e.$

$$3\text{DES}_{k_1,k_2}(x) = \text{DES}_{k_1}\left(\text{DES}_{k_2}^{-1}\left(\text{DES}_{k_1}(x)\right)\right).$$

2.2 Basic Building Blocks

We already mentioned that we use parallel 3DES as well as a kind of keyed swap. In order to further formalize our proposal, let us define the following three basic building blocks which refer to operations on 128-bit strings. For convenience, we split a 128-bit string x into two 64-bit halves x_h and x_l.

1. **Keyed Translation.** Let $k = k_h|k_l$ be a 128-bit string. We define

$$T_k(x) = x \oplus k.$$

2. **Keyed Swap.** Let k be a 64-bit string. We define

$$S_k(x) = (x_h \oplus u)|(x_l \oplus u)$$

where $u = (x_h \oplus x_l) \wedge k$. This actually consists of exchanging the bits which are masked by k in the two halves.

3. **Parallel Encryption.** Let $k = k_h|k_l$ be two concatenated keys for two keyed algorithms C and C'. We define

$$P_{k,C,C'}(x) = C_{k_h}(x_h)|C'_{k_l}(x_l).$$

Our algorithm is a combination of three rounds of products of these transformations with additional operations before the first and after the last encryption layer.

2.3 Our New DES and 3DES-Compliant Construction

Having defined the above components, let $m = \texttt{00000000ffffffff}_x$, and let $k' = k_1|k_2|k_3|k_4$ and $m' = m_1|m_2|m_3|m_4$ be respectively two 256-bit extended keys derived from k by the key schedule.

Definition 1.

$$\text{UES}_k^* = P_{k_1|k_3,\text{DES},\text{DES}} \circ S_m \circ P_{k_2|k_4,\text{DES}^{-1},\text{DES}^{-1}} \circ S_m \circ P_{k_1|k_3,\text{DES},\text{DES}}$$

See figure 1. Then the precise formula to encrypt a plaintext under key k using UES reads as follows:

Definition 2.

$$\text{UES}_k = S_{m_4} \circ T_{m_3|m_3} \circ \text{UES}_k^* \circ T_{m_2|m_2} \circ S_{m_1}$$

See figure 2. This algorithm has two interesting properties. Namely if we set $m' = 0$ and $k' = k$, we have

Property 1.

$$\text{UES}_{k_1|k_2|k_1|k_2}(x_l|x_l) = \text{UES}_{k_1|k_2|k_1|k_2}^*(x_l|x_l) = 3\text{DES}_{k_1,k_2}(x_l)|3\text{DES}_{k_1,k_2}(x_l)$$

and

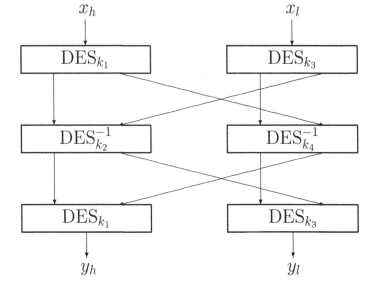

Fig. 1. UES*: Double-block length parallel triple DES

Property 2.

$$\mathrm{UES}_{k_1|k_1|k_1|k_1}(x_l|x_l) = \mathrm{UES}^*_{k_1|k_1|k_1|k_1}(x_l|x_l) = \mathrm{DES}_{k_1}(x_l)|\mathrm{DES}_{k_1}(x_l).$$

In addition it operates on 128-bit block messages. This makes the algorithm compatible with the forthcoming AES, and usable in DES or triple-DES mode. Finally, if we set $m = 0$, we can even run two full DES or 3DES encryptions in parallel, which doubles the encryption speed (two blocks are encrypted applying UES* only once).

Note that this scheme enables to construct double block-length encryption algorithms no matter what the underlying cipher is. For simplicity throughout this paper we will consider DES, but any other secure 64-bit block cipher could do the job. We will also focus on generic attacks that do not exploit the internal structure of the component encryption algorithm. Specific attacks such as differential [7] or linear cryptanalysis [20], truncated or higher order differentials [15] do not apply in this context as at least three layers of basic encryption are applied. We also believe that the best way to attack the scheme by a generic method is to try to create inner collisions.

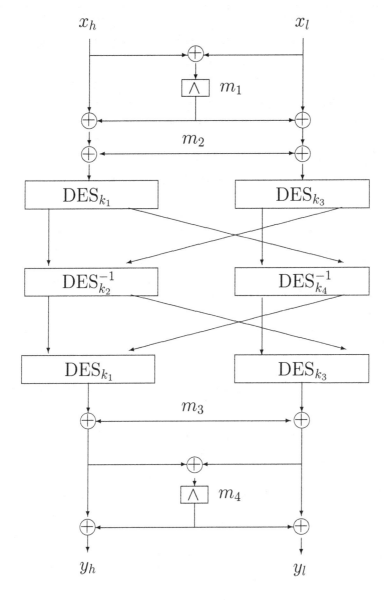

Fig. 2. Encryption with UES.

2.4 The Key-Schedule

In Table 1 below, we summarize in which different modes UES may be used.

Mode Key size	DES 56	3DES 112	AES 128/192/256
Block size 64 bits	$k' = k\|k\|k\|k$ $m' = 0,\, m = 0$	$k' = k\|k$ $m' = 0,\, m = 0$	-
Block size 128 bits	$k' = k\|k\|k\|k$ $m' = 0, x_h = x_l$	$k' = k\|k$ $m' = 0, x_h = x_l$	$k' = k_1\|k_2\|k_3\|k_4$ $m' = m_1\|m_2\|m_3\|m_4$

Table 1. Key-schedule for DES, 3DES and AES modes

The four subkeys and the four submasks used in AES-mode are derived from the user key using DEAL's key-schedule (for a 256-bit key). The user key is first divided into s subkeys of 64 bits each for $s = 2, 3, 4$. Then expand these s keys to 8 keys by repetition and exor the keys with a new constant for every repetition. Encrypt the expanded list of keys using DES in CBC mode with a fixed key $K = \texttt{0123456789abcdef}_x$ and with the initial value set to zero. In order to partially allow on the fly key generation, start by deriving m_1 and m_2, next derive the four DES keys forming k', and finally derive m_3 and m_4.

We are aware of Kelsey and Schneier's [13] key-schedule cryptanalysis of DEAL. It turns out UES may have a very small class of equivalent keys in the 192-bit key case, because of the use of 56-bit keys for the inner DES blocks, whereas 64 bit subkeys are generated by the key-schedule. We also worked out a similar related-key attack with John Kelsey, which recovers the keys in complexity 2^{64} using 2^{33} related keys. However, these attacks apply in a very limited number of practical settings. Developpers should still make sure an attacker is not allowed to choose the keys in such a way.

3 Collision Attacks on Parallel DES

In this section, we consider the variant of UES previously defined as:

$$\text{UES}_k^* = P_{k_1|k_3,\text{DES},\text{DES}} \circ S_m \circ P_{k_2|k_4,\text{DES}^{-1},\text{DES}^{-1}} \circ S_m \circ P_{k_1|k_3,\text{DES},\text{DES}}$$

We will show that this straightforward way of doubling the block size is not secure because a collision attack can be mounted against it (this phenomenon has been independently observed by Knudsen [17]). This is due to the fact that the construction is not a multipermutation. In other words, it may very well happen that if half of the input bits have a fixed value, half of the output bits also have, which would not be the case if the multipermutation property had been satisfied [22]. However, our intention is to prove that we can nevertheless use the structure if the input and output bits to this variant are unknown to the attacker. Therefore we begin by showing where the problem comes from, and justify our additional layers of swapping and masking in the final version of UES.

3.1 Public Intermediate Swapping

We first show how to break UES* by recovering the secret key with about 2^{34} chosen plaintexts, 2^{59} DES operations, and a memory of 16GB. The attack consists in the following steps.

Step 1. First fix $x_h = a$ to a constant and try many $x_l = u_i$ values for $i = 1, \ldots, n$. Request $y_i | z_i = \text{UES}^*(a|u_i)$.

Step 2. For any collision $y_i = y_j$, guess that this comes from collisions on the two inputs of the second and third internal DES higher permutations (these are called "good collisions"). The expected number of good collisions is $n^2 . 2^{-65}$, and the expected number of "natural" (bad) collisions is the same. Try all possible k_3 until there is a collision on both

$$\text{DES}_{k_3}(x_i) \wedge m = \text{DES}_{k_3}(x_j) \wedge m$$

and

$$\text{DES}_{k_3}^{-1}(z_i) \wedge m = \text{DES}_{k_3}^{-1}(z_j) \wedge m.$$

Note that a single (good) collision will always suggest the good k_3 value and an expected number of 2^{-8} random ones, and a bad collision will suggest 2^{-8} random values on average. It is thus likely that we get the k_3 key once a k_3 value is suggested twice (namely with a confidence of $2^{72} : 1$). We thus need only two good collisions. This requires $n \approx 2^{33}$.

Step 3. Perform a similar attack on k_1.

Step 4. Recover k_2, then k_4 by exhaustive search.

This shows that this algorithm is just a little more secure than DES, and far less secure than triple-DES. We add that Bart Preneel pointed out to us that in Step 1, a collision on the other half of the ciphertext occurs with the same probability, therefore we get an extra condition satisfied by k_3 as well as k_1 from the same number of chosen plaintexts. This slightly decreases the number of required chosen plaintexts.

As a matter of fact, the previous attack holds whenever m is any other public value. Namely let w denote the Hamming weight of m. Without loss of generality, let us assume that $w \leq 32$ (otherwise, let us consider the lower DES^{-1} operation). In the attack above, the number of expected good collisions is $n^2 . 2^{-2w-1}$, and the number of bad collisions is $n^2 . 2^{-65}$. The attack thus still holds but with a complexity of $n \approx 2^{w+1}$. In general, the complexity is thus $n \approx 2^{33 - |32-w|}$. Actually, the complexity is the highest for UES*, because m has a balanced Hamming weight. (Note that this analysis does not hold if $m = 0$ or $m = 0^{\ell=64}$ for which we have two triple-DES in parallel, and no possible collision.)

3.2 Keyed Intermediate Swapping

At first sight, one might think that introducing a keyed inner swap significantly increases the complexity of the attack. However this is not the case. Let us show why.

If m is a part of the key, we cannot exhaustively search for k_3 because we do not know m. In the worst case ($w = 32$) we have 2 good collisions and 2 bad ones. Let us assume we have guesses which are the good ones (this may lead to an overhead factor of 16). For each possible k_3 we can look on which bits $\mathrm{DES}_{k_3}(x_i)$ and $\mathrm{DES}_{k_3}(x_j)$ collide, as well as $\mathrm{DES}_{k_3}^{-1}(z_i)$ and $\mathrm{DES}_{k_3}^{-1}(z_j)$. For the good k_3 we will find $w + \frac{64-w}{4}$ bits on average with a standard deviation of $\sqrt{(64 - w)\frac{3}{16}}$. For a random k_3 we will find $16 \pm 2\sqrt{3}$ bits (which means that 16 is the average and $2\sqrt{3}$ the standard deviation). In order to simplify the analysis, let us consider the worst case where $w = 32$. So for the right key k_3 and for a good collision, the number of colliding bits is $40 \pm \sqrt{6}$.

Now for each possible k_3 count the collisions that have say more than $t = 30$ bits as they will much more likely result from the right key value rather than from a random key value. Then the key guess associated to the most such collisions will be the right one with high probability.

Let

$$\varphi(x) = \frac{1}{\sqrt{2\pi}} \int_{-\infty}^{x} e^{-\frac{t^2}{2}} dt. \tag{1}$$

Then as a matter of fact, the average number C_t of collisions on more than t bits is

$$C_t = n^2 . 2^{-65}(1 - \varphi) \pm n . 2^{-32.5}\sqrt{\varphi(1 - \varphi)} \tag{2}$$

where $\varphi = \varphi_1 = \varphi\left(\frac{t-16}{2\sqrt{3}}\right) \approx 1 - 10^{-4.6}$ for $t = 30$ in case of a random key value, and $\varphi = \varphi_2 = \varphi\left(\frac{t-40}{\sqrt{6}}\right) \approx 2^{-15.8}$ for the correct key guess.

So for $n = 2^{34}$ the average number of such collisions is $2^{-5.6}$ for a wrong guess, whereas it is about 4 for the right key.

As a result of this enhaced collision attack, we chose not to use any keyed inner swapping as it unnecessarily complicates the design (also more key materiel is needed) without significantly increasing its security. Instead of this, we chose to add the features described hereafter.

4 Introducing Pre- and Post-whitening

The scheme of the previous section is compliant with DES and 3DES, but is not secure enough against key recovery attacks. So the next most straightforward idea is to protect against the exhaustive key search (once a collision is found) by adding whitening keys before and after the current structure. This considerably increases the work factor and derives from a principle discussed in the construction of DESX [14].

Let us define this new variant of UES by:

Definition 3.

$$\mathrm{UES}_k^{**} = T_{m_3|m_3} \circ \mathrm{UES}_k^* \circ T_{m_2|m_2}$$

The complexity of exhaustive key search increases to about $2^{56+64} = 2^{120}$ offline encryptions given one single collision due to the DESX phenomenon (other trade-offs can be achieved if more than one collision is available). However, this variant can still be distinguished from a random permutation by the previous attack because collisions are far more likely in this setting (they occur twice more often). Note that a collision on one half of the output of UES* leads to a collision on the same half of the ciphertext because the value m_3 is kept constant. Therefore with the same complexity as the collision attack, this second variant may be distinguished from a random permutation, which is not a desirable feature.

5 On the Importance of Pre- and Post-swapping

Having solved the key recovery problem, we still face the distinguisher problem. Therefore the next and last step towards our final UES is to add yet another layer of swapping, but this time under control of the secret key. We will first show how the addition of m_4 increases the complexity of the collision attack, and next which additional workfactor is introduced by m_1.

5.1 Keyed Swap of the Output

Adding a keyed post-swapping, our current structure becomes:

Definition 4.

$$\mathrm{UES}_k^{***} = S_{m4} \circ \mathrm{UES}^{**} = S_{m4} \circ T_{m_3|m_3} \circ \mathrm{UES}^* \circ T_{m_2|m_2}$$

In order to build the same attack as the distinguisher of the previous section (key recovery is hopeless by now), we need to create collisions on one half of the ouput. However, this time these collisions are much harder to spot, as we do not know which output bits correspond say to the left half of the output of the butterfly structure.

Nevertheless, we can still use a property of S_{m_4}. Namely, if $x_h = x'_h$, we let $\Delta = S_{m_4}(x) \oplus S_{m_4}(x')$ and it holds that:

1. $\Delta_h \wedge \Delta_l = 0$
2. $(\Delta_h)_i \leq (m_4)_i$
3. $(\Delta_l)_i \leq (\overline{m_4})_i$

for any bit $i = 1, \ldots, 64$.

Proof. Let $y_h = (S_{m_4}(x))_h$, $y_l = (S_{m_4}(x))_l$, $y'_h = (S_{m_4}(x'))_h$ and $y'_l = (S_{m_4}(x'))_l$. Then we have the following results:

1. When $x_h = x'_h$, the following relations hold:
   $y_h \oplus y'_h = (x_l \wedge m_4) \oplus (x'_l \wedge m_4) = (x_l \oplus x'_l) \wedge m_4$
   $y_l \oplus y'_l = (x_l \wedge m_4) \oplus (x'_l \wedge m_4) \oplus x_l \oplus x'_l = (x_l \oplus x'_l) \wedge \overline{m_4}$
   Thus
   $\Delta_h \wedge \Delta_l = ((x_l \oplus x'_l) \wedge m_4) \wedge ((x_l \oplus x'_l) \wedge \overline{m_4}) = 0$

2. $\Delta_h = (x_l \oplus x'_l) \wedge m_4$ so when $(m_4)_i = 0$, $(\Delta_h)_i = 0$ and when $(m_4)_i = 1$, $(\Delta_h)_i = 0$ or 1. The result follows.
3. The third point is symmetric to the second.

Given the above properties, the attack consists in the following steps.

Step 1. First fix $x_h = a$ to a constant and try many $x_l = u_i$ values for $i = 1, \ldots, n$. Request $y_i = \text{UES}^{***}(a|u_i)$.

Step 2. For all (i, j) pairs, let $y_i \oplus y_j = z|t$. If we have $z \wedge t = 0$, guess that we have a collision as in the above attack. Guess that m_4 is an intermediate mask between z and t. (If $z_i = 1$, then $(m_4)_i = 1$, and if $t_i = 1$, then $(m_4)_i = 0$.) Thus the expected number of good events (the signal) is $n^2.2^{-2w-1}$ and the number of bad events (the noise) is $\frac{n^2}{2} \cdot \left(\frac{3}{4}\right)^{64} \approx n^2.2^{-27.5}$. One good event suggests $2/3$ of the bits of m_4 on average. One bad event also suggests $2/3$ of the bits of m_4 on average, but in a random way so that we can check for consistency. It is thus likely that we recover the right mask m_4 within four good events (mask bits suggested by bad events will happen to be inconsistent with the good ones with high probability).

Step 3. From m_4 and the above collisions, apply the same attack as before to distinguish UES^{***} from a random permutation.

Since we need four good events to occur, in the worst case ($w = 32$) we need $n \approx 2^{33.5}$, and considering all (i, j) pairs in Step 2 leads to a complexity of 2^{67}. (These are however very simple tests, so this complexity can actually be compared to an exhaustive search for DES.) We can expect to get $\frac{n^2}{2} \left(\frac{3}{4}\right)^{64} \approx 2^{39.4}$ bad events on average. Each event suggests a pattern for m_4 with determined bits (0 or 1), and undetermined ones. A pair of events may thus be consistent with probability $\left(\frac{7}{9}\right)^{64} \approx 2^{-23.2}$. We can thus expect to find $2^{77.8}.2^{-23.2} = 2^{54.6}$ consistent pairs of bad events. More generally speaking, we are looking for multiple events in which each pair is consistent with a unique mask m_4. This is the same problem as seeking k-cliques in the consistency graph of the bad events. Any k-clique will be consistent with probability $\left(\frac{2^{k+1}-1}{3^k}\right)^{64}$. And there are exactly $\frac{n^k}{k!}$ such cliques. Therefore, when k gets larger ($k \geq 11$), no k-clique in the consistency graph will survive this filtering process. The complexity of this algorithm is subject to combinatorial optimizations, and we believe that the bottleneck complexity will actually come from the exhaustive search of DES keys.

5.2 Keyed Swap of the Input

Taking into account what we just saw, our final construction must make it as hard as possible for the attacker to find the required 2^{34} different values entering say the right half of the structure. Therefore all we have to do is make it hard to find 34 bits entering the right half (else the attacker tries all the values of these 34 bits and keeps the rest constant which leads to the above result.

Adding a final extra layer of keyed swapping on input to the structure will lead to this result. The attacker now has to guess 34 bits that enter one half in order to subsequently attack m_4 and then be able to distinguish UES from a random permutation. The extra work factor is thus $\binom{128}{34}/\binom{64}{34}$ which is 2^{43}. Then the total complexity is $2^{43+35} = 2^{78}$.

We believe this security level is acceptable.

5.3 Other Alternatives

If the security level is still a concern to some people, one might also consider replacing the keyed outer swapping by a keyed permutation at the bit level. This will add a bit more complexity again. The attacker will have yet a harder time finding which 35 bits enter say the left part of the structure. However, bit permutations are very costly in terms of speed, therefore this alternative shall only be considered if execution time is not that much an issue.

We also considered byte permutations, but these are far too trivial to attack. The overhead complexity is only about 2^{12}.

Our final construction is therefore UES with keyed outer swapping and whitening "à la DESX".

6 Conclusion

We have investigated several variants of a double-block length encryption scheme based on DES which is compliant with DES, 3DES as well as with AES specifications. This may be useful for applications where DES or 3DES are still in use, but where people start to think about double block length and key sizes. Once the final AES is chosen and becomes a standard, it can be plugged into applications in place of our scheme with ease. Among several variants, we selected the best one in terms of security and simplicity, and showed that there is no practical attack that can endanger our scheme. Key recovery does not seem possible and in order to distinguish this new cipher from a random permutation, the workload is basically very high.

References

1. http://www.nist.gov/aes
2. ANSI draft X9.52, *"Triple Data Encryption Algorithm Modes of Operation,"* Revision 6.0, 1996.
3. E. Biham, "On modes of operation," *Fast Software Encryption'93, LNCS 809,* Springer-Verlag, 1994, pp. 116–120.
4. E. Biham, "Cryptanalysis of multiple modes of operation," *ASIACRYPT'94, LNCS 917,* Springer-Verlag, 1994, pp. 278–292.
5. E. Biham, "Cryptanalysis of triple-modes of operation," *Technion Technical Report CS0885,* 1996.
6. E. Biham, L. R. Knudsen, "Cryptanalysis of the ANSI X9.52 CBCM mode," *EUROCRYPT'98, LNCS 1403,* Springer-Verlag, 1998, pp. 100–111.
7. E. Biham, A. Shamir, *"Differential Cryptanalysis of the Data Encryption Standard,"* Springer-Verlag, 1993.

8. The Electronic Frontier Foundation, *"Cracking DES. Secrets of Encryption Research, Wiretap Politics & Chip Design,"* O'Reilly, May 1998.

9. FIPS 46, *"Data Encryption Standard,"* US Department of Commerce, National Bureau of Standards, 1977 (revised as FIPS 46–1:1988; FIPS 46–2:1993).

10. FIPS 81, *"DES Modes of Operation,"* US Department of Commerce, National Bureau of Standards, 1980.

11. H. Handschuh, B. Preneel, "On the security of double and 2-key triple modes of operation", *Fast Software Encryption'99,* Springer-Verlag, 1999, pp. 215–230.

12. B. S. Kaliski, M.J.B. Robshaw, "Multiple encryption: Weighing security and performance," *Dr. Dobb's Journal,* January 1996, pp. 123–127.

13. J. Kelsey, B. Schneier, "Key-Schedule Cryptanalysis of DEAL," in these proceedings.

14. J. Kilian, P. Rogaway, "How to protect DES against exhaustive key search, *CRYPTO'96, LNCS 1109,* Springer-Verlag, 1996, pp. 252–267.

15. L. R. Knudsen, *"Block Ciphers – Analysis, Design and Applications,"* PhD thesis, Aarhus University, Denmark, 1994.

16. L. R. Knudsen, *"DEAL: a 128-bit block cipher,"* AES submission, 1998.

17. L. Knudsen, "On Expanding the Block Length of DES," unpublished manuscript, nov. 98.

18. S. Lucks, "Attacking triple encryption," *Fast Software Encryption'98, LNCS 1372,* Springer-Verlag, 1998, pp. 239–253.

19. S. Lucks, "On the security of the 128-bit block cipher DEAL," preprint, 1998.

20. M. Matsui, "Linear cryptanalysis method for DES cipher," *EUROCRYPT'93, LNCS 765,* Springer-Verlag, 1993, pp. 386–397.

21. B. Schneier, *Applied Cryptography,* Wiley & Sons, 1995, pp. 364.

22. S. Vaudenay, "On the need for multipermutations: Cryptanalysis of MD4 and SAFER," *Fast Software Encryption 2, LNCS 1008,* Springer-Verlag, 1995, pp. 286–297.

23. P. C. van Oorschot, M. J. Wiener, "A known-plaintext attack on two-key triple encryption," *EUROCRYPT'90, LNCS 473,* 1990, pp. 318–325.

24. P. C. van Oorschot, M. J. Wiener, "Improving implementable meet-in-the-middle attacks by orders of magnitude," *CRYPTO'96, LNCS 1109,* 1996, pp. 229–236.

25. D. Wagner, "Cryptanalysis of some recently-proposed multiple modes of operation," *Fast Software Encryption'98, LNCS 1372,* Springer-Verlag, 1998, pp. 254–269.

26. M.J. Wiener, "Efficient DES key search," *Technical Report TR-244,* School of Computer Science, Carleton University, Ottawa, Canada, May 1994. Presented at the rump session of Crypto'93 and reprinted in W. Stallings, *Practical Cryptography for Data Internetworks,* IEEE Computer Society Press, 1996, pp. 31–79.

Yarrow-160:
Notes on the Design and Analysis of the Yarrow Cryptographic Pseudorandom Number Generator

John Kelsey, Bruce Schneier, and Niels Ferguson

Counterpane Systems; 101 E Minnehaha Parkway, Minneapolis, MN 55419, USA
{kelsey,schneier,niels}@counterpane.com

Abstract. We describe the design of Yarrow, a family of cryptographic pseudo-random number generators (PRNG). We describe the concept of a PRNG as a separate cryptographic primitive, and the design principles used to develop Yarrow. We then discuss the ways that PRNGs can fail in practice, which motivates our discussion of the components of Yarrow and how they make Yarrow secure. Next, we define a specific instance of a PRNG in the Yarrow family that makes use of available technology today. We conclude with a brief listing of open questions and intended improvements in future releases.

1 Introduction

Random numbers are critical in every aspect of cryptography. Cryptographers design algorithms such as RC4 and DSA, and protocols such as SET and SSL, with the assumption that random numbers are available. Even as straightforward an application as encrypting a file on a disk with a passphrase typically needs random numbers for the salt to be hashed in with the passphrase and for the initialization vector (IV) used in encrypting the file. To encrypt e-mail, digitally sign documents, or spend a few dollars worth of electronic cash over the internet, we need random numbers.

Specifically, random numbers are used in cryptography in the following applications:

- Session and message keys for symmetric ciphers, such as triple-DES or Blowfish.
- Seeds for routines that generate mathematical values, such as large prime numbers for RSA or ElGamal-style cryptosystems.
- Salts to combine with passwords, to frustrate offline password guessing programs.
- Initialization vectors for block cipher chaining modes.
- Random values for specific instances of many digital signature schemes, such as DSA.
- Random challenges in authentication protocols, such as Kerberos.

Howard Heys and Carlisle Adams (Eds.): SAC'99, LNCS 1758, pp. 13–33, 2000.
© Springer-Verlag Berlin Heidelberg 2000

- Nonces for protocols, to ensure that different runs of the same protocol are unique; e.g., SET and SSL.

Some of those random numbers will be sent out in the clear, such as IVs and random challenges. Other of those random numbers will be kept secret, and used as keys for block ciphers. Some applications require a large quantity of random numbers, such as a Kerberos server generating thousands of session keys every hour, and others only a few. In some cases, an attacker can even force the random generator to generate thousands of random numbers and send them to him.

Unfortunately, random numbers are very difficult to generate, especially on computers that are designed to be deterministic. We thus fall back on *pseudo-random*[1] numbers. These are numbers that are generated from some (hopefully random) internal values, and that are very hard for an observer to distinguish from random numbers.

Given the importance of generating pseudo-random numbers for cryptographic applications, it is somewhat surprising that little formal cryptanalysis of these generators exist. There are methodologies for generating randomness on computer systems [DIF94,ECS94], and ad hoc designs of generators [Gut98], but we are aware of only one paper cryptanalyzing these designs [KSWH98a].

1.1 What Is a Cryptographic PRNG?

In our context, a random number is a number that cannot be predicted by an observer before it is generated. If the number is to be in the range $0\ldots2^n - 1$, an observer cannot predict that number with probability any better than $1/2^n$. If m random numbers are generated in a row, an observer given any $m - 1$ of them still cannot predict the m'th with any better probability than $1/2^n$. More technical definitions are possible, but they amount to the same general idea.

A cryptographic pseudorandom number generator, or PRNG, is a cryptographic mechanism for processing somewhat-unpredictable inputs, and generating pseudorandom outputs. If designed, implemented, and used properly, even an attacker with enormous computational resources should not be able to distinguish a sequence of PRNG outputs from a random sequence of bits.

There are a great many PRNGs in use in cryptographic applications. Some of them (such as Peter Gutmann's PRNG in Cryptlib [Gut98], or Colin Plumb's PRNG in PGP [Zim95]) are apparently pretty well designed. Others (such as the RSAREF 2.0 PRNG [RSA94], or the PRNG specified in ANSI X9.17 [NIST92]) are appropriate for some applications, but fail badly when used in other applications [KSWH98a].

---

[1] It is important to distinguish between the meaning of pseudorandom numbers in normal programming contexts, where these numbers merely need to be reasonably random-looking, and in the context of cryptography, where these numbers must be indistinguishable from real random numbers, even to observers with enormous computational resources.

A PRNG can be visualized as a black box. Into one end flow all the internal measurements (samples) which the system designer believed might be unpredictable to an attacker. Out of the other end, once the PRNG believes it is in an unguessable state, flow apparently random numbers. An attacker might conceivably have some knowledge or even control over some of the input samples to the PRNG. An attacker might have compromised the PRNG's internal state at some point in the past. An attacker might have an extremely good model of the "unpredictable" values being used as input samples to the PRNG, and a great deal of computational power to throw at the problem of guessing the PRNG's internal state.

Internally, a PRNG needs to have a mechanism for processing those (hopefully) unpredictable samples, a mechanism for using those samples to update its internal state, and a mechanism to use some part of its internal state to generate pseudorandom outputs. In some PRNG designs, more-or-less the same mechanism does all three of these tasks; in others, the mechanisms are clearly separated.

1.2 Why Design a New PRNG?

We designed Yarrow because we are not satisfied with existing PRNG designs. Many have flaws that allowed attacks under some circumstances (see [KSWH98a] for details on many of these). Most of the others do not seem to have been designed with attacks in mind. None implement all the defenses we have worked out over the last two years of research into PRNGs.

Yarrow is an enhancement of a proprietary PRNG we designed several years ago for a client. We kept improving our design as we discovered new potential attacks.

1.3 A Guide to the Rest of the Paper

The remainder of this paper is as follows: In Section 2 we discuss the reasons behind our design choices for Yarrow. In Section 3 we discuss the various ways that cryptographic PRNGs can fail in practice. Then, in Section 4, we will discuss the basic components of Yarrow, and show how they resist the kinds of failures listed earlier. Section 5 gives the generic design ideas and their rationale. Finally, we will consider open questions relating to Yarrow, and plans for future releases.

In the full paper we will define Yarrow-160, a precisely defined PRNG, and discuss entropy calculation.

2 Yarrow Design Principles

Our goal for Yarrow is to make a PRNG that system designers can fairly easily incorporate into their own systems, and that is better at resisting the attacks we know about than the existing, widely-used alternatives.

We pose the following constraints on the design of Yarrow:

1. Everything is reasonably efficient. There is no point in designing a PRNG that nobody will use, because it slows down the application too much.
2. Yarrow is so easy to use that an intelligent, careful programmer with no background in cryptography has some reasonable chance of using the PRNG in a secure way.
3. Where possible, Yarrow re-uses existing building blocks.

Yarrow was created using an attack-oriented design process. This means we designed the PRNG with attacks in mind from the beginning. Block ciphers are routinely designed in this way, with structures intended to optimize their strength against commonly-used attacks such as differential and linear cryptanalysis. The Yarrow design was very much focused on potential attacks. This had to be tempered with other design constraints: performance, flexibility, simplicity, ease of use, portability, and even legal issues regarding the exportability of the PRNG were considered. The result is still a work-in-progress, but it resists every attack of which we are aware, while still being a usable tool for system designers.

We spent the most time working on a good framework for entropy-estimation and reseeding, because this is so critical for the ultimate security of the PRNG, and because it is so often done badly in fielded systems. Our cryptographic mechanisms are nothing very exciting, just various imaginative uses of a hash function and a block cipher. However, they do resist known attacks very well.

2.1 Terminology

At any point in time, a PRNG contains an internal state that is used to generate the pseudorandom outputs. This state is kept secret and controls much of the processing. Analogous to ciphers we call this state the key of the PRNG.

To update the key the PRNG needs to collect inputs that are truly random, or at least not known, predictable or controllable by the attacker. Often used examples include the exact timing of key strokes or the detailed movements of the mouse. Typically, there are a fairly large number of these inputs over time, and each of the input values is fairly small. We call these inputs the samples.

In many systems there are several sources that each produce samples. We therefore classify the samples according to the source they came from.

The process of combining the existing key and new sample(s) into a new key is called the reseeding.

If a system is shut down and restarted, it is desirable to store some high-entropy data (such as the key) in non-volatile memory. This allows the PRNG to be restarted in an unguessable state at the next restart. We call this stored data the seed file.

3   How Cryptographic PRNGs Fail

In this section, we consider some of the ways that a PRNG can fail in a real-world application. By considering how a PRNG can fail, we are able to recognize ways to prevent these failures in Yarrow. In other cases, the failures cannot be totally prevented, but we can make them less likely. In still other cases, we can only ensure a quick recovery from the compromised state.

3.1 How PRNGs Are Compromised

Once the key of a PRNG is compromised, its outputs are predictable; at least until it gets enough new samples to derive a new, unguessable key. Many PRNGs have the property that, once compromised, they will never recover, or they will recover only after a very long time.

For these reasons, it makes sense to consider how a PRNG's key can be compromised, and how, once keys are compromised, they may be exploited.

Entropy Overestimation and Guessable Starting Points. We believe that this is the most common failing in PRNGs in real-world applications. It is easy to look at a sequence of samples that appears random and has a total length of 128 bits, feed it into the PRNG, and then start generating output. If that sequence of samples turns out only to have 56 bits of entropy, then an attacker could feasibly perform an exhaustive search for the starting point of the PRNG.

This is probably the hardest problem to solve in PRNG design. We tried to solve it by making sure that the entropy estimate is very conservative. While it is still possible to seriously overestimate the starting entropy, it is much less likely to happen, and when it does the estimate is likely to be closer to the actual value. We also use a computationally-expensive reseeding process to raise the cost of attempting to guess the PRNG's key.

Mishandling of Keys and Seed Files. Keys and seed files are easy to mishandle in various ways, such as by letting them get written to the swap file by the operating system, or by opening a seed file, but failing to update it every time it is used. The Yarrow design provides some functions to simplify the management of seed files. An excellent discussion of some methods for avoiding key compromise appears in [Gut98].

Implementation Errors. Another way that the key of the PRNG can be compromised is by exploiting some implementation error. Errors in the implementation are impossible to prevent. The only preventative measures we found for Yarrow was to try to make the interface reasonably simple so that the programmer trying to use Yarrow in a real-world product can use it securely without understanding much about how the PRNG works.

This is an area we are still working on. It is notoriously difficult to make security products easy to use for most programmers, and of course, it is very hard to be certain there are no errors in the Yarrow generator itself.

One thing we can do is to make it easy to verify the correct implementation of a Yarrow PRNG. We have carefully designed Yarrow to be portable and precisely defined. This allows us to create test vectors that can be used to verify that a Yarrow implementation is in fact working correctly. Without such test vectors an implementor would never be able to ensure that her Yarrow implementation was indeed working correctly.

Cryptanalytic Attacks on PRNG Generation Mechanisms. Between re-seedings, the PRNG output generation mechanism is basically a stream cipher. Like any other stream cipher, it is possible that the one used in a PRNG will have some cryptanalytic weakness that makes the output stream somewhat predictable or at least recognizable. The process of finding weaknesses in this part of the PRNG is the same as finding them in a stream cipher.

We have not seen a lot of PRNGs that were easily vulnerable to this kind of attack. Most PRNGs' generation mechanisms are based on strong cryptographic mechanisms already. Thus, while this kind of attack is always a concern, it usually does not seem to break the PRNG. To be safe, we have designed Yarrow to be based on a block cipher; if the block cipher is secure, then so is the generation mechanism. This was done because there are quite a number of apparently-secure block ciphers available in the public domain.

Side-Channel Attacks. Side-channel attacks are attacks that use additional information about the inner workings of the implementation [KSWH98b]: timing attacks [Koc96], and power analysis [Koc98] are typical examples. Many PRNGs that are otherwise secure fall apart when any additional information about their internal operations are leaked. One example of this is the RSAREF 2.0 PRNG, which can be implemented in a way that is vulnerable to a timing attack.

It is probably not possible to protect against side-channel attacks in the design of algorithms. However, we do try to avoid obvious weaknesses, specifically any data-dependent execution paths.

Chosen-Input Attacks on the PRNG. An attacker is not always limited to just observing PRNG outputs. It is sometimes possible to gain control over some of the samples sent into the PRNG, especially in a tamper-resistant token. Some PRNGs, such as the RSAREF 2.0 PRNG, are vulnerable to such attacks. In the worst case the attacker can mount an adaptive attack in which the samples are selected based on the output that the PRNG provides. To avoid this kind of attack in Yarrow, all samples are processed by a cryptographic hash function, and are combined with the existing key using a secure update function.

3.2 How Compromises Are Exploited

Once the key is compromised, it is interesting to consider how this compromise is exploited. Since it is not always possible to prevent an attacker from learning the key, it is reasonable to spend some serious time and effort making sure the PRNG can recover its security from a key compromise.

Permanent Compromise Attacks. Some PRNGs, such as the one proposed in ANSI X9.17, have the property that once the key has been compromised, an attacker is forever after able to predict their outputs. This is a terrible property for a PRNG to have, and we have made sure that Yarrow can recover from a key compromise.

Iterative Guessing Attacks. If the samples are mixed in with the key as they arrive, an attacker who knows the PRNG key can guess the next "unpredictable" sample, observe the next PRNG output, and test his guess by seeing if they agree. This means that a PRNG which mixes in samples with 32 bits of entropy every few output words will not recover from a key compromise until the attacker is unable to see the effects of three or four such samples on the outputs. This is called an iterative guessing attack, and the only way to resist it is to collect entropy samples in a pool separate from the key, and only reseed the key when the contents of the entropy pool is unguessable to any real-world attacker. This is what Yarrow does.

Backtracking Attacks. Some PRNGs, such as the RSAREF 2.0 PRNG, are easy to run backwards as well as forward. This means that an attacker that has compromised the PRNG's key *after* a high-value RSA key pair was generated can still go back and learn that high-value key pair. We include a mechanism in Yarrow to limit backtracking attacks to a limited number of output bytes.

Compromise of High-Value Keys Generated From Compromised Key. Of course, the biggest cost of a compromised PRNG is that it leads to compromised system-keys if the key generation process uses the PRNG. If the key that is being generated is very valuable, the harm to the system owner can be very large. As we mentioned, the iterative guessing attacks require us to collect entropy in a pool before reseeding the generator with it. When we are about to generate a very valuable key, it is preferable to have whatever extra entropy there is in the PRNG's key. Therefore, the user can request an explicit reseed of the generator. This feature is intended to be used rarely and only for generating high-value secrets.

4   The Yarrow Design: Components

In this section, we discuss the components of Yarrow, and how they interact. A major design principle of Yarrow is that its components are more-or-less independent, so that systems with various design constraints can still use the general Yarrow design.

The use of algorithm-independent components in the top level design is a key concept in Yarrow. Our goal is not to increase the number of security primitives that a cryptographic system is based on, but to leverage existing primitives as much as possible. Hence, we rely on one-way hash functions and block ciphers,

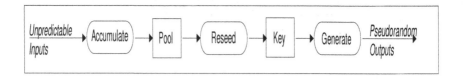

Fig. 1. Generic block diagram of Yarrow

two of the best-studied and most widely available cryptographic primitives, in our design.

There are four major components:

1. An **Entropy Accumulator** which collects samples from entropy sources, and collects them in the two pools.
2. A **Reseed Mechanism** which periodically reseeds the key with new entropy from the pools.
3. A **Generation Mechanism** which generates PRNG outputs from the key.
4. A **Reseed control** that determines when a reseed is to be performed.

Below, we specify each component's role in the larger PRNG design, we discuss the requirements for each component in terms of both security and performance, and we discuss the way each component must interact with each other component. Later in this paper, we will discuss specific choices for these components.

4.1 Design Philosophy

We have seen two basic design philosophies for PRNGs.

One approach assumes that it is usually possible to collect and distill enough entropy from the samples that each of the output bits should have one bit of real entropy. If more output is required than entropy has been collected from the samples, the PRNG either stops generating outputs or falls back on a cryptographic mechanism to generate the outputs. Colin Plumb's PGP PRNG and Gutmann's Cryptlib PRNG both fall into this category. In this kind of design, entropy is accumulated to be immediately reused as output, and the whole PRNG mechanism may be seen as a mechanism to distill and measure entropy from various sources on the machine, and a buffer to store this entropy until it is used.

Yarrow takes a different approach. We assume that we can accumulate enough entropy to get the PRNG into an unguessable state (without such an assumption, there is no point designing a PRNG). Once at that starting point, we believe we have cryptographic mechanisms that will generate outputs an attacker cannot distinguish from random outputs. In our approach, the purpose of accumulating entropy is to be able to recover from PRNG key compromises. The PRNG is designed so that, once it has a secure key, even if all other entropy accumulated is predictable by, or even under the control of, an attacker, the PRNG is still secure. This is also the approach taken by the RSAREF, DSA, and ANSI X9.17 PRNGs.

The strength of the first approach is that, if properly designed, it is possible to get unconditional security from the PRNG. That is, if the PRNG really does accumulate enough entropy to provide for all its outputs, even breaking some strong cipher like triple-DES will not be sufficient to let an attacker predict unknown PRNG outputs. The weakness of the approach is that the strength of the PRNG is based in a critical way on the mechanisms used to estimate and distill entropy. While this is inevitably true of all PRNGs, with a design like Yarrow we can afford to be far more conservative in our entropy estimates, since we are not expecting to be able to distill enough entropy to provide for all our outputs. In our opinion, entropy estimation is the hardest part of PRNG design. By contrast, the design of a generation mechanism that will resist cryptanalysis is a relatively easy task, making use of available cryptographic primitives such as a block cipher.

Practical cryptographic systems rely on the strength of various algorithms, such as block ciphers, stream ciphers, hash functions, digital signature schemes, and public key ciphers. We feel that basing the strength of our PRNG on well-trusted cryptographic mechanisms is as reasonable as basing the strength of our systems on them.

This approach raises two important issues, which should be made explicit:

1. Yarrow's outputs are cryptographically derived. Systems that use Yarrow's outputs are no more secure than the generation mechanism used. Thus, unconditional security is not available in systems like one-time pads, blind signature schemes, and threshold schemes. Those mechanisms are capable of unconditional security, but an attacker capable of breaking Yarrow's generation mechanism will be able to break a system that trust Yarrow outputs to be random. This is true even if Yarrow is accumulating far more entropy from the samples than it is producing as output.

2. Like any other cryptographic primitive, a Yarrow generator has a limited strength which we express in the size of the key. Yarrow-160 relies on the strength of three-key triple-DES and SHA-1, and has an effective key size of about 160 bits. Systems that have switched to new cryptographic mechanisms (such as the new AES cipher, when it is selected) in the interests of getting higher security should also use a different version of Yarrow to rely on those new mechanisms. If a longer key is necessary, then a future "larger" version of Yarrow should be used; it makes no sense to use a 160-bit PRNG to generate a 256-bit key for a block cipher, if 256 bits of security are actually required.

4.2 Entropy Accumulator

Entropy Accumulation. Entropy accumulation is the process by which a PRNG acquires a new, unguessable internal state. During initialization of the PRNG, and for reseeding during operation, it is critical that we successfully accumulate entropy from the samples. To avoid iterative guessing attacks and still regularly reseed the PRNG it is important that we correctly estimate the amount of entropy we have collected thus far. The entropy accumulation mechanism must also resist chosen-input attacks, in the sense that it must not be possible for an attacker who controls some of the samples, but does not know others, to cause the PRNG to lose the entropy from the unknown samples.

In Yarrow, entropy from the samples is collected into two *pools*, each a hashing context. The two pools are the *fast* pool and the *slow* pool; the fast pool provides frequent reseeds of the key, to ensure that key compromises have as short a duration as possible when our entropy estimates of each source are reasonably accurate. The slow pool provides rare, but extremely conservative, reseeds of the key. This is intended to ensure that even when our entropy estimates are very optimistic, we still eventually get a secure reseed. Alternating input samples are sent into the fast and slow pools.

Each pool contains the running hash of all inputs fed into it since it was last used to carry our a reseed.

In Yarrow-160, the pools are each SHA-1 contexts, and thus are 160 bits wide. Naturally, no more than 160 bits of entropy can be collected in these pools, and this determines the design strength of Yarrow-160 to be no greater than 160 bits.

The following are the requirements for the entropy accumulation component:

1. We must expect to accumulate nearly all entropy from the samples, up to the size of a pool, even when the entropy is distributed in various odd ways in those samples, e.g., always in the last bit, or no entropy in most samples, but occasional samples with nearly 100 bits of entropy in a 100-bit sample, etc.

2. An attacker must not be able to choose samples to undo the effects of those samples he does not know on a pool.

3. An attacker must not be able to force a pool into any kind of weak state, from which it cannot collect entropy successfully.

4. An attacker who can choose which bits in which samples will be unknown to him, but still has to allow n unknown bits, must not be able to narrow down the number of states in a pool to substantially fewer than 2^n.

Note that this last condition is a very strong requirement. This virtually requires the use of a cryptographic hash function.

Entropy Estimation. Entropy estimation is the process of determining how much work it would take an attacker to guess the current contents of our pools. The general method of Yarrow is to group the samples into sources and estimate the entropy contribution of each source separately. To do this we estimate the entropy of each sample separately, and then add these estimates of all samples that came from the same source.

The assumption behind this grouping into sources is that we do not want our PRNG's reseeding taking place based on only one source's effects. Otherwise, one source which appears to provide lots of entropy, but instead provides relatively little, will keep causing the PRNG to reseed, and will leave it vulnerable to an iterative guessing attack. We thus allow a single fast source to cause frequent reseeding from the fast pool, but not the slow pool. This ensures that we reseed frequently, but if our entropy estimates from our best source are wildly inaccurate, we still will eventually reseed from the slow pool, based on entropy estimates of a different source. Recall that samples from each source alternate between the two pools.

Implementors should be careful in determining their sources. The sources should not be closely linked or exhibit any significant correlations.

The entropy of each sample is measured in three ways:

- The programmer supplies an estimate of entropy in a sample when he writes the routine to collect data from that source. Thus, the programmer might send in a sample, with an estimate of 20 bits of entropy.
- For each source a specialized statistical estimator is used to estimate the entropy of the sample. This test is geared towards detecting abnormal situations in which the samples have a very low entropy.
- There is a system-wide maximum "density" of the sample, by considering the length of the sample in bits, and multiplying it by some constant factor less than one to get a maximum estimate of entropy in the sample. Currently, we use a multiplier of 0.5 in Yarrow-160.

We use the smallest of these three estimates as the entropy of the sample in question.

The specific statistical tests used depends on the nature of the source and can be changed in different implementations. This is just another component, which can be swapped out and replaced by better-suited components in different environments.

4.3 Generating Pseudorandom Outputs

The Generation Mechanism provides the PRNG output. The output must have the property that, if an attacker does not know the PRNG's key, he cannot distinguish the PRNG's output from a truly random sequence of bits.

The generation mechanism must have the following properties:

- Resistant to cryptanalytic attack,
- efficient,
- resistant to backtracking after a key compromise,
- capable of generating a very long sequence of outputs securely without reseeding.

4.4 Reseed Mechanism

The Reseed Mechanism connects the entropy accumulator to the generating mechanism. When the reseed control determines that a reseed is required, the reseeding component must update the key used by the generating mechanism with information from one or both of the pools being maintained by the entropy accumulator, in such a way that if either the key or the pool(s) are unknown to the attacker before the reseed, the key will be unknown to the attacker after the reseed. It must also be possible to make reseeding computationally expensive to add difficulty to attacks based on guessing unknown input samples.

Reseeding from the fast pool uses the current key and the hash of all inputs to the fast pool since the last reseed (or since startup) to generate a new key. After this is done, the entropy estimates for the fast pool are all reset to zero.

Reseeding from the slow pool uses the current key, the hash of all inputs to the fast pool, and the hash of all inputs to the slow pool, to generate a new key. After this is done, the entropy estimates for both pools are reset to zero.

4.5 Reseed Control

The Reseed Control mechanism must weigh various considerations. Frequent reseeding is desirable, but it makes an iterative guessing attack more likely. Infrequent reseeding gives an attacker that has compromised the key more information. The design of the reseed control mechanism is a compromise between these goals.

We keep entropy estimates for each source as the samples have gone into each pool. When any source in the fast pool has passed a threshhold value, we reseed from the fast pool. In many systems, we would expect this to happen many times per hour. When any k of the n sources have hit a higher threshhold in the slow pool, we reseed from the slow pool. This is a much slower process.

For Yarrow-160, the threshhold for the fast pool is 100 bits, and for the slow pool, is 160 bits. At least two different sources must be over 160 bits in the slow pool before the slow pool reseeds, by default. (This should be tunable for different environments; environments with three good and reasonably fast entropy sources should set $k = 3$.)

5 The Generic Yarrow Design and Yarrow-160

In this section, we describe the generic Yarrow design. This is a generic description, using an arbitrary block cipher and hash function. If both algorithms are secure, and the PRNG gets sufficient starting entropy, our construction results in a strong PRNG. We also discuss the specific parameters and primitives used in Yarrow-160.

We need two algorithms, with properties as follows:

- A one-way hash function, $h(x)$, with an m-bit output size,
- A block cipher, $E()$, with a k-bit key size and an n-bit block size.

The hash function is assumed to have the following properties:

- Collision intractable.
- One-way.

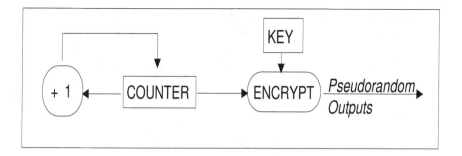

Fig. 2. Generation mechanism

- Given any set M of possible input values, the output values are distributed as $|M|$ selections of the uniform distribution over m-bit values.

The last requirements implies several things. Even if the attacker knows most of the input to the hash function, he still has no effective knowledge about the output unless he can enumerate the set of possible inputs. It also makes it impossible to control any property of the output value unless you have full control over the input.

The block cipher is assumed to have the following properties:

- It is resistant to known-plaintext and chosen-plaintext attacks, even those requiring enormous numbers of plaintexts and their corresponding cipher-texts,
- Good statistical properties of outputs, even given highly patterned inputs.

The strength (in bits) of the resulting PRNG is limited by $\min(m, k)$. In practice even this limit will not quite be reached. The reason is that if you take an m bit random value and apply a hash function that produces m bits of output, the result has less than m bits of entropy due to the collisions that occur. This is a very minor effect, and overall results in the loss of at most a few bits of entropy. We ignore this small constant factor, and say that the PRNG has a strength of $\min(m, k)$ bits.

Yarrow-160 uses the SHA1 hash function for $h()$, and three-key triple-DES for $E_K()$.

5.1 Generation Mechanism

Figure 2 shows the generator which is based on using the block cipher in counter mode.

We have an n-bit counter value C. To generate the next n-bit output block, we increment C and encrypt it with our block cipher, using the key K. To generate the next output block we thus do the following:

$$C \leftarrow (C + 1) \bmod 2^n$$
$$R \leftarrow E_K(C)$$

where R is the next output block and K is the current PRNG key.

If the key is compromised at a certain point in time, the PRNG must not leak too many 'old' outputs that were generated before the compromise. It is clear that this generation mechanism has no inherent resistance to this kind of attack. For that reason, we keep count of how many blocks we have output. Once we reach some limit P_g (a system security parameter, $1 \leq P_g \leq 2^{n/3}$), we generate k bits of PRNG output, and use them as the new key.

$$K \leftarrow \text{Next } k \text{ bits of PRNG output}$$

We call this operation a generator gate. Note that this is not a reseeding operation as no new entropy is introduced into the key.

In the interests of keeping an extremely conservative design, the maximum number of outputs from the generator between reseedings is limited to $\min\{2^n, 2^{k/3}P_g\}$ n-bit output blocks. The first term in the minimum prevents the value C from cycling. The second term makes it extremely unlikely that K will take on the same value twice. In practice, P_g should be set much lower than this, e.g. $P_g = 10$, in order to minimize the number of outputs that can be learned by backtracking.

In Yarrow-160, we use three-key triple-DES in counter mode to generate outputs, and plan to apply the generator gate every ten outputs. (That is, $P_g = 10$.)

Security Arguments.

Normal Operations. Consider an attacker who can, after seeing a long sequence of outputs from this generator under the same key K, extract the key. This can be converted into a chosen plaintext attack on the cipher to extract its key.

Consider an attacker who can, after seeing a long sequence of outputs from this generator under the same key, predict a single future or past output value. The algorithm used by the attacker performs a chosen-plaintext attack on the underlying block cipher, allowing the prediction of (part of) one ciphertext after some number of encryptions of chosen plaintexts have been seen. This is enough of a demonstrated weakness to rule the cipher out for many uses, e.g. in CBC-MAC.

Backtracking Protection. Consider an attacker who can use the outputs after a generator gate has taken place to mount an attack on the data generated before the generator gate. The same attacker can mount his attack on the generator without the generator gate by using k known bits of the generator output to form a new key, using that key to generate a sequence of outputs, and then applying the attack. (This is possible as the counter value C is assumed to be known to the attacker.) Thus, a generator gate cannot expose previous output values to attack without also demonstrating a weakness in the generation mechanism in general.

Consider an attacker who compromises the current key of the PRNG some-how. Suppose he can learn a previous key from the current key. To do this, he must be able to extract the key of the block cipher given a small number of bits of the generator's output. Thus, the attacker must defeat the generator mechanism to defeat the generator gate mechanism.

Consider an attacker who can predict the next key generated by the generator gate. The same method he uses to do this can be used to predict the next PRNG output, if the generator is used without generator gate.

Limits on Generator Outputs. As the number of output blocks from the basic generator available to the attacker grows closer to and beyond $2^{n/2}$ it becomes easier and easier to distinguish the cipher's outputs from a real random sequence. A random sequence should have collisions in some n-bit output blocks, but there will be no repetitions of output blocks in the output from running a block cipher in counter mode. This means that a conservative design should re-key long before this happens. This is the reason why we require the generator gate to be used at least once every $2^{n/3}$ output blocks. Note that P_g is a configurable parameter and can be set to smaller values. Smaller values of P_g increase the number of generator gates and thus decrease the amount of old data an attacker can retrieve if he were to find the current key. The disadvantage of very small P_g values is that performance suffers, especially if a block cipher is used that has an expensive key schedule.

Each time we use the generator gate, we generate a new key from the old key using a function that we can assume to behave as a random function. This function is not the same function for each generator gate, as the counter C changes in value. There are therefore no direct cycles for K to fall into. Any cycle would require C to wrap around, which we do not allow between reseedings. To be on the safe side we do restrict the number of generator gate operations to $2^{k/3}$ which makes it extremely unlikely that the same value K will be used twice between reseedings.

Implementation Ideas. The use of counter mode allows several output blocks to be computed together, or even in parallel. A hardware implementation can exploit this parallelism using a pipelined design, and software implementations could use a bit-sliced implementation of the block cipher for higher performance. Even for simple software implementations it might very well be more efficient to produce many blocks at a time and to buffer the output in a secure memory area. This improves the locality of the code, and can improve the cache-hit ratio of the program.

5.2 Entropy Accumulator

To accumulate the entropy from a sequence of inputs, we concatenate all the inputs. Once we have collected enough entropy we apply the hash function h to the concatenation of all inputs. We alternate applying samples from each source to each pool.

In Yarrow-160, we use the SHA1 hash function to accumulate inputs in this way. We alternate feeding inputs from each source into the fast and slow pools; each pool is its own SHA1 hash context, and thus effectively contains the SHA1 hash of all inputs fed into that pool.

Security Arguments. If we believe that an attacker cannot find collisions in the hash function, then we must also believe that an attacker cannot be helped by any collisions that exist.

Consider the situation of an attacker trying to predict the whole sequence of inputs to be fed into the user's entropy accumulator. The attacker's best strategy is to try to generate a list of the most likely input sequences, in order of decreasing probability. If he can generate a list that is feasible for him to search through which has a reasonable probability (say, a 10^{-6} chance) of containing the actual sequence of samples, he has a worthwhile attack. Ultimately, an attacker in this position cannot be resisted effectively by the design of the algorithm, though we do our best. He can only be resisted by the use of better entropy sources, and by better estimation of the entropy in the pool.

Now, how can the entropy accumulator help the attacker? Only by reducing the total number of different input sequences he must test. However, in order for the attacker to see a single pair of different input sequences that will lead to the same entropy pool contents he must find a pair of distinct input sequences that have the same hash value.

Implementation Ideas. All common hash functions can be computed in an incremental manner. The input string is usually partitioned into fixed size blocks, and these blocks are processed sequentially by the hash function. This allows an implementation to compute the hash of the sequence of inputs on the fly. Instead of concatenating all inputs and applying the hash function in one go (which would require an unbounded amount of memory) the software can use a fixed size buffer and compute the hash partially whenever the buffer is full.

As with the generator mechanism, the locality of the code can be improved by using a buffer that is larger than one hash function input block. The entropy accumulator would thus accumulate several blocks worth of samples before hashing the entire buffer.

The entropy accumulator should be careful not to generate any overflows while adding up the entropy estimates. As there is no limit on the number of samples the accumulator might have to process between two reseeds the implementation has to handle this case.

5.3   Reseed Mechanism

The reseeding mechanism generates a new key K for the generator from the entropy accumulator's pool and the existing key. The execution time of the reseed mechanism depends on a parameter $P_t \geq 0$. This parameter can either be fixed for the implementation or be dynamically adjusted.

The reseed process consists of the following steps:

1. The entropy accumulator computes the hash on the concatenation of all the inputs into the fast pool. We call the result v_0.
2. Set $v_i := h(v_{i-1}|v_0|i)$ for $i = 1, \ldots, t$.
3. Set $K \leftarrow h'(h(v_{P_t}|K), k)$.
4. Set $C \leftarrow E_K(0)$.
5. Reset all entropy estimate accumulators of the entropy accumulator to zero.
6. Wipe the memory of all intermediate values
7. If a seed file is in use, the next $2k$ bits of output from the generator are written to the seed file, overwriting any old values.

Step 1 gathers the output from the entropy accumulator. Step 2 uses an iterative formula of length P_t to make the reseeding computationally expensive if desired. Step 3 uses the hash function h and a function h', which we will define shortly, to create a new key K from the existing key and the new entropy value v_{P_t}. Step 4 defines the new value of the counter C.

The function h' is defined in terms of h. To compute $h'(m, k)$ we construct

$$s_0 := m$$
$$s_i := h(s_0|\ldots|s_{i-1}) \qquad i = 1, \ldots$$
$$h'(m, k) := \text{first } k \text{ bits of } (s_0|s_1|\ldots)$$

This is effectively a 'size adaptor' function that converts an input of any length to an output of the specified length. If the input is larger than the desired output, the function takes the leading bits of the input. If the input is the same size as the output the function is the identity function. If the input is smaller than the output the extra bits are generated using the hash function. This is a very expensive type of PRNG, but for the small sizes we are using this is not a problem.

There is no security reason why we would set a new value for the counter C. This is done to allow more implementation flexibility and still maintain compatibility between different implementations. Setting the counter C makes it simple for an implementation to generate a whole buffer of output from the generator at once. If a reseed occurs, the new output should be derived from the new seed and not from the old output buffer. Setting a new C value makes this simple: any data in the output buffer is simply discarded. Simply re-using the existing counter value is not compatible as different implementations have different sizes of output buffers, and thus the counter has been advanced to different points. Rewinding the counter to the virtual 'current' position is error-prone.

To reseed the slow pool, we feed the hash of the slow pool into the fast pool, and then do a reseed. In general, this slow reseed should have P_t set as high as is tolerable.

In Yarrow-160, this is done as described above, but using SHA1 and triple-DES. We generate a three-key triple-DES key from the hash of the contents of the pool or pools used, and the current key.

Security Arguments. Consider an attacker who starts out knowing the generator key but not the contents of the entropy pool hash v_0. The value v_{P_t} is a pure function of v_0, so the attacker has no real information about v_{P_t}. This value is then hashed with K, and the result is size-adjusted to be the new key. As the result of the hash has as much entropy as v_{P_t} has, the attacker loses his knowledge about K.

Consider an attacker in the opposite situation: he starts out knowing the samples that have been processed, but not the current generator key. The attacker thus knows v_{P_t}. However, an attacker with no knowledge of the key K cannot predict the result of the hash, and thus ends up knowing nothing about the new key.

5.4 Reseed Control

The reseed control module determines when a reseed is to be performed. An explicit reseed occurs when some application explicitly asks for a reseed operation. This is intended to be used only rarely, and only by applications that generate very high-valued random secrets. Access to the explicit reseed function should be restricted in many cases.

The reseed periodically occurs automatically. The fast pool is used to reseed whenever any of its sources have an entropy estimate of over some threshhold value. The slow pool is used to reseed whenever at least two of its sources have entropy estimates above some other threshhold value.

In Yarrow-160, the fast pool threshhold is 100 bits, and the slow pool threshhold is 160 bits. Two sources must pass the threshhold for the slow pool to reseed.

6 Open Questions and Plans for the Future

Yarrow-160, our current construction, is limited to at most 160 bits of security by the size of its entropy accumulation pools. Three-key triple-DES has known attacks considerably better than brute-force; however, the backtracking prevention mechanism changes keys often enough that the cipher still has about 160 bits of security in practice.

At some point in the future, we expect to see a new block cipher standard, the AES. Yarrow's basic design can easily accommodate a new block cipher. However, we will also have to either change hash functions, or come up with some special hash function construction to provide more than 160 bits of entropy pool. For AES with 128 bits, this will not be an issue; for AES with 192 bits or 256 bits, it will have to be dealt with. We note that the generic Yarrow framework will accomodate the AES block cipher and a 256-bit hash function (perhaps constructed from the AES block cipher) with no problems.

In practice, we expect any weaknesses in Yarrow-160 to come from poorly estimating entropy, not from cryptanalysis. For that reason, we hope to continue to improve the Yarrow entropy estimation mechanisms. This is the subject of ongoing research; as better estimation tools become available, we will upgrade Yarrow to use them.

We still have to create a reference implementation of Yarrow-160, and create test vectors for various parameter sets. These test vectors will test all aspects of the generator. This will probably require the use of Yarrow-160 versions with different parameters then the ones used in Yarrow-160; the details of this remain to be investigated.

The reseed control rules are still an ad-hoc design. Further study might yield an improves set of reseed control rules. This is the subject of ongoing research.

7   On the Name "Yarrow"

Yarrow is a flowering perennial with distinctive flat flower heads and lacy leaves, like Queen Anne's Lace or wild carrot. Yarrow stalks have been used for divination in China since the Hsia dynasty, in the second millennium B.C.E. The fortuneteller would divide a set of 50 stalks into piles, then repeatedly use modulo arithmetic to generate two bits of random information (but with a nonuniform distribution).

Here is the full description of the method: The most notable things are: one, it takes an amazing amount of effort to generate two random bits; and two, it does not produce a flat output distribution, but, apparently, 1/16 - 3/16 - 5/16 - 7/16.

The oracle is consulted with the help of yarrow stalks. These stalks are short lengths of bamboo, about four inches in length and an eighth inch in diameter. Fifty stalks are used for this purpose. One is put aside and plays no further part. The remaining 49 stalks are first divided into two random heaps. One stalk is then taken from the right-hand heap and put between the ring finger and the little finger of left hand. Then the left-hand heap is placed in the left hand, and the right hand takes from it bundles of 4, until there are 4 or fewer stalks remaining. This remainder is placed between the ring finger and the middle finger of the left hand. Next the right-hand heap is counted off by fours, and the remainder is placed between the middle finger and the forefinger of the left hand. The sum of the stalks now between the fingers of the left hand is either 9 or 5. (The various possibilities are 1 + 4 + 4, or 1 + 3 + 1, or 1 + 2 + 2, or 1 + 1 + 3; it follows that the number 5 is easier to obtain than the number 9.) At this first counting off of the stalks, the first stalk—held between the little finger and the ring finger—is disregarded as supernumerary, hence one reckons as follows: 9 = 8, or 5 = 4. The number 4 is regarded as a complete unit, to which the numerical value 3 is assigned. The number 8, on the other hand, is regarded as a double unit and is reckoned as having only the numerical value 2.Therefore, if at the first count 9 stalks are left over, they count as 2; if 5 are left, they count as 3. These stalks are now laid aside for the time being.

Then the remaining stalks are gathered together again and divided anew. Once more one takes a stalk from the pile on the right and places it between the ring finger and the little finger of the left hand; then one counts off the stalks as before. This time the sum of the remainders is either 8 or 4, the possible combinations being $1 + 4 + 3$, or $1 + 3 + 4$, or $1 + 1 + 2$, or $1 + 2 + 1$, so that this time the chances of obtaining 8 or 4 are equal. The 8 counts as a 2, the 4 counts as a 3. The procedure is carried out a third time with the remaining stalks, and again the sum of the remainders is 8 or 4.

Now from the numerical values assigned to each of the three composite remainders, a line is formed with a total value of 6, 7, 8, or 9.

Yarrow stalks are still used for fortunetelling in China, but with a greatly simplified method: shake a container of 100 numbered yarrow stalks until one comes out. This random number is used as an index into a table of fortunes.

Acknowledgements

We wish to thank Christopher Allen, Steve Bellovin, Matt Blaze, Jon Callas, Bram Cohen, Dave Grawrock, Alexey Kirichenko, David Wagner, and James Wallner for useful comments on the Yarrow design. We would also like to thank Ari Y. Benbasat for implementing the preliminary Windows version of Yarrow.

References

Agn88.   G. B. Agnew, "Random Source for Cryptographic Systems," *Advances in Cryptology—EUROCRYPT '87 Proceedings,* Springer-Verlag, 1988, pp. 77–81.

ANSI85.   ANSI X 9.17 (Revised), "American National Standard for Financial Institution Key Management (Wholesale)," American Bankers Association, 1985.

Bal96.   R.W. Baldwin, "Proper Initialization for the BSAFE Random Number Generator," *RSA Laboratories Bulletin,* n. 3, 25 Jan 1996.

BDR+96.   M. Blaze, W. Diffie, R. Rivest, B. Schneier, T. Shimomura, E. Thompson, and M. Wiener, "Minimal Key Lengths for Symmetric Ciphers to Provide Adequate Commercial Security," January 1996.

Dai97.   W. Dai, Crypto++ library,
         `http://www.eskimo.com/~weidai/cryptlib.html`.

DIF94.   D. Davis, R. Ihaka, and P. Fenstermacher, "Cryptographic Randomness from Air Turbulence in Disk Drives," *Advances in Cryptology — CRYPTO '94 Proceedings,* Springer-Verlag, 1994, pp. 114–120.

ECS94.   D. Eastlake, S.D. Crocker, and J.I. Schiller, "Randomness Requirements for Security," RFC 1750, Internet Engineering Task Force, Dec. 1994.

FMK85.   R.C. Fairchild, R.L. Mortenson, and K.B. Koulthart, "An LSI Random Number Generator (RNG)," *Advances in Cryptology: Proceedings of CRYPTO '84,* Springer-Verlag, 1985, pp. 203–230.

Gud85.   M. Gude, "Concept for a High-Performance Random Number Generator Based on Physical Random Noise," *Frequenz,* v. 39, 1985, pp. 187–190.

Gut98.   P. Gutmann, "Software Generation of Random Numbers for Cryptographic Purposes," *Proceedings of the 1998 Usenix Security Symposium,* USENIX Association, 1998, pp. 243–257.

Kah67.   D. Kahn, *The Codebreakers, The Story of Secret Writing*, Macmillan Publishing Co., New York, 1967.

Koc95.   P. Kocher, post to `sci.crypt` Internet newsgroup (message-ID pck-DIr4Ar.L4z@netcom.com), 4 Dec 1995.

Koc96.   P. Kocher, "Timing Attacks on Implementations of Diffie-Hellman, RSA, DSS, and Other Systems," *Advances in Cryptology—CRYPTO '96 Proceedings*, Springer-Verlag, 1996, pp. 104–113.

Koc98.   P. Kocher, "Differential Power Analysis," available online from `http://www.cryptography.com/dpa/`.

KSWH98a.   J. Kelsey, B. Schneier, D. Wagner, and C. Hall, "Cryptanalytic Attacks on Pseudorandom Number Generators," *Fast Software Encryption, 5th International Workshop Proceedings*, Springer-Verlag, 1998, pp. 168–188.

KSWH98b.   J. Kelsey, B. Schneier, D. Wagner, and C. Hall, "Side Channel Cryptanalysis of Product Ciphers," *ESORICS '98 Proceedings*, Springer-Verlag, 1998, pp. pp 97–110.

LMS93.   J.B. Lacy, D.P. Mitchell, and W.M. Schell, "CryptoLib: Cryptography in Software," *USENIX Security Symposium IV Proceedings*, USENIX Association, 1993, pp. 237–246.

Luc98.   S. Lucks, Private Communication, 1998.

NIS80.   National Institute of Standards and Technology. *DES Modes of Operation*, December 2, 1980. FIPS PUB 81, available from `http://www.itl.nist.gov/div897/pubs/fip81.htm`.

NIS93.   National Institute of Standards and Technology. *Data Encryption Standard (DES)*, December 30, 1993. FIPS PUB 46-2, available from `http://www.itl.nist.gov/div897/pubs/fip46-2.htm`.

NIS95.   National Institute of Standards and Technology. *Secure Hash Standard*, April 17, 1995. FIPS PUB 180-1, available from `http://www.itl.nist.gov/div897/pubs/fip180-1.htm`.

NIS99.   National Institute of Standards and Technology. *Data Encryption Standard (DES)*, 1999. DRAFT FIPS PUB 46-3.

NIST92.   National Institute for Standards and Technology, "Key Management Using X9.17," NIST FIPS PUB 171, U.S. Department of Commerce, 1992.

Plu94.   C. Plumb, "Truly Random Numbers, *Dr. Dobbs Journal*, v. 19, n. 13, Nov 1994, pp. 113-115.

Ric92.   M. Richterm "Ein Rauschgenerator zur Gweinnung won quasi-idealen Zufallszahlen fur die stochastische Simulation," Ph.D. dissertation, Aachen University of Technology, 1992. (In German.)

RSA94.   RSA Laboratories, RSAREF cryptographic library, Mar 1994, `ftp://ftp.funet.fi/pub/crypt/cryptography/asymmetric/rsa/rsaref2.tar.gz`.

SV86.   M. Santha and U.V. Vazirani, "Generating Quasi-Random Sequences from Slightly Random Sources," *Journal of Computer and System Sciences*, v. 33, 1986, pp. 75–87.

Sch96.   B. Schneier, *Applied Cryptography,* John Wiley & Sons, 1996.

Zim95.   P. Zimmermann, *The Official PGP User's Guide,* MIT Press, 1995.

Elliptic Curve Pseudorandom Sequence Generators

Guang Gong[1], Thomas A. Berson[2], and Douglas R. Stinson[3]

[1] Department of Combinatorics and Optimization
University of Waterloo
Waterloo, Ontario N2L 3G1, Canada
ggong@cacr.math.uwaterloo.ca
[2] Anagram Laboratories, P.O. Box 791
Palo Alto, CA 94301, USA
berson@anagram.com
[3] Department of Combinatorics & Optimization
University of Waterloo
Waterloo, Ontario N2L 3G1, CANADA
dstinson@cacr.math.uwaterloo.ca

Abstract. In this paper, we introduce a new approach to the generation of binary sequences by applying trace functions to elliptic curves over $GF(2^m)$. We call these sequences *elliptic curve pseudorandom sequences* (EC-sequence). We determine their periods, distribution of zeros and ones, and linear spans for a class of EC-sequences generated from supersingular curves. We exhibit a class of EC-sequences which has half period as a lower bound for their linear spans. EC-sequences can be constructed algebraically and can be generated efficiently in software or hardware by the same methods that are used for implementation of elliptic curve public-key cryptosystems.

1 Introduction

It is a well-known result that any periodic binary sequence can be decomposed as a sum of linear feedback shift register (LFSR) sequences and can be considered as a sequence arising from operating a trace function on a Reed-Solomon codeword [22], [24]. More precisely, let α be a primitive element of a finite field $\mathbb{F}_{2^n}$ and let $C = \{r_1, \cdots, r_s\}, 0 < r_i < 2^n - 1$, be the null spectrum set of a Reed-Solomon code. If we want to transmit a message $m = (m_1, \cdots, m_s), m_i \in \mathbb{F}_{2^n}$, over a noisy channel, then first we form a polynomial $g(x) = \sum_{i=0}^{s} m_i x^{r_i}$ and then compute $c_j = g(\alpha^j)$. The codeword is $c = (c_0, c_1, \cdots, c_{2^n-2})$. Now we apply the trace function from $\mathbb{F}_{2^n}$ to $\mathbb{F}_2$ to this codeword, i.e., we compute

$$a_i = Tr(c_i) = Tr(g(\alpha^i)), i = 0, 1, \cdots, 2^n - 2. \tag{1}$$

Then the resulting sequence $A = \{a_i\}$ is a binary sequence having period which is a factor of $2^n - 1$. All periodic binary sequences can be reduced to this model. Note that if $g(x) = x$, then A is an m-sequence of period $2^n - 1$. A lot of research

Howard Heys and Carlisle Adams (Eds.): SAC'99, LNCS 1758, pp. 34–48, 2000.

has been done concerning ways to choose the function $g(x)$ such that the resulting sequence has the good statistical properties. Examples include filter function generators [15], [11], [18], combinatorial function generators [14], [25], [23], and clock controlled generators and shrinking generators[1], [5]. Unfortunately, the trace function destroys the structure of Reed-Solomon code. It is difficult to get sequences satisfying cryptographic requirements from this approach. If one can specify the linear span, then there is no obvious method to determine the statistical properties of the resulting sequences. Examples include many conjectured sequences with two-level autocorrelation or lower level cross correlation [21], [27]. If one can fix the parameters for good statistical properties, then all known sequences have low linear spans in the sense that ratio of linear span to the period is much less than $1/2$.

Note that if a binary sequence of period 2^n has the property that each n-tuple occurs exactly once in one period, then it is called a *de Bruijn sequence* [3]. Chan et al. proved that de Bruijn sequences have large linear spans [4]. From a de Bruijn sequence of period 2^n one can construct a binary sequence of period $2^n - 1$ by deleting one zero from the unique run of zeros of length n. The resulting sequence is called a *modified de Bruijn sequence*, see [10]. There is no theoretical result on the linear spans of such sequences except for m-sequences. Experimental computation on the linear spans of the modified sequences have only been done for the sequences with period 15, 31 and 63 [10]. Another problem that de Bruijn sequences have is that they are difficult to implement. All algorithms for constructing de Bruijn sequences (except for a class constructed from the m-sequences of period $2^n - 1$) require a huge memory space. It is infeasible to construct a de Bruijn sequence or a nonlinear modified de Bruijn sequence with period 2^n when $n > 30$ [6], [7], [9]. (It is a well known fact that in design of secure systems, if one sequence can be obtained by removing or inserting one bit from another sequence, and the resulting sequence has a large linear span, then it is not considered as secure. Consequently, the de Bruijn sequences of period 2^n constructed from m-sequences of period $2^n - 1$ by inserting one zero into the run of zeros of length $n - 1$ of the m-sequence are not considered to be good pseudorandom sequences.)

In this paper, we introduce a new method for generating binary sequences. We will replace a Reed-Solomon codeword in (1) by the points on an elliptic curve over $\mathbb{F}_{2^n}$. The resulting binary sequences are called *elliptic curve pseudorandom sequences*, or EC-sequences for short. We will discuss constructions and representation of EC-sequences, their statistical properties, their periods and linear spans. We exhibit a class of EC-sequences which may be suitable for use as a key generator in stream cipher cryptosystems. These EC-sequences have period equal to 2^{n+1}, the bias for unbalance is $\lfloor 2^{n/2} \rfloor$ and lower bound and upper bounds on their linear spans are 2^n and $2^{n+1} - 2$, respectively. It is worth pointing out that EC-sequences can be constructed algebraically and they can be generated efficiently in software or hardware by the same method that are used for implementation of elliptic curve public-key cryptosystems [20].

The paper is organized as follows. In Section 2, we introduce some concepts and and preliminary results from sequence analysis and the definition of the elliptic curves over $\mathbb{F}_{2^n}$. In Section 3, we give a method for construction of EC-sequences and their representation by interleaved structure. In Section 4, we discuss statistical properties of EC-sequences constructed from supersingular elliptic curves. In Section 5, we determine the periods of EC-sequences constructed from supersingular elliptic curves. In Section 6, we derive a lower bound and an upper bound for EC-sequences constructed from a class of supersingular elliptic curves with order $2^n + 1$. Section 7 shows a class of EC-sequences which are suitable for use as a key generator in stream cipher cryptosystems. A comparison of this class of EC sequence generators with the other known pseudo-random sequence generators is also included in this section.

Remark. Kaliski discussed how to generate a pseudo-random sequence from elliptic curves in [16], where he used randomness criteria based on the computational difficulty of the discrete logarithm over the elliptic curves [26]. In this paper our approach is completely different. We use the unconditional randomness criteria to measure the EC-sequences and use the trace function to obtain binary sequences. A set of the unconditional randomness measurements for pseudorandom sequence generators is described as follows:

- Long period
- Balance property (Golomb Postulate 1 [9])
- Run property (Golomb Postulate 2)
- n-tuple distribution
- Two-level auto correlation (Golomb Postulate 3)
- Low-level cross correlation
- Large linear span and smooth increased linear span profiles

2 Preliminaries

In this section, we introduce some concepts and preliminary results on sequence analysis.

Let $q = 2^n$, let
F_q be a finite field and let $\mathbb{F}_q[x]$ be the ring of polynomials over $\mathbb{F}_q$.

2.1 Trace Function from $\mathbb{F}_q$ to $\mathbb{F}_2$

$$Tr(x) = x + x^2 + \cdots + x^{2^{n-1}}, x \in F_q.$$

Property: $Tr(x^{2^k}) = Tr(x)$ for any positive integer k.
For $x \in \mathbb{F}_q$, this can be written as

$$x = x_0\alpha + x_1\alpha^2 + \cdots + x_{n-1}\alpha^{2^{n-1}}, x_i \in \{0, 1\}$$

where $\{\alpha, \alpha^2, \cdots, \alpha^{2^{n-1}}\}$ is a normal basis of $\mathbb{F}_{2^n}$. In this representation, $Tr(x)$ can be computed as follows

$$Tr(x) = x_0 + x_1 + \cdots + x_{n-1}.$$

2.2 Periods, Characteristic Polynomials, and Minimal Polynomials of Sequences

Let $A = \{a_i\}$ be a binary sequence. If v is a positive integer such that

$$a_i = a_{v+i}, \ i = 0, 1, \cdots, \tag{2}$$

then v is called a length of A. We also write $A = (a_0, a_1, \cdots, a_{v-1})$, denote $v = length(A)$. Note the index is reduced modulo v. If p is the smallest positive integer satisfying (2), then we say p is the period of A, denoted as $per(A)$. It is easy to see that $p|v$.

Let $f(x) = x^l + c_{l-1}x^{l-1} + \cdots + c_1 x + c_0 \in \mathbb{F}_2[x]$. If $f(x)$ satisfies the following recursive relation:

$$a_{l+k} = \sum_{i=0}^{l-1} c_i a_{i+k} = c_{l-1}a_{l-1+k} + \cdots + c_1 a_{1+k} + c_0 a_k, \ k = 0, 1, \cdots$$

then we say $f(x)$ is a characteristic polynomial of A over $\mathbb{F}_2$.

The left shift operator L is defined as

$$L(A) = a_1, a_2, \cdots,$$

For any $i > 0$,

$$L^i(A) = a_i, a_{i+1}, \cdots,$$

We denote $L^0(A) = A$ for convention. If $f(x)$ is a characteristic polynomial of A over $\mathbb{F}_2$, then

$$f(L)A = \sum_{i=0}^{l} c_i L^i(A) = 0$$

where 0 represents a sequence consisting of all zeros. (Note 0 represents a number 0 or a sequence consisting of all zeros depending on the context.) Let

$$G(A) = \{f(x) \in \mathbb{F}_2[x] | f(L)A = 0\}.$$

The polynomial in $G(A)$ with the smallest degree, say $m(x)$, is called the minimal polynomial of A over $\mathbb{F}_2$. Note that $G(A)$ is a principle ideal of $\mathbb{F}_2[x]$ and $G(A) = < m(x) >$. So, if $f(x)$ is a characteristic polynomial of A over $\mathbb{F}_2$, then $f(x) = m(x)h(x)$ where $h(x) \in \mathbb{F}_2[x]$. The linear span of A over $\mathbb{F}_2$, denoted as $LS(S)$, is defined as $LS(A) = deg(m(x))$.

2.3 Interleaved Sequences

We can arrange the elements of the sequence A into a t by s array as follows:

$$\begin{pmatrix} a_0 & a_t & \cdots & a_{(s-1)t} \\ a_1 & a_{t+1} & \cdots & a_{(s-1)t+1} \\ a_2 & a_{t+2} & \cdots & a_{(s-1)t+2} \\ \vdots & & & \\ a_{t-1} & a_{t+t-1} & \cdots & a_{(s-1)t+t-1} \end{pmatrix}$$

Let A_i denote the ith row of the above array. Then we also write the sequence $A = (A_0, A_1, \cdots, A_{t-1})^T$ where T is a transpose of a vector. In reference [12], A is called an *interleaved sequence* if A_i, $0 \le i \le t-1$, has the same minimal polynomial over $\mathbb{F}_2$. Here we generalize this concept to any structures of A_is. We still refer to A as a (t, s) interleaved sequence. By using the same approach as used in [12], we can have the following proposition.

Proposition 1 *Let v be a length of A and A be a (t, s) interleaved sequence where $v = ts$. Let $m_i(x) \in \mathbb{F}_2[x]$ be the minimal polynomial of A_i, $1 \le i \le t$ and $m(x) \in \mathbb{F}_2[x]$ be the minimal polynomial of A, then*

$$m(x)|m_j(x^t), 0 \le j \le t-1.$$

2.4 Elliptic Curves over $\mathbb{F}_{2^n}$

An elliptic curve E over $\mathbb{F}_{2^n}$ can be written in the following standard form (see [19]):

$$y^2 + y = x^3 + c_4 x + c_6, c_i \in \mathbb{F}_{2^n} \tag{3}$$

if E is supersingular, or

$$y^2 + xy = x^3 + c_2 x^2 + c_6, c_i \in \mathbb{F}_{2^n} \tag{4}$$

if E is non-supersingular. The points $P = (x, y)$, $x, y \in \mathbb{F}_{2^n}$, that satisfy this equation, together with a "point at infinity" denoted O, form an Abelian group $(E, +, O)$ whose identity element is O.

Let $P = (x_1, y_1)$ and $Q = (x_2, y_2)$ be two different points in E and both P and Q are not equal to the infinity point.

Addition Law for E supersingular For $2P = P + P = (x_3, y_3)$,

$$x_3 = x_1^4 + c_4^2 \tag{5}$$
$$y_3 = (x_1^2 + c_4)(x_1 + x_3) + y_1 + 1 \tag{6}$$

For $P + Q = (x_3, y_3)$, if $x_1 = x_2$, then $P + Q = O$. Otherwise,

$$x_3 = \lambda^2 + x_1 + x_2$$
$$y_3 = \lambda(x_1 + x_3) + y_1 + 1$$

where $\lambda = (y_1 + y_2)/(x_1 + x_2)$.

Remark 1 *For a detailed treatment of sequence analysis and an introduction to elliptic curves, the reader is referred to [9], [19].*

3 Constructions of Pseudorandom Sequences from Elliptic Curves over $\mathbb{F}_q$

In this section, we give a construction of binary sequences from an elliptic curve over $\mathbb{F}_q$.

Let E be an elliptic curve over $\mathbb{F}_q$, denoted as $E(\mathbb{F}_q)$ or simply E if there is no confusion for the field that we work with, and let $|E|$ be the number of points of E over $\mathbb{F}_q$. Let $P = (x_1, y_1)$ be a point of E with order $v + 1$. Note that $v + 1 || E|$. Let $\Gamma = (P, 2P, \cdots, vP)$ where $iP = (x_i, y_i)$, $1 \le i \le v$. Note that v is even if E is supersingular. v may be odd or even if E is non-supersingular. So, we can write $v = 2l$ if E is supersingular and $v = 2l + e, e \in F_2$ if E is non-supersingular.

3.1 Construction

Let

$$a_i = Tr(x_i) \text{ and } b_i = Tr(y_i), i = 1, 2, \cdots, v, \tag{7}$$

$$S_0 = (a_1, \cdots, a_v) \text{ and } S_1 = (b_1, \cdots, b_v). \tag{8}$$

Let $S = (S_0, S_1)^T$ be a $(2, v)$ interleaved sequence, i.e., the elements of $S = \{s_i\}_{i \ge 1}$ are given by

$$s_{2i-1} = a_i \text{ and } s_{2i} = b_i, i = 1, \cdots, v \tag{9}$$

where $length(S) = 2v$. For a convenient discussion in the following sections, we write S starting from 1, we denote 0 as $2v$ when the index is computed modulo $2v$. We call S a *binary elliptic curve pseudorandom sequence generated by* $E(\mathbb{F}_q)$ *of type I*, an *EC-sequence* for short.

Remark 2 *In the full paper [13], we discuss two other methods of constructing sequences from elliptic curves.*

Let $A = (a_1, a_2, \cdots, a_l)$ and $B = (b_1, b_2, \cdots, b_l)$. If $U = (u_1, u_2, \cdots, u_t)$, then we denote $\overleftarrow{U} = (u_t, u_{t-1}, \cdots, u_1)$, i.e., U written backwards.

Theorem 1 *With the above notation. Let $v + 1 || E|$, and let $S = (S_0, S_1)^T$ be a EC-sequence generated by $E(\mathbb{F}_q)$ of length $2v$ whose elements are given by (9). Let E be supersingular. Then*

$$S = \begin{pmatrix} A \ \overleftarrow{A} \\ B \ \overleftarrow{B} +1 \end{pmatrix} \tag{10}$$

Proof. Let E be supersingular. Note that y and $y + 1$ are two roots of (3) in $\mathbb{F}_q$ under the condition $Tr(x^3 + c_4 x + c_6) = 0$. Since the order of P is $v + 1$, then

$$iP + (2l + 1 - i)P = O \implies x_{l+i} = x_{l+1-i} \implies y_{l+i} = y_{l+1-i} + 1, i = 1, \cdots, l.$$

Thus we have $S_0 = (A, \overleftarrow{A})$ and $S_1 = (B, \overleftarrow{B} +1)$.

4 Statistical Properties of Supersingular EC-Sequences

In this section, we discuss the statistical properties of EC-sequences generated by supersingular curves over $\mathbb{F}_{2^n}$ where n is odd. Let $A = (a_0, \cdots, a_{p-1})$, $w(A)$ represent the Hamming weight of sequence A. i.e.,

$$w(A) = |\{i \mid a_i = 1, 0 \leq i < p\}|.$$

For convenience, we generalize the notation of Hamming weight of binary sequences to functions from $\mathbb{F}_q$ to $\mathbb{F}_2$. Let $g(x)$ be a function from $\mathbb{F}_q$ to $\mathbb{F}_2$, the weight of g is defined as $w(g) = |\{x \in \mathbb{F}_q | g(x) = 1\}|$. For two isomorphic curves $E(\mathbb{F}_q)$ and $T(\mathbb{F}_q)$, denote this by $E \cong T$. From [19], there are three different isomorphism classes for supersingular curves over $\mathbb{F}_q$ ($q = 2^n$) for n odd.

1. $E_1 = \{E(\mathbb{F}_q) | E(\mathbb{F}_q) \cong y^2 + y = x^3\}$ and $|E_1| = 2^{2n-1}$ and for any $E(\mathbb{F}_q) \in E_1$, $|E| = q + 1$.
2. $E_2 = \{E(\mathbb{F}_q) | E(\mathbb{F}_q) \cong y^2 + y = x^3 + x\}$.
3. $E_3 = \{E(\mathbb{F}_q) | E(\mathbb{F}_q) \cong y^2 + y = x^3 + x + 1\}$.

Here $|E_2| = |E_3| = 2^{2n-2}$. For any $E(\mathbb{F}_q) \in E_2$ or E_3, $|E| = 2^n \pm 2^{(n+1)/2} + 1$. Let

$$E : y^2 + y = x^3 + c_4 x + c_6, c_4, c_6 \in \mathbb{F}_q.$$

Theorem 2 *Let n be odd. Let $S = \begin{pmatrix} A & \overleftarrow{A} \\ B & \overleftarrow{B} + 1 \end{pmatrix}$ be an EC-sequence generated by a supersingular elliptic curve E where $length(S) = 2v$ and $v = |E| - 1$. Then $w(S_0) = 2w(A)$, $w(S_1) = v/2$ and $w(S) = 2w(A) + v/2$, where $w(A) = 2^{n-2} \pm 2^{(n-3)/2}$.*

In order to prove this result, we need the following lemma. If we denote $h(x) = x^3 + c_4 x + c_6$, then E can be written as $y^2 + y = h(x)$.

Lemma 1 *Let E and $h(x)$ be defined as above. Then we have*

$$\sum_{x \in \mathbb{F}_{2^n}} (-1)^{Tr(h(x))} = |E| - 2^n - 1.$$

Proof.

$$\sum_{x \in \mathbb{F}_{2^n}} (-1)^{Tr(h(x))} = |\{x \in \mathbb{F}_{2^n} : Tr(h(x)) = 0\}| - |\{x \in \mathbb{F}_{2^n} : Tr(h(x)) = 1\}|$$

$$= 2|\{x \in \mathbb{F}_{2^n} : Tr(h(x)) = 0\}| - 2^n$$

$$= (|E| - 1) - 2^n.$$

For $i, j = 0, 1$, define

$$n_{i,j} = |\{x \in \mathbb{F}_{2^n} : Tr(x) = i, Tr(h(x)) = j\}|.$$

Next we determine $n_{1,0}$. Let F denote the elliptic curve $y^2 + y = h(x) + x$. Then the following equations hold:

$$n_{1,0} + n_{1,1} = 2^{n-1}$$
$$n_{0,0} + n_{0,1} = 2^{n-1}$$
$$n_{0,0} + n_{1,0} = (|E| - 1)/2$$
$$n_{0,0} + n_{1,1} - (n_{0,1} + n_{1,0}) = |F| - 1 - 2^n.$$

Note that the last equation follows easily from Lemma 1 since

$$n_{0,0} + n_{1,1} - (n_{0,1} + n_{1,0}) = |\{x \in \mathbb{F}_{2^n} : Tr(x + h(x))$$
$$= 0\}| - |\{x \in \mathbb{F}_{2^n} : Tr(x + h(x)) = 1\}|.$$

Now, this system of four equations in four unknowns is easily seen to have a unique solution. The value of $n_{1,0}$ is as stated in the following lemma:

Lemma 2 *Let E, F and $n_{1,0}$ be defined as above. Then we have*

$$n_{1,0} = 2^{n-2} + \frac{|E| - |F|}{4}.$$

It is known that $|E| - |F| = \pm 2^{(n+1)/2}$ for any values of c_4 and c_6 (This is shown in [8]; alternatively it follows easily from [19], p.40 and 47.) Thus we have the following corollary:

Corollary 1 *Let $n_{1,0}$ be defined as above; then $n_{1,0} = 2^{n-2} \pm 2^{(n-3)/2}$.*

Proof (Proof of Theorem 2). Since $length(S) = 2v$, from Theorem 1, we have $w(S_0) = 2w(A)$ and $w(S_1) = v/2$. So,

$$w(S) = 2w(A) + v/2. \tag{11}$$

According to the definition of $n_{i,j}$, we have $w(A) = n_{10}$. From Corollary 1, $w(A) = 2^{n-2} \pm 2^{(n-3)/2}$.

Remark 3 *The value of $w(A)$ depends on the values of c_4 and c_6. For further results on this, we refer the reader to the full version of this work [13].*

5 Periods of Supersingular EC-Sequences

In this section, we discuss the periods of EC-sequences generated by supersingular curves.

Lemma 3 *Let $S = (S_0, S_1)^T$ be a EC-sequence generated by a supersingular elliptic curve $E(\mathbb{F}_q)$ where $S_0 = (a_1, a_2, \cdots, a_v)$ and $v = |E| - 1 = 2l$. Then*

$$a_{2i} = a_i + Tr(c_4), i = 1, 2, \cdots, l.$$

Proof. Recall that $a_i = Tr(x_i)$. From formula (5) in Section 1,

$$x_{2i} = x_i^4 + c_4^2, i = 1, \cdots, l. \tag{12}$$

$$\Longrightarrow a_{2i} = Tr(x_{2i}) = Tr(x_i^4 + c_4^2) = Tr(x_i) + Tr(c_4) = a_i + Tr(c_4).$$

Definition 1 *Let $U = (u_1, u_2, \cdots, u_{2k})$ be a binary sequence of length $2k$. Then U is called a coset fixed palindrome sequence of length $2k$, CFP-sequence of length $2k$ for short, if it satisfies the following two conditions.*

(i) *Palindrome Condition (P)*
$U = (U_0, \overleftarrow{U_0})$ where $U_0 = (u_1, u_2, \cdots, u_k)$.
(ii) *Coset Fixed Condition (CF)*
$u_{2i} = u_i + c$, for each $1 \le i \le k$ where c is a constant in $\mathbb{F}_2$.

Lemma 4 *Let U be a CFP sequence of length $2d$ and $0 < w(U) < 2d$. Then $per(U) = 2d$.*

Proof. We claim that $per(U) \ne 2$. Otherwise, from the coset fixed condition $u_{2i} = u_i$, $1 \le i \le d$, we get $w(U) = 0$ or $w(U) = 2d$, which is a contradiction with the given condition. Therefore we can write $per(U) = t$ where $2 < t$ and $t|2d$. If $t < 2d$, let $2d = ts$. Then

$$u_{t+i} = u_i, i = 1, 2, \cdots. \tag{13}$$

Since U is a CFP sequence, from condition (i) in Definition 1, we have

$$u_{d-i} = u_{d+1+i}, 0 \le i \le d - 1. \tag{14}$$

From (13) and (14), we get

$$u_{l-i} = u_{l+1+i}, 0 \le i \le l - 1 \tag{15}$$

where $l = t/2$ if t is even and

$$u_{l-i} = u_{l+i}, 1 \le i \le l - 1 \tag{16}$$

$l = (t+1)/2$ if t is odd. From condition 2 in Definition 1,

$$u_{2i} = u_i + c, 1 \le i \le t. \tag{17}$$

Since $0 < w(U) < 2d$ and U satisfies the CF condition, there exists $k : 0 \le k < l$ such that
$$(u_{t+2k+1}, u_{t+2k+2}) = (1, 0) \text{ or } (0, 1). \tag{18}$$

(For a detailed proof of existence of such k, please see the full version of this paper [13].)

Case 1 $t = 2l$. Applying the above identities,

$$u_{l+k+1} \overset{(17)}{=} u_{2l+2k+2} + c = u_{t+2k+2} + c. \tag{19}$$

On the other hand,

$$u_{l+k+1} \overset{(15)}{=} u_{l-k} \overset{(17)}{=} u_{2l-2k} + c = u_{t-2k} + c \overset{(14)}{=} u_{t+2k+1} + c \tag{20}$$

(19) and (20) $\Longrightarrow u_{t+2k+1} = u_{t+2k+2}$ which contradicts with (18). Thus $per(U) = 2d$.

Case 2 $t = 2l - 1$.

$$u_{l+k+1} \overset{(17)}{=} u_{2l+2k+2} + c = u_{t+2k+1} + c. \tag{21}$$

$$u_{l+k+1} \overset{(16)}{=} u_{l-k-1} \overset{(17)}{=} u_{2l-2k-2} + c = u_{t-2k-1} + c \overset{(14)}{=} u_{t+2k+2} + c \tag{22}$$

(21) and (22) $\Longrightarrow u_{t+2k+1} = u_{t+2k+2}$ which contradicts with (18). Thus $per(U) = 2d$.

Lemma 5 *Let* $S = (S_0, S_1)^T$ *be a EC-sequence of length* $2v$, *generated by a supersingular elliptic curve* $E(\mathbb{F}_q)$, *where* $v|(|E| - 1)$ *and* $0 < w(S_0) < v$. *Then* $per(S_0) = v$.

Proof. From Theorem 1, we have $S_0 = (A, \overleftarrow{A})$, where $length(A) = v/2$. Together with Lemma 3, S_0 is a CFP sequence of length v. Since $0 < w(S_0) < v$, applying Lemma 4, we get $per(S_0) = v$.

Lemma 6 *Let* $S = (S_0, S_1)^T$ *be a EC-sequence of length* $2v$, *generated by an elliptic curve* $E(\mathbb{F}_q)$, *where* $v|(|E| - 1)$. *Then* $per(S)$ *is an even number.*

Proof. Assume that $per(S) = 2t + 1$. Then we have $s_1 = s_{2t+2} = b_{t+1}$ and $b_{v-t+1} = s_{2v-2(t+1)} = s_1 \Longrightarrow b_{v-t+1} = b_{t+1}$. From Theorem 1, $b_{v-t+1} = b_{t+1} + 1$ which is a contradiction. So, $per(S)$ is even.

Theorem 3 *Let* $S = (S_0, S_1)^T$ *be a EC-sequence of length* $2v$, *generated by a supersingular elliptic curve* $E(\mathbb{F}_q)$, *where* $v|(|E| - 1)$ *and* $0 < w(S_0) < v$. *Then* $per(S) = 2v$.

Proof. Since $length(S) = 2v$, then $per(S)|2v$. According to Lemma 6, $per(S) = 2t$ where $t|v$. Assume that $t < v$. Then

$$a_{t+j} = s_{2(t+j)-1} = s_{2t+2j-1} = s_{2j-1} = a_j, j = 1, 2, \cdots.$$

Thus, t is a length of $S_0 \Longrightarrow per(S_0)|t$. According to Lemma 5, $per(S_0) = v$. Thus $t = per(S_0) = v \Longrightarrow per(S) = 2v$.

Corollary 2 *Let n be odd. Let $S = (S_0, S_1)^T$ be a EC-sequence of length $2v$, generated by a supersingular elliptic curve $E(\mathbb{F}_q)$, where $v|(|E|-1)$. Then $per(S) = 2v$.*

Proof. From Theorem 4, we have $0 < w(S_0) < v$. Applying Theorem 5, the result follows.

6   Linear Span of Supersingular EC-Sequences

In this section, we derive a lower bound and an upper bound on the linear span of the EC-sequences generated by supersingular elliptic curves in the isomorphic class E_1. For convenience in using Proposition 1, from now on we will write S, S_0 and S_1 with the starting index at 0, i.e., $S = (s_0, s_1, \cdots, s_{2^{n+1}-1})$, $S_0 = (a_0, a_1, \cdots, a_{2^n-1})$ and $S_1 = (b_0, b_1, \cdots, b_{2^n-1})$ ($v = 2^n$ in this case). So,

$$a_i = s_{2i}, i = 0, 1, \cdots,$$
$$b_i = s_{2i+1}, i = 0, 1, \cdots.$$

Lemma 7 *Let $U = (u_0, \cdots, u_{2^k-1})$ where $per(U) = 2^k$ and $w(U) \equiv 0 \bmod 2$. Then, the linear span of U, $LS(U)$, is bounded as follows:*

$$2^{k-1} < LS(U) \leq 2^k - 1$$

Proof. Let $h(x)$ be the minimal polynomial of U over $\mathbb{F}_2$. Let $f(x) = x^{2^k} + 1$, then $f(L)(S) = 0$. Thus $h(x)|f(x)$. Since

$$f(x) = x^{2^k} + 1 = (x+1)^{2^k},$$

we have $h(x) = (x+1)^t$ where t is in the range of $1 \leq t \leq 2^k$. Since $w(U) \equiv 0 \bmod 2$, let $p = 2^k$, we have

$$u_{p+j} = \sum_{i=0}^{p-1} u_{j+i}, j = 0, 1, \cdots.$$

$\implies g(x) = \sum_{i=0}^{p-1} x^i$ is a characteristic polynomial of U over $\mathbb{F}_2$. So $h(x)|g(x) \implies$ $LS(U) \leq 2^k - 1$.

On the other hand, if $r < 2^{k-1}$, then $h(x)|(x+1)^{2^{k-1}} = x^{2^{k-1}} + 1 \implies$ $x^{2^{k-1}} + 1$ is a characteristic polynomial of U over $\mathbb{F}_2 \implies$

$$(L^{2^{k-1}} + 1)U = u_{2^{k-1}+i} + u_i = 0, i = 0, 1, \cdots$$

$\implies per(U)|2^{k-1}$. This contradicts $per(U) = 2^k$. So, $r = LS(U) > 2^{k-1}$.

Theorem 4 *Let n be odd. Let S be an EC-sequence of length $2v$, generated from a supersingular elliptic curve $E(\mathbb{F}_q)$ which is isomorphic to $y^2 + y = x^3$, where $v = |E| - 1$. Then*

$$2^n \leq LS(S) \leq 2(2^n - 1).$$

Proof. From Corollary 2, we have $per(S) = 2^{n+1}$. According to Theorem 2, $w(S) \equiv 0 \mod 2$. So, S satisfies the conditions of Lemma 7. Applying Lemma 7,

$$2^n < LS(S) < 2^{n+1} - 1.$$

Now, we only need to prove that $LS(S) \leq 2(2^n - 1)$. Let $m(x)$ and $m_0(x)$ be the minimal polynomials of S and S_0 over $\mathbb{F}_2$, respectively, where $S = (S_0, S_1)^T$. According to Proposition 1, we have

$$m(x)|m_0(x^2) \implies deg(m(x)) \leq 2deg(m_0(x)).$$

Since S_0 also satisfies the condition of Lemma 7, we get $deg(m_0(x)) = LS(S_0) \leq 2^n - 1$. So,

$$LS(S) = deg(m(x)) \leq 2deg(m_0(x)) \leq 2(2^n - 1).$$

7 Applications

In this section, using the theoretical results that we obtained in the previous sections, we construct a class of EC-sequences with large linear spans and small bias unbalance, point out its implementation and give a comparison of ECPSG I with other known pseudorandom sequence generators.

7.1 ECPSG I

(a) Choose a finite field $K = \mathbb{F}_{2^n}$ where n is odd
(b) Randomly choose a super singular curve $E : y^2 + y = x^3 + c_4 x + c_6$ over $\mathbb{F}_{2^n}$ in the isomorphism class E_1 of the curve $y^2 + y = x^3$. ($|E_1| = 2^{2n-1}$.)
(c) Randomly choose a point $P = (x, y)$ on the curve E such that the order of P is $2^n + 1$.
(d) Compute $iP = (x_i, y_i)$, $i = 1, \cdots, 2^n$.
(e) Map iP into a binary pair by using the trace function

$$a_i = Tr(x_i) \text{ and } b_i = Tr(y_i)$$

(f) Concatenate the pair (a_i, b_i) to construct the sequence $S = (a_1, b_1, a_2, b_2, \cdots, a_{2^n}, b_{2^n})$.

Let

$$G(E_1) = \{S = \{s_i\}|S \text{ generated by } E(\mathbb{F}_{2^n}) \in E_1\}.$$

$G(E_1)$ is called an *elliptic curve pseudorandom sequence generator of type I (ECPSG I)*. Any sequence in $G(E_1)$ satisfies that $per(S) = 2^{n+1}$, $w(S) = 2^n \pm 2^m$ and $2^n < LS(S) \leq 2(2^n - 1)$.

Example Let $n = 5$.

(a) Construct a finite field $\mathbb{F}_{2^5}$ which is generated by a primitive polynomial $f(x) = x^5 + x^3 + 1$. Let α be a root of $f(x)$. We represent the elements in $\mathbb{F}_{2^5}$ as a power of α. For zero element, we write as $0 = \alpha^{\infty}$.

(b) Choose a curve $E : y^2 + y = x^3$.

(c) Choose $P = (\alpha, \alpha^{23})$ with order 33.

(d) Compute $iP = (x_i, y_i)$, $i = 1, \cdots, 32$, and the exponents of α for each point iP are listed in Table 1.

Table 1. $\{iP\}$

(1, 23)	(4, 13)	(18, 7)	(16, 27)	(13, 5)	
(10, 2)	(26, 6)	(2, 22)	(5, 14)	(21, 12)	
$(\infty, 0)$	(9, 19)	(22, 17)	(11, 9)	(20, 25)	
(8, 29)	(8 , 26)	(20, 4)	(11, 24)	(22, 18)	
(9, 8)	(∞, ∞)	(21, 20)	(5 , 1)	(2, 15)	
(26, 10)	(10, 28)	(13, 3)	(16, 21)	(18, 16)	
(4, 30)	(1, 11)				

(e) Map the point iP into two bits by the trace function:

x-coordinate sequence

$$\{a_i = Tr(x_i)\} = 00101110110111100111101101110100$$

and y-coordinate sequence

$$\{b_i = Tr(y_i)\} = 01101001101101101001001001101001$$

(f) Interleave (a_i, b_i):

$S = (a_1, b_1, a_2, b_2, \cdots, a_{32}, b_{32})$

$= 0001110011101001111001111011110001101011100011100011111001100001$

According to Theorems 3, 2 and 4, we have

- $per(S) = 64$.
- $w(S) = 2^5 + 2^2 = 36$. The bias of unbalance is equal to 4 for S.
- Linear span: $32 < LS(S) \leq 62$.

Remark 4 1. *The actual linear span of S is 62 and it has the minimal polynomial $m(x) = (x + 1)^{62}$.*

2. *The linear span of a periodic sequence is invariant under the cyclic shift operation on the sequence. We computed the supersingular EC-sequences over $\mathbb{F}_{2^5}$ and $\mathbb{F}_{2^7}$ for all phase shifts of the sequences. Experimental data shows that the profile of linear spans of any supersingular EC-sequence increases smoothly for each phase shift of the sequence.*

7.2   Implementation of ECPSG I

Implementation of ECPSG relies only on implementation of elliptic curves over $\mathbb{F}_{2^n}$, we can borrow software/hardware from elliptic curve public-key cryptosystems to implement ECPSG.

7.3 A Table

In Table 2, we compare the period, frequency range of 1 occurrence, unbalance range, and linear span (LS) of ECPSG I with other sequence generators, such as filter function generators (FFG), combinatorial function generators (CFG), and clock controlled generators (CCG). We also include data for de Bruijn sequences. We conclude that ECPSG I may be suitable for use as a key generator in a stream cipher cryptosystem.

Table 2. Comparison of ECPSG I with Other Sequence Generators

Type of Generator	Period	Frequency Range of 1 occurrence	Unbalance Range	Linear Span
FFG	$2^n - 1$	$[1, 2^{n-1}]$	$[1, 2^{n-1}]$	unclear
CFG	$\leq 2^n - 1$	$[1, 2^{n-1}]$	$[1, 2^{n-1}]$	unclear
CCG	$(2^n - 1)^2$	$2^{n-1}(2^n - 1)$	$2^n - 1$	$n(2^n - 1)$
de Bruijn	2^{n+1}	2^n	0	$\geq 2^n + n + 1$ $\leq 2^{n+1} - 1$
ECPSG I	2^{n+1}	$2^n \pm 2^{(n-1)/2}$	$\pm 2^{(n-1)/2}$	$\geq 2^n$ $\leq 2^{n+1} - 2$

Acknowledgment

The authors would like to acknowledge useful discussions with Alfred Menezes.

References

1. T. Beth and F.Piper, The stop-and-go generator, *Advances in Cryptology, Proc. of EUROCRYPT'84*, vol. 209, Springer-Verlag, 1985, pp. 88-92.
2. M. Blum and S. Micali, How to generate cryptographically strong sequences of pseudo-random bits, *SIAM Journal of Computing* **13**(4), pp. 850-864, 1984.
3. N.G. de Bruijn, A combinatorial problem, *Kononklijke Nederlands Akademi van Wetenchappen, Proc.*, vol. 49, Pr. 2, 1946, pp. 758-764.
4. A.H. Chan, R.A. Games and E.L. Key, On the complexities of de Bruijn sequences, *J. Combin. Theory*, vol. 33, pp. 233-246, Nov. 1982.
5. D. Coppersmith, H. Krawczys and Y. Mansour, The shrinking generator, *Advances in Cryptology-Crypt'93*, Lecture Notes in Computer Science, vol. 773, Springer-Verlag, 1994, pp. 22-39.
6. H. Fredrickson, A survey of full length nonlinear shift register cycle algorithms, *SIAM Rev.*, Vol. 24, pp. 195-229, Apr. 1982.
7. R.A. Games, A generalized recursive construction for de Bruijn sequences, *IEEE Trans- on Inform. Theory* vol. IT-29, No. 6, Nov. 1983, pp. 843-850.
8. R. Gold, Maximal recursive sequences with 3-valued recursive cross-correlation functions, *IEEE Trans. on Inform. Theory*, January 1968, pp. 154-156.

9. S.W. Golomb, *Shift Register Sequences*, Revised Edition, Aegean Park Press, 1982, pp. 39.

10. G.L. Mayhew and S.W. Golomb, Linear spans of modified de Bruijn sequences, *IEEE Trans. Inform. Theory*, vol. IT-36, No. 5, September 1990, pp. 1166-1167.

11. G. Gong, *An Analysis and Synthesis of Phases and Linear Complexity of Nonlinear Feed-forward Sequences*, Ph. D. dissertation, Institute of Information Systems, Univ. of Electronic Sci. & Tech. of China, Chengdu, Sichuan, China, 1990.

12. G. Gong, Theory and applications of q-ary interleaved sequences, *IEEE Trans. on Inform. Theory*, vol. IT-41, No. 2, March 1995, pp. 400-411.

13. G. Gong, T.A. Berson, and D.R. Stinson, Elliptic curve pseudorandom sequence generators, Technical Report, University of Waterloo, December 1998, http://www.cacr.math.uwaterloo.ca.

14. E.J. Groth, Generation of binary sequences with controllable complexity, *IEEE Trans. on Inform. Theory* vol. IT-17, No. 3, May 1971, pp. 288-296.

15. E.L. Key, An analysis of the structure and complexity of nonlinear binary sequence generators, *IEEE Trans. on Inform. Theory* vol. IT-22, No. 6, November 1976, pp. 732-736.

16. Jr. B. Kaliski, A pseudo-random bit generator based on elliptic logarithms, *Advances in Cryptology-Crypto'86*, Lecture Notes in Computer Science, vol. 263 , Springer-Verlag, Berlin, 1986. pp. 84-103.

17. F.J. MacWilliams and N.J.A. Sloane, *The Theory of Error-Correcting Codes*, North-Holland, New York, 1977.

18. J.L. Massey and S. Serconek, The linear complexity of periodic sequences: a general theory, *Advances in Cryptology-Crypto'96*, Lecture Notes in Computer Science, vol. 1109 , Springer-Verlag, Berlin, 1996. pp. 358-372.

19. A.J. Menezes, *Elliptic Curve Public Key Cryptosystems*, Kluwer Academic Publishers, 1993.

20. A.J. Menezes and S.A. Vanstone, Elliptic curve cryptosystems and their implementation, *Journal of Cryptology,* **6**(1993), pp.209-224.

21. J.S. No, S.W. Golomb, G. Gong, H.K. Lee, and P. Gaal, New binary pseudorandom sequences of period $2^n - 1$ with ideal autocorrelation, *IEEE Trans. on Inform. Theory*, vol. 44, No. 2, March 1998, pp.814-817.

22. I.R. Reed and G. Solomon, Polynomial codes over certain finite fields, *J. SIAM*, **8**(1960), pp. 300-304.

23. R.A. Rueppel, Products of linear recurring sequences with maximum complexity, *IEEE Trans. on Inform. Theory* vol. IT-33, No. 1, January 1987, pp. 124-131.

24. D.V. Sarwate, Optimum PN sequences for CDMA systems, *Proceedings of IEEE Third International Symposium on Spread Spectrum Techniques and Applications (IEEE ISSSTA'94)*, pp. 27-35.

25. T. Siegenthaler, Correlation-immunity of nonlinear combining functions for cryptographic applications, *IEEE Trans. Inform. Theory*, vol. IT-30, Sep. 1984, pp. 776-780.

26. Andrew C. Yao, Theory and applications of trapdoor functions , *23rd Annual Symposium of Foundations of Computer Science*, pp. 80-91.

27. D.V. Sarwate and M.B. Pursley, Cross correlation properties of pseudo-random and related sequences, *Proc. of the IEEE*, vol. 68, No. 5, May 1980.

Adaptive-Attack Norm for Decorrelation and Super-Pseudorandomness

Serge Vaudenay[*]

Ecole Normale Supérieure — CNRS
Serge.Vaudenay@ens.fr

Abstract. In previous work, security results of decorrelation theory was based on the infinity-associated matrix norm. This enables to prove that decorrelation provides security against non-adaptive iterated attacks. In this paper we define a new matrix norm dedicated to adaptive chosen plaintext attacks. Similarly, we construct another matrix norm dedicated to chosen plaintext and ciphertext attacks.

The formalism from decorrelation enables to manipulate the notion of best advantage for distinguishers so easily that we prove as a trivial consequence a somewhat intuitive theorem which says that the best advantage for distinguishing a random product cipher from a truly random permutation decreases exponentially with the number of terms.

We show that several of the previous results on decorrelation extend with these new norms. In particular, we show that the Peanut construction (for instance the DFC algorithm) provides security against adaptive iterated chosen plaintext attacks with unchanged bounds, and security against adapted iterated chosen plaintext and ciphertext attacks with other bounds, which shows that it is actually super-pseudorandom.

We also generalize the Peanut construction to any scheme instead of the Feistel one. We show that one only requires an equivalent to Luby–Rackoff's Lemma in order to get decorrelation upper bounds.

Since the beginning of conventional cryptography, theory on the formal security of encryption algorithms hardly got foundations. Decorrelation theory enables to deal with randomness and d-wise independence in connection with security. This provides a way for proving the security against restricted attacks. Other approaches treats unconditional security for encryption in a group structure (see Pliam [11]).

Decorrelation theory provides new directions to design block ciphers with provable security against some classes of standard attacks. Decorrelating to an order of d a block cipher C_K which depends on a random key K roughly consists in making sure that for all d plaintexts $(x_1, \ldots, x_d)$, the corresponding ciphertexts $(C_K(x_1), \ldots, C_K(x_d))$ are uncorrelated. This way, decorrelated functions are generalizations of Maurer's locally random functions [9]. Although the notion of decorrelation is quite intuitive, there is no formal definition of it, but instead several ways to measure it. Decorrelation theory has usually four tasks.

---

[*] Part of this work was done while the author was visiting the NTT Laboratories.

Howard Heys and Carlisle Adams (Eds.): SAC'99, LNCS 1758, pp. 49–61, 2000.

1. Defining a measurement for the decorrelation. This usually relies on a matrix norm.
2. Constructing a simple primitive (also called "decorrelation module") with a quite good decorrelation.
3. Constructing cryptographic algorithms with decorrelation modules in such a way that the decorrelation of the primitive can be inherited by the algorithm.
4. Proving that the decorrelation provides security against classes of attacks.

In [13,14,17,18], these issues have been treated with the infinity-associated matrix norm (denoted $|||.|||_\infty$). In particular, it was shown that this norm corresponds to the best advantage of a non-adaptive chosen plaintext attack. The present paper proves the results, but with a quite non-intuitive norm which corresponds to the best advantage of adaptive chosen plaintext attacks, and of adaptive chosen plaintext and ciphertext attacks. In particular we show that previous results on Peanut constructions extend to this setting. In particular, DFC has the same provable security against adaptive iterated chosen plaintext and ciphertext attacks.

This paper address the first three tasks, but hardly deals with the fourth one which may deserve further research.

1 Previous Results

The goal of decorrelation theory is to provide some kinds of formal proof of security on block ciphers. Earlier results was due to Shannon [12] (who show the limits of unconditional security) and Luby and Rackoff [8] (who show how the randomness theory is applicable to provide provable security). Decorrelation theory is mainly based on Carter-Wegman's universal hashing paradigm [2]. As was shown by Wegman and Carter [20], this enables to provide provably secure Message Authentication Codes.

Results on decorrelation have first been published in STACS'98 [13].[1] In this paper, decorrelation bias was formally defined.

Definition 1. *Given a random function F from a given set M_1 to a given set M_2 and an integer d, we define the "d-wise distribution matrix" $[F]^d$ of F as a $M_1^d \times M_2^d$-matrix where the (x, y)-entry of $[F]^d$ corresponding to the multi-points $x = (x_1, \ldots, x_d) \in M_1^d$ and $y = (y_1, \ldots, y_d) \in M_2^d$ is defined as the probability that we have $F(x_i) = y_i$ for $i = 1, \ldots, d$.*

Definition 2. *Given a random function F from a given set M_1 to a given set M_2, an integer d, and a distance D over the matrix space $\mathbf{R}^{M_1^d \times M_2^d}$, we define the "d-wise decorrelation bias of function F" as being the distance*

$$\mathrm{DecF}_D^d(F) = D([F]^d, [F^*]^d)$$

---

[1] A more complete version (with some error fixed in it) is available in [14].

where F^* is a uniformly distributed random function from $\mathcal{M}_1$ to $\mathcal{M}_2$. Similarly, for $\mathcal{M}_1 = \mathcal{M}_2$, if C is a random permutation over $\mathcal{M}_1$ we define the "d-wise decorrelation bias of permutation C" as being the distance

$$\mathrm{DecP}_D^d(C) = D([C]^d, [C^*]^d)$$

where C^* is a uniformly distributed random permutation over $\mathcal{M}_1$.

In [13,14], the infinity-associated matrix norm denoted $|||.|||_\infty$ and defined by

$$|||A|||_\infty = \max_{\text{row } i} \sum_{\text{col } j} |A_{i,j}|$$

was considered. For an injection r from $\{0,1\}^m$ to $\mathrm{GF}(q)$ and a surjection π from $\mathrm{GF}(q)$ to $\{0,1\}^m$, it was shown that the random function F defined on $\{0,1\}^m$ by

$$F(x) = \pi\left(r(K_0) + r(K_1)x + \ldots + r(K_{d-1})x^{d-1}\right)$$

for $(K_0, \ldots, K_{d-1})$ uniformly distributed in $\{0,1\}^{dm}$ provides a quite good decorrelation. Namely,

$$\mathrm{DecF}^d_{|||.|||_\infty}(F) \leq 2(q^d.2^{-md} - 1).$$

This construction is called the "NUT-IV decorrelation module" on [16] since there are three other ones.

It was shown that this decorrelation could be inherited by a Feistel network [3] in a construction called "Peanut". Namely, when the round functions of an r-round Feistel network ($r \geq 3$) has a d-wise decorrelation bias less than ϵ, the d-wise decorrelation bias of the whole permutation is less than

$$\left(3\epsilon + 3\epsilon^2 + \epsilon^3 + d^2.2^{1-\frac{m}{2}}\right)^{\lfloor \frac{r}{3} \rfloor}. \tag{1}$$

It was also shown that decorrelation to the order 2 provides security against differential and linear attacks.

In SAC'98 [15], the Euclidean norm (denoted $||.||_2$) was proposed, and it was shown that the same results hold for the $d = 2$ case with other upper bounds. These bounds unfortunately provide worse bounds than for the $|||.|||_\infty$ ones, but are applicable to the following decorrelation module for which the $|||.|||_\infty$ is not:

$$F(x) = (K_0 + K_1 x) \bmod p$$

with $(K_0, K_1) \in_U \{0, \ldots, 2^m - 1\}^2$ and a prime $p < 2^m$.

Based on the Peanut construction, an algorithm called "DFC" [4,5,1] was submitted to the Advanced Encryption Standard process.

In Eurocrypt'99 [18], the family of iterated attacks of order d was considered. It was shown that decorrelation to the order $2d$ provides security against iterated attacks of order d.

2 A New Decorrelation Measurement Dedicated to Adaptive Attacks

Let us consider a distinguisher $\mathcal{A}$ which is limited to d queries to an oracle $\mathcal{O}$. Its computation power is unlimited, and its output (0 or 1) can be probabilistic. Its aim is to distinguish if $\mathcal{O}$ implements a random function F_1 or a random function F_2. For this we consider the advantage

$$\mathrm{Adv}^{\mathcal{A}}(F_1, F_2) = \left| \Pr\left[\mathcal{A}^{\mathcal{O}=F_1} = 1\right] - \Pr\left[\mathcal{A}^{\mathcal{O}=F_2} = 1\right] \right|.$$

We say that $\mathcal{A}$ is non-adaptive if all queries can be sent simultaneously to the oracle (in particular, no query depend on the answer to a previous query). A well known result shows that the largest advantage of a non-adaptive chosen plaintext attack corresponds to the $|||.|||_\infty$ norm of $[F_1]^d - [F_2]^d$. Namely, we have

$$\max_{\substack{\mathcal{A} \text{ non-adaptive} \\ \text{chosen plaintext} \\ d-\text{limited}}} \mathrm{Adv}^{\mathcal{A}}(F_1, F_2) = \frac{1}{2}|||[F_1]^d - [F_2]^d|||_\infty.$$

We adapt this result in order to define a new norm which will be denoted $||.||_a$.

Definition 3. *Let $\mathcal{M}_1$ and $\mathcal{M}_2$ be two sets, and d be an integer. For a matrix $A \in \mathbf{R}^{\mathcal{M}_1^d \times \mathcal{M}_2^d}$ we define*

$$||A||_a = \max_{x_1} \sum_{y_1} \max_{x_2} \sum_{y_2} \ldots \max_{x_d} \sum_{y_d} |A_{(x_1,\ldots,x_d),(y_1,\ldots,y_d)}|.$$

Theorem 4. *For any random functions F_1 and F_2 from a set $\mathcal{M}_1$ to a set $\mathcal{M}_2$ and any integer d, we have*

$$\max_{\substack{\mathcal{A} \text{ distinguisher} \\ d-\text{limited}}} \mathrm{Adv}^{\mathcal{A}}(F_1, F_2) = \frac{1}{2}||[F_1]^d - [F_2]^d||_a.$$

Proof. Let $\mathcal{A}$ be a distinguisher. It first queries with a random X_1 (where the randomness comes from $\mathcal{A}$ only), then get a random Y_1 (whose randomness also comes from $\mathcal{O}$). Then it queries a random X_2 which depends on X_1 and Y_2, and get a Y_2, ... At the end, $\mathcal{A}$ answers a random value $A = 0$ or 1. We have

$$\Pr\left[\mathcal{A}^{\mathcal{O}} = 1\right] = \sum_{x_1,y_1,\ldots,x_d,y_d} \Pr[x_1]\Pr[y_1/x_1]\ldots\Pr[A = 1/x_1\ldots y_d].$$

Let $p_i = \Pr\left[\mathcal{A}^{\mathcal{O}=F_i} = 1\right]$. Since the randomness of $\mathcal{A}$ and F_i are independent, we have

$$p_i = \sum_{x_1,y_1,\ldots,x_d,y_d} \Pr[x_1]\Pr[x_2/x_1,y_1]\ldots\Pr[A = 1/x_1\ldots y_d][F_i]^d_{x,y}$$

where $x = (x_1, \ldots, x_d)$ and $y = (y_1, \ldots, y_d)$. This is a sum of terms of the form $\Pr[x_1]f(x_1)$. Obviously, the advantage is maximal when $\Pr[x_1] = 1$ for the maximal $f(x_1)$. Actually, we show that this sum is maximal for some deterministic distinguisher in which x_j is a function of $y_1, \ldots, y_{j-1}$ only. We have

$$p_1 - p_2 = \sum_y a_y \left([F_1]^d_{x,y} - [F_2]^d_{x,y} \right)$$

where a_y is 0 or 1. Obviously, this difference is maximal if a_y is 1 for the positive terms, and 0 for the negative terms. We notice that the sum of all terms is 0. Hence we have

$$|p_1 - p_2| = \frac{1}{2} \sum_y \left| [F_1]^d_{x,y} - [F_2]^d_{x,y} \right|$$

when it is maximal. The choice of x which maximizes this sum completes the proof. $\qquad\square$

In order to deal with decorrelation biases, it is pleasant to have matrix norms, *i.e.* norms such that $||A \times B|| \leq ||A|| \cdot ||B||$. If we have such a norm, we actually have the following property

$$\mathrm{DecP}^d_{||\cdot||}(C_1 \circ C_2) \leq \mathrm{DecP}^d_{||\cdot||}(C_1) . \mathrm{DecP}^d_{||\cdot||}(C_2) \tag{2}$$

and the same for $\mathrm{DecF}_{||\cdot||}$. The following result says it is applicable for the $||\cdot||_a$ norm.

Theorem 5. $||\cdot||_a$ *is a matrix norm.*

Proof. We make an induction on d. Let A be a matrix in $\mathbf{R}^{\mathcal{M}_1^d \times \mathcal{M}_2^d}$. To each $x_1 \in \mathcal{M}_1$ and each $x_2 \in \mathcal{M}_2$ we associate a submatrix $\pi_{x_1,y_1}(A)$ in $\mathbf{R}^{\mathcal{M}_1^{d-1} \times \mathcal{M}_2^{d-1}}$ defined by

$$(\pi_{x_1,y_1}(A))_{(x_2,\ldots,x_d),(y_2,\ldots,y_d)} = A_{(x_1,\ldots,x_d),(y_1,\ldots,y_d)}.$$

These submatrices actually define a matrix $\pi(A)$ which is basically a different way of viewing A. We have the following property which links the corresponding norms for the parameters d and $d-1$

$$||A||_a = \max_{x_1} \sum_{y_1} ||\pi_{x_1,y_1}(A)||_a.$$

Let A and B be two matrices. We have

$$||A \times B||_a = \max_{x_1} \sum_{y_1} ||\pi_{x_1,y_1}(A \times B)||_a.$$

Straightforward computations show that

$$\pi_{x_1,y_1}(A \times B) = \sum_{t_1} \pi_{x_1,t_1}(A) \times \pi_{t_1,y_1}(B).$$

Thus by induction we have

$$\|A \times B\|_a = \max_{x_1} \sum_{y_1} \sum_{t_1} \|\pi_{x_1,t_1}(A) \times \pi_{t_1,y_1}(B)\|_a$$

$$\leq \max_{x_1} \sum_{y_1} \sum_{t_1} \|\pi_{x_1,t_1}(A)\|_a \cdot \|\pi_{t_1,y_1}(B)\|_a.$$

This last expression is actually a $\||.\||_\infty$ norm of the product of two matrices A' and B' defined by

$$(A')_{x_1,t_1} = \|\pi_{x_1,t_1}(A)\|_a$$

and

$$(B')_{t_1,y_1} = \|\pi_{t_1,y_1}(B)\|_a.$$

We already know that $\||.\||_\infty$ is a matrix norm. Therefore we have

$$\|A \times B\|_a \leq \||A' \times B'\||_\infty$$

$$\leq \||A'\||_\infty \cdot \||B'\||_\infty$$

which is $\|A\|_a \cdot \|B\|_a$. □

As in [13,14], this theorem implies the following properties.

Corollary 6. *For any random function $F_1, \ldots, F_4$, if F^* denotes a random function with uniform distribution, the following properties hold.*

$$\mathrm{DecF}^d_{\|.\|_a}(F_1 \circ F_2) \leq \mathrm{DecF}^d_{\|.\|_a}(F_1).\mathrm{DecF}^d_{\|.\|_a}(F_2) \tag{3}$$

$$\|[F_1 \circ F_2]^d - [F_1 \circ F_3]^d\|_a \leq \mathrm{DecF}^d_{\|.\|_a}(F_1).\|[F_2]^d - [F_3]^d\|_a \tag{4}$$

$$\|[F_1 \circ F_2]^d - [F_3 \circ F_4]^d\|_a \leq \mathrm{DecF}^d_{\|.\|_a}(F_1).\|[F_2]^d - [F_4]^d\|_a$$

$$+\mathrm{DecF}^d_{\|.\|_a}(F_4).\|[F_1]^d - [F_3]^d\|_a \tag{5}$$

Similar properties hold for permutations.

We outline that Equation (3) means that if F_1 and F_2 are two independent random functions with the same distribution and if α is the best advantage of a d-limited distinguisher between F_1 and a uniformly distributed random function F^*, then the best advantage of a d-limited distinguisher between $F_1 \circ F_2$ and F^* is less than $2\alpha^2$. Similarly, for r rounds, the best advantage is less than $\frac{1}{2}(2\alpha)^r$: the advantage decreases exponentially with the number of rounds.

3 On the NUT-IV Decorrelation Module

The DFC algorithm is a Peanut construction which uses the following decorrelation module.

$$F(x) = (Ax + B) \bmod (2^{64} + 13) \bmod 2^{64}$$

where $(A, B) \in_U \{0, \ldots, 2^{64} - 1\}^2$. This is a particular case of the NUT-IV decorrelation module for which we prove the same bound for its decorrelation bias, but with the $\|.\|_a$ norm.

Theorem 7. *For an integer m, let $q = 2^m(1 + \delta)$ be a prime power with $\delta > 0$. We consider an injection r from $\{0, 1\}^m$ to $\mathrm{GF}(q)$, and a surjection π from $\mathrm{GF}(q)$ to $\{0, 1\}^m$. We define the following random function on $\{0, 1\}^m$.*

$$F(x) = \pi \left(r(A_0) + r(A_1).r(x) + \ldots + r(A_{d-1}).r(x)^{d-1} \right)$$

where $(A_0, \ldots, A_{d-1}) \in \{0, 1\}^{md}$. We have

$$\mathrm{DecF}^d_{||.||_a}(F) \leq 2 \left((1 + \delta)^d - 1 \right).$$

Proof. We adapt the proof of [14]. We let F^* be a uniformly distributed random function. In the computation of $||[F]^d - [F^*]^d||_a$, let x_1, $x_2 = f_2(y_1)$, ... $x_d = f_d(y_1, \ldots, y_{d-1})$ such that

$$\sum_{y=(y_1,\ldots,y_d)} |[F]^d_{x,y} - [F^*]^d_{x,y}|$$

is maximal, where $x = (x_1, \ldots, x_d)$.

For some terms in the sum, some x_i may be equal to each other. For this we need to make a transformation in order to assume that all x_is are pairwise different. For any (x, y) term, let c be the total number of different x_is. Let σ be a monotone injection from $\{1, \ldots, c\}$ to $\{1, \ldots, d\}$ such that all $x_{\sigma(i)}$ are different. We notice that if $x_i = x_j$, we can restrict the sum to $y_i = y_j$ (because the other terms will be all zero). We thus still have $x'_i = x_{\sigma(i)} = f'_i(y'_1, \ldots, y'_{i-1})$ where $y'_i = y_{\sigma(i)}$, and all x'_i are pairwise different for $i = 1, \ldots, c$. We can now define $x'_{c+1}, \ldots, x'_d$ with some new arbitrary functions $f'_{c+1}, \ldots, f'_d$ in such a way that all x'_i are pairwise different. We have

$$\mathrm{DecF}^d_{||.||_a}(F) = \sum_{y'_1,\ldots,y'_c} \left| \sum_{y'_{c+1},\ldots,y'_d} ([F]^d_{x',y'} - [F^*]^d_{x',y'}) \right|$$

$$\leq \sum_{y'_1,\ldots,y'_d} |[F]^d_{x',y'} - [F^*]^d_{x',y'}|$$

where $x' = (x'_1, \ldots, x'_d)$ and $y' = (y'_1, \ldots, y'_d)$. Hence we can assume without loss of generality that all x_is are pairwise different.

Obviously, $[F]^d_{x,y}$ can be written $j.2^{-md}$ where j is an integer. Let N_j be the number of y such that $[F]^d_{x,y} = j.2^{-md}$. We have

$$\mathrm{DecF}^d_{||.||_a}(F) \leq \sum_{j=0}^{+\infty} N_j |j - 1| 2^{-md}$$

$$= 2N_0.2^{-md} + \sum_{j=0}^{+\infty} N_j j.2^{-md} - \sum_{j=0}^{+\infty} N_j.2^{-md}.$$

The first sum is equal to

$$\sum_y [F]^d_{x,y}$$

which is equal to 1. The second sum is 2^{-md} times the total number of y, which is also 1. Thus we have $\text{DecF}^d_{||.||_a}(F) \le 2N_0.2^{-md}$.

Let A be the set of all (x, y) such that $[F]^d_{x,y} = 0$. Let B be the set of all $(a_0, \ldots, a_{d-1})$ in $GF(q)^d$ such that for at least one j we have $a_j \notin r(\{0, 1\}^m)$. From usual interpolation tricks, we know that for any (x, y) in A there exists at least one $(a_0, \ldots, a_{d-1})$ in $GF(q)^d$ such that

$$\pi(a_0 + a_1.r(x_j) + \ldots + a_{d-1}.r(x_j)^{d-1}) = y_j$$

for $j = 1, \ldots, d$. Since $[F]^d_{x,y} = 0$ this must be in B. Furthermore this mapping from A to B must be an injection. Hence N_0, which is the cardinality of A is less than the cardinality of B which is $q^d - 2^{md}$. □

4 Decorrelation of Peanut-Like Constructions

We show here that the decorrelation of internal decorrelation modules in a cipher can be inherited by the whole scheme.

Lemma 8. *Let d be an integer, and $F_1, \ldots, F_r$ be r random functions which are use in order to define a random function $\Omega(F_1, \ldots, F_r)$. We assume that the Ω structure is such that for any x, computing $\Omega(F_1, \ldots, F_r)(x)$ requires a_i computations of F_i for $i = 1, \ldots, r$. We have*

$$||[\Omega(F_1, \ldots, F_r)]^d - [\Omega(F_1^*, \ldots, F_r^*)]^d||_a \le \sum_{i=1}^r \text{DecF}^{a_i d}_{||.||_a}(F_i)$$

where $F_1^*, \ldots, F_r^*$ are uniformly distributed random functions.

Proof. By triangular inequalities, we have

$$||[\Omega(F_1, \ldots, F_r)]^d - [\Omega(F_1^*, \ldots, F_r^*)]^d||_a \le$$

$$\sum_{i=1}^r ||[\Omega(F_1, \ldots, F_{i-1}, F_i^*, \ldots, F_d^*)]^d - [\Omega(F_1, \ldots, F_i, F_{i+1}^*, \ldots, F_d^*)]^d||_a.$$

From Theorem 4, each term corresponds to the best distinguisher between $\Omega(F_1, \ldots, F_{i-1}, F_i^*, \ldots, F_d^*)$ and $\Omega(F_1, \ldots, F_i, F_{i+1}^*, \ldots, F_d^*)$. This attack can be transformed into a distinguisher between F_i and F_i^* by simulating the other functions. Hence this attack cannot have an advantage greater than the best attack for distinguishing F_i from F_i^* with the same number of queries. The number of queries for this attack is at most $a_i d$. By applying back Theorem 4, we obtain the result. □

This lemma can be considered as a "meta-theorem" which is applicable to any product cipher construction. For instance, for the Feistel construction $\Psi(F_1, \ldots, F_r)$, we have $a_i = 1$ for all i. The Peanut construction consists of picking decorrelated modules as round functions. In order to finish to estimate the decorrelation of Feistel structures, we need a lemma in order to estimate the decorrelation of Feistel ciphers with truly random functions. This is precisely the Luby–Rackoff [8] Lemma.

Lemma 9 (Luby–Rackoff 1988). *Let F_1^*, F_2^*, F_3^* be three random function on $\{0,1\}^{\frac{m}{2}}$ with uniform distribution. We have*

$$\text{DecP}^d_{||\cdot||_a}(\Psi(F_1^*, F_2^*, F_3^*)) \le 2d^2.2^{-\frac{m}{2}}.$$

(This is a straightforward translation of the original result by using Theorem 4.) We can thus upper bound the decorrelation bias in a Peanut construction.

Corollary 10. *If $F_1, \ldots, F_r$ are r random function ($r \ge 3$) on $\{0,1\}^{\frac{m}{2}}$ such that $\text{DecF}^d_{||\cdot||_a}(F_i) \le \epsilon$, we have*

$$\text{DecP}^d_{||\cdot||_a}(\Psi(F_1, \ldots, F_r)) \le (3\epsilon + 2d^2.2^{-\frac{m}{2}})^{\lfloor \frac{r}{3} \rfloor}.$$

We note that this slightly improves Equation (1) taken from [13,14].

Proof. Since the best advantage cannot increase when we make a product of independent ciphers, Lemma 9 holds for any Feistel cipher with at least three rounds. We write $\Psi(F_1, \ldots, F_r)$ as a product of $\lfloor \frac{r}{3} \rfloor$ Feistel ciphers with at least 3 rounds. We apply Lemma 8 and Lemma 9 to each of it, and we finally apply Equation (2). □

As another example, we mention this lemma taken from [10].

Lemma 11 (Patarin 1992). *Let ζ be a permutation on $\{0,1\}^{\frac{m}{2}}$ such that for any y there exists at least λ values x such that $x \oplus \zeta(x) = y$. Given a uniformly distributed random function F^* on $\{0,1\}^{\frac{m}{2}}$ and an integer d, we have*

$$\text{DecP}^d_{||\cdot||_a}(\Psi(F^*, F^*, F^* \circ \zeta \circ F^*)) \le 13d^2 2^{-\frac{m}{2}} + 2\lambda d 2^{-\frac{m}{2}}$$

Corollary 12. *Let ζ be a permutation on $\{0,1\}^{\frac{m}{2}}$ such that for any y there exists at least λ values x such that $x \oplus \zeta(x) = y$. Given independent random functions $F_1, \ldots, F_r$ on $\{0,1\}^{\frac{m}{2}}$ and an integer d, we have*

$$\text{DecP}^d_{||\cdot||_a}(\Psi(F_1, F_1, F_1 \circ \zeta \circ F_1, \ldots, F_r, F_r, F_r \circ \zeta \circ F_r))$$
$$\le \left(13d^2 2^{-\frac{m}{2}} + 2\lambda d 2^{-\frac{m}{2}} + \epsilon\right)^r$$

where $\epsilon = \max_i \text{DecF}^{4d}_{||\cdot||_a}(F_i)$.

Other product constructions require an equivalent to Lemma 9. For instance, the Lai-Massey scheme which is used in IDEA [7,6] has an equivalent result. (See [19].)

5 Super-Pseudorandomness

We now address the problem of d-limited adaptive chosen plaintext and ciphertext distinguishers. Since the proofs are essentially the same, we do not give all details here. We first define the corresponding norm.

Definition 13. *Let $\mathcal{M}_1$ and $\mathcal{M}_2$ be two sets, and d be an integer. For a matrix $A \in \mathbf{R}^{\mathcal{M}_1^d \times \mathcal{M}_2^d}$ we let $\pi_{x_1, y_2}(A)$ denote the matrix in $\mathbf{R}^{\mathcal{M}_1^{d-1} \times \mathcal{M}_2^{d-1}}$ defined by*

$$(\pi_{x_1, y_1}(A))_{(x_2,\ldots,x_d),(y_2,\ldots,y_d)} = A_{(x_1,\ldots,x_d),(y_1,\ldots,y_d)}.$$

By induction on d we define

$$||A||_s = \max\left(\max_{x_1} \sum_{y_1} ||\pi_{x_1,y_2}(A)||_s, \max_{y_1} \sum_{x_1} ||\pi_{x_1,y_2}(A)||_s\right)$$

with the convention that $||A||_s = |A_{(),()}|$ for $d = 0$.

Since chosen ciphertext makes sense for permutation only, all the following results hold for permutations.

Theorem 14. *For any random permutation C_1 and C_2 over a set $\mathcal{M}$ and any integer d, we have*

$$\max_{\substack{A \text{ distinguisher} \\ \text{chosen plaintex and ciphertext} \\ d-\text{limited}}} \mathrm{Adv}^{\mathcal{A}}(C_1, C_2) = \frac{1}{2}||[C_1]^d - [C_2]^d||_s.$$

The proof is a straightforward adaptation of the proof of Theorem 4.

Theorem 15. $||.||_s$ *is a matrix norm.*

For this proof, we adapt the proof of Theorem 5 and notice that

$$\max_{y_1} \sum_{x_1} |M_{x_1,y_1}| = |||M|||_1$$

where $|||.|||_1$ is the matrix norm associated to the L_1 vector norm. Therefore Corollary 6 holds for the $||.||_s$ norm with permutations.

We can also extend Lemma 8.

Lemma 16. *Let d be an integer, $F_1, \ldots, F_r$ be r random functions and let $C_1, \ldots, C_s$ be s random permutations which are used in order to define a random permutation $C = \Omega(F_1, \ldots, F_r, C_1, \ldots, C_s)$. We assume that the Ω structure is such that for any x and y, computing $C(x)$ or $C^{-1}(y)$ requires a_i computations of F_i for $i = 1, \ldots, r$ and b_i computations of C_i or C_i^{-1} for $i = 1, \ldots, s$. We have*

$$||[\Omega(F_1, \ldots, F_r, C_1, \ldots, C_s)]^d - [\Omega(F_1^*, \ldots, F_r^*, C_1^*, \ldots, C_s^*)]^d||_s$$
$$\leq \sum_{i=1}^{r} \mathrm{DecF}_{||.||_a}^{a_i d}(F_i) + \sum_{i=1}^{s} \mathrm{DecP}_{||.||_s}^{b_i d}(C_i)$$

where $F_1^*, \ldots, F_r^*$ are uniformly distributed random functions and $C_1^*, \ldots, C_s^*$ are uniformly distributed random permutations.

For instance, in the Peanut construction, we have $s = 0$ and $a_i = 1$ for all i. However Lemma 9 is not applicable with the $||.||_s$ norm. We thus use a similar lemma for 4-round Feistel ciphers.

Lemma 17 (Luby–Rackoff 1988). *Let $F_1^*, F_2^*, F_3^*, F_4^*$ be four random function tion on $\{0,1\}^{\frac{m}{2}}$ with uniform distribution. We have*

$$\mathrm{DecP}^d_{||.||_s}(\Psi(F_1^*, F_2^*, F_3^*, F_4^*)) \leq 2d^2.2^{-\frac{m}{2}}.$$

We can therefore measure the decorrelation in the sense of $||.||_s$ of Peanut constructions.

Corollary 18. *If $F_1, \ldots, F_r$ are r random function $(r \geq 4)$ on $\{0,1\}^{\frac{m}{2}}$ such that $\mathrm{DecF}^d_{||.||_a}(F_i) \leq \epsilon$, we have*

$$\mathrm{DecP}^d_{||.||_s}(\Psi(F_1, \ldots, F_r)) \leq (4\epsilon + 2d^2.2^{-\frac{m}{2}})^{\lfloor \frac{r}{4} \rfloor}.$$

This shows how much super-pseudorandom a Peanut construction is.

6 Security by Decorrelation with the New Norms

We already know that the decorrelation with the $|||.|||_\infty$ norm enables to prove the security against differential, linear distinguishers and non-adaptive chosen plaintext iterated attacks. Since we have $||.||_s \geq ||.||_a \geq |||.|||_\infty$, all these results are applicable to the decorrelation with the $||.||_a$ and $||.||_s$ norms.

From the proofs in [18] it is quite clear that all results on iterated attack extends to $||.||_a$-decorrelation when each iteration is adaptive, and to $||.||_s$-decorrelation when they can use chosen ciphertexts in addition.

One open question remains from the iterated attacks results. In [18] it was shown that the security proof requires some assumption on the distribution of the queries to the oracle. This was meaningful when we addresses the known plaintext non-adaptive attacks. But now adaptive attacks are chosen plaintext in essence. It thus remains to improve the results from [18] in order to get provable security against these attacks.

7 Conclusion

We have shown which matrix norm adaptive attacks and chosen plaintext and ciphertext attacks was related to. These norms define a much stronger notion of decorrelation. We have shown that previous upper bounds on the decorrelation extends to these new norms, in particular for the Peanut construction and the NUT-IV decorrelation module. We also generalized the Peanut construction to any scheme which is not necessarily a Feistel one. We have shown that if it is a product scheme, then we can upper bound the decorrelation of the whole scheme from the decorrelation of its internal functions, provided that we can extend the Luby–Rackoff Lemma to this scheme.

Our formalism happens to be practical enough in order to make trivial the exponential decreasing of the best advantage of a distinguisher between a product cipher and a truly random cipher.

Acknowledgment

I wish to thank NTT and Tatsuaki Okamoto for providing a good environment for research activities, and his team for enjoyable meetings and fruitful discussions.

References

1. O. Baudron, H. Gilbert, L. Granboulan, H. Handschuh, R. Harley, A. Joux, P. Nguyen, F. Noilhan, D. Pointcheval, T. Pornin, G. Poupard, J. Stern, S. Vaudenay. DFC Update. In Proceedings from the Second Advanced Encryption Standard Candidate Conference, National Institute of Standards and Technology (NIST), March 1999.
2. L. Carter, M. Wegman. Universal Classes of Hash Functions. *Journal of Computer and System Sciences*, vol. 18, pp. 143–154, 1979.
3. H. Feistel. Cryptography and Computer Privacy. *Scientific American*, vol. 228, pp. 15–23, 1973.
4. H. Gilbert, M. Girault, P. Hoogvorst, F. Noilhan, T. Pornin, G. Poupard, J. Stern, S. Vaudenay. Decorrelated Fast Cipher: an AES Candidate. (Extended Abstract.) In *Proceedings from the First Advanced Encryption Standard Candidate Conference*, National Institute of Standards and Technology (NIST), August 1998.
5. H. Gilbert, M. Girault, P. Hoogvorst, F. Noilhan, T. Pornin, G. Poupard, J. Stern, S. Vaudenay. Decorrelated Fast Cipher: an AES Candidate. Submitted to the Advanced Encryption Standard process. In *CD-ROM "AES CD-1: Documentation"*, National Institute of Standards and Technology (NIST), August 1998.
6. X. Lai. *On the Design and Security of Block Ciphers*, ETH Series in Information Processing, vol. 1, Hartung-Gorre Verlag Konstanz, 1992.
7. X. Lai, J. L. Massey. A Proposal for a New Block Encryption Standard. In *Advances in Cryptology EUROCRYPT'90*, Aarhus, Denmark, Lectures Notes in Computer Science 473, pp. 389–404, Springer-Verlag, 1991.
8. M. Luby, C. Rackoff. How to Construct Pseudorandom Permutations from Pseudorandom Functions. *SIAM Journal on Computing*, vol. 17, pp. 373–386, 1988.
9. U. M. Maurer. A Simplified and Generalized Treatment of Luby–Rackoff Pseudorandom permutation generators. In *Advances in Cryptology EUROCRYPT'92*, Balatonfüred, Hungary, Lectures Notes in Computer Science 658, pp. 239–255, Springer-Verlag, 1993.
10. J. Patarin. How to Construct Pseudorandom and Super Pseudorandom Permutations from One Single Pseudorandom Function. In *Advances in Cryptology EUROCRYPT'92*, Balatonfüred, Hungary, Lectures Notes in Computer Science 658, pp. 256–266, Springer-Verlag, 1993.
11. J. O. Pliam. Bounding Guesswork and Variation Distance: A New Technique for Provable Cipher Security. In these proceedings.
12. C. E. Shannon. Communication Theory of Secrecy Systems. *Bell system technical journal*, vol. 28, pp. 656–715, 1949.
13. S. Vaudenay. Provable Security for Block Ciphers by Decorrelation. In *STACS 98*, Paris, France, Lectures Notes in Computer Science 1373, pp. 249–275, Springer-Verlag, 1998.
14. S. Vaudenay. Provable Security for Block Ciphers by Decorrelation. (Full Paper.) Technical report LIENS-98-8, Ecole Normale Supérieure, 1998.
    URL: ftp://ftp.ens.fr/pub/reports/liens/liens-98-8.A4.ps.Z

15. S. Vaudenay. Feistel Ciphers with L_2-Decorrelation. In *Selected Areas in Cryptography*, Kingston, Ontario, Canada, Lectures Notes in Computer Science 1556, pp. 1–14, Springer-Verlag, 1999.

16. S. Vaudenay. The Decorrelation Technique Home-Page.
    URL:http://www.dmi.ens.fr/~vaudenay/decorrelation.html

17. S. Vaudenay. *Vers une Théorie du Chiffrement Symétrique*, Dissertation for the diploma of "habilitation to supervise research" from the University of Paris 7, Technical Report LIENS-98-15 of the Laboratoire d'Informatique de l'Ecole Normale Supérieure, 1998.

18. S. Vaudenay. Resistance Against General Iterated Attacks. In *Advances in Cryptology EUROCRYPT'99*, Prague, Czech Republic, Lectures Notes in Computer Science 1592, pp. 255–271, Springer-Verlag, 1999.

19. S. Vaudenay. On the Lai-Massey Scheme. Technical report LIENS-99-3, Ecole Normale Supérieure, 1999. To appear in Asiacrypt'99, LNCS, Springer-Verlag.
    URL: ftp://ftp.ens.fr/pub/reports/liens/liens-99-3.A4.ps.Z

20. M. N. Wegman, J. L. Carter. New Hash Functions and their Use in Authentication and Set Equality. *Journal of Computer and System Sciences*, vol. 22, pp. 265–279, 1981.

Adaptive-Attack Norm for Decorrelation and Super-Pseudorandomness

Serge Vaudenay[*]

Ecole Normale Supérieure — CNRS
Serge.Vaudenay@ens.fr

Abstract. In previous work, security results of decorrelation theory was based on the infinity-associated matrix norm. This enables to prove that decorrelation provides security against non-adaptive iterated attacks. In this paper we define a new matrix norm dedicated to adaptive chosen plaintext attacks. Similarly, we construct another matrix norm dedicated to chosen plaintext and ciphertext attacks.

The formalism from decorrelation enables to manipulate the notion of best advantage for distinguishers so easily that we prove as a trivial consequence a somewhat intuitive theorem which says that the best advantage for distinguishing a random product cipher from a truly random permutation decreases exponentially with the number of terms.

We show that several of the previous results on decorrelation extend with these new norms. In particular, we show that the Peanut construction (for instance the DFC algorithm) provides security against adaptive iterated chosen plaintext attacks with unchanged bounds, and security against adapted iterated chosen plaintext and ciphertext attacks with other bounds, which shows that it is actually super-pseudorandom.

We also generalize the Peanut construction to any scheme instead of the Feistel one. We show that one only requires an equivalent to Luby–Rackoff's Lemma in order to get decorrelation upper bounds.

Since the beginning of conventional cryptography, theory on the formal security of encryption algorithms hardly got foundations. Decorrelation theory enables to deal with randomness and d-wise independence in connection with security. This provides a way for proving the security against restricted attacks. Other approaches treats unconditional security for encryption in a group structure (see Pliam [11]).

Decorrelation theory provides new directions to design block ciphers with provable security against some classes of standard attacks. Decorrelating to an order of d a block cipher C_K which depends on a random key K roughly consists in making sure that for all d plaintexts $(x_1, \ldots, x_d)$, the corresponding ciphertexts $(C_K(x_1), \ldots, C_K(x_d))$ are uncorrelated. This way, decorrelated functions are generalizations of Maurer's locally random functions [9]. Although the notion of decorrelation is quite intuitive, there is no formal definition of it, but instead several ways to measure it. Decorrelation theory has usually four tasks.

---

[*] Part of this work was done while the author was visiting the NTT Laboratories.

Howard Heys and Carlisle Adams (Eds.): SAC'99, LNCS 1758, pp. 49–61, 2000.
© Springer-Verlag Berlin Heidelberg 2000

1. Defining a measurement for the decorrelation. This usually relies on a matrix norm.
2. Constructing a simple primitive (also called "decorrelation module") with a quite good decorrelation.
3. Constructing cryptographic algorithms with decorrelation modules in such a way that the decorrelation of the primitive can be inherited by the algorithm.
4. Proving that the decorrelation provides security against classes of attacks.

In [13,14,17,18], these issues have been treated with the infinity-associated matrix norm (denoted $|||.|||_\infty$). In particular, it was shown that this norm corresponds to the best advantage of a non-adaptive chosen plaintext attack. The present paper proves the results, but with a quite non-intuitive norm which corresponds to the best advantage of adaptive chosen plaintext attacks, and of adaptive chosen plaintext and ciphertext attacks. In particular we show that previous results on Peanut constructions extend to this setting. In particular, DFC has the same provable security against adaptive iterated chosen plaintext and ciphertext attacks.

This paper address the first three tasks, but hardly deals with the fourth one which may deserve further research.

1 Previous Results

The goal of decorrelation theory is to provide some kinds of formal proof of security on block ciphers. Earlier results was due to Shannon [12] (who show the limits of unconditional security) and Luby and Rackoff [8] (who show how the randomness theory is applicable to provide provable security). Decorrelation theory is mainly based on Carter-Wegman's universal hashing paradigm [2]. As was shown by Wegman and Carter [20], this enables to provide provably secure Message Authentication Codes.

Results on decorrelation have first been published in STACS'98 [13].[1] In this paper, decorrelation bias was formally defined.

Definition 1. *Given a random function F from a given set $\mathcal{M}_1$ to a given set $\mathcal{M}_2$ and an integer d, we define the "d-wise distribution matrix" $[F]^d$ of F as a $\mathcal{M}_1^d \times \mathcal{M}_2^d$-matrix where the (x, y)-entry of $[F]^d$ corresponding to the multi-points $x = (x_1, \ldots, x_d) \in \mathcal{M}_1^d$ and $y = (y_1, \ldots, y_d) \in \mathcal{M}_2^d$ is defined as the probability that we have $F(x_i) = y_i$ for $i = 1, \ldots, d$.*

Definition 2. *Given a random function F from a given set $\mathcal{M}_1$ to a given set $\mathcal{M}_2$, an integer d, and a distance D over the matrix space $\mathbf{R}^{\mathcal{M}_1^d \times \mathcal{M}_2^d}$, we define the "d-wise decorrelation bias of function F" as being the distance*

$$\mathrm{DecF}_D^d(F) = D([F]^d, [F^*]^d)$$

---

[1] A more complete version (with some error fixed in it) is available in [14].

where F^* is a uniformly distributed random function from $\mathcal{M}_1$ to $\mathcal{M}_2$. Similarly, for $\mathcal{M}_1 = \mathcal{M}_2$, if C is a random permutation over $\mathcal{M}_1$ we define the "d-wise decorrelation bias of permutation C" as being the distance

$$\mathrm{DecP}^d_D(C) = D([C]^d, [C^*]^d)$$

where C^* is a uniformly distributed random permutation over $\mathcal{M}_1$.

In [13,14], the infinity-associated matrix norm denoted $|||.|||_\infty$ and defined by

$$|||A|||_\infty = \max_{\text{row } i} \sum_{\text{col } j} |A_{i,j}|$$

was considered. For an injection r from $\{0,1\}^m$ to $\mathrm{GF}(q)$ and a surjection π from $\mathrm{GF}(q)$ to $\{0,1\}^m$, it was shown that the random function F defined on $\{0,1\}^m$ by

$$F(x) = \pi\left(r(K_0) + r(K_1)x + \ldots + r(K_{d-1})x^{d-1}\right)$$

for $(K_0, \ldots, K_{d-1})$ uniformly distributed in $\{0,1\}^{dm}$ provides a quite good decorrelation. Namely,

$$\mathrm{DecF}^d_{|||.|||_\infty}(F) \le 2(q^d.2^{-md} - 1).$$

This construction is called the "NUT-IV decorrelation module" on [16] since there are three other ones.

It was shown that this decorrelation could be inherited by a Feistel network [3] in a construction called "Peanut". Namely, when the round functions of an r-round Feistel network ($r \ge 3$) has a d-wise decorrelation bias less than ϵ, the d-wise decorrelation bias of the whole permutation is less than

$$\left(3\epsilon + 3\epsilon^2 + \epsilon^3 + d^2.2^{1-\frac{m}{2}}\right)^{\lfloor \frac{r}{3} \rfloor}. \tag{1}$$

It was also shown that decorrelation to the order 2 provides security against differential and linear attacks.

In SAC'98 [15], the Euclidean norm (denoted $||.||_2$) was proposed, and it was shown that the same results hold for the $d = 2$ case with other upper bounds. These bounds unfortunately provide worse bounds than for the $|||.|||_\infty$ ones, but are applicable to the following decorrelation module for which the $|||.|||_\infty$ is not:

$$F(x) = (K_0 + K_1 x) \bmod p$$

with $(K_0, K_1) \in_U \{0, \ldots, 2^m - 1\}^2$ and a prime $p < 2^m$.

Based on the Peanut construction, an algorithm called "DFC" [4,5,1] was submitted to the Advanced Encryption Standard process.

In Eurocrypt'99 [18], the family of iterated attacks of order d was considered. It was shown that decorrelation to the order $2d$ provides security against iterated attacks of order d.

2 A New Decorrelation Measurement Dedicated to Adaptive Attacks

Let us consider a distinguisher $\mathcal{A}$ which is limited to d queries to an oracle $\mathcal{O}$. Its computation power is unlimited, and its output (0 or 1) can be probabilistic. Its aim is to distinguish if $\mathcal{O}$ implements a random function F_1 or a random function F_2. For this we consider the advantage

$$\text{Adv}^{\mathcal{A}}(F_1, F_2) = \left| \Pr\left[\mathcal{A}^{\mathcal{O}=F_1} = 1 \right] - \Pr\left[\mathcal{A}^{\mathcal{O}=F_2} = 1 \right] \right|.$$

We say that $\mathcal{A}$ is non-adaptive if all queries can be sent simultaneously to the oracle (in particular, no query depend on the answer to a previous query). A well known result shows that the largest advantage of a non-adaptive chosen plaintext attack corresponds to the $||| . |||_{\infty}$ norm of $[F_1]^d - [F_2]^d$. Namely, we have

$$\max_{\substack{\mathcal{A} \text{ non-adaptive} \\ \text{chosen plaintext} \\ d-\text{limited}}} \text{Adv}^{\mathcal{A}}(F_1, F_2) = \frac{1}{2} ||| [F_1]^d - [F_2]^d |||_{\infty}.$$

We adapt this result in order to define a new norm which will be denoted $|| . ||_a$.

Definition 3. *Let $\mathcal{M}_1$ and $\mathcal{M}_2$ be two sets, and d be an integer. For a matrix $A \in \mathbf{R}^{\mathcal{M}_1^d \times \mathcal{M}_2^d}$ we define*

$$||A||_a = \max_{x_1} \sum_{y_1} \max_{x_2} \sum_{y_2} \ldots \max_{x_d} \sum_{y_d} |A_{(x_1, \ldots, x_d), (y_1, \ldots, y_d)}|.$$

Theorem 4. *For any random functions F_1 and F_2 from a set $\mathcal{M}_1$ to a set $\mathcal{M}_2$ and any integer d, we have*

$$\max_{\substack{\mathcal{A} \text{ distinguisher} \\ d-\text{limited}}} \text{Adv}^{\mathcal{A}}(F_1, F_2) = \frac{1}{2} || [F_1]^d - [F_2]^d ||_a.$$

Proof. Let $\mathcal{A}$ be a distinguisher. It first queries with a random X_1 (where the randomness comes from $\mathcal{A}$ only), then get a random Y_1 (whose randomness also comes from $\mathcal{O}$). Then it queries a random X_2 which depends on X_1 and Y_2, and get a Y_2, ... At the end, $\mathcal{A}$ answers a random value $A = 0$ or 1. We have

$$\Pr\left[\mathcal{A}^{\mathcal{O}} = 1 \right] = \sum_{x_1, y_1, \ldots, x_d, y_d} \Pr[x_1] \Pr[y_1/x_1] \ldots \Pr[A = 1/x_1 \ldots y_d].$$

Let $p_i = \Pr\left[\mathcal{A}^{\mathcal{O}=F_i} = 1 \right]$. Since the randomness of $\mathcal{A}$ and F_i are independent, we have

$$p_i = \sum_{x_1, y_1, \ldots, x_d, y_d} \Pr[x_1] \Pr[x_2/x_1, y_1] \ldots \Pr[A = 1/x_1 \ldots y_d][F_i]^d_{x,y}$$

where $x = (x_1, \ldots, x_d)$ and $y = (y_1, \ldots, y_d)$. This is a sum of terms of the form $\Pr[x_1] f(x_1)$. Obviously, the advantage is maximal when $\Pr[x_1] = 1$ for the maximal $f(x_1)$. Actually, we show that this sum is maximal for some deterministic distinguisher in which x_j is a function of $y_1, \ldots, y_{j-1}$ only. We have

$$p_1 - p_2 = \sum_y a_y \left([F_1]_{x,y}^d - [F_2]_{x,y}^d \right)$$

where a_y is 0 or 1. Obviously, this difference is maximal if a_y is 1 for the positive terms, and 0 for the negative terms. We notice that the sum of all terms is 0. Hence we have

$$|p_1 - p_2| = \frac{1}{2} \sum_y \left| [F_1]_{x,y}^d - [F_2]_{x,y}^d \right|$$

when it is maximal. The choice of x which maximizes this sum completes the proof. $\qquad\square$

In order to deal with decorrelation biases, it is pleasant to have matrix norms, *i.e.* norms such that $||A \times B|| \leq ||A||.||B||$. If we have such a norm, we actually have the following property

$$\mathrm{DecP}_{||.||}^d (C_1 \circ C_2) \leq \mathrm{DecP}_{||.||}^d (C_1).\mathrm{DecP}_{||.||}^d (C_2) \qquad (2)$$

and the same for $\mathrm{DecF}_{||.||}$. The following result says it is applicable for the $||.||_a$ norm.

Theorem 5. $||.||_a$ *is a matrix norm.*

Proof. We make an induction on d. Let A be a matrix in $\mathbf{R}^{\mathcal{M}_1^d \times \mathcal{M}_2^d}$. To each $x_1 \in \mathcal{M}_1$ and each $x_2 \in \mathcal{M}_2$ we associate a submatrix $\pi_{x_1, y_1}(A)$ in $\mathbf{R}^{\mathcal{M}_1^{d-1} \times \mathcal{M}_2^{d-1}}$ defined by

$$(\pi_{x_1, y_1}(A))_{(x_2, \ldots, x_d), (y_2, \ldots, y_d)} = A_{(x_1, \ldots, x_d), (y_1, \ldots, y_d)}.$$

These submatrices actually define a matrix $\pi(A)$ which is basically a different way of viewing A. We have the following property which links the corresponding norms for the parameters d and $d - 1$

$$||A||_a = \max_{x_1} \sum_{y_1} ||\pi_{x_1, y_1}(A)||_a.$$

Let A and B be two matrices. We have

$$||A \times B||_a = \max_{x_1} \sum_{y_1} ||\pi_{x_1, y_1}(A \times B)||_a.$$

Straightforward computations show that

$$\pi_{x_1, y_1}(A \times B) = \sum_{t_1} \pi_{x_1, t_1}(A) \times \pi_{t_1, y_1}(B).$$

Thus by induction we have

$$||A \times B||_a = \max_{x_1} \sum_{y_1} \sum_{t_1} ||\pi_{x_1,t_1}(A) \times \pi_{t_1,y_1}(B)||_a$$

$$\leq \max_{x_1} \sum_{y_1} \sum_{t_1} ||\pi_{x_1,t_1}(A)||_a.||\pi_{t_1,y_1}(B)||_a.$$

This last expression is actually a $|||.|||_\infty$ norm of the product of two matrices A' and B' defined by

$$(A')_{x_1,t_1} = ||\pi_{x_1,t_1}(A)||_a$$

and

$$(B')_{t_1,y_1} = ||\pi_{t_1,y_1}(B)||_a.$$

We already know that $|||.|||_\infty$ is a matrix norm. Therefore we have

$$||A \times B||_a \leq |||A' \times B'|||_\infty$$

$$\leq |||A'|||_\infty.|||B'|||_\infty$$

which is $||A||_a.||B||_a$. $\qquad\square$

As in [13,14], this theorem implies the following properties.

Corollary 6. *For any random function $F_1, \ldots, F_4$, if F^* denotes a random function with uniform distribution, the following properties hold.*

$$\mathrm{DecF}^d_{||.||_a}(F_1 \circ F_2) \leq \mathrm{DecF}^d_{||.||_a}(F_1).\mathrm{DecF}^d_{||.||_a}(F_2) \qquad (3)$$

$$||[F_1 \circ F_2]^d - [F_1 \circ F_3]^d||_a \leq \mathrm{DecF}^d_{||.||_a}(F_1).||[F_2]^d - [F_3]^d||_a \qquad (4)$$

$$||[F_1 \circ F_2]^d - [F_3 \circ F_4]^d||_a \leq \mathrm{DecF}^d_{||.||_a}(F_1).||[F_2]^d - [F_4]^d||_a$$

$$+\mathrm{DecF}^d_{||.||_a}(F_4).||[F_1]^d - [F_3]^d||_a \qquad (5)$$

Similar properties hold for permutations.

We outline that Equation (3) means that if F_1 and F_2 are two independent random functions with the same distribution and if α is the best advantage of a d-limited distinguisher between F_1 and a uniformly distributed random function F^*, then the best advantage of a d-limited distinguisher between $F_1 \circ F_2$ and F^* is less than $2\alpha^2$. Similarly, for r rounds, the best advantage is less than $\frac{1}{2}(2\alpha)^r$: the advantage decreases exponentially with the number of rounds.

3   On the NUT-IV Decorrelation Module

The DFC algorithm is a Peanut construction which uses the following decorrelation module.

$$F(x) = (Ax + B) \bmod (2^{64} + 13) \bmod 2^{64}$$

where $(A, B) \in_U \{0, \ldots, 2^{64} - 1\}^2$. This is a particular case of the NUT-IV decorrelation module for which we prove the same bound for its decorrelation bias, but with the $||.||_a$ norm.

Theorem 7. *For an integer m, let $q = 2^m(1 + \delta)$ be a prime power with $\delta > 0$. We consider an injection r from $\{0,1\}^m$ to $\mathrm{GF}(q)$, and a surjection π from $\mathrm{GF}(q)$ to $\{0,1\}^m$. We define the following random function on $\{0,1\}^m$.*

$$F(x) = \pi\left(r(A_0) + r(A_1).r(x) + \ldots + r(A_{d-1}).r(x)^{d-1}\right)$$

where $(A_0, \ldots, A_{d-1}) \in \{0,1\}^{md}$. We have

$$\mathrm{DecF}^d_{||\cdot||_a}(F) \leq 2\left((1+\delta)^d - 1\right).$$

Proof. We adapt the proof of [14]. We let F^* be a uniformly distributed random function. In the computation of $||[F]^d - [F^*]^d||_a$, let $x_1, x_2 = f_2(y_1), \ldots x_d = f_d(y_1, \ldots, y_{d-1})$ such that

$$\sum_{y=(y_1,\ldots,y_d)} |[F]^d_{x,y} - [F^*]^d_{x,y}|$$

is maximal, where $x = (x_1, \ldots, x_d)$.

For some terms in the sum, some x_i may be equal to each other. For this we need to make a transformation in order to assume that all x_is are pairwise different. For any (x, y) term, let c be the total number of different x_is. Let σ be a monotone injection from $\{1, \ldots, c\}$ to $\{1, \ldots, d\}$ such that all $x_{\sigma(i)}$ are different. We notice that if $x_i = x_j$, we can restrict the sum to $y_i = y_j$ (because the other terms will be all zero). We thus still have $x'_i = x_{\sigma(i)} = f'_i(y'_1, \ldots, y'_{i-1})$ where $y'_i = y_{\sigma(i)}$, and all x'_i are pairwise different for $i = 1, \ldots, c$. We can now define $x'_{c+1}, \ldots, x'_d$ with some new arbitrary functions $f'_{c+1}, \ldots, f'_d$ in such a way that all x'_i are pairwise different. We have

$$\mathrm{DecF}^d_{||\cdot||_a}(F) = \sum_{y'_1,\ldots,y'_c} \left| \sum_{y'_{c+1},\ldots,y'_d} ([F]^d_{x',y'} - [F^*]^d_{x',y'}) \right|$$

$$\leq \sum_{y'_1,\ldots,y'_d} |[F]^d_{x',y'} - [F^*]^d_{x',y'}|$$

where $x' = (x'_1, \ldots, x'_d)$ and $y' = (y'_1, \ldots, y'_d)$. Hence we can assume without loss of generality that all x_is are pairwise different.

Obviously, $[F]^d_{x,y}$ can be written $j.2^{-md}$ where j is an integer. Let N_j be the number of y such that $[F]^d_{x,y} = j.2^{-md}$. We have

$$\mathrm{DecF}^d_{||\cdot||_a}(F) \leq \sum_{j=0}^{+\infty} N_j |j - 1| 2^{-md}$$

$$= 2N_0.2^{-md} + \sum_{j=0}^{+\infty} N_j j.2^{-md} - \sum_{j=0}^{+\infty} N_j.2^{-md}.$$

The first sum is equal to

$$\sum_y [F]^d_{x,y}$$

which is equal to 1. The second sum is 2^{-md} times the total number of y, which is also 1. Thus we have $\mathrm{DecF}^d_{||.||_a}(F) \leq 2N_0.2^{-md}$.

Let A be the set of all (x, y) such that $[F]^d_{x,y} = 0$. Let B be the set of all $(a_0, \ldots, a_{d-1})$ in $\mathrm{GF}(q)^d$ such that for at least one j we have $a_j \notin r(\{0, 1\}^m)$. From usual interpolation tricks, we know that for any (x, y) in A there exists at least one $(a_0, \ldots, a_{d-1})$ in $\mathrm{GF}(q)^d$ such that

$$\pi(a_0 + a_1.r(x_j) + \ldots + a_{d-1}.r(x_j)^{d-1}) = y_j$$

for $j = 1, \ldots, d$. Since $[F]^d_{x,y} = 0$ this must be in B. Furthermore this mapping from A to B must be an injection. Hence N_0, which is the cardinality of A is less than the cardinality of B which is $q^d - 2^{md}$. □

4 Decorrelation of Peanut-Like Constructions

We show here that the decorrelation of internal decorrelation modules in a cipher can be inherited by the whole scheme.

Lemma 8. *Let d be an integer, and $F_1, \ldots, F_r$ be r random functions which are use in order to define a random function $\Omega(F_1, \ldots, F_r)$. We assume that the Ω structure is such that for any x, computing $\Omega(F_1, \ldots, F_r)(x)$ requires a_i computations of F_i for $i = 1, \ldots, r$. We have*

$$||[\Omega(F_1, \ldots, F_r)]^d - [\Omega(F_1^*, \ldots, F_r^*)]^d||_a \leq \sum_{i=1}^{r} \mathrm{DecF}^{a_i d}_{||.||_a}(F_i)$$

where $F_1^*, \ldots, F_r^*$ are uniformly distributed random functions.

Proof. By triangular inequalities, we have

$$||[\Omega(F_1, \ldots, F_r)]^d - [\Omega(F_1^*, \ldots, F_r^*)]^d||_a \leq$$
$$\sum_{i=1}^{r} ||[\Omega(F_1, \ldots, F_{i-1}, F_i^*, \ldots, F_d^*)]^d - [\Omega(F_1, \ldots, F_i, F_{i+1}^*, \ldots, F_d^*)]^d||_a.$$

From Theorem 4, each term corresponds to the best distinguisher between $\Omega(F_1, \ldots, F_{i-1}, F_i^*, \ldots, F_d^*)$ and $\Omega(F_1, \ldots, F_i, F_{i+1}^*, \ldots, F_d^*)$. This attack can be transformed into a distinguisher between F_i and F_i^* by simulating the other functions. Hence this attack cannot have an advantage greater than the best attack for distinguishing F_i from F_i^* with the same number of queries. The number of queries for this attack is at most $a_i d$. By applying back Theorem 4, we obtain the result. □

This lemma can be considered as a "meta-theorem" which is applicable to any product cipher construction. For instance, for the Feistel construction $\Psi(F_1, \ldots, F_r)$, we have $a_i = 1$ for all i. The Peanut construction consists of picking decorrelated modules as round functions. In order to finish to estimate the decorrelation of Feistel structures, we need a lemma in order to estimate the decorrelation of Feistel ciphers with truly random functions. This is precisely the Luby–Rackoff [8] Lemma.

Lemma 9 (Luby–Rackoff 1988). *Let F_1^*, F_2^*, F_3^* be three random function on $\{0,1\}^{\frac{m}{2}}$ with uniform distribution. We have*

$$\mathrm{DecP}^d_{||\cdot||_a}(\Psi(F_1^*, F_2^*, F_3^*)) \leq 2d^2 . 2^{-\frac{m}{2}}.$$

(This is a straightforward translation of the original result by using Theorem 4.) We can thus upper bound the decorrelation bias in a Peanut construction.

Corollary 10. *If $F_1, \ldots, F_r$ are r random function $(r \geq 3)$ on $\{0,1\}^{\frac{m}{2}}$ such that $\mathrm{DecF}^d_{||\cdot||_a}(F_i) \leq \epsilon$, we have*

$$\mathrm{DecP}^d_{||\cdot||_a}(\Psi(F_1, \ldots, F_r)) \leq (3\epsilon + 2d^2 . 2^{-\frac{m}{2}})^{\lfloor \frac{r}{3} \rfloor}.$$

We note that this slightly improves Equation (1) taken from [13,14].

Proof. Since the best advantage cannot increase when we make a product of independent ciphers, Lemma 9 holds for any Feistel cipher with at least three rounds. We write $\Psi(F_1, \ldots, F_r)$ as a product of $\lfloor \frac{r}{3} \rfloor$ Feistel ciphers with at least 3 rounds. We apply Lemma 8 and Lemma 9 to each of it, and we finally apply Equation (2). □

As another example, we mention this lemma taken from [10].

Lemma 11 (Patarin 1992). *Let ζ be a permutation on $\{0,1\}^{\frac{m}{2}}$ such that for any y there exists at least λ values x such that $x \oplus \zeta(x) = y$. Given a uniformly distributed random function F^* on $\{0,1\}^{\frac{m}{2}}$ and an integer d, we have*

$$\mathrm{DecP}^d_{||\cdot||_a}(\Psi(F^*, F^*, F^* \circ \zeta \circ F^*)) \leq 13d^2 2^{-\frac{m}{2}} + 2\lambda d2^{-\frac{m}{2}}$$

Corollary 12. *Let ζ be a permutation on $\{0,1\}^{\frac{m}{2}}$ such that for any y there exists at least λ values x such that $x \oplus \zeta(x) = y$. Given independent random functions $F_1, \ldots, F_r$ on $\{0,1\}^{\frac{m}{2}}$ and an integer d, we have*

$$\mathrm{DecP}^d_{||\cdot||_a}(\Psi(F_1, F_1, F_1 \circ \zeta \circ F_1, \ldots, F_r, F_r, F_r \circ \zeta \circ F_r))$$
$$\leq \left(13d^2 2^{-\frac{m}{2}} + 2\lambda d2^{-\frac{m}{2}} + \epsilon\right)^r$$

where $\epsilon = \max_i \mathrm{DecF}^{4d}_{||\cdot||_a}(F_i)$.

Other product constructions require an equivalent to Lemma 9. For instance, the Lai-Massey scheme which is used in IDEA [7,6] has an equivalent result. (See [19].)

5   Super-Pseudorandomness

We now address the problem of d-limited adaptive chosen plaintext and ciphertext distinguishers. Since the proofs are essentially the same, we do not give all details here. We first define the corresponding norm.

Definition 13. *Let $\mathcal{M}_1$ and $\mathcal{M}_2$ be two sets, and d be an integer. For a matrix $A \in \mathbf{R}^{\mathcal{M}_1^d \times \mathcal{M}_2^d}$ we let $\pi_{x_1, y_2}(A)$ denote the matrix in $\mathbf{R}^{\mathcal{M}_1^{d-1} \times \mathcal{M}_2^{d-1}}$ defined by*

$$(\pi_{x_1, y_1}(A))_{(x_2, \ldots, x_d), (y_2, \ldots, y_d)} = A_{(x_1, \ldots, x_d), (y_1, \ldots, y_d)}.$$

By induction on d we define

$$\|A\|_s = \max\left(\max_{x_1} \sum_{y_1} \|\pi_{x_1, y_2}(A)\|_s, \max_{y_1} \sum_{x_1} \|\pi_{x_1, y_2}(A)\|_s\right)$$

with the convention that $\|A\|_s = |A_{(),()}|$ for $d = 0$.

Since chosen ciphertext makes sense for permutation only, all the following results hold for permutations.

Theorem 14. *For any random permutation C_1 and C_2 over a set $\mathcal{M}$ and any integer d, we have*

$$\max_{\substack{\mathcal{A} \text{ distinguisher} \\ \text{chosen plaintex and ciphertext} \\ d-\text{limited}}} \mathrm{Adv}^{\mathcal{A}}(C_1, C_2) = \frac{1}{2}\|[C_1]^d - [C_2]^d\|_s.$$

The proof is a straightforward adaptation of the proof of Theorem 4.

Theorem 15. *$\|.\|_s$ is a matrix norm.*

For this proof, we adapt the proof of Theorem 5 and notice that

$$\max_{y_1} \sum_{x_1} |M_{x_1, y_1}| = \||M\||_1$$

where $\||.\||_1$ is the matrix norm associated to the L_1 vector norm. Therefore Corollary 6 holds for the $\|.\|_s$ norm with permutations.

We can also extend Lemma 8.

Lemma 16. *Let d be an integer, $F_1, \ldots, F_r$ be r random functions and let $C_1, \ldots, C_s$ be s random permutations which are used in order to define a random permutation $C = \Omega(F_1, \ldots, F_r, C_1, \ldots, C_s)$. We assume that the Ω structure is such that for any x and y, computing $C(x)$ or $C^{-1}(y)$ requires a_i computations of F_i for $i = 1, \ldots, r$ and b_i computations of C_i or C_i^{-1} for $i = 1, \ldots, s$. We have*

$$\|[\Omega(F_1, \ldots, F_r, C_1, \ldots, C_s)]^d - [\Omega(F_1^*, \ldots, F_r^*, C_1^*, \ldots, C_s^*)]^d\|_s$$
$$\leq \sum_{i=1}^{r} \mathrm{DecF}_{\|.\|_a}^{a_i d}(F_i) + \sum_{i=1}^{s} \mathrm{DecP}_{\|.\|_s}^{b_i d}(C_i)$$

where $F_1^*, \ldots, F_r^*$ are uniformly distributed random functions and $C_1^*, \ldots, C_s^*$ are uniformly distributed random permutations.

For instance, in the Peanut construction, we have $s = 0$ and $a_i = 1$ for all i. However Lemma 9 is not applicable with the $||.||_s$ norm. We thus use a similar lemma for 4-round Feistel ciphers.

Lemma 17 (Luby–Rackoff 1988). *Let $F_1^*, F_2^*, F_3^*, F_4^*$ be four random function tion on $\{0,1\}^{\frac{m}{2}}$ with uniform distribution. We have*

$$\text{DecP}^d_{||.||_s}(\Psi(F_1^*, F_2^*, F_3^*, F_4^*)) \leq 2d^2 . 2^{-\frac{m}{2}}.$$

We can therefore measure the decorrelation in the sense of $||.||_s$ of Peanut constructions.

Corollary 18. *If $F_1, \dots, F_r$ are r random function ($r \geq 4$) on $\{0,1\}^{\frac{m}{2}}$ such that $\text{DecF}^d_{||.||_a}(F_i) \leq \epsilon$, we have*

$$\text{DecP}^d_{||.||_s}(\Psi(F_1, \dots, F_r)) \leq (4\epsilon + 2d^2 . 2^{-\frac{m}{2}})^{\lfloor \frac{r}{4} \rfloor}.$$

This shows how much super-pseudorandom a Peanut construction is.

6   Security by Decorrelation with the New Norms

We already know that the decorrelation with the $|||.|||_\infty$ norm enables to prove the security against differential, linear distinguishers and non-adaptive chosen plaintext iterated attacks. Since we have $||.||_s \geq ||.||_a \geq |||.|||_\infty$, all these results are applicable to the decorrelation with the $||.||_a$ and $||.||_s$ norms.

From the proofs in [18] it is quite clear that all results on iterated attack extends to $||.||_a$-decorrelation when each iteration is adaptive, and to $||.||_s$-decorrelation when they can use chosen ciphertexts in addition.

One open question remains from the iterated attacks results. In [18] it was shown that the security proof requires some assumption on the distribution of the queries to the oracle. This was meaningful when we addresses the known plaintext non-adaptive attacks. But now adaptive attacks are chosen plaintext in essence. It thus remains to improve the results from [18] in order to get provable security against these attacks.

7   Conclusion

We have shown which matrix norm adaptive attacks and chosen plaintext and ciphertext attacks was related to. These norms define a much stronger notion of decorrelation. We have shown that previous upper bounds on the decorrelation extends to these new norms, in particular for the Peanut construction and the NUT-IV decorrelation module. We also generalized the Peanut construction to any scheme which is not necessarily a Feistel one. We have shown that if it is a product scheme, then we can upper bound the decorrelation of the whole scheme from the decorrelation of its internal functions, provided that we can extend the Luby–Rackoff Lemma to this scheme.

Our formalism happens to be practical enough in order to make trivial the exponential decreasing of the best advantage of a distinguisher between a product cipher and a truly random cipher.

Acknowledgment

I wish to thank NTT and Tatsuaki Okamoto for providing a good environment for research activities, and his team for enjoyable meetings and fruitful discussions.

References

1. O. Baudron, H. Gilbert, L. Granboulan, H. Handschuh, R. Harley, A. Joux, P. Nguyen, F. Noilhan, D. Pointcheval, T. Pornin, G. Poupard, J. Stern, S. Vaudenay. DFC Update. In Proceedings from the Second Advanced Encryption Standard Candidate Conference, National Institute of Standards and Technology (NIST), March 1999.
2. L. Carter, M. Wegman. Universal Classes of Hash Functions. *Journal of Computer and System Sciences*, vol. 18, pp. 143–154, 1979.
3. H. Feistel. Cryptography and Computer Privacy. *Scientific American*, vol. 228, pp. 15–23, 1973.
4. H. Gilbert, M. Girault, P. Hoogvorst, F. Noilhan, T. Pornin, G. Poupard, J. Stern, S. Vaudenay. Decorrelated Fast Cipher: an AES Candidate. (Extended Abstract.) In *Proceedings from the First Advanced Encryption Standard Candidate Conference*, National Institute of Standards and Technology (NIST), August 1998.
5. H. Gilbert, M. Girault, P. Hoogvorst, F. Noilhan, T. Pornin, G. Poupard, J. Stern, S. Vaudenay. Decorrelated Fast Cipher: an AES Candidate. Submitted to the Advanced Encryption Standard process. In *CD-ROM "AES CD-1: Documentation"*, National Institute of Standards and Technology (NIST), August 1998.
6. X. Lai. *On the Design and Security of Block Ciphers*, ETH Series in Information Processing, vol. 1, Hartung-Gorre Verlag Konstanz, 1992.
7. X. Lai, J. L. Massey. A Proposal for a New Block Encryption Standard. In *Advances in Cryptology EUROCRYPT'90*, Aarhus, Denmark, Lectures Notes in Computer Science 473, pp. 389–404, Springer-Verlag, 1991.
8. M. Luby, C. Rackoff. How to Construct Pseudorandom Permutations from Pseudorandom Functions. *SIAM Journal on Computing*, vol. 17, pp. 373–386, 1988.
9. U. M. Maurer. A Simplified and Generalized Treatment of Luby–Rackoff Pseudorandom permutation generators. In *Advances in Cryptology EUROCRYPT'92*, Balatonfüred, Hungary, Lectures Notes in Computer Science 658, pp. 239–255, Springer-Verlag, 1993.
10. J. Patarin. How to Construct Pseudorandom and Super Pseudorandom Permutations from One Single Pseudorandom Function. In *Advances in Cryptology EUROCRYPT'92*, Balatonfüred, Hungary, Lectures Notes in Computer Science 658, pp. 256–266, Springer-Verlag, 1993.
11. J. O. Pliam. Bounding Guesswork and Variation Distance: A New Technique for Provable Cipher Security. In these proceedings.
12. C. E. Shannon. Communication Theory of Secrecy Systems. *Bell system technical journal*, vol. 28, pp. 656–715, 1949.
13. S. Vaudenay. Provable Security for Block Ciphers by Decorrelation. In *STACS 98*, Paris, France, Lectures Notes in Computer Science 1373, pp. 249–275, Springer-Verlag, 1998.
14. S. Vaudenay. Provable Security for Block Ciphers by Decorrelation. (Full Paper.) Technical report LIENS-98-8, Ecole Normale Supérieure, 1998. URL: `ftp://ftp.ens.fr/pub/reports/liens/liens-98-8.A4.ps.Z`

15. S. Vaudenay. Feistel Ciphers with L_2-Decorrelation. In *Selected Areas in Cryptography*, Kingston, Ontario, Canada, Lectures Notes in Computer Science 1556, pp. 1–14, Springer-Verlag, 1999.

16. S. Vaudenay. The Decorrelation Technique Home-Page. URL:`http://www.dmi.ens.fr/~vaudenay/decorrelation.html`

17. S. Vaudenay. *Vers une Théorie du Chiffrement Symétrique*, Dissertation for the diploma of "habilitation to supervise research" from the University of Paris 7, Technical Report LIENS-98-15 of the Laboratoire d'Informatique de l'Ecole Normale Supérieure, 1998.

18. S. Vaudenay. Resistance Against General Iterated Attacks. In *Advances in Cryptology EUROCRYPT'99*, Prague, Czech Republic, Lectures Notes in Computer Science 1592, pp. 255–271, Springer-Verlag, 1999.

19. S. Vaudenay. On the Lai-Massey Scheme. Technical report LIENS-99-3, Ecole Normale Supérieure, 1999. To appear in Asiacrypt'99, LNCS, Springer-Verlag. URL: `ftp://ftp.ens.fr/pub/reports/liens/liens-99-3.A4.ps.Z`

20. M. N. Wegman, J. L. Carter. New Hash Functions and their Use in Authentication and Set Equality. *Journal of Computer and System Sciences*, vol. 22, pp. 265–279, 1981.

Guesswork and Variation Distance as Measures of Cipher Security

John O. Pliam

Department of Control Science & Dynamical Systems,
University of Minnesota
Minneapolis, MN 55455, U.S.A.
pliam@ima.umn.edu

Abstract. Absolute lower limits to the cost of cryptanalytic attacks are quantified, via a theory of guesswork. Conditional guesswork naturally expresses limits to known and chosen plaintext attacks. New inequalities are derived between various forms of guesswork and variation distance. The machinery thus offers a new technique for establishing the security of a cipher: When the work-factor of the optimal known or chosen plaintext attack against a cipher is bounded below by a prohibitively large number, then no practical attack against the cipher can succeed. As an example, we apply the technique to iterated cryptosystems, as the Markov property which results from an independent subkey assumption makes them particularly amenable to analysis.

1 Introduction

Research on provably secure ciphers often focuses on specific cipher properties or resistance to specific families of attacks (see e.g. [16], [9] and [17]). When general attacks are considered, the adversary's resource limitations are typically built into the equation. In the Luby-Rackoff model (see [11] or more recently [15]), the adversary is assumed to have bounded computational resources. In the *Decorrelation Theory* of Vaudenay (see e.g. [21] and the references in [22]), the adversary may have restricted data complexity (such as a bound on the number of plaintext-ciphertext pairs) or may be carrying out a constrained attack (such as *Differential Cryptanalysis* [2]). In this paper, we summarize a different approach to provable cipher security which is developed more fully in [18]. Our approach is to model a cipher as a group-valued random variable — following Shannon — and derive absolute lower limits on the work-factor for discovering its secret key.

This technique naturally applies to product ciphers and iterated cryptosystems. Figure 1 below depicts a hypothetical security profile for the behavior of the product of finitely many ciphers as a function of the number of terms. In order to begin to quantify this profile, we must find a meaningful measure of security for which establishing the profile's shape in certain places is a tractable problem. Our primary interest is in the non-asymptotic shape of the curve — because iterated cryptosystems cannot iterate forever.

Howard Heys and Carlisle Adams (Eds.): SAC'99, LNCS 1758, pp. 62–77, 2000.

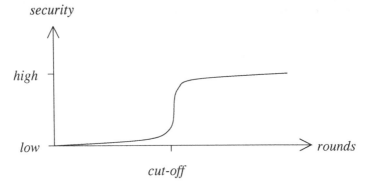

Fig. 1. A hypothetical profile of security as a function of the number of terms in a product, or equivalently the number of rounds in an iterated cryptosystems, assuming subkey independence.

We posit that a reasonable security measure is the expected work involved in "guessing" the cipher's key from the set of all keys which remain consistent with acquired plaintext-ciphertext pairs. We call this measure *guesswork* (or more generally *conditional guesswork*) and demonstrate its tractability by making use of techniques from the modern theory of random walks on symmetric structures.

Starting in Sect. 3 and continuing in Sect. 4, a formal theory of guesswork is developed which parallels information theory in a number of interesting ways. In particular, (logarithmically) tight bounds involving guesswork are derived in Theorem 1, and variation distance plays a role similar to Kullback-Leibler distance. With the help of these tools, we turn our attention in Sect. 5 to quantifying the shape of the security profile of Fig. 1 *non-asymptotically*. That is to say, rather than in some unknown neighborhood of the point at infinity, we establish provable security after a finite number of rounds.

2 Preliminaries

A basic familiarity with group theory [19], and random variables and probability spaces [8] is assumed. We develop an abstract form of Shannon's model of private key ciphers [20], in which the invertible encryption functions are taken as elements of a group G. For a block cipher with a message space $\mathcal{M}$ consisting of all n-bit strings, the group G is naturally seen as a subgroup of the symmetric group $\mathfrak{S}_{\mathcal{M}}$ (whose elements consist of all permutations of $\mathcal{M}$).

2.1 Shannon's Model

Secret keys and messages must be considered random from the viewpoint of a cryptanalytic adversary. Thus, the eavesdropper on an insecure channel may be thought of as performing a probabilistic experiment in which the message and key are values drawn at random according to certain probability distributions. It is assumed that the key is statistically independent of the message, and that the individual plaintext blocks of the message are statistically independent of one another[1]. This allows the cipher itself to be treated as an independent random variable. Furthermore, we may dispense with a distinction between the key space and the group G generated by the encryption functions. Each possible key corresponds to an element of G, and any element of G which is not identified with a key is taken to have probability 0. We may now formally define a cipher.

Definition 1. *Given a finite message space $\mathcal{M}$ and a subgroup $G \leq \mathfrak{S}_{\mathcal{M}}$, a G-cipher or a cipher over G is a G-valued random variable.*

Shannon wrote down a cipher as a linear combination of encryption functions, with the coefficients taken to be the probabilities of the corresponding functions. He naturally defined the product of ciphers by merely enforcing the distributive laws. Shannon was essentially defining what is now commonly called the *group algebra*. The natural product in the group algebra is equivalent to a kind of convolution of probability distributions.

2.2 Product Ciphers and Convolution

Consider the situation where an encryption operation is the composition of two independent encryption operations. This leads to the formal notion of the product of two ciphers over a group. Let X and Y be independent G-ciphers with probability distributions $x(g) = \mathsf{P}\left[X = g\right]$ and $y(g) = \mathsf{P}\left[Y = g\right]$. The G-cipher $Z = XY$ is called a *product cipher*, Y is called the *first component* and X is called the *second component*.

Let us examine the distribution $z(g) = \mathsf{P}\left[Z = g\right]$:

$$z(g) = \sum_{h \in G} \mathsf{P}\left[X = gh^{-1} \mid Y = h\right] \mathsf{P}\left[Y = h\right]$$

$$= \sum_{h \in G} \mathsf{P}\left[X = gh^{-1}\right] \mathsf{P}\left[Y = h\right] = \sum_{h \in G} x(gh^{-1})y(h).$$

Notice how much this last expression looks like convolution. In fact, if G were the abelian group of integers modulo n and the multiplicative notation were replaced by additive notation, $z(g)$ would literally be the *circular convolution* of the functions x and y. So, $z(g)$ is a kind of generalized convolution and will be written

$$x * y(g) = \sum_{h \in G} x(gh^{-1})y(h). \tag{1}$$

Thus the distribution of a product is described by the convolution of the component distributions. Intuitively, convolutions "smooth out" distributions.

---

[1] Technically, plaintext blocks are typically independent only in the limit of large block length, but the emphasis here is on chosen plaintext attacks which are always faster than known plaintext attacks

2.3 Variation Distance

Let $\mathscr{X}$ be a finite set with probability distributions p and q defined on it. Recall ([4] or [5]) the *variation distance* between p and q defined by

$$\|p - q\| = \max_{\mathscr{Y} \subseteq \mathscr{X}} |p(\mathscr{Y}) - q(\mathscr{Y})|. \tag{2}$$

It is a standard observation that variation distance is half of the ℓ_1-norm, i.e.

$$\|p - q\| = \frac{1}{2}\|p - q\|_1,$$

and that the maximum in (2) is achieved on the set

$$\mathscr{Y} = \{x \in \mathscr{X} \mid p(x) \geq q(x)\}.$$

If X is a G-cipher and u is the uniform distribution on G, then the closer p_X is to uniformity, the harder it will be for any adversary to determine the value of X. This general statement, which holds whether or not the adversary is in possession of plaintext-ciphertext pairs, is formalized in Theorem 1 and Corollary 2 below.

3   Guesswork: The Uncertainty of Guessing

In this section, we develop the means to quantify fundamental statistical limits to the amount of work required to determine the value of a random variable. The notions of work discussed here have appeared before. In a broad sense they are intimately connected to Lorenz's theory of wealth distribution [10] (see also [12]). Massey [13] was the first to formulate, in open cryptology, what we shall call the *guesswork* of a random variable.[2] While it has correctly been pointed out (e.g. [3]) that guesswork is not a meaningful predictor of practical attack performance, we shall show that it is a very useful and tractable measure of the fundamental limits to practical attacks.

3.1   Optimal Brute-Force Attacks

Let $\mathscr{X}$ be a finite set and suppose that X is the $\mathscr{X}$-valued random variable determined by probability distribution p. We may arrange $\mathscr{X}$ so that the probabilities $p_i = p(x_i)$ satisfy

$$p_1 \geq p_2 \geq \ldots \geq p_{|\mathscr{X}|}. \tag{3}$$

---

[2] We resist calling guesswork "guessing entropy", as is done in [3], because Theorem 1 below is so closely analogous to Shannon's First Theorem [4] that the natural analogue of guesswork is really the expected codeword length of Shannon's theorem, as discussed in Remark 1 below. It perhaps makes more sense to call variation distance a kind of (relative) entropy, because *it* appears in the upper and lower bounds of Theorem 1, just as entropy does in Shannon's theorem. Thus to call guesswork "guessing entropy" might lead to confusion.

Many situations in cryptology and computer security force an adversary to conduct a brute-force attack in which the values of $\mathscr{X}$ are enumerated and tested for a certain success condition. The only possible luxury afforded the adversary is that he or she may know which events are more likely. For example, UNIX passwords are routinely guessed with the aid of a public-domain software package called `crack` [14], which can be configured to test the most likely passwords first. The safest bet for the cryptographer is to assume that the adversary has complete knowledge of p and will conduct any brute-force attack *optimally*, i.e. in the order given by (3). This suggests the following definitions.

Definition 2. *Let X be an $\mathscr{X}$-valued random variable whose probabilities are arranged according to (3). The* **guesswork** *of X is given by*

$$W(X) = \sum_{i=1}^{|\mathscr{X}|} i p_i.$$

The following simple algorithm demonstrates the computational meaning behind guesswork. The adversary is assumed to have access to the necessary optimal enumerator and an oracle which tells whether they have guessed correctly.

Algorithm 1. *Optimal brute-force attack against X which will always succeed and has expected time complexity $O(W(X))$.*

> **input:** *(i). An enumerator of the values of $\mathscr{X}$ in order of nonincreasing probability. (ii). An oracle which answers whether $X = x$.*
> **output:** *The value of X.*

> **for** $x \in \mathscr{X}$ **do**
>   **if** $X = x$ **then**
>   **return** x.
>   **endif**
> **done**

Clearly, the average computation time of Algorithm 1 is $W(X)$. Thus, guesswork may be interpreted as the optimal expected work involved in guessing the value of a random variable.

3.2 Guesswork and Variation Distance

It is easily seen that guesswork is bounded above by

$$W(X) \le \frac{|\mathscr{X}| + 1}{2}, \tag{4}$$

and that equality is achieved if and only if X is uniformly distributed on $\mathscr{X}$ (see [12] or [18]). The next theorem offers tight upper and lower bounds on the difference between guesswork and its maximum. The situation is analogous to

Shannon's First Theorem in which the average codeword length (the thing you want to know) is bounded above and below by expressions involving entropy (the thing you can often compute).

Theorem 1. *Let $\mathcal{X}$ be a set of size n, and let X be an $\mathcal{X}$-valued random variable defined by probability distribution p. Then,*

$$\frac{n}{2}\|p - u\| \leq \frac{n+1}{2} - W(X) \leq n\|p - u\|. \tag{5}$$

The theorem is proved in [18]. Note that when $\|p - u\|$ is sufficiently small, the upper and lower bounds of

$$\frac{n+1}{2} - n\|p - u\| \leq W(X) \leq \frac{n+1}{2} - \frac{n}{2}\|p - u\|, \tag{6}$$

are both positive. We see that as $\|p - u\| \to 0$, $W(X)$ approaches its maximum within increasingly tight bounds.

Remark 1. For small values of the variation distance, (6) admits the approximation

$$W(X) \approx \frac{n}{2}(1 - \|p - u\|).$$

In this form, an analogy to Shannon's First Theorem [4] is rather apt, because the optimal expected codeword length L^* may similarly be approximated by

$$L^* \approx \log(n) - D(p\|u),$$

where $D(p\|u) = \log(n) + H(p)$ is the *Kullback-Leibler* distance to uniformity, and $H(p)$ is the *entropy* of p. Notice that $\|p - u\|$ has a supremum of 1, while $D(p\|u)$ has a maximum of $\log(n)$.

Furthermore in Shannon's theorem, the optimal codeword length is within 1 bit of the entropy. However entropy is a logarithmic quantity relative to guesswork. In that sense, (5) says that the cost of being naive in a non-optimal search is within 1 bit of the quantity $\log(n\|p - u\|)$.

4 Security Measures for Known and Chosen Plaintext Attacks

In this section we consider a cipher's capacity for resisting known and chosen plaintext attacks.

4.1 Conditional Guesswork and the Security Factors

In a known or chosen plaintext attack, a single encryption key is used to encrypt a number of different plaintexts. An adversary who observes the corresponding plaintext-ciphertext pairs is privy to partial information about the key. In this section we quantify the intuitive notion that the resilience of a cipher against known or chosen plaintexts attacks can be measured by the amount of work required to guess the key *after* information about the plaintext-ciphertext pairs has been taken into account.

Formally if G is a subgroup of $\mathfrak{S}_{\mathcal{M}}$, let X be a G-cipher representing a single choice of a cipher's key. Again let $x(g) = \mathsf{P}\,[X = g]$, and let $P^\ell = (P_1, P_2, \dots, P_\ell)$ be an ℓ-tuple of i.i.d. random variables describing a sequence of *distinct* plaintexts in $\mathcal{M}$. Following [6], let $\mathcal{M}^{(\ell)}$ denote the set of ℓ-tuples with distinct elements of $\mathcal{M}$. $\mathfrak{S}_{\mathcal{M}}$ and hence G acts on $\mathcal{M}^{(\ell)}$ in the natural way, namely $\sigma(m_1, \dots, m_\ell) = (\sigma m_1, \dots, \sigma m_\ell)$. Now define

$$C^\ell = (X P_1, X P_2, \dots, X P_\ell) = (C_1, C_2, \dots, C_\ell).$$

In other words, P^ℓ and C^ℓ are $\mathcal{M}^{(\ell)}$-valued random variables. We write $p, c \in \mathcal{M}^{(\ell)}$ for instances of P^ℓ and C^ℓ. When contemplating the loss of security due to observations of plaintext-ciphertext pairs, it is natural to define, by analogy to conditional entropy, notions of conditional guesswork.

Definition 3. *Given the quantities described above, the* **conditional guesswork** *of X given C^ℓ and P^ℓ is defined as*

$$W(X|C^\ell, P^\ell) = \sum_{c, p \in \mathcal{M}^{(\ell)}} W(X|C^\ell = c, P^\ell = p) p_j(c, p).$$

The **conditional guesswork** *of X given C^ℓ and that $P^\ell = p$ is defined as*

$$W(X|C^\ell, P^\ell = p) = \sum_{c \in \mathcal{M}^{(\ell)}} W(X|C^\ell = c, P^\ell = p) p_c(c|p).$$

Here $p_j(c, p)$ is the joint distribution of C^ℓ and P^ℓ, while $p_c(c|p)$ is the conditional distribution of C^ℓ given P^ℓ. These are respectively given by

$$p_j(c, p) = \mathsf{P}\,\left[C^\ell = c, P^\ell = p \right], \quad \text{and} \quad p_c(c|p) = \mathsf{P}\,\left[C^\ell = c \mid P^\ell = p \right].$$

The two kinds of conditional guesswork will be used to quantify the performances of optimal known and chosen plaintext attacks, justifying the following definitions.

Definition 4. *The* **known plaintext security factor** *of X against the observation of ℓ plaintext-ciphertext pairs is defined as*

$$\nu_\ell(X) = W(X|C^\ell, P^\ell),$$

and the **chosen plaintext security factor** *of X against a choice of ℓ plaintext-ciphertext pairs is defined as*

$$\theta_\ell(X) = \min_{p \in \mathcal{M}^{(\ell)}} W(X|C^\ell, P^\ell = p).$$

Finally, we define $\nu_0(X) = \theta_0(X) = W(X)$.

Notice that the chosen plaintext security factor is independent of the plaintext statistics, as one would expect. The next proposition establishes $\theta_\ell(X)$ as a principal figure of merit.

Proposition 1. $\theta_\ell(X) \leq \nu_\ell(X)$.

Proof. Simply expand out the formulas,

$$\nu_\ell(X) = \sum_{p \in \mathcal{M}^{(\ell)}} W(X|C^\ell, P^\ell = p) p_P(p) \geq \sum_{p \in \mathcal{M}^{(\ell)}} \theta_\ell(X) p_P(p) = \theta_\ell(X),$$

where $p_P(p) = \mathsf{P}\left[P^\ell = p\right]$. $\qquad\square$

4.2 Observing Plaintext-Ciphertext Pairs

An elementary observation about group action leads to a fundamental fact. Put simply, the guesswork $W(X|C^\ell = c, P^\ell = p)$ is entirely determined by the distribution of X on a coset of a certain subgroup of G.

Lemma 1 (Coset Work Lemma). *With X, C^ℓ, P^ℓ and $c, p \in \mathcal{M}^{(\ell)}$ defined as before, there is a $g_{cp} \in G$ such that $c = g_{cp}p$. The conditional guesswork*

$$W(X|C^\ell = c, P^\ell = p),$$

is determined by the distribution of X on the left coset $g_{cp}H$, where H is the stabilizer subgroup $\mathrm{Stab}_G(p)$.

Proof. The proof uses familiar group action observations discussed in [18]. Let g_{cp} be the value of X. By definition $c = g_{cp}p$, and it is standard that

$$\{g \in G \,|\, c = gp\} = g_{cp}\,\mathrm{Stab}_G(p) = g_{cp}H.$$

If $\widehat{X}$ is the random variable $(X|C^\ell = c, P^\ell = p)$, we have

$$\mathsf{P}\left[\widehat{X} = g\right] = \begin{cases} \dfrac{x(g)}{x(g_{cp}H)}, & \text{if } g \in g_{cp}H, \\ 0, & \text{otherwise,} \end{cases}$$

by Bayes's theorem. Now $W(\widehat{X}) = W(X|C^\ell = c, P^\ell = p)$, which completes the proof. $\qquad\square$

The coset work lemma suggests optimal algorithms for attacking a cipher X. Given ℓ plaintext-ciphertext pairs $c, p \in \mathcal{M}^{(\ell)}$, we may restrict the optimal search for the value of X in Algorithm 1 to a coset of $H = \mathrm{Stab}_G(p)$. Thus we have the following algorithms.

Algorithm 2 (Optimal Known Plaintext Attack). *Defines algorithm* kpa_ℓ.

    1. Collect into tuple p, ℓ random plaintexts according to their natural statistics.
    2. Collect into tuple c, the corresponding ciphertexts.
    3. Invoke Algorithm 1 to optimally search $g_{cp}\,\text{Stab}_G(p)$ for the value of X, where $c = g_{cp}p$.

Algorithm 3 (Optimal Chosen Plaintext Attack). *Defines algorithm* cpa_ℓ.

    1. Let $\widehat{p}$ minimize $W(X|C^\ell, P^\ell = \widehat{p})$.
    2. Let $c = X\widehat{p}$.
    3. Invoke Algorithm 1 to optimally search $\widehat{g}\,\text{Stab}_G(\widehat{p})$ for the value of X, where $c = \widehat{g}\widehat{p}$.

The next proposition justifies the definitions of security factors $\nu_\ell(X)$ and $\theta_\ell(X)$. See [18] for a formal proof of this intuitive statement.

Proposition 2. *Under the assumption that the various oracles respond instantaneously, the expected computation time of attacks kpa_ℓ and cpa_ℓ against X are given by $\nu_\ell(X)$ and $\theta_\ell(X)$, respectively.*

4.3 Uniformly Distributed and (Conditionally) Perfect Ciphers

Ciphers for which every achievable message permutation is equally likely have extraordinary properties, making them worthy of special attention. There is one such cipher for every subgroup G of the symmetric group $\mathfrak{S}_\mathcal{M}$. Their security factors greatly simplify and can often be explicitly computed. When $G = \mathfrak{S}_\mathcal{M}$, we shall show that the resulting uniformly distributed cipher is *perfect* in meaningful ways.

Definition 5. *For any $G \leq \mathfrak{S}_\mathcal{M}$, the uniformly distributed G-cipher denoted U_G is called the* **uniform G-cipher**. *In case $G = \mathfrak{S}_\mathcal{M}$, $U_{\mathfrak{S}_\mathcal{M}}$ will simply be denoted U and called the* **perfect cipher**.

The coset work lemma admits an immediate simplification for uniform ciphers.

Theorem 2. *For every $p \in \mathcal{M}^{(\ell)}$,*

$$W(U_G|C^\ell, P^\ell = p) = \frac{1}{2}\left(1 + |\text{Stab}_G(p)|\right).$$

Proof. For specific $c, p \in \mathcal{M}^{(\ell)}$, the coset work lemma tells us that

$$W(U_G|C^\ell = c, P^\ell = p) = W(\widehat{U_G}),$$

where $\widehat{U_G}$ is uniformly distributed on a coset of $H = \text{Stab}_G(p)$. By (4),

$$W(\widehat{U_G}) = \frac{1}{2}(1 + |g_{cp}H|) = \frac{1}{2}(1 + |H|),$$

which is independent of c. The desired result follows. $\qquad\square$

For a uniform cipher, we immediately have that the chosen plaintext security factor is a function *only* of the size of the smallest ℓ-message stabilizer.

Corollary 1. *For any $G \leq \mathfrak{S}_{\mathscr{M}}$,*

$$\theta_\ell(U_G) = \frac{1}{2}\left(1 + \min_{p \in \mathscr{M}^{(\ell)}} |\mathrm{Stab}_G(p)|\right).$$

For the perfect cipher U, which is uniformly distributed over the entire symmetric group, we can obtain precise formulas for $\nu_\ell(U)$ and $\theta_\ell(U)$.

Proposition 3.

$$\nu_\ell(U) = \theta_\ell(U) = \frac{1 + (|\mathscr{M}| - \ell)!}{2}.$$

Proof. For any tuple $p \in \mathscr{M}^{(\ell)}$, the stabilizer subgroup of p in $\mathfrak{S}_{\mathscr{M}}$ is the symmetric group on the remaining messages $\mathscr{M} - \{p\}$. Each stabilizer therefore has $(|\mathscr{M}| - \ell)!$ elements, and we may apply Corollary 1 to obtain $\theta_\ell(U)$. Furthermore, we have

$$\nu_\ell(U) = \sum_{p \in \mathscr{M}^{(\ell)}} W(U|C^\ell, P^\ell = p)p_P(p) = \theta_\ell(U)\sum_{p \in \mathscr{M}^{(\ell)}} p_P(p) = \theta_\ell(U).$$

$\square$

What Proposition 3 tells us is that we can determine exactly the expected performance of the optimal known and chosen plaintext attacks $\mathbf{kpa}_\ell$ and $\mathbf{cpa}_\ell$ against a perfect cipher. Provided $\ell \ll |\mathscr{M}|$, these attacks reduce to very long brute-force searches. The addition of a new plaintext-ciphertext pair reduces the size, in bits, of the effective search space by

$$\log\theta_\ell(U) - \log\theta_{\ell+1}(U) \approx \log\left[\frac{(|\mathscr{M}| - \ell)!}{(|\mathscr{M}| - \ell - 1)!}\right] < \log|\mathscr{M}|.$$

Thus, for a cipher of block length n, $|\mathscr{M}| = 2^n$ and each new plaintext-ciphertext pair reduces the search space by no more than n bits. But by Stirling's formula

$$\log\theta_0(U) \approx \log|\mathfrak{S}_{\mathscr{M}}| \approx n2^n \text{ bits.}$$

In other words, in order to reduce the search space to within a reasonably attackable size, on the order of 2^n distinct plaintext-ciphertext pairs must be obtained. By that time the adversary has a table of all 2^n possible ciphertexts from which they can look up any desired target plaintext. One cannot expect a block cipher to perform better than this. We now explicitly prove what this discussion suggests, namely that the perfect cipher is as secure as any cipher.

Theorem 3. *For any G-cipher with $G \leq \mathfrak{S}_{\mathscr{M}}$,*

$$\nu_\ell(X) \leq \nu_\ell(U), \quad and \quad \theta_\ell(X) \leq \theta_\ell(U).$$

Proof. Since $G \leq \mathfrak{S}_{\mathcal{M}}$, $\mathrm{Stab}_G(p) \leq \mathrm{Stab}_{\mathfrak{S}_{\mathcal{M}}}(p)$, so that any distribution on a coset of $\mathrm{Stab}_G(p)$ can be thought of as distribution on a coset of $H = \mathrm{Stab}_{\mathfrak{S}_{\mathcal{M}}}(p)$. Once again invoking the coset work lemma along with the fact that the uniform distribution is majorized by any other distribution (see [12] or [18]), we obtain

$$W(X|C^\ell = c, P^\ell = p) \leq W(U|C^\ell = c, P^\ell = p) = \frac{1 + |H|}{2}.$$

The theorem is essentially proved. Pedantically, one should expand out the formulas for $\nu_\ell(X)$ and $\theta_\ell(X)$ (see [18]). $\qquad\square$

4.4 The Security Factors and Variation Distance

Theorem 1 gave us, in terms of variation distance, tight bounds on the difference between guesswork and its maximum value. If we wish variation distance to have a deeper security meaning, it is natural to seek similar bounds on conditional guesswork.

Theorem 4. *For permutation group $G \leq \mathfrak{S}_{\mathcal{M}}$, let X be a G-cipher with probability distribution x. If $p \in \mathcal{M}^{(\ell)}$ and $H = \mathrm{Stab}_G(p)$, then*

$$W(X|C^\ell, P^\ell = p) \geq \frac{1 + |H|}{2} - |G| \, \|x - u\|.$$

The proof of Theorem 4, which is presented in detail in [18], is essentially based on the decomposition of the group algebra $\mathbb{R}G$ into a direct sum of vector spaces isomorphic to the smaller group algebra $\mathbb{R}H$. This is a special case of a very important construction called the *induced representation* (see [7] and [18]).

We may bound $\theta_\ell(X)$ by an expression which is a function of the variation distance $\|x - u\|$, and as in Corollary 1, the size of the smallest ℓ-message stabilizer.

Corollary 2. *For any $G \leq \mathfrak{S}_{\mathcal{M}}$ and any G-cipher X with probability distribution x,*

$$\theta_\ell(X) \geq \frac{1}{2}\left(1 + \min_{p \in \mathcal{M}^{(\ell)}} |\mathrm{Stab}_G(p)|\right) - |G| \, \|x - u\|.$$

Proof. By definition, $\theta_\ell(X) = W(X|C^\ell, P^\ell = \hat{p})$, where $\hat{p}$ minimizes the conditional guesswork. Writing $\hat{H} = \mathrm{Stab}_G(\hat{p})$, we observe

$$\theta_\ell(X) = W(X|C^\ell, P^\ell = \hat{p})$$
$$\geq \frac{1 + |\hat{H}|}{2} - |G| \, \|x - u\|$$
$$\geq \frac{1}{2}\left(1 + \min_{p \in \mathcal{M}^{(\ell)}} |\mathrm{Stab}_G(p)|\right) - |G| \, \|x - u\|,$$

which was to be proved. $\qquad\square$

Just as the lower bound on $W(X)$ of (6) is vacuously negative unless $\|x - u\|$ is smaller than $1/2$, so too the lower bound given in Corollary 2 will be negative unless $\|x - u\|$ is sufficiently small. To see when this happens, let H be one of the smallest ℓ-message stabilizers, and rearrange the inequality of the corollary as

$$\theta_\ell(X) \geq \frac{|H|}{2}(1 - 2[G:H]\|x - u\|). \tag{7}$$

When represented in this way, the lower bound on $\theta_\ell(X)$ becomes meaningful only when $\|x - u\|$ is less than $1/(2[G:H])$. It is not terribly surprising that resistance to chosen plaintext attacks should come at some measurable cost.

5 Applications to Iterated Cryptosystems

5.1 Generalized Markov Ciphers and the Cut-Off Phenomenon

Under the assumption of subkey independence, an iterated cryptosystem is equivalent to the product of finitely many independent and identically distributed G-ciphers. The sequence of all such products — as the number of rounds r ranges from 0 to ∞ — defines a random walk on G whose underlying Markov chain has many important security properties.

Formally, let $(X_i)_{i=1}^\infty$ be an infinite sequence of i.i.d. G-ciphers, each with probability distribution $x(g) = \mathsf{P}[X_i = g]$. Define the sequence $(Z_r)_{r=0}^\infty$ of G-ciphers by $Z_0 = 1$ and $Z_r = X_r \cdots X_2 X_1$. Applying (1), we see that the distribution of Z_r is given by an r-fold convolution of x with itself

$$\mathsf{P}[Z_r = g] = x^{*r}(g).$$

The next result follows from Proposition 5 below.

Proposition 4. *The sequence (Z_i) is a Markov chain with state space G.*

This fact allows us to generalize the definition of a Markov cipher given by Lai, Massey and Murphy [9]. Our motivation is itself a generalization of theirs. The idea of a Markov cipher in [9] was used to model resistance to Differential Cryptanalysis as a function of the number of rounds. Similarly we seek to quantify the resistance of an iterated cryptosystem to *all* known and chosen plaintext attacks, as a function of the number of rounds.

Definition 6. *With x and (X_i) defined as above, the G-cipher $Z_r = X_r \cdots X_2 X_1$, is called the (**generalized**) **Markov cipher** generated by r rounds of x, and (Z_i) will be called the **Markov chain** generated by x.*

There are a multitude of different Markov chains resulting from the action of (Z_i) on various G-sets. The following proposition is proved in [18].

Proposition 5. *Let x be a probability distribution on a finite group G, and let (Z_i) be the Markov chain generated by x. If $\mathscr{Y}$ is a G-set, and Y_0 is an independent $\mathscr{Y}$-valued random variable, then the sequence $(Y_i = Z_i Y_0)_{i \geq 0}$, is a Markov chain on the state space $\mathscr{Y}$. The transition matrix is doubly stochastic and is completely determined by x.*

Recent decades have witnessed a renaissance in Markov chain research spearheaded by Aldous and Diaconis (see [1], [5]). An important frequent observation of this research has been that many random walks on groups and other discrete structures exhibit *cut-off phenomena*, in which there is a rapid transition from order to uniform randomness. The phenomena is often quantified in terms the variation distance $\|x^{*r} - u\|$, and in fact $1 - \|x^{*r} - u\|$ often follows a profile like the one in Fig. 1. Proofs of cut-off phenomena for special cases abound in the literature. They sometimes employ representation theoretic arguments as in [5], and they sometimes employ more probabilistic arguments as in [1].

In the next section, we explore how probabilistic arguments can establish the non-asymptotic behavior of an iterated cryptosystem. In [18] some cryptological implications of the representation theoretic approach are explored.

5.2 Strong Uniform Times

Following [1] and [5, Chap. 4], we introduce some basic definitions useful in making probabilistic arguments for establishing the behavior of $\|x^{*r} - u\|$.

Let $\mathbb{N} = \{1, 2, \ldots\}$, and take $G^{\mathbb{N}}$ to be the set of infinite sequences of elements of G. A *stopping rule* is a function

$$t : G^{\mathbb{N}} \longrightarrow \mathbb{N} \cup \{\infty\},$$

such that if $t(g_1, g_2, \ldots) = i$, then $t(\widehat{g}_1, \widehat{g}_2, \ldots) = i$ whenever $\widehat{g}_j = g_j$, $j \leq i$. If Z_i is a sequence of G-valued random variables, then the $\mathbb{N}$-valued random variable $T = t(Z_1, Z_2, \ldots)$ is called a *stopping time*. In essence, the stopping rule identifies the first time that a certain condition is met in a sequence of group elements, and the stopping time describes random fluctuations in the first occurrence of that condition.

Of course, we are interested in the evolution of Markov ciphers and their approach to uniformity. Let Z_r be the Markov cipher generated by r rounds of x. If the condition being met by a stopping time T is sufficient to guarantee uniformity of Z_r, in other words if

$$P\left[Z_r = g \mid T \leq r\right] = \frac{1}{|G|}, \quad \text{for all } g \in G,$$

then T is called a *strong uniform time (for x)*. As one might intuitively expect, the statistics of a strong uniform time can characterize the approach to uniformity of the Markov cipher.

Lemma 2 (Aldous, Diaconis [1]). *Let x be a probability distribution on a finite group G, and let T be a strong uniform time for x. Then*

$$\|x^{*r} - u\| \leq P\left[T > r\right], \quad \text{for all } r \geq 0.$$

5.3 An Example: Top-to-Random Shuffle

Consider shuffling a deck of k cards by repeatedly removing the top card and returning it to a random position in the deck. Each step can be modeled by choosing a random permutation in $\mathfrak{S}_k$ of the form $\gamma_i = (i \ldots 21)$ with probability $x(\gamma_i) = 1/k$, $1 \leq i \leq k$. There is a strong uniform time for x defined in the following way. Let t_1 be a stopping rule expressing the first time that γ_k is chosen. At this point the specific card j has been moved from the top to the bottom of the deck. Let t_{k-1} be the first time after t_1 that j returns to the top of the deck. At this point each permutation of the remaining cards is equally likely. At $t_k = t_{k-1} + 1$, in other words after the j on top of the deck is placed at random within the deck, each permutation of the deck is equally likely. If (Z_i) is the Markov chain generated by x, then the random time $T = t_k(Z_1, Z_2, \ldots)$ is a strong uniform time for x.

Aldous and Diaconis show in [1] that the probability $\mathsf{P}[T > r]$ is governed by the "coupon-collector's problem" and is bounded by

$$\mathsf{P}[T > k \log k + ck] \leq e^{-c}, \quad c \geq 0, \ k \geq 0.$$

Thus we have a cut-off point $r_0 = k \log k$, and

$$\|x^{*r} - u\| \leq e^{-(r - r_0)/k}, \quad r \geq r_0.$$

The simplicity of the top-to-random shuffle allows it to be implemented as an iterated cryptosystem. Consider the shuffle permutations acting on the $k = 2^n$ bit strings of length n. By considering these bit strings as binary representations of the integers $\{0, \ldots, 2^n - 1\}$, the following algorithm implements one round of the shuffle.

Algorithm 4. *Defines function* TopToRand (n, i), *which implements one round of the top-to-random shuffle. We assume the existence of a pseudo-random number generator (PRNG) satisfying* $1 \leq$ random$(n) \leq n$, *and uniformly distributed thereon.*

>**input:** *The block length n, and the plaintext input, represented as*
>   *an integer $0 \leq i < 2^n$.*
>**output:** *The ciphertext output.*
>
>**function** TopToRand (n, i):
> $m \leftarrow$ random(2^n).
>   **if** $i < m$ **then**
>   **return** $i - 1 \bmod m$.
>   **else**
>   **return** i.
>   **endif**

Unfortunately, the previous algorithm does not achieve security within a practical number of rounds because for a reasonable block length, the cut-off point $r_0 = n2^n$ is too large. Nevertheless, the example shows that there exists a cipher with an efficient round function, and for which an explicit cut-off point can be computed. Furthermore, using (6) and (7), we can also compute explicit bounds on the guesswork and chosen plaintext security factor. For $r \geq r_0$,

$$W(Z_r) \geq \frac{2^n!}{2} \left[1 - 2e^{-(r-r_0)/2^n} \right],$$

and

$$\theta_\ell(Z_r) \geq \frac{(2^n - \ell)!}{2} \left[1 - 2^{n\ell+1} e^{-(r-r_0)/2^n} \right].$$

The lower bound on $\theta_\ell(Z_r)$ makes use of the fact that all ℓ-message stabilizers of $\mathfrak{S}_{2^n}$ have size $(2^n - \ell)!$. As soon as the quantities in brackets are positive, the lower bounds on $W(Z_r)$ and $\theta_\ell(Z_r)$ grow quickly toward intractably large quantities, forcing even the most endowed adversary to work "forever" guessing the key.

6 Conclusion

We have successfully demonstrated that inequalities involving guesswork, conditional guesswork and variation distance can be used to establish the number of rounds necessary to achieve provable security in an iterated cryptosystem. Though in the example given here, that number of rounds grows exponentially with the block length, the iterations could still be applied to a smaller message space to produce provably secure S-boxes. Ongoing research suggests that iterated cryptosystems exist in which the round function is computationally efficient and number of rounds required for provable security is a polynomial in the block length. Some caveats to this approach include:

- We assume the existence of a cryptographically strong pseudo-random function. To date such functions are based on hard open problems and bounded computational resources.
- Variation distance is relatively sensitive to small deviations away from uniformity. It may therefore prove to be overly conservative as a security measure.
- Direct application of these techniques to existing block ciphers such as DES is not expected to be fruitful because it is known that keys of nonzero probability are sparse in a large group. Furthermore, it took several decades of open research to establish (finally in [23]) the precise group for DES. Nevertheless, in the design of new ciphers, the group G is easily treated as a design parameter. Large candidate groups which are smaller than $\mathfrak{S}_{2^n}$ include various wreath products.

References

1. David J. Aldous and Persi Diaconis. Shuffling cards and stopping times. *Amer. Math. Monthly*, 93:333–348, 1986.
2. Eli Biham and Adi Shamir. *Differential Cryptanalysis of the Data Encryption Standard.* Springer-Verlag, New York, 1993.
3. Christian Cachin. *Entropy Measures and Unconditional Security in Cryptography.* PhD thesis, ETH Zürich, 1997.
4. Thomas M. Cover and Joy A. Thomas. *Elements of Information Theory.* John Wiley & Sons, New York, 1991.
5. Persi Diaconis. *Group Representations in Probability and Statistics.* Institute of Mathematical Statistics, Hayward, CA, 1988.
6. John D. Dixon and Brian Mortimer. *Permutation Groups.* Springer-Verlag, New York, 1996.
7. William Fulton and Joe Harris. *Representation Theory: A First Course.* Springer-Verlag, New York, 1991.
8. G. R. Grimmett and D. R. Stirzaker. *Probability and Random Processes.* Oxford University Press, Oxford, 2nd edition, 1992.
9. Xuejia Lai, James L. Massey, and Sean Murphy. Markov ciphers and differential cryptanalysis. In D. W. Davies, editor, *Advances in Cryptology - EUROCRYPT '91*, pages 17–38, Berlin, 1991. Springer-Verlag.
10. M. O. Lorenz. Methods of measuring concentration of wealth. *J. Amer. Statist. Assoc.*, 9:209–219, 1905.
11. Michael Luby and Charles Rackoff. How to construct pseudorandom permutations from pseudorandom functions. *SIAM Jour. Comput.*, 75(2), 1988.
12. Albert W. Marshall and Ingram Olkin. *Inequalities: Theory of Majorization and Its Applications.* Academic Press, San Diego, 1979.
13. James L. Massey. Guessing and entropy. *Proc. 1994 IEEE Int'l Symp. on Information Theory*, page 204, 1994.
14. Alec Muffett. *Crack Version 5.0a User Manual.*
    URL: ftp://ftp.cert.org/pub/tools/crack/.
15. Moni Naor and Omer Reingold. On the construction of pseudorandom permutations: Luby-Rackoff revisited. *Journal of Cryptology*, 12:29–66, 1999.
16. Kaisa Nyberg and Lars Ramkilde Knudsen. Provable security against a differential attack. *Journal of Cryptology*, 8:27–37, 1995.
17. Luke O'Connor and Jovan Dj. Golić. A unified Markov approach to differential and linear cryptanalysis. In Josef Pieprzyk and Reihanah Safavi-Naini, editors, *Advances in Cryptology - ASIACRYPT '94*, pages 387–397, New York, 1994. Springer-Verlag.
18. John O. Pliam. *Ciphers and their Products: Group Theory in Private Key Cryptography.* PhD thesis, University of Minnesota, July 1999.
19. Joseph J. Rotman. *An Introduction to the Theory of Groups.* Wm. C. Brown, Dubuque, IA, 3rd edition, 1988.
20. Claude E. Shannon. Communication theory of secrecy systems. *Bell System Tech. Jour.*, 28:656–715, 1949.
21. Serge Vaudenay. Provable security for block ciphers by decorrelation. In *STACS '98*, pages 249–275, Berlin, 1998. Springer-Verlag.
22. Serge Vaudenay. The decorrelation technique, 1999.
    URL: http://www.dmi.ens.fr/~vaudenay/decorrelation.html.
23. Ralph Wernsdorf. The one-round functions of DES generate the alternating group. In R.A. Reuppel, editor, *Advances in Cryptology - EUROCRYPT '92*, pages 99–112, Berlin, 1993. Springer-Verlag.

Modeling Linear Characteristics of Substitution-Permutation Networks

Liam Keliher[1], Henk Meijer[1], and Stafford Tavares[2]

[1] Department of Computing and Information Science
Queen's University, Kingston, Ontario, Canada
{keliher,henk}@cs.queensu.ca
[2] Department of Electrical and Computer Engineering
Queen's University, Kingston, Ontario, Canada
stafford@eleceng.ee.queensu.ca

Abstract. In this paper we present a model for the bias values associated with linear characteristics of substitution-permutation networks (SPN's). The first iteration of the model is based on our observation that for sufficiently large s-boxes, the best linear characteristic usually involves one active s-box per round. We obtain a result which allows us to compute an upper bound on the probability that linear cryptanalysis using such a characteristic is feasible, as a function of the number of rounds. We then generalize this result, upper bounding the probability that linear cryptanalysis is feasible when any linear characteristic may be used (no restriction on the number of active s-boxes). The work of this paper indicates that the basic SPN structure provides good security against linear cryptanalysis based on linear characteristics after a reasonably small number of rounds.

1 Introduction

A substitution-permutation network (SPN) is a basic cryptosystem architecture which implements Shannon's principles of "confusion" and "diffusion" [15], and which was first proposed by Feistel [4]. An SPN is in some sense the simplest implementation of Shannon's principles. Its basic structural elements of substitution and linear transformation are the foundation of many modern block ciphers, as can be seen from the current AES candidates (for example, Serpent uses a straight SPN structure [1]). Viewing the basic SPN architecture as a "canonical" cryptosystem has provided a useful model for study, yielding a range of analytical and experimental results [6,7,17].

In this paper we consider the linear cryptanalysis of SPN's, developing a model which allows us to bound the probability that a linear attack based on linear characteristics will succeed. The result is of interest because, in practice, linear cryptanalysis often relies on carefully chosen linear characteristics. It should be noted, however, that to achieve "provable security" against linear cryptanalysis, resistance to linear hulls, the counterpart of differentials in differential cryptanalysis, must be demonstrated (see Nyberg [13]).

Howard Heys and Carlisle Adams (Eds.): SAC'99, LNCS 1758, pp. 78–91, 2000.

2 Substitution-Permutation Networks

A substitution-permutation network processes an N-bit plaintext through a series of R rounds, each round consisting of a *substitution stage* followed by a *permutation stage*. In the substitution stage, the current block is viewed as M n-bit subblocks, each of which is fed into a bijective $n \times n$ substitution box (s-box), i.e., a bijective function mapping $\{0,1\}^n \to \{0,1\}^n$. This is followed by a permutation stage, originally a bit-wise permutation, but more generally an invertible linear transformation [5,7]. The permutation stage is usually omitted from the last round. An example of an SPN with $N = 16$, $M = n = 4$, and $R = 3$ is shown in Figure 1. Incorporation of key bits typically involves the derivation

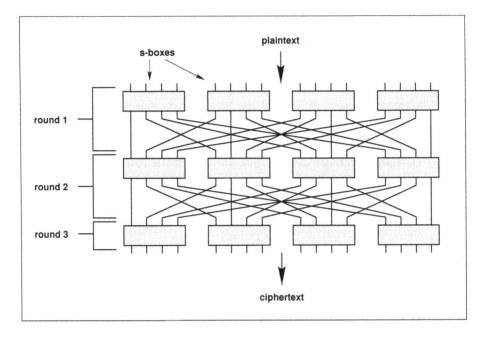

Fig. 1. Example SPN with $N = 16$, $M = n = 4$, $R = 3$

of $(R+1)$ N-bit *subkeys*, denoted $\mathbf{K}^1, \mathbf{K}^2, \ldots, \mathbf{K}^R, \mathbf{K}^{R+1}$, from the original key, $\mathbf{K}$, via a *key scheduling algorithm*. Subkey $\mathbf{K}^r$ is XOR'd with the current block before round r, and subkey $\mathbf{K}^{R+1}$ is XOR'd with the output of the last round to form the ciphertext. For the purpose of what follows, we will assume that $\mathbf{K}$ is an *independent key* [2], a concatenation of $(R + 1)$ N-bit subkeys which are not necessarily derivable from some master key via a key-scheduling algorithm (therefore $\mathbf{K} \in \{0,1\}^{N(R+1)}$).

Decryption is accomplished by running the SPN "backwards," reversing the order of the rounds, and in each round performing the inverse linear transformation followed by application of the inverse s-boxes (subkey $\mathbf{K}^{R+1}$ is first XOR'd with the ciphertext, and each subkey $\mathbf{K}^r$ is XOR'd with the current block *after* decryption round r).

For the purpose of this paper, we adopt an SPN structure with $M = n$ s-boxes of size $n \times n$ $(n \geq 2)$ in each round (therefore $N = n^2$), and an inter-round permutation $\pi : \{0,1\}^N \rightarrow \{0,1\}^N$ which connects output bit j of s-box i in round r to input bit i of s-box j in round $r+1$ [8], as in Figure 1. (We use the convention that all numbering proceeds from left to right, beginning at 1.)

In our model, each s-box in the SPN is chosen uniformly and independently from the set of all bijective $n \times n$ s-boxes. In addition, we make the assumption that the input to each encryption round is uniformly and independently distributed over $\{0,1\}^N$. This allows the use of Matsui's Piling-up Lemma [9] in Sections 4 and 5. This assumption does in fact hold if we observe the inputs to the various rounds while varying over all plaintexts *and all keys* $\mathbf{K} \in \{0,1\}^{N(R+1)}$. However, in practice, $\mathbf{K}$ is fixed and only the plaintexts vary. Nyberg [13] provides a rigorous analysis of this issue.

3   Nonlinearity Measures

The linear approximation table (LAT) [9] of an s-box $S : \{0,1\}^n \rightarrow \{0,1\}^n$ is defined as follows: for $\alpha, \beta \in \{0,1\}^n$,

$$\text{LAT}[\alpha, \beta] = \#\left\{\mathbf{X} \in \{0,1\}^n : \alpha \bullet \mathbf{X} = \beta \bullet S(\mathbf{X})\right\} - 2^{n-1} \;,$$

where $\bullet$ is the inner product summed over $GF(2)$. It follows that $\text{LAT}[0,0] = 2^{n-1}$, and if S is bijective, as is the case in an SPN, then $\text{LAT}[\alpha, \beta] = 0$ if exactly one of α, β is 0. These entries are of no cryptographic significance; in the discussion below we consider only $\text{LAT}[\alpha, \beta]$ for $\alpha, \beta \neq 0$.

If $\text{LAT}[\alpha, \beta] = 0$, then the function $f_\beta(\mathbf{X}) = \beta \bullet S(\mathbf{X})$ is at equal Hamming distance (2^{n-1}) from the affine functions $g_\alpha(\mathbf{X}) = \alpha \bullet \mathbf{X}$ and $g'_\alpha(\mathbf{X}) = (\alpha \bullet \mathbf{X}) \oplus 1$ (here we view functions mapping $\{0,1\}^n \rightarrow \{0,1\}$ as 2^n-bit vectors for the purpose of measuring Hamming distance). A positive value of $\text{LAT}[\alpha, \beta]$ indicates that f_β is closer to g_α, and a negative value indicates that f_β is closer to g'_α. In fact f_β can be approximated by g_α with probability

$$p_{\alpha,\beta} = \frac{\#\left\{\mathbf{X} \in \{0,1\}^n : g_\alpha(\mathbf{X}) = f_\beta(\mathbf{X})\right\}}{2^n} = \frac{\text{LAT}[\alpha, \beta] + 2^{n-1}}{2^n} \;, \tag{1}$$

and by g'_α with probability $(1 - p_{\alpha,\beta})$, computed over the uniform distribution of $\mathbf{X} \in \{0,1\}^n$. It is also useful to define the *bias* associated with $\text{LAT}[\alpha, \beta]$:

$$b_{\alpha,\beta} = p_{\alpha,\beta} - \frac{1}{2} = \frac{\text{LAT}[\alpha, \beta]}{2^n} \;. \tag{2}$$

Obviously $b_{\alpha,\beta} \in \left[-\frac{1}{2}, \frac{1}{2}\right]$. A value of $b_{\alpha,\beta}$ which is (relatively) large in absolute value indicates a (relatively) high probability of success in approximating f_β by an affine function. It is such approximations that are exploited by linear cryptanalysis (Section 4). (Conversely, a bias value of 0 yields no information to the cryptanalyst.) One measure of the resistance of an s-box S to approximation by affine functions is the *nonlinearity* of S, $\mathrm{NL}(S)$:

$$\mathrm{NL}(S) = 2^{n-1} - \max\left\{|\mathrm{LAT}[\alpha, \beta]| : \alpha, \beta \in \{0,1\}^n, \ \alpha, \beta \neq 0\right\}.$$

Another useful value is the minimum nonlinearity over the s-boxes of the SPN, $\mathrm{NL}_{\min}$:

$$\mathrm{NL}_{\min} = \min\left\{\mathrm{NL}(S) : S \in \mathrm{SPN}\right\}.$$

4 Linear Cryptanalysis of SPN's

Linear cryptanalysis is a known-plaintext attack (ciphertext-only under certain conditions) which was introduced by Matsui in 1993 [9]. Matsui demonstrated that linear cryptanalysis could break DES using 2^{43} known plaintexts [11]. Here we present linear cryptanalysis in the context of SPN's where (absent the complexities of DES) the basic concepts are more easily stated. Linear cryptanalysis of SPN's has been considered to some extent by, among others, Heys and Tavares [7] and Youssef [17].

The basic linear attack attempts to extract the equivalent of one key bit, expressed as the XOR sum of a subset of key bits, using a linear equation which relates subsets of the plaintext ($\mathbf{P}$), ciphertext($\mathbf{C}$) and key ($\mathbf{K}$) bits:

$$\mathbf{P}_{i_1} \oplus \mathbf{P}_{i_2} \oplus \cdots \oplus \mathbf{P}_{i_a} \oplus \mathbf{C}_{j_1} \oplus \mathbf{C}_{j_2} \oplus \cdots \oplus \mathbf{C}_{j_b} = \mathbf{K}_{k_1} \oplus \mathbf{K}_{k_2} \oplus \cdots \oplus \mathbf{K}_{k_c} \quad (3)$$

(here $\mathbf{P}_{i_1}$, for example, denotes the i_1^{th} bit of $\mathbf{P}$, numbering from left to right). Such an equation holds with some probability p (and associated bias $b = p - \frac{1}{2}$), computed over the uniform distribution of plaintexts. Matsui's Algorithm 1 [9] extracts the key bit represented by the right-hand side of (3) (with success rate 97.7%) by encrypting $\mathcal{N}_L$ random plaintexts, where

$$\mathcal{N}_L = \frac{1}{b^2} \quad (4)$$

(increasing (reducing) the number of random plaintexts encrypted increases (reduces) the probability that the key bit will be determined correctly).

One-Round Linear Characteristics
A system linear approximation such as (3) can be constructed from one-round linear approximations, also known as *linear characteristics* [2]. Specifically, a one-round characteristic for round r is a tuple

$$\Omega_r = \langle \Gamma_{\mathrm{P}}^r, \ \Gamma_{\mathrm{C}}^r, \ \Gamma_{\mathrm{K}}^r, \ b_r \rangle, \quad (5)$$

where $\Gamma_{\mathrm{P}}^r, \Gamma_{\mathrm{C}}^r \in \{0,1\}^N$ and $\Gamma_{\mathrm{K}}^r \in \{0,1\}^{N(R+1)}$; Γ_{K}^r contains Γ_{P}^r in its rth N-bit subblock, and is zero elsewhere; and bias $b_r \in \left[-\frac{1}{2}, \frac{1}{2}\right]$. Let $S^r(\cdot)$ denote application of the round r s-boxes, which are indexed left to right as $S_1^r, S_2^r, \ldots, S_n^r$.

We can view Γ_P^r (Γ_C^r) as an input (output) mask for round r, and specifically as the concatenation of n n-bit input (output) masks for the S_i^r, denoted $\Gamma_{P,1}^r$, $\Gamma_{P,2}^r, \ldots, \Gamma_{P,n}^r$ ($\Gamma_{C,1}^r, \Gamma_{C,2}^r, \ldots, \Gamma_{C,n}^r$). For $1 \leq i \leq n$, if both $\Gamma_{P,i}^r$ and $\Gamma_{C,i}^r$ are nonzero, then S_i^r is called an *active* s-box [2]. If the active s-boxes in round r are $S_{i_1}^r, S_{i_2}^r, \ldots, S_{i_A}^r$, and $b_{i_a}^r$ is the bias associated with LAT $[\Gamma_{P,i_a}^r, \Gamma_{C,i_a}^r]$ for $S_{i_a}^r$ ($1 \leq a \leq A$), then

$$b_r = 2^{A-1} \prod_{a=1}^{A} b_{i_a}^r \qquad (6)$$

by Matsui's Piling-up Lemma [9]. Note that $|b_r| \leq |b_{i_a}^r|$ for $1 \leq a \leq A$.

It follows from the above, and from equations (1) and (2), that for any independent key $\mathbf{K} \in \{0,1\}^{N(R+1)}$, and uniformly chosen $\mathbf{X} \in \{0,1\}^N$,

$$\text{Prob}\{(\Gamma_P^r \bullet \mathbf{X}) \oplus (\Gamma_C^r \bullet S^r(\mathbf{X} \oplus \mathbf{K}^r)) = (\Gamma_K^r \bullet \mathbf{K})\} = b_r + \frac{1}{2}.$$

Multi-round Linear Characteristics

Given T one-round characteristics $\Omega_1, \Omega_2, \ldots, \Omega_T$ satisfying $\pi(\Gamma_C^t) = \Gamma_P^{t+1}$ for $1 \leq t \leq (T-1)$ (recall that $\pi(\cdot)$ is the inter-round permutation), a single T-round characteristic may be formed from their concatenation:

$$\Omega = \langle \Gamma_P^1, \Gamma_C^T, \Gamma_K, b \rangle,$$

where $\Gamma_K = \Gamma_K^1 \oplus \Gamma_K^2 \oplus \cdots \oplus \Gamma_K^T$, and

$$b = 2^{T-1} \prod_{t=1}^{T} b_t \qquad (7)$$

(again from the Piling-up Lemma). If $T = R$, and if Γ_K' is derived from Γ_K by setting the $(R+1)^{st}$ (i.e., last) N-bit subblock of Γ_K to Γ_C^R, then the linear equation represented by $\Omega' = \langle \Gamma_P^1, \Gamma_C^T, \Gamma_K', b \rangle$, namely

$$\Gamma_P^1 \bullet \mathbf{P} \oplus \Gamma_C^R \bullet \mathbf{C} = \Gamma_K' \bullet \mathbf{K}, \qquad (8)$$

has the form of (3) (holding with probability $p = b + \frac{1}{2}$, over the uniform distribution of plaintexts, $\mathbf{P}$).

In order to break DES, Matsui used auxiliary techniques which allowed a single linear characteristic to be used for the extraction of more than one key bit [9,11]. Since such techniques are not relevant to the discussion which follows, we do not present them here.

5 Model for Distribution of Biases

For the purpose of linear cryptanalysis, clearly the attacker is interested in the R-round linear characteristic whose accompanying bias is maximum in absolute value, termed the *best* linear characteristic (such a characteristic is not necessarily unique), since it minimizes $\mathcal{N}_L$ (see (4)). (For the auxiliary techniques mentioned in Section 4 and applied to SPN's, $(R-q)$-round characteristics are used, for certain integers $q \geq 1$). We limit our consideration to linear characteristics which activate one or more s-boxes in each round, since this is a necessary condition for the accompanying bias (computed using the Piling-up Lemma) to be nonzero. Note that this condition need not be enforced for linear characteristics of ciphers based on the Feistel network architecture, such as DES.

Let $\mathcal{L}_R$ be the set of all R-round linear characteristics. For a fixed SPN, i.e., for a fixed set of s-boxes, and for a given $\Omega \in \mathcal{L}_R$, let $b(\Omega)$ be the bias associated with Ω. Define

$$B_R = \max\left\{|b(\Omega)| : \Omega \in \mathcal{L}_R\right\}.$$

Clearly $B_R \in \left[0, \frac{1}{2}\right]$. In addition, let $\mathcal{L}_R^A$ be the set of all R-round linear characteristics which activate a total of A s-boxes $(A \geq R)$, and define

$$B_R^A = \max\left\{|b(\Omega)| : \Omega \in \mathcal{L}_R^A\right\}.$$

5.1 Modeling Biases of Characteristics in $\mathcal{L}_R^R$

We began our research by creating a computer program to search for the best R-round linear characteristic of a given SPN, for varying values of n and R. The program, tailored to the SPN structure, is based on Matsui's algorithm which finds the best linear characteristic of DES [10]. We quickly observed that the best characteristic almost always involved one active s-box in each round (i.e., it belonged to $\mathcal{L}_R^R$), especially as the s-box dimension was increased. In fact, when 500 16-round SPN's with 8×8 s-boxes were generated at random, the best linear characteristic for the first r rounds, $1 \leq r \leq 16$, was always found to be in $\mathcal{L}_R^R$.

This is not fully intuitive—increasing the number of active boxes in a given round allows the search algorithm more choices for the input mask to the next round, potentially increasing the absolute value of the bias associated with that round; but it also decreases the absolute value of the bias for the round having multiple active s-boxes, by increasing the number of terms in the product of the Piling-up Lemma (see (6)).

In this section, in keeping with the above observation, we derive information about the distribution of values of B_R^R. We begin with the following result [14,16]:

Lemma 1. *Let S be a bijective $n \times n$ s-box, $n \geq 2$, and let $\alpha, \beta \in \{0,1\}^n$, with $\alpha, \beta \neq 0$. Then the set of possible values for the bias associated with $\mathrm{LAT}[\alpha, \beta]$ is*

$$\left\{\frac{\pm 2\ell}{2^n} : \ell \text{ an integer, } 0 \leq \ell \leq 2^{n-2}\right\},$$

where the biases $\frac{\pm 2\ell}{2^n}$ each occur with probability

$$\frac{\binom{2^{n-1}}{2^{n-2}+\ell}^2}{\binom{2^n}{2^{n-1}}},$$

computed over the uniform distribution of bijective $n \times n$ s-boxes.

The probability distribution given by Lemma 1 for $n = 8$ is plotted in Figure 2 (using a $\log_{10}$ scale on the vertical axis).

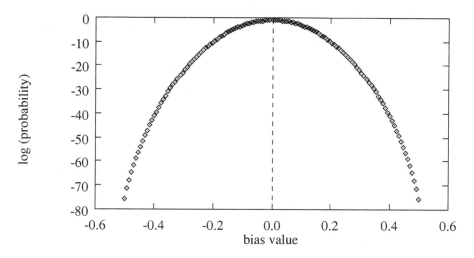

Fig. 2. Probability distribution for bias value of single LAT entry (8×8 bijective s-box)

Before proceeding to the next lemma, it is useful to define the following two sets, for $R \geq 1$ and $n \geq 2$:

$$\mathcal{H}_n = \{1, \ldots, 2^{n-2}\}$$
$$\mathcal{H}_n^R = \{\ell_1 \ell_2 \cdots \ell_R : \ell_r \in \mathcal{H}_n \text{ for } 1 \leq r \leq R\}.$$

Lemma 2. *Let $\Omega \in \mathcal{L}_R^R$. Then the set of possible nonzero values for $b(\Omega)$ is*

$$\left\{ \pm \frac{h}{2^{(n-2)R+1}} : h \in \mathcal{H}_n^R \right\}, \tag{9}$$

where the biases $\pm \frac{h}{2^{(n-2)R+1}}$ each occur with probability

$$2^{R-1} \sum_{\substack{\ell_1, \ell_2, \ldots, \ell_R \in \mathcal{H}_n \\ \ell_1 \ell_2 \cdots \ell_R = h}} \prod_{r=1}^{R} \frac{\binom{2^{n-1}}{2^{n-2}+\ell_r}^2}{\binom{2^n}{2^{n-1}}}, \tag{10}$$

computed over all R-round SPN's with s-boxes chosen uniformly and independently from the set of bijective $n \times n$ s-boxes. The probability that $b(\Omega) = 0$ is *given by*

$$\left(\frac{\binom{2^{n-1}}{2^{n-2}}^2}{\binom{2^n}{2^{n-1}}}\right)^R + \sum_{T=1}^{R-1}\left[\binom{R}{T}2^{T-1}\left(\sum_{\ell_1,\ldots,\ell_T\in\mathcal{H}_n}\prod_{t=1}^{T}\frac{\binom{2^{n-1}}{2^{n-2}+\ell_t}^2}{\binom{2^n}{2^{n-1}}}\right)\left(\frac{\binom{2^{n-1}}{2^{n-2}}^2}{\binom{2^n}{2^{n-1}}}\right)^{R-T}\right].$$

Proof. Each $\Omega \in \mathcal{L}_R^R$ represents a "chain" of active s-boxes through the SPN. Since Ω uniquely determines the n-bit input/output masks for each active s-box, the bias associated with each s-box is determined by a single LAT entry. Let b_r be the bias associated with the active s-box in round r, for $1 \le r \le R$. It follows that b_r takes on the values (with the corresponding probabilities) of Lemma 1.

Now suppose that $b(\Omega) \ne 0$ (therefore each $b_r \ne 0$). Let $s = s(\Omega)$ be the number of active s-boxes whose bias is *negative*. Then from (7), $b(\Omega)$ is of the form

$$2^{R-1}\prod_{r=1}^{R} b_r = (-1)^s\, 2^{R-1}\left(\frac{2\ell_1}{2^n}\right)\left(\frac{2\ell_2}{2^n}\right)\cdots\left(\frac{2\ell_R}{2^n}\right), \quad \text{for some } \ell_1,\ldots,\ell_R \in \mathcal{H}_n$$

$$= (-1)^s\,\frac{\ell_1\ell_2\cdots\ell_R}{2^{(n-2)R+1}}$$

$$= (-1)^s\,\frac{h}{2^{(n-2)R+1}}, \quad h = \ell_1\ell_2\cdots\ell_R \in \mathcal{H}_n^R\,,$$

which gives (9).

Consider the case that $b(\Omega)$ is positive, i.e., $b(\Omega) = \frac{h}{2^{(n-2)R+1}}$ for some $h \in \mathcal{H}_n^R$ (so $s(\Omega)$ is even). We have $|b_r| = \frac{2\ell_r}{2^n}$, for some $\ell_r \in \mathcal{H}_n$ ($1 \le r \le R$), with $\ell_1\ell_2\cdots\ell_R = h$. Keeping the ℓ_r fixed, there are 2^{R-1} ways of assigning $+/-$ signs to the b_r such that $s(\Omega)$ is even. For any such assignment, it follows from Lemma 1 that the probability that the active s-boxes will yield the sequence of biases $b_1, b_2, \ldots, b_R$ is

$$\prod_{r=1}^{R}\frac{\binom{2^{n-1}}{2^{n-2}+\ell_r}^2}{\binom{2^n}{2^{n-1}}}.$$

Summing over all $\ell_1, \ell_2, \ldots, \ell_R$ such that $\ell_1\ell_2\cdots\ell_R = h$, we get (10). It is easy to see that the case $b(\Omega) = \frac{-h}{2^{(n-2)R+1}}$ occurs with the same probability.

The proof in the case $b(\Omega) = 0$ is based on the observation that a sequence of bias values $b_1, b_2, \ldots, b_R$ whose product is 0 must consist of T nonzero values (and $(R-T)$ zero values), for some T, with $0 \le T \le (R-1)$. The details are omitted here.

Lemma 3. $\#\mathcal{L}_R^R = n^R\,(2^n-1)^2.$

Proof. The number of ways to choose one active s-box per round is n^R. For a given choice of active s-boxes, the n-bit output mask for the active s-box in round r, $1 \le r \le (R-1)$, is determined: it consists of all zeros with a 1 in position j, where j is the index of the active s-box in round $r+1$. Similarly, the n-bit input masks for the active s-boxes in rounds $2\ldots R$ are determined. All that remains is the choice of input mask for the active s-box in round 1, and the output mask for the active s-box in round R. Since each such n-bit mask must be nonzero, we have $(2^n - 1)^2$ choices, and the result follows.

The main result of this section is given in Theorem 1. First, however, it is useful to have the following intermediate result. For $\Omega \in \mathcal{L}_R^A$ and $\lambda \in (0, \frac{1}{2}]$, define

$$p_R^A(\lambda) = \text{Prob}\left\{|b(\Omega)| \geq \lambda\right\},$$

computed over all R-round SPN's with s-boxes chosen uniformly and independently from the set of bijective $n \times n$ s-boxes. Arguing as in the proof of Lemma 2, it can be shown that $p_R^A(\lambda)$ is independent of the choice of $\Omega \in \mathcal{L}_R^A$.

Lemma 4. Let $\lambda \in \left(0, \frac{1}{2}\right]$, and define $\Lambda = \lambda \cdot 2^{(n-2)R+1}$. Then

$$p_R^R(\lambda) = 2^R \sum_{\substack{h \in \mathcal{H}_n^R \\ h \geq \Lambda}} \left[\sum_{\substack{\ell_1,\ldots,\ell_R \in \mathcal{H}_n \\ \ell_1 \cdots \ell_R = h}} \prod_{r=1}^R \frac{\binom{2^{n-1}}{2^{n-2}+\ell_r}^2}{\binom{2^n}{2^{n-1}}} \right].$$

Proof. Let $\Omega \in \mathcal{L}_R^R$. Then $p_R^R(\lambda) = \text{Prob}\left\{|b(\Omega)| \geq \lambda\right\} = 2 \cdot \text{Prob}\left\{b(\Omega) \geq \lambda\right\}$, since the distribution of probabilities corresponding to the possible values of $b(\Omega)$ is symmetric about 0, by Lemma 2. Therefore, we can assume that $b(\Omega)$ is positive, and write $b(\Omega) = \frac{h}{2^{(n-2)R+1}}$, for some $h \in \mathcal{H}_n^R$. It follows that

$$p_R^R(\lambda) = 2 \cdot \text{Prob}\left\{b(\Omega) \geq \lambda\right\}$$

$$= 2 \cdot \text{Prob}\left\{h \geq \lambda \cdot 2^{(n-2)R+1}\right\}$$

$$= 2 \cdot \text{Prob}\left\{h \geq \Lambda\right\}$$

$$= 2^R \sum_{\substack{h \in \mathcal{H}_n^R \\ h \geq \Lambda}} \left[\sum_{\substack{\ell_1,\ldots,\ell_R \in \mathcal{H}_n \\ \ell_1 \cdots \ell_R = h}} \prod_{r=1}^R \frac{\binom{2^{n-1}}{2^{n-2}+\ell_r}^2}{\binom{2^n}{2^{n-1}}} \right], \tag{11}$$

where (11) follows from (10) in Lemma 2.

Theorem 1. *Consider an R-round SPN with $n \times n$ s-boxes, n per round, and assume that each s-box is chosen uniformly and independently from the set of all bijective $n \times n$ s-boxes. Let the inter-round permutation, $\pi(\cdot)$, be as above. If $\lambda \in \left(0, \frac{1}{2}\right]$, and $\Lambda = \lambda \cdot 2^{(n-2)R+1}$ then*

$$\text{Prob}\left\{B_R^R \geq \lambda\right\} \leq (2n)^R (2^n - 1)^2 \sum_{\substack{h \in \mathcal{H}_n^R \\ h \geq \Lambda}} \left[\sum_{\substack{\ell_1,\ldots,\ell_R \in \mathcal{H}_n \\ \ell_1 \cdots \ell_R = h}} \prod_{r=1}^R \frac{\binom{2^{n-1}}{2^{n-2}+\ell_r}^2}{\binom{2^n}{2^{n-1}}} \right]. \tag{12}$$

Proof. We have

$$\text{Prob}\left\{B_R^R \geq \lambda\right\} = \text{Prob}\left\{\exists\, \Omega \in \mathcal{L}_R^R \text{ such that } |b(\Omega)| \geq \lambda\right\}$$

$$\leq \sum_{\Omega \in \mathcal{L}_R^R} \text{Prob}\left\{|b(\Omega)| \geq \lambda\right\} \tag{13}$$

$$= \#\mathcal{L}_R^R \cdot p_R^R(\lambda)\,, \tag{14}$$

where (14) follows from (13) because the distribution of $b(\Omega)$ is independent of the choice of Ω. Substituting the results from Lemma 3 and Lemma 4 into (14) and combining constant terms gives (12), finishing the proof.

5.2 An Improved Result

Since the initial submission of this paper, we have been able to generalize the main result (Theorem 1). The improved result, given in Theorem 2 below, upper bounds the probability that linear cryptanalysis of an SPN using linear characteristics is feasible, with no restriction on the number of active s-boxes (of course, we still require a *minimum* of one active s-box per round).

Theorem 2. *Consider an R-round SPN with $n \times n$ s-boxes, n per round, and assume that each s-box is chosen uniformly and independently from the set of all bijective $n \times n$ s-boxes. Let the inter-round permutation, $\pi(\cdot)$, be as above. If $\lambda \in \left(0, \frac{1}{2}\right]$, and $\Lambda = \lambda \cdot 2^{(n-2)R+1}$ then*

$$\text{Prob}\left\{B_R \geq \lambda\right\} \leq \sum_{A=R}^{nR} \#\mathcal{L}_R^A \cdot p_R^A(\lambda)\,. \tag{15}$$

Comment on Proof and Computation

Arguing as in the proof of Theorem 1, it follows that each term in the sum of (15) of the form $\#\mathcal{L}_R^A \cdot p_R^A(\lambda)$ is an upper bound on the probability that linear cryptanalysis is feasible using characteristics from $\mathcal{L}_R^A$. Therefore the sum of all such terms is an upper bound on the probability that linear cryptanalysis using any $\Omega \in \mathcal{L}_R$ is feasible.

In order to extract useful values from (15), it is necessary to transform the right-hand side into an expression which can be evaluated. The sub-terms p_R^A can be evaluated using a slightly modified version of Lemma 4. The main work lies in computing the sub-terms $\#\mathcal{L}_R^A$. We solved this in a recursive fashion. The key observation is that if $\Omega \in \mathcal{L}_R^A$ activates α s-boxes in round R, then the sub-characteristic Ω' obtained by removing round R is an element of $\mathcal{L}_{R-1}^{A-\alpha}$. Counting the number of ways that an Rth round with α active s-boxes can be added to Ω', and summing over all values of α, completes the computation. The details can be found in the full version of this paper.

6 Computational Results

The second computer program created to carry out this research computes the distribution of biases associated with an R-round characteristic $\Omega \in \mathcal{L}_R^R$, as given by Lemma 2. The program works iteratively, computing the distribution for a given round r before proceeding to round $(r+1)$. For $n = 8$ and $R = 3$, the resulting distribution has 28451 bias values. These are plotted in Figure 3, using a $\log_{10}$ scale for the y-axis.

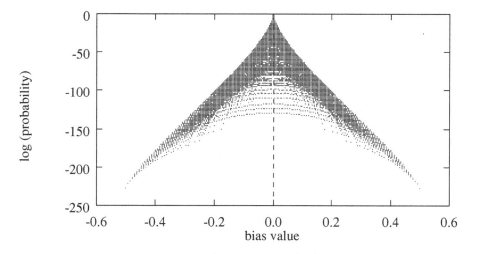

Fig. 3. Distribution of $b(\Omega)$ for $\Omega \in \mathcal{L}_R^R$, with $n = 8$, $R = 3$

Linear cryptanalysis of an N-bit SPN using an R-round linear characteristic $\Omega \in \mathcal{L}_R^R$ is *feasible* if the number of plaintexts required in the best case is at most 2^N, the number of plaintexts available, i.e., if

$$\mathcal{N}_L = \frac{1}{\left(B_R^R\right)^2} \leq 2^N \iff B_R^R \geq 2^{-N/2} \tag{16}$$

(this is for Matsui's Algorithm 1, with a success rate of 97.7% [9]). Setting $\lambda = 2^{-N/2}$, Theorem 1 gives an upper bound on the probability that (16) holds. A modified version of the program used to determine the distribution of $b(\Omega)$ above, for $\Omega \in \mathcal{L}_R^R$, was used to evaluate this upper bound, by computing (14). Results for the case $n = 8$, $N = 64$ (so $\lambda = 2^{-32}$), and $R = 10\ldots16$ are presented in the second column of Table 1. The third column of Table 1 gives the upper bound from the improved result of Theorem 2. In addition, the fourth column of Table 1 gives the experimental probability that (16) holds, obtained by generating 500 16-round, 64-bit SPN's with random 8×8 s-boxes, and computing B_R^R for the first r rounds, for $10 \leq r \leq 16$. (In fact we computed B_R, and found that in each case it was identical to B_R^R, as mentioned in Section 5.)

It is quite interesting that the generalized upper bound of Theorem 2 yields values which are very close to the values obtained from Theorem 1 (in fact, for $R \geq 13$ they are identical to four decimal places). This is evidence that the first term of the sum in (15) (which is exactly the upper bound of Theorem 1) is the dominant term, supporting our earlier observation that the best linear characteristic is usually found in $\mathcal{L}_R^R$.

Number of rounds	Restricted upper bound (Theorem 1)	Unrestricted upper bound (Theorem 2)	Experimental (500 trials)	$\mathcal{N}_L$ lower bound (older result)
10	–	–	1.000	2^{30}
11	–	–	0.962	2^{33}
12	4.3823×10^{-3}	4.3824×10^{-3}	0.000	2^{36}
13	4.6480×10^{-10}	4.6480×10^{-10}	0.000	2^{39}
14	8.8615×10^{-19}	8.8615×10^{-19}	0.000	2^{42}
15	2.8796×10^{-29}	2.8796×10^{-29}	0.000	2^{44}
16	1.5177×10^{-41}	1.5177×10^{-41}	0.000	2^{47}

Table 1. Probability that linear cryptanalysis is feasible, for $n = 8$, $R = 10 \ldots 16$ (contrasted with lower bound on $\mathcal{N}_L$)

We have placed the values of Table 1 in the context of an earlier related result. In [7], Heys and Tavares, using the same SPN structure, give an expression which provides a lower bound on $\mathcal{N}_L$ in terms of $\mathrm{NL}_{\min}$, namely

$$\mathcal{N}_L \geq 2^{2(1-R)} \left(\frac{2^n}{2^{n-1} - \mathrm{NL}_{\min}} \right)^{2R}. \tag{17}$$

This is based on the worst-case scenario (from the perspective of the cipher designer): the existence of an R-round linear characteristic in $\mathcal{L}_R^R$, such that the absolute value of the bias associated with each active s-box is the maximum possible, namely $\left|\left(2^{n-1} - \mathrm{NL}_{\min}\right)/2^n\right|$. Evaluating (17) in the case $n = 8$ ($N = 64$), with $\mathrm{NL}_{\min} = 80$, gives the values in the rightmost column of Table 1. Taken alone, these lower bounds seem to imply that linear cryptanalysis of at least 16 rounds is feasible (in fact, (17) does not tell us that linear cryptanalysis becomes infeasible until $R \geq 22$). However, the result of Theorem 2 shows this to be excessively pessimistic—the probability that linear cryptanalysis of an SPN is feasible, using any characteristic $\Omega \in \mathcal{L}_R$, is small for $R \geq 12$ (computed over all SPN's, as per our model). This evidence of resistance to linear cryptanalysis is especially interesting when compared to a result of Chen [3], who showed that under certain assumptions about the XOR tables of the s-boxes, the same 64-bit SPN is also resistant to differential cryptanalysis for $R \geq 12$.

7 Conclusion

In this paper we have presented a model for the bias values associated with linear characteristics of substitution-permutation networks. We first considered linear characteristics which activate one s-box in each round, since experimentally these usually provide the best bias value. We determined the distribution of bias values which can be associated with such characteristics. This allowed us to evaluate an upper bound on the probability that linear cryptanalysis using such linear characteristics is feasible, as a function of the number of rounds. This probability is computed over all SPN's with s-boxes chosen uniformly and independently from the set of all bijective $n \times n$ s-boxes.

We then gave a generalization of the above result, stating an upper bound on the probability that linear cryptanalysis of an SPN is feasible, with no restriction on the number of s-boxes activated by the linear characteristics used. Experimental data indicates that the restricted and the generalized upper bounds yield nearly identical values, supporting the observation that the best linear characteristics almost always activate one s-box per round.

The work of this paper further supports the idea that the basic SPN structure merits study, both as a source of theoretical results, and as a practical cipher architecture with good security properties after a relatively small number of rounds.

Acknowledgment

This work was funded in part by Communications and Information Technology Ontario (CITO), and by the Natural Sciences and Engineering Research Council (NSERC), Canada.

References

1. R. Anderson, E. Biham and L. Knudsen, *Serpent: A flexible block cipher with maximum assurance,* The First Advanced Encryption Standard Candidate Conference, Proceedings, Ventura, California, August 1998.
2. E. Biham, *On Matsui's linear cryptanalysis,* Advances in Cryptology—EUROCRYPT'94, Springer-Verlag, Berlin, pp. 341–355, 1995.
3. Z.G. Chen and S.E. Tavares, *Towards provable security of substitution-permutation encryption networks,* Fifth Annual International Workshop on Selected Areas in Cryptography—SAC'98, Springer-Verlag, Berlin, LNCS 1556, pp. 43–56, 1999.
4. H. Feistel, *Cryptography and computer privacy,* Scientific American, Vol. 228, No. 5, pp. 15–23, May 1973.
5. H.M. Heys, *The design of substitution-permutation network ciphers resistant to cryptanalysis,* Ph.D. Thesis, Queen's University, Kingston, Canada, 1994.
6. H.M. Heys and S.E. Tavares, *Avalanche characteristics of substitution-permutation encryption networks,* IEEE Transactions on Computers, Vol. 44, No. 9, pp. 1131–1139, September 1995.

7. H.M. Heys and S.E. Tavares, *Substitution-permutation networks resistant to differential and linear cryptanalysis,* Journal of Cryptology, Vol. 9, No. 1, pp. 1–19, 1996.

8. J.B. Kam and G.I. Davida, *Structured design of substitution-permutation encryption networks,* IEEE Transactions on Computers, Vol. C-28, No. 10, pp. 747–753, October 1979.

9. M. Matsui, *Linear cryptanalysis method for DES cipher,* Advances in Cryptology—Proceedings of EUROCRYPT'93, Springer-Verlag, Berlin, pp. 386–397, 1994.

10. M. Matsui, *On correlation between the order of s-boxes and the strength of DES,* Advances in Cryptology—EUROCRYPT'94, Springer-Verlag, Berlin, pp. 366–375, 1995.

11. M. Matsui, *The first experimental cryptanalysis of the Data Encryption Standard,* Advances in Cryptology—CRYPTO'94, Springer-Verlag, Berlin, pp. 1–11, 1994.

12. National Institute of Standards and Technology, Information Technology Laboratory, The First Advanced Encryption Standard Candidate Conference, Proceedings, Ventura, California, August 1998.

13. K. Nyberg, *Linear approximation of block ciphers,* Advances in Cryptology—EUROCRYPT'94, Springer-Verlag, Berlin, pp. 439–444, 1995.

14. L. O'Connor, *Properties of linear approximation tables,* Fast Software Encryption: Second International Workshop, Springer-Verlag, Berlin, pp. 131–136, 1995.

15. C.E. Shannon, *Communication theory of secrecy systems,* Bell System Technical Journal, Vol. 28, no. 4, pp. 656–715, 1949.

16. A.M. Youssef and S.E. Tavares, *Resistance of balanced s-boxes to linear and differential cryptanalysis,* Information Processing Letters, Vol. 56, pp. 249–252, 1995.

17. A.M. Youssef *Analysis and design of block ciphers* Ph.D. Thesis, Queen's University, Kingston, Canada, 1997.

Strong Linear Dependence and Unbiased Distribution of Non-propagative Vectors

Yuliang Zheng[1] and Xian-Mo Zhang[2]

[1] School of Comp & Info Tech, Monash University
McMahons Road, Frankston, Melbourne, VIC 3199, Australia
yuliang@pscit.monash.edu.au
http://www.pscit.monash.edu.au/links/
[2] School of Info Tech & Comp Sci
The University of Wollongong, Wollongong
NSW 2522, Australia
xianmo@cs.uow.edu.au

Abstract. This paper proves (i) in any $(n-1)$-dimensional linear subspace, the non-propagative vectors of a function with n variables are linearly dependent, (ii) for this function, there exists a non-propagative vector in any $(n-2)$-dimensional linear subspace and there exist three non-propagative vectors in any $(n-1)$-dimensional linear subspace, except for those functions whose nonlinearity takes special values.
Keywords: Cryptography, Boolean Function, Propagation, Nonlinearity.

1 Introduction

In examining the nonlinearity properties of a function f with n variables, it is important to understand $\Re_f$, the set of so-called non-propagative vectors where f does not satisfy the propagation criterion. In this work, we are concerned with both $\#\Re_f$ (the number of non-propagative vectors in $\Re_f$) and the distribution of $\Re_f$. More specifically, we prove two properties of $\Re$. One is called the strong linear dependence and the other the unbiased distribution, of $\Re$.

The strong linear dependence property states that if W is a $(n-1)$-dimensional linear subspace satisfying $\#(\Re \cap W) \geq 4$, then the non-zero vectors in $\Re \cap W$ are linearly dependent. This improves a previously known result. The unbiased distribution property says that any function f with n variables, except for those whose nonlinearity takes the special value of $2^{n-1} - 2^{\frac{1}{2}(n-1)}$, $2^{n-1} - 2^{\frac{1}{2}n}$ or $2^{n-1} - 2^{\frac{1}{2}n-1}$, fulfills the condition that every $(n-2)$-dimensional linear subspace contains a non-zero vector in $\Re_f$ and every $(n-1)$-dimensional linear subspace contains at least three non-zero vectors in $\Re_f$. In special cases, $\#(\Re \cap W)$ may significantly effect other cryptographic properties of a function. The strong linear dependence and the unbiased distribution are helpful for the design of cryptographic functions as these conclusions provide more information on the number and the status of non-propagative vectors in any $(n-1)$-dimensional linear subspace.

Howard Heys and Carlisle Adams (Eds.): SAC'99, LNCS 1758, pp. 92–105, 2000.

2 Cryptographic Criteria of Boolean Functions

We consider functions from V_n to $GF(2)$ (or simply functions on V_n), V_n is the vector space of n tuples of elements from $GF(2)$. The *truth table* of a function f on V_n is a $(0,1)$-sequence defined by $(f(\alpha_0), f(\alpha_1), \ldots, f(\alpha_{2^n-1}))$, and the *sequence* of f is a $(1,-1)$-sequence defined by $((-1)^{f(\alpha_0)}, (-1)^{f(\alpha_1)}, \ldots, (-1)^{f(\alpha_{2^n-1})})$, where $\alpha_0 = (0,\ldots,0,0)$, $\alpha_1 = (0,\ldots,0,1)$, $\ldots$, $\alpha_{2^{n-1}-1} = (1,\ldots,1,1)$. The *matrix* of f is a $(1,-1)$-matrix of order 2^n defined by $M = ((-1)^{f(\alpha_i \oplus \alpha_j)})$ where $\oplus$ denotes the addition in $GF(2)$. f is said to be *balanced* if its truth table contains an equal number of ones and zeros.

Given two sequences $\tilde{a} = (a_1, \cdots, a_m)$ and $\tilde{b} = (b_1, \cdots, b_m)$, their *component-wise product* is defined by $\tilde{a} * \tilde{b} = (a_1 b_1, \cdots, a_m b_m)$. In particular, if $m = 2^n$ and $\tilde{a}$, $\tilde{b}$ are the sequences of functions f and g on V_n respectively, then $\tilde{a} * \tilde{b}$ is the sequence of $f \oplus g$ where $\oplus$ denotes the addition in $GF(2)$.

Let $\tilde{a} = (a_1, \cdots, a_m)$ and $\tilde{b} = (b_1, \cdots, b_m)$ be two sequences or vectors, the *scalar product* of $\tilde{a}$ and $\tilde{b}$, denoted by $\langle \tilde{a}, \tilde{b} \rangle$, is defined as the sum of the component-wise multiplications. In particular, when $\tilde{a}$ and $\tilde{b}$ are from V_m, $\langle \tilde{a}, \tilde{b} \rangle = a_1 b_1 \oplus \cdots \oplus a_m b_m$, where the addition and multiplication are over $GF(2)$, and when $\tilde{a}$ and $\tilde{b}$ are $(1,-1)$-sequences, $\langle \tilde{a}, \tilde{b} \rangle = \sum_{i=1}^{m} a_i b_i$, where the addition and multiplication are over the reals.

An *affine* function f on V_n is a function that takes the form of $f(x_1, \ldots, x_n) = a_1 x_1 \oplus \cdots \oplus a_n x_n \oplus c$, where $a_j, c \in GF(2)$, $j = 1, 2, \ldots, n$. Furthermore f is called a *linear* function if $c = 0$.

A $(1,-1)$-matrix N of order n is called a *Hadamard* matrix if $NN^T = nI_n$, where N^T is the transpose of N and I_n is the identity matrix of order n. A Sylvester-Hadamard matrix of order 2^n, denoted by H_n, is generated by the following recursive relation

$$H_0 = 1, \quad H_n = \begin{bmatrix} H_{n-1} & H_{n-1} \\ H_{n-1} & -H_{n-1} \end{bmatrix}, \quad n = 1, 2, \ldots.$$

Let ℓ_i, $0 \le i \le 2^n - 1$, be the i row of H_n. It is known that ℓ_i is the sequence of a linear function $\varphi_i(x)$ defined by the scalar product $\varphi_i(x) = \langle \alpha_i, x \rangle$, where α_i is the ith vector in V_n according to the ascending alphabetical order.

The *Hamming weight* of a $(0,1)$-sequence ξ, denoted by $W(\xi)$, is the number of ones in the sequence. Given two functions f and g on V_n, the *Hamming distance* $d(f, g)$ between them is defined as the Hamming weight of the truth table of $f(x) \oplus g(x)$, where $x = (x_1, \ldots, x_n)$.

Definition 1. *The nonlinearity of a function f on V_n, denoted by N_f, is the minimal Hamming distance between f and all affine functions on V_n, i.e., $N_f = \min_{i=1,2,\ldots,2^{n+1}} d(f, \varphi_i)$ where $\varphi_1, \varphi_2, \ldots, \varphi_{2^{n+1}}$ are all the affine functions on V_n.*

The following characterisations of nonlinearity will be useful (for a proof see for instance [2]).

Lemma 1. *The nonlinearity of f on V_n can be expressed by*

$$N_f = 2^{n-1} - \frac{1}{2}\max\{|\langle \xi, \ell_i \rangle|, 0 \le i \le 2^n - 1\}$$

where ξ is the sequence of f and $\ell_0, \ldots, \ell_{2^n-1}$ are the rows of H_n, namely, the sequences of linear functions on V_n.

Definition 2. *Let f be a function on V_n. For a vector $\alpha \in V_n$, denote by $\xi(\alpha)$ the sequence of $f(x \oplus \alpha)$. Thus $\xi(0)$ is the sequence of f itself and $\xi(0) * \xi(\alpha)$ is the sequence of $f(x) \oplus f(x \oplus \alpha)$. Set*

$$\Delta_f(\alpha) = \langle \xi(0), \xi(\alpha) \rangle,$$

the scalar product of $\xi(0)$ and $\xi(\alpha)$. $\Delta(\alpha)$ is called the auto-correlation of f with a shift α. Write

$$\Delta_M = \max\{|\Delta(\alpha)| \, | \, \alpha \in V_n, \alpha \ne 0\}$$

We omit the subscript of $\Delta_f(\alpha)$ if no confusion occurs.

Definition 3. *Let f be a function on V_n. We say that f satisfies the* propagation criterion *with respect to α if $f(x) \oplus f(x \oplus \alpha)$ is a balanced function, where $x = (x_1, \ldots, x_n)$ and α is a vector in V_n. Furthermore f is said to satisfy the propagation criterion of degree k if it satisfies the propagation criterion with respect to every non-zero vector α whose Hamming weight is not larger than k (see [3]).*

The *strict avalanche criterion (SAC)* [5] is the same as the propagation criterion of degree one.

Obviously, $\Delta(\alpha) = 0$ if and only if $f(x) \oplus f(x \oplus \alpha)$ is balanced, i.e., f satisfies the propagation criterion with respect to α.

Definition 4. *Let f be a function on V_n. $\alpha \in V_n$ is called a* linear structure *of f if $|\Delta(\alpha)| = 2^n$ (i.e., $f(x) \oplus f(x \oplus \alpha)$ is a constant).*

For any function f, $\Delta(\alpha_0) = 2^n$, where α_0 is the zero vector on V_n. It is easy to verify that the set of all linear structures of a function f form a linear subspace of V_n, whose dimension is called the *linearity* of f. It is also well-known that if f has non-zero linear structures, then there exists a nonsingular $n \times n$ matrix B over $GF(2)$ such that $f(xB) = g(y) \oplus h(z)$, where $x = (y, z)$, $y \in V_p$, $z \in V_q$, g is a function on V_p that has no non-zero linear structures, and h is an affine function on V_q.

The following lemma is the re-statement of a relation proved in Section 2 of [1].

Lemma 2. *For every function f on V_n, we have*

$$(\Delta(\alpha_0), \Delta(\alpha_1), \ldots, \Delta(\alpha_{2^n-1}))H_n = (\langle \xi, \ell_0 \rangle^2, \langle \xi, \ell_1 \rangle^2, \ldots, \langle \xi, \ell_{2^n-1} \rangle^2).$$

where ξ denotes the sequence of f and ℓ_i is the ith row of H_n, $i = 0, 1, \ldots, 2^n - 1$.

The balance and the nonlinearity are necessary in most cases. The propagation or especially the SAC, is an important cryptographic criterion.

3 Introduction to $\Re$

Notation 1. *Let f be a function on V_n. Set $\Re_f = \{\alpha \mid \Delta(\alpha) \neq 0, \, \alpha \in V_n\}$, $\Delta_M = \max\{|\Delta(\alpha)| \, | \, \alpha \in V_n, \, \alpha \neq 0\}$.*

We simply write $\Re_f$ as $\Re$ if no confusion occurs. It is easy to verify that $\#\Re$ and Δ_M are invariant under any nonsingular linear transformation on the variables, where $\#$ denotes the cardinal number of a set.

$\#\Re$ and the distribution of $\Re$ reflects the propagation characteristics, while Δ_M forecasts the avalanche property of the function. Therefore information on $\Re$ and Δ_M is useful in determining important cryptographic characteristics of f. Usually, small $\#\Re$ and Δ_M are desirable.

Definition 5. *A function f on V_n is called a bent function [4] if $\langle \xi, \ell_i \rangle^2 = 2^n$ for every $i = 0, 1, \ldots, 2^n - 1$, where ℓ_i is the ith row of H_n.*

A bent function on V_n exists only when n is even, and it achieves the highest possible nonlinearity $2^{n-1} - 2^{\frac{1}{2}n-1}$. The algebraic degree of bent functions on V_n is at most $\frac{1}{2}n$ [4]. From [4] and Parseval's equation, we have the following:

Theorem 1. *Let f be a function on V_n. Then the following statements are equivalent: (i) f is bent, (ii) $\#\Re = 1$, (iii) $\Delta_M = 0$, (iv) the nonlinearity of f, N_f, satisfies $N_f = 2^{n-1} - 2^{\frac{1}{2}n-1}$, (v) the matrix of f is an Hadamard matrix.*

The following result is called *the linear dependence theorem* that can be found in [7]

Theorem 2. *Let f be a function on V_n that satisfies the propagation criterion with respect to all but $k + 1$ vectors $0, \beta_1, \ldots, \beta_k$ in V_n, where $k \geq 2$. Then $\beta_1, \ldots, \beta_k$ are linearly dependent, namely, there exist k constants $c_1, \ldots, c_k \in GF(2)$, not all of which are zeros, such that $c_1\beta_1 \oplus \cdots \oplus c_k\beta_k = 0$.*

Note that $n + 1$ non-zero vectors in V_n must be linearly dependent. Hence if $\#\Re \geq n+2$ (i.e., $\#(\Re - \{0\}) \geq n+1$) then Theorem 2 is trivial. For this reason, we improve Theorem 2 in this paper. We prove two properties of $\Re$: the strong linear dependence and the unbiased distribution of $\Re$.

4 The Strong Linear Dependence Theorem

Note the ith (i.e., the α_ith) row of H_n, where $\alpha_i \in V_n$ is the binary representation of integer j, $j = 0, 1, \ldots, 2^n - 1$, is the sequence of linear function $\varphi_i(x) = \langle \alpha_i, x \rangle$. Lemma 4 of [7] can be restated as follows:

Lemma 3. *Let Q be the $2^n \times q$ that consists of the α_{j_1}th, $\ldots$, the α_{j_q}th rows of H_n, where each $\alpha_j \in V_n$ is the binary representation of integer j, $0 \leq j \leq 2^n - 1$. If $\alpha_{j_1}, \ldots, \alpha_{j_q}$ are linearly independent then each $(a_1, \ldots, a_q)^T$, where each $a_j = \pm 1$, appears as a column in Q precisely 2^{n-q} times.*

The following Lemma can be found in [7].

Lemma 4. *Let $n \geq 3$ be a positive integer and $2^n = \sum_{j=1}^{4} a_j^2$ where $a_1 \geq a_2 \geq a_3 \geq a_4 \geq 0$ and each a_j is an integer. We have the following statements:*

(i) if n is add, then $a_1^2 = a_2^2 = 2^{n-1}$, $a_3 = a_4 = 0$,
(ii) if n is even, then $a_1^2 = 2^n$, $a_2 = a_3 = a_4 = 0$ or $a_1^2 = a_2^2 = a_3^2 = a_4^2 = 2^{n-2}$.

Lemma 5. *For every function f on V_n, we have*

$$2(\Delta(\alpha_0), \Delta(\alpha_2), \ldots, \Delta(\alpha_{2^n-2}))H_{n-1}$$
$$= (\langle \xi, \ell_0 \rangle^2 + \langle \xi, \ell_1 \rangle^2, \langle \xi, \ell_2 \rangle^2 + \langle \xi, \ell_3 \rangle^2, \ldots, \langle \xi, \ell_{2^n-2} \rangle^2 + \langle \xi, \ell_{2^n-1} \rangle^2)$$

where ξ denotes the sequence of f and ℓ_i is the ith row of H_n, $i = 0, 1, \ldots, 2^n - 1$.

Proof. From Lemma 2,

$$2^n(\Delta(\alpha_0), \Delta(\alpha_1), \ldots, \Delta(\alpha_{2^n-1})) = (\langle \xi, \ell_0 \rangle^2, \langle \xi, \ell_1 \rangle^2, \ldots, \langle \xi, \ell_{2^n-1} \rangle^2)H_n \quad (1)$$

Comparing the 0th, the 2nd, ..., the $(2^n - 2)$th terms in the two sides of equality (1), we obtain

$$2^n(\Delta(\alpha_0), \Delta(\alpha_2), \ldots, \Delta(\alpha_{2^n-2}))$$
$$= (\langle \xi, \ell_0 \rangle^2 + \langle \xi, \ell_1 \rangle^2, (\langle \xi, \ell_2 \rangle^2 + \langle \xi, \ell_3 \rangle^2, \ldots, \langle \xi, \ell_{2^n-2} \rangle^2 + \langle \xi, \ell_{2^n-1} \rangle^2)H_{n-1}$$

This proves the lemma. □

The following theorem is called *the strong linearly dependence theorem* which is an improvement on Theorem 2 (the linearly dependence theorem).

Theorem 3. *Let f be a function on V_n, and W be a $(n-1)$-dimensional linear subspace satisfying $\Re \cap W = \{0, \beta_1, \ldots, \beta_k\}$ $(k \geq 3)$. Then $\beta_1, \ldots, \beta_k$ are linearly dependent, namely, there exist k constants $c_1, \ldots, c_k \in GF(2)$ with $(c_1, \ldots, c_k) \neq (0, \ldots, 0)$, such that $c_1\beta_1 \oplus \cdots \oplus c_k\beta_k = 0$.*

Proof. The theorem is obviously true if $k > n$. Now we prove the theorem for $k \leq n$. We only need to prove the lemma in the special case when W is composed of $\alpha_0, \alpha_2, \ldots, \alpha_{2^n-2}$, where $\alpha_{2j} \in V_n$ is the binary representation of an even number $2j$, $j = 0, 1, \ldots, 2^{n-1} - 1$. In other words, W is composed of all the vectors in V_n, that can be expressed in the form $(a_1, \ldots, a_{n-1}, 0)$, where each $a_j \in GF(2)$. In the general case, we can use a nonsingular linear transformation on the variables so as to change W into the special case. Let ξ be the sequence of f.

Since $\beta_j \in W$, $j = 1, \ldots, k$, β_j can be expressed as $\beta_j = (\gamma_j, 0)$ where $\gamma_j \in V_{n-1}$, $j = 1, \ldots, k$, and $0 \in GF(2)$.

Let P be a $(k+1) \times 2^{n-1}$ matrix composed of the 0th, the γ_1th, ..., the γ_kth rows of H_{n-1}. Set $a_j^2 = \langle \xi, \ell_j \rangle^2$, $j = 0, 1, \ldots, 2^n - 1$. Note that $\Delta(\alpha) = 0$ if $\alpha \notin \{0, \beta_1, \ldots, \beta_k\}$. Hence the equality in Lemma 5 can be specialized as

$$2(\Delta(0), \Delta(\beta_1), \ldots, \Delta(\beta_k))P = (a_0^2 + a_1^2, a_2^2 + a_3^2, \ldots, a_{2^n-2}^2 + a_{2^n-1}^2) \qquad (2)$$

where $\Delta(0)$ is identical to $\Delta(\alpha_0)$ where $\alpha_0 = 0$.

Write $P = (p_{ij})$, $i = 0, 1, \ldots k$, $j = 0, 1, \ldots, 2^{n-1} - 1$. As the top row of P is $(1, 1, \ldots, 1)$, from (2),

$$2(\Delta(0) + \sum_{i=1}^{k} p_{ij}\Delta(\beta_i)) = a_{2j}^2 + a_{2j+1}^2 \qquad (3)$$

$j = 0, 1, \ldots, 2^{n-1} - 1$. Let P^* be the submatrix of P obtained by removing the top row from P.

We now prove the theorem by contradiction. Suppose k vectors in V_n, β_1, ..., β_k, are linearly independent. Hence k vectors in V_{n-1}, $\gamma_1, \ldots, \gamma_k$, are also linearly independent and hence $k \leq n - 1$.

Applying Lemma 3 to matrix P^*, we conclude that each k-dimensional $(1, -1)$-vector appears in P^*, as a column vector of P^* precisely 2^{n-1-k} times. Thus for each fixed j there exists a number j_0, $0 \leq j_0 \leq 2^{n-1} - 1$, such that $(p_{1j_0}, \ldots, p_{kj_0}) = -(p_{1j}, \ldots, p_{kj})$ and hence

$$2(\Delta(0) - \sum_{i=1}^{k} p_{ij_0}\Delta(\beta_i)) = a_{j_0}^2 + a_{2j_0+1}^2 \qquad (4)$$

Adding (3) and (4) together, we have $4\Delta(0) = a_j^2 + a_{2j+1}^2 + a_{j_0}^2 + a_{2j_0+1}^2$. Hence $a_j^2 + a_{2j+1}^2 + a_{j_0}^2 + a_{2j_0+1}^2 = 2^{n+2}$. There are two cases to be considered: even n and odd n.

Case 1: n is odd. By using Lemma 4,

$$\{a_j^2, a_{2j+1}^2, a_{j_0}^2, a_{2j_0+1}^2\} = \{2^{n+1}, 2^{n+1}, 0, 0\}, j = 0, 1, \ldots, 2^{n-1} \qquad (5)$$

Hence from (3), we have $\Delta(0) + \sum_{i=1}^{k} p_{ij}\Delta(\beta_i) = 2^{n+1}, 2^n, 0$ and hence

$$\sum_{i=1}^{k} p_{ij}\Delta(\beta_i) = 2^n, 0, -2^n, j = 0, 1, \ldots, 2^n - 1 \qquad (6)$$

For each fixed j, rewrite (6) as

$$p_{1j}\Delta(\beta_1) + \sum_{i=2}^{k} p_{ij}\Delta(\beta_i) = 2^n, 0, -2^n \qquad (7)$$

By using Lemma 3, there exists a number j_1, $0 \leq j_1 \leq 2^{n-1} - 1$, such that $(p_{1j_1}, p_{2j_1}, \ldots, p_{kj_i}) = (p_{1j}, -p_{2j}, \ldots, -p_{kj})$.

Hence

$$p_{1j_1}\Delta(\beta_1) - \sum_{i=2}^{k} p_{ij_1}\Delta(\beta_i) = 2^n, 0, -2^n \tag{8}$$

Adding (7) and (8) together, we have

$$p_{1j}\Delta(\beta_1) = \pm 2^n, \pm 2^{n-1}, 0$$

Since $\Delta(\beta_1) \neq 0$, we conclude $\Delta(\beta_1) = \pm 2^n, \pm 2^{n-1}$. By the same reasoning we can prove

$$\Delta(\beta_j) = \pm 2^n, \pm 2^{n-1}, j = 1, 2, \ldots, k \tag{9}$$

Thus we can write

$$(\Delta(\beta_1), \ldots, \Delta(\beta_k)) = 2^{n-1}(b_1, \ldots, b_k) \tag{10}$$

where each $b_j = \pm 1, \pm 2$. By using Lemma 3, there exists a number s, $0 \leq s \leq 2^{n-1} - 1$, such that

$$(p_{1s}, \ldots, p_{ks}) = \left(\frac{b_1}{|b_1|}, \ldots, \frac{b_k}{|b_j|}\right). \tag{11}$$

Due to (10) and (11),

$$\sum_{i=1}^{k} p_{is}\Delta(\beta_i) = \sum_{i=1}^{k} \frac{b_i}{|b_i|}\Delta(\beta_i) = \sum_{i=1}^{k} \frac{b_i^2}{|b_i|}2^{n-1} = 2^{n-1}\sum_{i=1}^{k}|b_i| \geq k2^{n-1}. \tag{12}$$

Since $k \geq 3$, (12) contradicts (6).

Case 2: n is even. By using Lemma 4,

$$\{a_j^2, a_{2j+1}^2, a_{j_0}^2, a_{2j_0+1}^2\} = \{2^{n+2}, 0, 0, 0\} \text{ or}$$
$$\{a_j^2, a_{2j+1}^2, a_{j_0}^2, a_{2j_0+1}^2\} = \{2^n, 2^n, 2^n, 2^n\}, j = 0, 1, \ldots, 2^{n-1} \tag{13}$$

Hence from (3), we have $\Delta(0) + \sum_{i=1}^{k} p_{ij}\Delta(\beta_i) = 2^{n+1}, 2^n, 0$, and hence

$$\sum_{i=1}^{k} p_{ij}\Delta(\beta_i) = 2^n, 0, -2^n$$

Repeating the same deduction as in Case 1, we obtain a contradiction in Case 2.

Summarizing Cases 1 and 2, we conclude that the assumption that $\beta_1, \ldots, \beta_k$ are linearly independent is wrong. This proves the theorem. □

Theorem 3 shows that $\Re$ is subject to crucial restrictions. We now compare Theorem 3 with Theorem 2. Since $n + 1$ non-zero vectors in V_n must be linearly dependent, Theorem 2 is trivial when $\#\Re \geq n + 2$ (i.e., $\#(\Re - \{0\}) \geq n + 1$). In contrast, in Theorem 3 the linear dependence of vectors takes place in each $\Re \cap W$ not only in $\Re$.

We notice that there exist $n - 1$ $(n - 1)$-dimensional linear subspaces. Hence Theorem 3 is more profound than Theorem 2.

5 The Unbiased Distribution of $\mathfrak{R}$

In this section we focus on the distribution of $\mathfrak{R}$ for the functions on V_n, whose nonlinearity does not take the special value $2^{n-1} - 2^{\frac{1}{2}(n-1)}$ or $2^{n-1} - 2^{\frac{1}{2}n}$ or $2^{n-1} - 2^{\frac{1}{2}n-1}$.

The next result is from [6] (Theorem 18).

Lemma 6. *Let f be a function on V_n $(n \geq 2)$, ξ be the sequence of f, and p is an integer, $2 \leq p \leq n$. If $\langle \xi, \ell_j \rangle \equiv 0 \pmod{2^{n-p+2}}$, where ℓ_j is the jth row of H_n, $j = 0, 1, \ldots, 2^n - 1$, then the algebraic degree of f is at most $p - 1$.*

Lemma 7. *For every function f on V_n, we have*

$$4(\Delta(\alpha_0), \Delta(\alpha_4), \ldots, \Delta(\alpha_{2^n-4}))H_{n-2}$$

$$= (\sum_{j=0}^{3}\langle \xi, \ell_j \rangle^2, \sum_{j=4}^{7}\langle \xi, \ell_j \rangle^2, \ldots, \sum_{j=2^n-4}^{2^n-1}\langle \xi, \ell_j \rangle^2)$$

Where ξ denotes the sequence of f and ℓ_i is the ith row of H_n, $i = 0, 1, \ldots, 2^n - 1$.

Proof. Comparing the $4j$th terms, $j = 0, 1, \ldots, 2^{n-2} - 1$, in the two sides of equality (1), we obtain

$$2^n(\Delta(\alpha_0), \Delta(\alpha_4), \ldots, \Delta(\alpha_{2^n-4}))$$

$$= (\sum_{j=0}^{3}\langle \xi, \ell_j \rangle^2, \sum_{j=4}^{7}\langle \xi, \ell_j \rangle^2, \ldots, \sum_{j=2^n-4}^{2^n-1}\langle \xi, \ell_j \rangle^2)H_{n-2}$$

This proves the lemma. $\qquad \square$

Theorem 4. *Let f be a function on V_n, and U be a $(n-2)$-dimensional linear subspace satisfying $\#(\mathfrak{R} \cap U) = 1$ (i.e., $\mathfrak{R} \cap U = \{0\}$). Then we have*

(i) if n is odd, then the nonlinearity of f satisfies $N_f = 2^{n-1} - 2^{\frac{1}{2}(n-1)}$ and the algebraic degree of f is at most $2^{\frac{1}{2}(n+1)}$,

(ii) if n is even, then f is bent or the nonlinearity of f satisfies $N_f = 2^{n-1} - 2^{\frac{1}{2}n}$ and the algebraic degree of f is at most $2^{\frac{1}{2}n+1}$.

Proof. We only need to prove the theorem in the special case when U is composed of $\alpha_0, \alpha_4, \alpha_8, \ldots, \alpha_{2^n-4}$, where $\alpha_{4j} \in V_n$ is the binary representation of even number $4j$, $j = 0, 1, 2, \ldots, 2^{n-2} - 1$. In other words, U is composed of all the vectors in V_n, that can be expressed in the form $(a_1, \ldots, a_{n-2}, 0, 0)$, where each $a_j \in GF(2)$. For U in general case, we can use a nonsingular linear transformation on the variables so as to change U into the special case. Let ξ be the sequence of f. Set $a_j^2 = \langle \xi, \ell_j \rangle^2$, $j = 0, 1, \ldots, 2^n - 1$.

Since $\Delta(0) = 2^n$ and $\Delta(\alpha_{4j}) = 0$, $j = 1, 2, \ldots, 2^{n-2} - 1$, the equality in Lemma 7 is specialized as

$$2^{n+2}(1, \ldots, 1) = (\sum_{j=0}^{3} a_j^2, \sum_{j=4}^{7} a_j^2, \ldots, \sum_{j=2^n-4}^{2^n-1} a_j^2) \tag{14}$$

$j = 0, 1, \ldots, 2^{n-2} - 1$.

(i) When n is odd, by using Lemma 4,

$$\{a_{4j}^2, a_{4j+1}^2, a_{4j+3}^2, a_{4j+3}^2\} = \{2^{n+1}, 2^{n+1}, 0, 0\}, j = 0, 1, \ldots, 2^{n-2}$$

By using Lemma 1, we have proved the nonlinearity of f satisfies $N_f = 2^{n-1} - 2^{\frac{1}{2}(n-1)}$, and by using Lemma 6, we have proved that the algebraic degree of f is at most $2^{\frac{1}{2}(n+1)}$.

(ii) When n is even. By using Lemma 4,

$$\{a_{4j}^2, a_{4j+1}^2, a_{4j+3}^2, a_{4j+3}^2\} = \{2^n, 2^n, 2^n, 2^n\} \text{ or } \{2^{n+2}, 0, 0, 0\},$$

$j = 0, 1, \ldots, 2^{n-2} - 1$.

If there exists a number j_0, $0 \leq j_0 \leq 2^{n-2} - 1$, such that

$$\{a_{4j_0}^2, a_{4j_0+1}^2, a_{4j_0+2}^2, a_{4j_0+3}^2\} = \{2^{n+2}, 0, 0, 0\}$$

then by using Lemma 1, we have proved that the nonlinearity of f satisfies $N_f = 2^{n-1} - 2^{\frac{1}{2}n}$, and by using Lemma 6, we have proved that the algebraic degree of f is at most $2^{\frac{1}{2}(n+1)}$.

If there exists no such j_0, mentioned as above, i.e., $\{a_{4j}^2, a_{4j+1}^2, a_{4j+3}^2, a_{4j+3}^2\} = \{2^n, 2^n, 2^n, 2^n\}$, $j = 0, 1, \ldots, 2^{n-2} - 1$. Then f is bent.

$\square$

To emphasise the distribution of $\Re$ we modify Theorem 4 as follows:

Theorem 5. *Let f be a function on V_n. If the nonlinearity of f does not take the special value $2^{n-1} - 2^{\frac{1}{2}(n-1)}$ or $2^{n-1} - 2^{\frac{1}{2}n}$ or $2^{n-1} - 2^{\frac{1}{2}n-1}$, then $\#(\Re \cap U) \geq 2$ where U is any $(n-2)$-dimensional linear subspace, in other words, every $(n-2)$-dimensional linear subspace U contains a non-zero vector in $\Re$.*

There exist many methods to locate all the $(n-1)$-dimensional linear subspaces and all the $(n-2)$-dimensional linear subspaces in V_n. For example, let φ_α denote the linear function on V_n, where $\alpha \in V_n$, such that $\varphi_\alpha(x) = \langle \alpha, x \rangle$. Hence $W = \{\gamma | \alpha \in V_n, \varphi_\alpha(\gamma) = 0\}$ is a $(n-1)$-dimensional linear subspace and each $(n-1)$-dimensional linear subspace can be expressed in this form.

Also for any $\alpha, \alpha' \in V_n$ with $\alpha \neq \alpha'$, $U = \{\gamma | \alpha \in V_n, \varphi_\alpha(\gamma) = 0, \varphi_{\alpha'}(\gamma) = 0\}$ is a $(n-2)$-dimensional linear subspace and each $(n-2)$-dimensional linear subspace can be expressed in this form.

Lemma 8. *Let Ω be a subset of V_k with $0 \notin \Omega$. If there exists a positive integer p such that $\#(\Omega \cap U) \geq p$ holds for every $(k-1)$-dimensional linear subspace U, then $\#\Omega \geq 2p + 1$.*

Proof. Note that each non-zero vector is included in precisely $2^{k-1} - 1$ $(k-1)$-dimensional linear subspaces, on the other hand, there exist exactly $2^k - 1$ $(k-1)$-dimensional linear subspaces. Hence $(2^{k-1} - 1)\#\Omega = \sum_U \#(\Omega \cap U)$. From $\#(\Omega \cap U) \geq p$, we conclude that $(2^{k-1} - 1)\#\Omega \geq (2^k - 1)p$. Since $\frac{2^k-1}{2^{k-1}-1} > 2$, $\#\Omega > 2p$ or $\#\Omega \geq 2p + 1$. $\square$

Theorem 6. *Let f be a function on V_n. If the nonlinearity of f does not take the special values $2^{n-1} - 2^{\frac{1}{2}(n-1)}$ or $2^{n-1} - 2^{\frac{1}{2}n}$ or $2^{n-1} - 2^{\frac{1}{2}n-1}$, then $\#(\Re \cap W) \geq 4$ for every $(n-1)$-dimensional linear subspace W, in other words, every $(n-1)$-dimensional linear subspace W contains at least three non-zero vectors in $\Re$.*

Proof. Let W be an arbitrary $(n-1)$-dimensional linear subspace and U be an arbitrary $(n-2)$-dimensional linear subspace with $U \subset W$. Note that the inequality in Theorem 5 can be rewritten as

$$\#((\Re - \{0\}) \cap U) \geq 1 \tag{15}$$

and $((\Re - \{0\}) \cap W) \cap U = (\Re - \{0\}) \cap U$. Applying Lemma 8, we have proved $\#((\Re - \{0\}) \cap W) \geq 3$. Since $0 \in \Re \cap W$, $\#(\Re \cap W) \geq 4$. $\square$

Theorems 5 and 6 are helpful to locate the non-propagative vectors.

The properties mentioned together in Theorems 5 and 6 are called *the unbiased distribution of $\Re$*, with respect to every $(n-2)$-dimensional linear subspace and every $(n-1)$-dimensional linear subspace.

6 Distribution of $\Re$ in Special Cases

We now turn to the case $\#(\Re_f \cap W) \leq 3$ where W is an $(n-1)$-dimensional linear subspace. The following Lemma can be found in [7]:

Lemma 9. *Let $n \geq 2$ be a positive integer and $2^n = a^2 + b^2$ where $a \geq b \geq 0$ and both a and b are integers. Then $a^2 = 2^n$ and $b = 0$ when n is even, and $a^2 = b^2 = 2^{n-1}$ when n is odd.*

Theorem 7. *Let f be a function on V_n, and W be an $(n-1)$-dimensional linear subspace satisfying $\#(\Re \cap W) = 1$ (i.e., $\Re \cap W = \{0\}$). We have*

(i) f has at most one non-zero linear structure,
(ii) if n is odd, then the nonlinearity of f satisfies $N_f = 2^{n-1} - 2^{\frac{1}{2}(n-1)}$ and the algebraic degree of f is at most $2^{\frac{1}{2}(n+1)}$,
(iii) if n is even, then f is bent.

Proof. (i) Let $\alpha^* \in V_n$ and $\alpha^* \notin W$, From linear algebra, $V_n = W \cup (\alpha^* \oplus W)$, where $\alpha^* \oplus W = \{\alpha^* \oplus \alpha | \alpha \in W\}$, W and $\alpha^* \oplus W$ are disjoint. We now prove that f has at most one non-zero linear structure by contradiction. Suppose f has two non-zero linear structures, β_1 and β_2 with $\beta_1 \neq \beta_2$. Since all linear structures of f form a linear subspace of V_n, $\beta_1 \oplus \beta_2$ is also a non-zero linear structures of f and hence $\beta_1 \oplus \beta_2 \in \Re$. Since $\Re \cap W = \{0\}$, $\beta_1, \beta_2 \in \alpha^* \oplus W$. Obviously $\beta_1 \oplus \beta_2 \in W$ and hence $\beta_1 \oplus \beta_2 \in \Re \cap W$. This contradicts the condition $\Re \cap W = \{0\}$. The contradiction proves that f has at most one non-zero linear structure.

Recall the proof of Theorem 3, (3) can be specialized as $2\Delta(0) = a_{2j}^2 + a_{2j+1}^2$ and hence $a_{2j}^2 + a_{2j+1}^2 = 2^{n+1}$, where $j = 0, 1, \ldots, 2^{n-1} - 1$.

(ii) If n be odd, from Lemma 9, $\{a_{2j}^2, a_{2j+1}^2\} = \{2^{n+1}, 0\}$, where $j = 0, 1, \ldots,$ $2^{n-1} - 1$. From Lemma 1, the nonlinearity of f satisfies $N_f = 2^{n-1} - 2^{\frac{1}{2}(n-1)}$. By using Lemma 6 we conclude that the algebraic degree of f is at most $2^{\frac{1}{2}(n+1)}$.

(iii) If n is even, due to Lemma 9, $a_{2j}^2 = a_{2j+1}^2 = 2^n$, where $j = 0, 1, \ldots, 2^{n-1} - 1$. This proves that f is bent.

$\square$

Example 1. Let n be a positive odd number and $f(x_1, \ldots, x_n) = x_1 \oplus g(x_2, \ldots, x_n)$ where g is a bent function in V_{n-1}. Let W be an $(n-1)$-dimensional linear subspace of V_n, composed of all the vectors in V_n, that can be expressed in the form $(0, a_2, \ldots, a_n)$, where each $a_j \in GF(2)$. It is easy to see $\alpha^* = (1, 0, \ldots, 0) \in V_n$ is a non-zero linear structure of f and $\Re \cap W = \{0\}$. Due to (ii) of Theorem 7, $N_f = 2^{n-1} - 2^{\frac{1}{2}(n-1)}$.

We can restate (iii) of Theorem 7 as follows:

Proposition 1. *Let f be a function on V_n where n is even. If there exists an $(n-1)$-dimensional linear subspace W_0 satisfying $\#(\Re \cap W_0) = 1$ (i.e., $\Re \cap W_0 = \{0\}$), then f satisfies $\Re \cap W = \{0\}$, for every $(n-1)$-dimensional linear subspace W.*

Next we examine the case of $\#(\Re \cap W) = 2$.

Theorem 8. *Let f be a function on V_n. If there exists a $(n-1)$-dimensional linear subspace W satisfying $\Re \cap W = \{0, \beta_1\}$, then we have*

(i) β_1 is a non-zero linear structure of f,
(ii) if n is odd, then the nonlinearity of f satisfies $N_f = 2^{n-1} - 2^{\frac{1}{2}(n-1)}$ and the algebraic degree of f is at most $2^{\frac{1}{2}(n+1)}$,
(iii) if n is even, then $N_f = 2^{n-1} - 2^{\frac{1}{2}n}$ and the algebraic degree of f is at most $2^{\frac{1}{2}n+1}$.

Proof. Since any single non-zero vector is linearly independent, we can keep the deduction in the proof of Theorem 3 until inequality (12) where we need the condition $k \geq 3$.

(i) Recall the proof of Theorem 3, (6) can be specialized as $p_{1j}\Delta(\beta_1) = 2^n, 0, -2^n, j = 0, 1, \ldots, 2^n - 1$. Since $\beta_1 \in \Re$, $\Delta(\beta_1) \neq 0$. Hence $\Delta(\beta_1) = \pm 2^n$. This proves that β_1 is a non-zero linear structure.

(ii) If n is odd, from (5) we conclude that $\langle \xi, \ell_i \rangle^2 = 2^{n+1}, 0, i = 0, 1, \ldots, 2^n - 1$, and hence by using Lemma 1, we have proved $N_f = 2^{n-1} - 2^{\frac{1}{2}(n-1)}$. By using Lemma 6 we conclude that the algebraic degree of f is at most $2^{\frac{1}{2}(n+1)}$.

(iii) If n is even, from (13), $\langle \xi, \ell_i \rangle^2 = 2^{n+2}, 0, 2^n$. Since $\#\Re > 1$, f is not bent. Hence $\langle \xi, \ell_i \rangle^2 = 2^n$ cannot hold for all i and hence there exists a number $i_0, 0 \le i_0 \le 2^n - 1$, such that $\langle \xi, \ell_i \rangle^2 = 2^{n+2}$. By using Lemma 1, we have proved $N_f = 2^{n-1} - 2^{\frac{1}{2}n}$, if n is even. By using Lemma 6 we conclude that the algebraic degree of f is at most $2^{\frac{1}{2}n+1}$.

$\square$

Example 2. Let n be a positive odd number and $f(x_1, \ldots, x_n)$ be the same with that in Example 1. Let W be an $(n-1)$-dimensional linear subspace of V_n, composed of all the vectors in V_n, that can be expressed in the form $(a_1, \ldots, a_{n-1}, 0)$, where each $a_j \in GF(2)$. It is easy to see $\alpha^* = (1, 0, \ldots, 0) \in V_n$ is a non-zero linear structure of f and $\Re \cap W = \{0, \alpha^*\}$. Due to (ii) of Theorem 8, $N_f = 2^{n-1} - 2^{\frac{1}{2}(n-1)}$.

Let k be a positive even number with $k \ge 4$ and $h(x_1, \ldots, x_k) = x_1 \oplus x_2 \oplus q(x_3, \ldots, x_k)$ where q is a bent function on V_{k-2}. Let U be an $(n-1)$-dimensional linear subspace of V_n, composed of all the vectors in V_n, that can be expressed in the form $(0, a_2, \ldots, a_k)$, where each $a_j \in GF(2)$. It is easy to see $\alpha_1^* = (0, 1, 0, \ldots, 0)$ is a non-zero linear structures of h and $\Re \cap U = \{0, \alpha_1^*\}$. Due to (iii) of Theorem 8, $N_h = 2^{k-1} - 2^{\frac{1}{2}k}$.

It is interesting that by using Theorem 8, we have determined N_h only from the condition $\#(\Re \cap U) = 2$ for an $(n-1)$-dimensional linear subspace U although we do not search other vectors in $\Re$.

Finally, we consider the case when $\#(\Re \cap W) = 3$.

Theorem 9. *Let f be a function on V_n. If there exists a $(n-1)$-dimensional linear subspace W satisfying $\Re \cap W = \{0, \beta_1, \beta_2\}$, then the following statements hold:*

(i) $\Delta(\beta_j) = \pm 2^{n-1}, j = 1, 2,$

(ii) if n is odd, then the nonlinearity of f satisfies $N_f = 2^{n-1} - 2^{\frac{1}{2}(n-1)}$ and the algebraic degree of f is at most $2^{\frac{1}{2}(n+1)}$,

(iii) if n is even, then $N_f = 2^{n-1} - 2^{\frac{1}{2}n}$ and the algebraic degree of f is at most $2^{\frac{1}{2}n+1}$.

Proof. Since any two non-zero vectors are linearly independent, we can keep the deduction in the proof of Theorem 3 until inequality (12) where we need the condition $k \ge 3$.

Recall the proof of Theorem 3, (9) can be specialized as $\Delta(\beta_j) = \pm 2^n, \pm 2^{n-1}$, $j = 1, 2$.

On the other hand, (10), (11) and (12) can be rewritten as $(\Delta(\beta_1), \Delta(\beta_2)) = 2^{n-1}(b_1, b_2)$ where each $b_j = \pm 1, \pm 2$, $(p_{1s}, p_{2s}) = (\frac{b_1}{|b_1|}, \frac{b_2}{|b_2|})$. and

$$p_{1s}\Delta(\beta_1) + p_{2s}\Delta(\beta_2) = (|b_1| + |b_2|)2^{n-1} \qquad (16)$$

respectively. It is easy to prove $b_1, b_2 = \pm 1$. Otherwise, for example, $b_1 = \pm 2$, from (16), $p_{1s}\Delta(\beta_1) + p_{2s}\Delta(\beta_2) \geq 3 \cdot 2^{n-1}$. This contradicts (6). Since $b_1, b_2 = \pm 1$, $\Delta(\beta_1), \Delta(\beta_2) = \pm 2^{n-1}$. This proves (i).

The rest proof is the same with the proof of Theorem 8. $\quad\square$

Example 3. Let n be a positive odd number with $n \geq 7$, $h(x_1, x_2, x_3, x_4, x_5) = (x_1 \oplus x_2 \oplus x_3)x_4 x_5 \oplus x_1 x_5 \oplus x_2 x_4 \oplus x_1 \oplus x_2 \oplus x_3$ and $g(x_6, \ldots, x_n)$ be a bent function on V_{n-5}. Set $f(x_1, \ldots, x_n) = h(x_1, x_2, x_3, x_4, x_5) \oplus g(x_6, \ldots, x_n)$.

Let W be an $(n-1)$-dimensional linear subspace of V_n, composed of all the vectors in V_n, that can be expressed in the form $(0, a_2, \ldots, a_n)$, where each $a_j \in GF(2)$. Write $\alpha_1^* = (0, 0, 1, 0, \ldots, 0)$, $\alpha_2^* = (0, 1, 0, \ldots, 0) \in V_n$, It is easy to verify $\alpha_1^*, \alpha_2^* \in \Re$ and $\Re \cap W = \{0, \alpha_1^*, \alpha_2^*\}$. Due to (i) and (ii) of Theorem 9, we conclude $\Delta(\alpha_1^*) = \pm 2^{n-1}$, $\Delta(\alpha_2^*) = \pm 2^{n-1}$ and $N_f = 2^{n-1} - 2^{\frac{1}{2}(n-1)}$.

We notice that by using Theorem 9, we have determined N_h, $\Delta(\alpha_1^*)$ and $\Delta(\alpha_2^*)$ only from the information about $\#(\Re \cap W)$ for an $(n-1)$-dimensional linear subspace W although we do not search other the vectors in $\Re$.

We can also find an example corresponding to (iii) of Theorem 9. All Theorems 7, 8 and 9 and Examples 1, 2 and 3 show that we can determine the nonlinearity of a function only from some information about $\#(\Re \cap W)$, where W is an $(n-1)$-dimensional linear subspace. It is interesting that [7] has proved that there exists no a function with $\#\Re = 3$ while Example 3 gives a function satisfying $\#(\Re \cap W) = 3$ for an $(n-1)$-dimensional linear subspace W.

7 Conclusions

The strong linear dependence is an improvement on a previously known result. The unbiased distribution of non-propagation vectors is valid for most functions. These results provide more information on the non-propagative vectors in any $(n-1)$-dimensional linear subspace of V_n, and hence they are helpful for designing cryptographic functions.

Acknowledgement

The second author was supported by a Queen Elizabeth II Fellowship (227 23 1002).

References

1. Claude Carlet. Partially-bent functions. *Designs, Codes and Cryptography*, 3:135–145, 1993.
2. W. Meier and O. Staffelbach. Nonlinearity criteria for cryptographic functions. In *Advances in Cryptology - EUROCRYPT'89*, volume 434, Lecture Notes in Computer Science, pages 549–562. Springer-Verlag, Berlin, Heidelberg, New York, 1990.

3. B. Preneel, W. V. Leekwijck, L. V. Linden, R. Govaerts, and J. Vandewalle. Propagation characteristics of boolean functions. In *Advances in Cryptology - EUROCRYPT'90*, volume 437, Lecture Notes in Computer Science, pages 155–165. Springer-Verlag, Berlin, Heidelberg, New York, 1991.

4. O. S. Rothaus. On "bent" functions. *Journal of Combinatorial Theory*, Ser. A, 20:300–305, 1976.

5. A. F. Webster and S. E. Tavares. On the design of S-boxes. In *Advances in Cryptology - CRYPTO'85*, volume 219, Lecture Notes in Computer Science, pages 523–534. Springer-Verlag, Berlin, Heidelberg, New York, 1986.

6. Y. Zheng X. M. Zhang and Hideki Imai. Duality of boolean functions and its cryptographic significance. In *Advances in Cryptology - ICICS'97*, volume 1334, Lecture Notes in Computer Science, pages 159–169. Springer-Verlag, Berlin, Heidelberg, New York, 1997.

7. X. M. Zhang and Y. Zheng. Characterizing the structures of cryptographic functions satisfying the propagation criterion for almost all vectors. *Design, Codes and Cryptography*, 7(1/2):111–134, 1996. special issue dedicated to Gus Simmons.

Security of E2 against
Truncated Differential Cryptanalysis

Shiho Moriai, Makoto Sugita, Kazumaro Aoki, and Masayuki Kanda

NTT Laboratories
1-1 Hikarinooka, Yokosuka, 239-0847, Japan
shiho@isl.ntt.co.jp,sugita@pcs.wslab.ntt.co.jp
maro@isl.ntt.co.jp,kanda@sucaba.isl.ntt.co.jp

Abstract. This paper studies the security offered by the block cipher E2 against truncated differential cryptanalysis. At FSE'99 Matsui and Tokita showed a possible attack on an 8-round variant of E2 without *IT*-Function (the initial transformation) and *FT*-Function (the final transformation) based on byte characteristics. To evaluate the security against attacks using truncated differentials, which mean bytewise differentials in this paper, we searched for all truncated differentials that lead to possible attacks for reduced-round variants of E2. As a result, we confirmed that there exist no such truncated differentials for E2 with more than 8 rounds. However, we found another 7-round truncated differential which lead to another possible attack on an 8-round variant of E2 without *IT*- or *FT*-Function *with less complexity*. We also found that the 7-round truncated differential is useful to distinguish a 7-round variant of E2 *with IT*- and *FT*-Functions from a random permutation. In spite of our severe examination, this type of cryptanalysis fails to break the full E2. We believe that this means that the full E2 offers strong security against this truncated differential cryptanalysis.

1 Introduction

The attacks using truncated differentials were introduced by Knudsen [K95]. It deals with truncated differentials, i.e. differentials where only a part of the difference can be predicted. Although the notion of truncated differentials he introduced is wide, with a byte-oriented cipher it is natural to study bytewise differentials as truncated differentials. The truncated differential can partly deal with the so called multiple-path for a Markov cipher [LMM91], which is a set of differential characteristics with the same input difference pattern and the same output difference pattern, hence the maximum probability of *truncated differential* can be higher than that of differential characteristics. Moreover, the truncated differentials can allow the attackers more freedom in choosing plaintexts or ciphertexts. Therefore, studying the security against truncated differential cryptanalysis can provide a more strict evaluation of the security against differential cryptanalysis.

A truncated differential cryptanalysis of reduced-round variants of E2 was presented by Matsui and Tokita at FSE'99 [MT99]. Their analysis was based on

Howard Heys and Carlisle Adams (Eds.): SAC'99, LNCS 1758, pp. 106–117, 2000.

the "byte characteristic," where the values to the difference in a byte are distinguished between non-zero and zero. They found a 7-round byte characteristic, which leads to a possible attack on an 8-round variant of E2 without IT-Function (the initial transformation) and FT-Function (the final transformation).

This paper studies the security of E2 against this type of cryptanalysis. We show an algorithm which searches for all effective truncated differentials that lead to possible attacks of Feistel ciphers, which Matsui et al. didn't go into details about in [MT99]. Here "effective" means that the probability of the truncated differential for the cipher is higher than the probability of the truncated differential for a random permutation. To run the algorithm above, we have to compute all non-zero probabilities of truncated differentials of the round function. Since the round function of E2 has the SPN (Substitution Permutation Network) structure, we made use of the method for computing the maximum average of differential probability of general SPN structures shown by Sugita et al. [SKI99].

As a result, we found another 7-round truncated differential, which leads to a possible attack on an 8-round variant of E2 without IT- or FT-Function *with less complexity* than that offered by Matsui et al. Moreover, this truncated differential was also useful in distinguishing a 7-round variant of E2 *with IT- and FT-Functions* from a random function. However, no flaw by the cryptanalysis above was discovered for the full 12-round E2, i.e. E2 in the specification submitted to NIST as an AES candidate [E2].

The contents of this paper are as follows. First, in Section 2, we describe an algorithm to compute the probabilities for all truncated differentials of the round function with the SPN structure. Second, we show a search algorithm for the truncated differentials of E2 in Section 3. This algorithm is applicable to other ciphers with the Feistel structure. Section 4 describes possible scenarios of attacks on reduced-round variants of E2 using the truncated differentials found in Section 3 and estimates the required complexity for attacking.

2 Truncated Differentials of Round Function

First, we show examples of the transition rules between the input and output bytewise differences of the round function of E2 and define the truncated differential used in this paper. Throughout this paper we follow the notations used in the specification of E2 [E2] (see also Figure 1). The linear transformation in the round function (P-Function) is represented as follows.

$$^t(z_1', z_2', \ldots, z_8') = P\, ^t(z_1, z_2, \ldots, z_8)$$

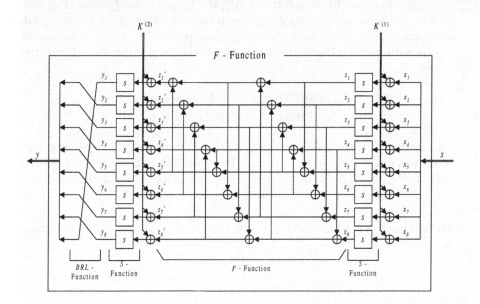

Fig. 1. The round function of E2

$$P = \begin{pmatrix} 0 & 1 & 1 & 1 & 1 & 1 & 1 & 0 \\ 1 & 0 & 1 & 1 & 0 & 1 & 1 & 1 \\ 1 & 1 & 0 & 1 & 1 & 0 & 1 & 1 \\ 1 & 1 & 1 & 0 & 1 & 1 & 0 & 1 \\ 1 & 1 & 0 & 1 & 1 & 1 & 0 & 0 \\ 1 & 1 & 1 & 0 & 0 & 1 & 1 & 0 \\ 0 & 1 & 1 & 1 & 0 & 0 & 1 & 1 \\ 1 & 0 & 1 & 1 & 1 & 0 & 0 & 1 \end{pmatrix} \tag{1}$$

Let $x = (x_1, x_2, \ldots, x_8)$, $y = (y_2, \ldots, y_8, y_1)$, and $z = (z_1, z_2, \ldots, z_8)$ be the input of the round function, the output of the round function, and the input of P-Function, respectively, and let $\Delta x \in (\mathrm{GF}(2)^8)^8$, $\Delta y \in (\mathrm{GF}(2)^8)^8$, and $\Delta z \in (\mathrm{GF}(2)^8)^8$ be the differences of x, y, and z, respectively.

$$\begin{aligned} \Delta x &= (\Delta x_1, \Delta x_2, \ldots, \Delta x_8), & \Delta x_i &\in \mathrm{GF}(2)^8 \\ \Delta y &= (\Delta y_2, \ldots, \Delta y_8, \Delta y_1), & \Delta y_i &\in \mathrm{GF}(2)^8 \qquad (i = 1, 2, \ldots, 8) \\ \Delta z &= (\Delta z_1, \Delta z_2, \ldots, \Delta z_8), & \Delta z_i &\in \mathrm{GF}(2)^8 \end{aligned}$$

For example, when two bytes of the input x_1 and x_5 are changed, if $\Delta z_1 = \Delta z_5$, then three bytes of the output y_2, y_6, and y_1 are changed. Otherwise (i.e., if $\Delta z_1 \neq \Delta z_5$) all bytes except y_7 are changed. Assuming that the input values $x_1, x_2, \ldots, x_8$ and the input differences Δx_1 and Δx_5 are given randomly (while the other Δx_i's are fixed to 0 $(i \neq 1, 5)$), the former event $(\Delta z_1 = \Delta z_5)$ occurs with approximate probability 2^{-8} (though the exact value is $\frac{1}{255}$), and the latter event $(\Delta z_1 \neq \Delta z_5)$ occurs with approximate probability $1 - 2^{-8}$. We describe the transition rules above between the input and output bytewise differences as follows.

$$(10001000) \rightarrow (10001001) \quad p \approx 2^{-8}$$
$$(10001000) \rightarrow (11111011) \quad p \approx 1 - 2^{-8}$$

The transition rules above are generalized to the transition rules between the input and output t-bitwise differences for a function with $m \times t$ bits input and output. We call these transition rules the truncated differentials of a function $f : (GF(2)^t)^m \mapsto (GF(2)^t)^m$. Formally, we define them as follows.

Definition 1 (χ-Function). *Let χ be the function $GF(2)^t \rightarrow GF(2)$ defined as follows.*

$$\chi(x) = \begin{cases} 0 & \text{if } x = 0 \\ 1 & \text{if } x \neq 0 \end{cases}$$

Let $\chi(x_1, x_2, \ldots, x_m) = (\chi(x_1), \chi(x_2), \ldots, \chi(x_m))$.

Definition 2 (Truncated Differential). *Let δx, $\delta y \in GF(2)^m$ denote the input differential and output differential of the truncated differential of the function f, respectively.*

$$\delta x = (\delta x_1, \delta x_2, \ldots, \delta x_m), \quad \delta x_i \in GF(2) \quad (i = 1, 2, \ldots, m)$$
$$\delta y = (\delta y_1, \delta y_2, \ldots, \delta y_m), \quad \delta y_i \in GF(2)$$

where $\delta x_i = \chi(\Delta x_i)$ and $\delta y_i = \chi(\Delta y_i)$.
Let $p_f(\delta x, \delta y)$ denote the probability of the truncated differential of the function f. $p_f(\delta x, \delta y)$ is defined by

$$p_f(\delta x, \delta y) = \max_{\substack{\Delta x \neq 0 \\ \chi(\Delta x) = \delta x}} \Pr_{x \in (GF(2)^t)^m} [\, \chi(f(x) \oplus f(x \oplus \Delta x)) = \delta y \,] \qquad (2)$$

We define the pair of δx and δy as the truncated differential of the function f and represent it as follows:

$$\delta x \rightarrow \delta y \quad \text{with probability } p_f(\delta x, \delta y).$$

To search exhaustively for the effective truncated differentials of the whole cipher, we need to derive all possible truncated differentials of the round function with non-zero probability. Sugita [SKI99] showed a method for calculating the maximum average of differential probability of the SPN structure, assuming that the differential probability of the s-boxes is uniformly distributed for any nonzero input difference and any nonzero output difference*. According to [SKI99, Section 5], we can calculate efficiently the probabilities of the truncated differentials of the round function of E2, $p_F(\delta x, \delta y)$, for every $\delta x, \delta y \in \mathrm{GF}(2)^8$. We begin by introducing the following semi-order $\preceq$ in $\mathrm{GF}(2)^m$.

Definition 3 (Semi-order). *For every $\delta x, \delta y \in \mathrm{GF}(2)^m$, we define the semi-order $\preceq$ in $\mathrm{GF}(2)^m$ as follows.*

$$\delta x \preceq \delta y \overset{\text{def}}{\iff} \forall i\, (1 \le i \le m); \quad \delta y_i = 0 \Rightarrow \delta x_i = 0,$$

where $\delta x = (\delta x_1, \delta x_2, \ldots, \delta x_m)$ and $\delta y = (\delta y_1, \delta y_2, \ldots, \delta y_m)$.

Algorithm 1 (Calculation of the Probabilities of Truncated Differentials of the Round Function of E2).

1. For every $\delta z, \delta z' \in \mathrm{GF}(2)^8$, we define $\mathrm{M}(\delta z, \delta z')$ for P-Function as follows.

$$\mathrm{M}(\delta z, \delta z')$$
$$= \#\{(\Delta z, \Delta z') \in ((\mathrm{GF}(2)^8)^8 \setminus \{\mathbf{0}\})^2 \mid \Delta z' = P\Delta z, \chi(\Delta z) \preceq \delta z, \chi(\Delta z') \preceq \delta z'\},$$

where
$$\delta z = (\delta z_1, \delta z_2, \ldots, \delta z_8), \quad \delta z_i = \chi(\Delta z_i)$$
$$\delta z' = (\delta z'_1, \delta z'_2, \ldots, \delta z'_8), \quad \delta z'_i = \chi(\Delta z'_i)$$

$\mathrm{M}(\delta z, \delta z')$ can be easily calculated by a simple rank calculation as follows.

$$\mathrm{M}(\delta z, \delta z') = 2^{8(16 - \mathrm{rank}\left(\mathcal{F}(\overline{\delta z}, \overline{\delta z}')\begin{pmatrix} P & E \end{pmatrix}\right))} - 1,$$

where $\overline{\delta z}$ and $\overline{\delta z}'$ are the complements of δz and $\delta z'$, respectively. P denotes the matrix represented by Equation (1), E denotes the 8×8 identity matrix, and $\mathcal{F}(\overline{\delta z}, \overline{\delta z}')$ denotes the 16×16 diagonal matrix whose (i, i) component equals $\overline{\delta z}_i$ for $i = 1, \cdots, 8$, and $\overline{\delta z}'_{i-8}$ for $i = 9, \cdots, 16$.

2. For every $\delta z, \delta z' \in \mathrm{GF}(2)^8$, we define $\mathrm{N}(\delta z, \delta z')$ for P-Function as follows.

$$\mathrm{N}(\delta z, \delta z')$$
$$= \#\{(\Delta z, \Delta z') \in ((\mathrm{GF}(2)^8)^8 \setminus \{\mathbf{0}\})^2 \mid \Delta z' = P\Delta z, \chi(\Delta z) = \delta z, \chi(\Delta z') = \delta z'\}$$

$\mathrm{N}(\delta z, \delta z')$ can be calculated recursively, using the following relation [SKI99].

$$\mathrm{N}(\delta z, \delta z') = \mathrm{M}(\delta z, \delta z') - \sum_{(\widetilde{\delta z}, \widetilde{\delta z}') \prec (\delta z, \delta z')} \mathrm{N}(\widetilde{\delta z}, \widetilde{\delta z}') \tag{3}$$

---

* Strictly speaking, let $n_s(\Delta x, \Delta y) = \#\{x \mid s(x) \oplus s(x \oplus \Delta x) = \Delta y\}$ and the following is assumed:

$$n_s = \begin{cases} \frac{1}{2^t - 1} & \text{if } \Delta x \Delta y \ne 0 \\ 1 & \text{if } \Delta x = \Delta y = 0 \\ 0 & \text{otherwise.} \end{cases}$$

3. For every $\delta x, \delta y \in \mathrm{GF}(2)^8$, calculate the probability of truncated differential of the round function $p_F(\delta x, \delta y)$ according to the following relations [SKI99].

$$p_F(\delta x, \delta y) = \sum_{\delta z} \mathrm{N}(\delta z, \delta z') q^{w_\mathrm{H}(\delta y)} p_S(\delta x, \delta z) \tag{4}$$

$$p_S(\delta x, \delta z) = \max_{\substack{\Delta x \neq 0 \\ \chi(\Delta x) = \delta x}} \Pr_{x \in (\mathrm{GF}(2)^8)^8} [\, \chi(S(x) \oplus S(x \oplus \Delta x)) = \delta z \,] \tag{5}$$

where $w_\mathrm{H}(\delta y)$ denotes the Hamming weight of δy and q is the maximum average of the differential probability of s-box. We have $q = 1/(2^8 - 1)$ under the assumption that differential probability of the s-boxes is uniformly distributed for any nonzero input difference and any nonzero output difference.

3 The Search for Truncated Differentials of E2

In this section we search for all truncated differentials that lead to possible attacks on (reduced-round variants of) E2. Below we show a search algorithm for all "effective" truncated differentials of a Feistel cipher with R rounds and blocksize $2mt$ bits. In this paper, "effective" means that the truncated differential could lead to possible attacks, in other words, the probability of the truncated differential is equal or higher than the probability with which the truncated differential holds for a random permutation[**].

This search algorithm consists of recursive procedures. Note that the search algorithm is the depth first search rather than the breadth first search considering the required memory. The "depth" corresponds to the number of rounds of the Feistel cipher.

Algorithm 2 (Search for all Effective Truncated Differentials of Feistel Cipher with R Rounds and Blocksize $2mt$ Bits)

Let $X^{(r)}, Y^{(r)} \in \mathrm{GF}(2)^m$ be the input and output differences of the truncated differential of the r-th round function. Thus $(X^{(0)}, X^{(1)})$ is the truncated differential of the plaintext. Let $\mathcal{P}_r$ be the variable which holds the probability of the r-round truncated differential. $\mathcal{P}_0$ should be initialized to be 1, $i.e., \mathcal{P}_0 := 1$.

1. Calculate all the probabilities of the truncated differentials of the round function $p_F(\delta x, \delta y)$. They should be sorted in order of the probability of truncated differentials for each input difference.

2. For all truncated differential of the plaintext, $(i.e., {}^\forall X^{(0)} \in \mathrm{GF}(2)^m$ and ${}^\forall X^{(1)} \in \mathrm{GF}(2)^m)$ call the procedure [THE 1ST ROUND], i.e., the procedure [THE r-TH ROUND] for $r = 1$. After finishing the procedure [THE 1ST ROUND] for all $X^{(0)}$ and $X^{(1)}$, exit the program.

[**] Although there is a claimed attack on the first 16 rounds of Skipjack using the truncated differential with smaller probability than a random permutation [KRW99], we are not concerned here with this case.

3. [THE r-TH ROUND] For each $X^{(r)}$, set the output truncated differential of the round function $Y^{(r)} \in GF(2)^m$ in order of the probability of the truncated differential.

    – Let $p_r := p_F(X^{(r)}, Y^{(r)})$.

    – If $\mathcal{P}_{r-1} \times p_r < 2^{-2mt}$, then try another $X^{(r)}$.

    – Call the procedure [THE r-TH XOR].

If $r \neq 1$, return to the procedure [THE $(r-1)$-ST XOR], otherwise (*i.e.*, $r = 1$), return to Step 2.

4. [THE r-TH XOR] At the XOR operation of the r-th round in the Feistel cipher, $X^{(r+1)}$ is derived from $X^{(r-1)}$ and $Y^{(r)}$. Here the difference may be canceled out: $1 \oplus 1 = 0$ with probability $\frac{1}{255} (\approx 2^{-t})$, while $1 \oplus 1 = 1$ with probability $\frac{254}{255}$, assuming that the difference is independent and uniformly distributed. When the cancelation occurs c times, the probability is approximately $(2^{-t})^c$. The number of all possible values of $X^{(r+1)}$ is $2^{w_H(X^{(r-1)} \wedge Y^{(r)})}$. For each $X^{(r+1)}$, call the following procedure.

    – Let $\mathcal{P}_r := \mathcal{P}_{r-1} \times p_r \times (2^{-t})^c$, where $c = w_H(X^{(r-1)} \vee Y^{(r)}) - w_H(X^{(r+1)})$.

    – If $\mathcal{P}_r < 2^{-2mt}$, then try another $X^{(r+1)}$.

    – If $\mathcal{P}_r$ is lower than the probability for a random function, i.e., if $\mathcal{P}_r < 2^{t \times (w_H(X^{(r)}) + w_H(X^{(r+1)})) - 2mt}$, then try another $X^{(r+1)}$.

    – If $r < R$, call the procedure [THE $(r+1)$-ST ROUND], else print the truncated differential:

$$(X^{(0)}, X^{(1)}) \rightarrow (X^{(R+1)}, X^{(R)}) \quad \text{with probability } \mathcal{P}_R.$$

Return to the procedure [THE $(r-1)$-ST ROUND].

At the procedure [THE r-TH XOR] of each round in the algorithm above, if the probability of the r-round truncated differential is lower than the probability with which the truncated differential holds for a random permutation, we don't have to continue the search for the truncated differential for longer rounds. This makes the search efficient by pruning off unnecessary candidates. This is because the following theorem holds for Feistel ciphers.

Theorem 1.

$$\mathcal{P}_r < 2^{t(w_H(X^{(r)}) + w_H(X^{(r+1)})) - 2mt} \tag{6}$$

$$\implies \mathcal{P}_{r+1} < 2^{t(w_H(X^{(r+1)}) + w_H(X^{(r+2)})) - 2mt} \tag{7}$$

Proof) We have

$$\mathcal{P}_{r+1} = \mathcal{P}_r \times p_{r+1} \times (2^{-t})^c.$$

From Equation (6) and since $c = w_H(X^{(r)} \vee Y^{(r+1)}) - w_H(X^{(r+2)})$ holds, where c is the number of times when the cancelation happens in the procedure [THE $r + 1$-TH XOR], *we have*

$$\mathcal{P}_{r+1} < 2^{t(w_H(X^{(r)}) + w_H(X^{(r+1)})) - 2mt} \times p_{r+1} \times 2^{-t(w_H(X^{(r)} \vee Y^{(r+1)}) - w_H(X^{(r+2)}))}$$

$$= 2^{t(w_H(X^{(r+1)}) + w_H(X^{(r+2)})) - 2mt} \times p_{r+1} \times 2^{t(w_H(X^{(r)}) - (w_H(X^{(r)} \vee Y^{(r+1)})))}$$

We have $p_{r+1} \le 1$ and $2^{t(w_H(X^{(r)}) - (w_H(X^{(r)} \vee Y^{(r+1)})))} \le 1$, since

$$w_H(X^{(r)}) - (w_H(X^{(r)} \vee Y^{(r+1)})) \le 0$$

holds. Therefore,

$$\mathcal{P}_{r+1} < 2^{t(w_H(X^{(r)}) + w_H(X^{(r+1)})) - 2mt}$$

holds. The proof is complete.

4 Attacks on Reduced-Round Variants of E2

Using Algorithm 2 we searched for all truncated differentials that lead to possible attacks for reduced-round variants of E2. As a result, we confirmed that there exist no such truncated differentials for E2 with more than 7 rounds. The best[***] 7-round truncated differential that leads to possible attacks on reduced-round variants of E2 is shown in Figure 2. This 7-round truncated differential holds with probability of about $2^{-104\dagger}$; for a random round function the probability of the truncated differential is expected to be $(2^{-8})^{14} = 2^{-112}$, which is significantly smaller. Therefore, this truncated differential is useful to derive subkey information of the last round and to distinguish from a random permutation.

Moreover, this 7-round truncated differential is connected with the truncated differentials of IT- and FT-Functions with probability about 1. In IT- and FT-Functions, 32-bit multiplications with subkeys are used. Since this multiplication is modulo 2^{32} (roughly speaking, the upper 32-bit of the resultant 64-bit is discarded), this multiplication has the following trivial truncated differential as shown in [MT99].

$$(1000) \rightarrow (1000) \qquad p \approx 1$$

[***] Here the "best" means that the ratio of the probability of the truncated differential to the probability for a random permutation is the highest.

[†] The more strict probability we computed was $248q^{14} + 18q^{15} + 39q^{16} + 157q^{17} + 22q^{18} + 62q^{19} + 225q^{20} + 158q^{21} + 172q^{22} + 191q^{23} + 205q^{24} + 202q^{25} + 189q^{26} + 194q^{27} + 246q^{28} + 137q^{29} + 10q^{30} + 93q^{31} + 37q^{32} + 173q^{33} + 9q^{34} + 162q^{35} + 74q^{36} + 95q^{37} + 156q^{38} + 28q^{39} + \cdots$, while the probability of the best known truncated differential [MT99] was computed as $q^{14} + 231q^{15} + 168q^{16} + 135q^{17} + 115q^{18} + 157q^{19} + 163q^{20} + 217q^{21} + 90q^{22} + 208q^{23} + 59q^{24} + 91q^{25} + 80q^{26} + 158q^{27} + 41q^{28} + 130q^{29} + 250q^{30} + 227q^{31} + 102q^{32} + 118q^{33} + 40q^{34} + 246q^{35} + 13q^{36} + 146q^{37} + 98q^{38} + 153q^{39} + 8q^{40} + \cdots$, where q is the maximum average of the differential probability of s-box. Under our assumption $q = 1/(2^8 - 1)$ for any nonzero input difference and any nonzero output difference of s-box.

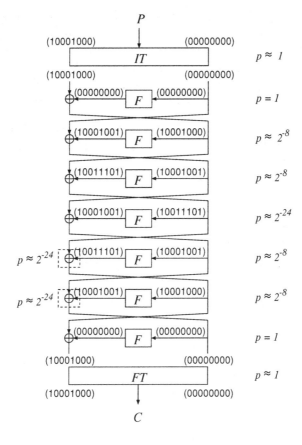

Fig. 2. The best 7-round truncated differential of E2

Hence the 7-round truncated differential shown in Figure 2 can skip IT- and FT-Functions with probability about 1. Additionally, the positions of the bytes which have a non-zero difference are not changed by BP-Function (or BP^{-1}-Function) in IT-Function (or FT-Function). It follows that we have the following truncated differential connecting the plaintext and ciphertext for a 7-round variant of E2.

$$(10001000\ 00000000) \to (10001000\ 00000000) \qquad p \approx 2^{-104}$$

4.1 E2 Reduced to 8 Rounds without IT- or FT-Function

We show a possible scenario of an attack of E2 reduced to 8 rounds without IT- or FT-Function. Below we show an attack to derive the last round key (the round key the 8-th round) without FT-Function.

Prepare the chosen plaintexts with the difference pattern (10001000 00000000) and guess the last round keys and get the output of the 7-th round using the ciphertexts. According to [MT99, Section 5, Lemma 1], when we have 2^{109} chosen plaintext pairs, if the number of pairs whose output differences follow the difference pattern (10001000 00000000) is more than 20, we can judge the guessed key is right and otherwise we can judge the guessed key is wrong. For a correct key the probability that the number of pairs whose output differences follow the difference pattern (10001000 00000000) is more than 20 is 99%, while the probability is 2^{-121} for a wrong key.

The required 2^{109} chosen plaintext pairs can be generated from 2^{94} chosen plaintext blocks ($94 = 109 - 16 + 1$). The attack on an 8-round variant of E2 without IT- and FT-Functions shown in [MT99] required 2^{100} chosen plaintext blocks. Moreover, we do not have to choose special plaintexts [MT99, Section 5.2] since the probability that correct pairs are detected is much larger than the probability that wrong pairs appear.

Note that the complexity of the procedure above for deriving the last round keys (128 bits) exceeds the complexity of exhaustive search $O(2^{128})$. We've not confirmed whether an improved attack with complexity less than $O(2^{128})$ is possible.

4.2 E2 Reduced to 7 Rounds with IT- and FT-Function

The 7-round truncated differential shown in Figure 2 is also useful to distinguish the 7-round variant of E2 with IT- and FT-Functions from a random permutation.

Prepare the chosen plaintexts with the difference pattern (10001000 00000000) and observe the differences of the ciphertexts. According to Matsui et al.'s theory, when we have 2^{106} chosen plaintext pairs, if at least one pair follows the difference pattern (10001000 00000000), we can regard it as the 7-round variant of E2 with IT- and FT-Functions, otherwise we regard it as a random permutation. The probability that the number of pairs whose output differences follow the difference pattern (10001000 00000000) is more than 1 is 98%, while the probability is 2% for a random permutation. The required 2^{106} chosen plaintext pairs can be generated from 2^{91} plaintext blocks ($91 = 106 - 16 + 1$).

5 Conclusion

This paper introduced search algorithms for finding effective truncated differentials useful in truncated differential cryptanalysis. Applying to E2, we found an attack on an 8-round variant of E2 without IT- or FT-Function requiring 2^{94} chosen plaintexts, which is fewer than that required by the best known attack. We also found that it is possible to distinguish a 7-round variant of E2 *with IT-* and FT-Functions from a random function using 2^{91} chosen plaintexts.

In spite of our severe examination, this type of cryptanalysis fails to break the full E2. We believe that this means that the full E2 offers strong security against truncated differential cryptanalysis.

Table 1. Attacks on reduced-round variants of E2

Attack 1: Extract the last round key information

Matsui et al.'s result	8-round E2 without IT and FT
	2^{100} chosen plaintexts
Our result	8-round E2 without IT or FT
	2^{94} chosen plaintexts

Note) The attack complexities may be above $O(2^{128})$.

Attack 2: Distinguish from a random permutation

Matsui et al.'s result	7-round E2 without IT and FT
	2^{97} chosen plaintexts
Our result	7-round E2 with IT and FT
	2^{91} chosen plaintexts

Appendix: Truncated Differentials of Rijndael

We also searched for truncated differentials of Rijndael [DR98] under the similar condition that the differential probability of the S-boxes is uniformly distributed for any nonzero input difference and any nonzero output difference. In [DR98] the designers stated that, for 6 rounds or more, no attacks faster than exhaustive key search have been found. For differential characteristics of Rijndael, they stated that it can be proven that there are no 4-round differential trails with a predicted prop ratio (probability) above 2^{-150}.

As the result of our search, there existed no truncated differentials for Rijndael with more than 4 rounds that has higher probability than a randomly chosen permutation. There existed 218,700,000 4-round truncated differentials that has the same probability as a randomly chosen permutation. For differentials of Rijndael, we found a 5-round differential with probability 1.06×2^{-128}, and there existed no differentials for Rijndael with more than 5 rounds that have higher probability than $\frac{1}{2^{128}-1}$.

References

DR98. J.Daemen and V.Rijmen, "The Rijndael Block Cipher," 1998, available at `http://www.esat.kuleuven.ac.be/~rijmen/rijndael/`.

K95. L.R.Knudsen, "Truncated and Higher Order Differentials," Fast Software Encryption — Second International Workshop, Lecture Notes in Computer Science 1008, pp.196–211, Springer-Verlag, 1995.

KRW99. L.R.Knudsen, M.J.B.Robshaw, and D.Wagner, "Truncated Differentials and Skipjack," Advances in Cryptology — CRYPTO'99, Lecture Notes in Computer Science 1666, pp.165–180, Springer-Verlag, 1999.

LMM91. X.Lai, J.L.Massey, and S.Murphy, "Markov Ciphers and Differential Cryptanalysis," Advances in Cryptology — EUROCRYPT'91, Lecture Notes in Computer Science 547, pp.17–38, Springer-Verlag, 1991.

MT99. M.Matsui and T.Tokita, "Cryptanalysis of a Reduced Version of the Block Cipher E2," in pre-proceedings of Fast Software Encryption'99, pp.70–79, 1999.

E2. Nippon Telegraph and Telephone Corporation, "Specification of E2 — a 128-bit Block Cipher," 1999, available at `http://info.isl.ntt.co.jp/e2/`.

SKI99. M.Sugita, K.Kobara, and H.Imai, "Pseudorandomness and Maximum Average of Differential Probability of Block Ciphers with SPN-Structures like E2," in proceedings of the second Advanced Encryption Standard candidate conference, pp.200–214, 1999.

V99. S.Vaudenay, "On the Security of CS-Cipher," in pre-proceedings of Fast Software Encryption'99, pp.259–274, 1999.

Key-Schedule Cryptanalysis of DEAL

John Kelsey and Bruce Schneier

Counterpane Systems
101 E. Minnehaha Pkwy
Minneapolis, MN 55419
{kelsey,schneier}@counterpane.com

Abstract. DEAL is a six- or eight-round Luby-Rackoff cipher that uses DES as its round function, with allowed key lengths of 128, 192, and 256 bits. In this paper, we discuss two new results on the DEAL key schedule. First, we discuss the existence of equivalent keys for all three key lengths; pairs of equivalent keys in DEAL-128 require about 2^{64} DES encryptions to find, while equivalent keys in DEAL-192 and DEAL-256 require only six or eight DES encryptions to find. Second, we discuss a new related-key attack on DEAL-192 and DEAL-256. This attack requires 2^{33} related key queries, the same 3 plaintexts encrypted under each key, and may be implemented with a variety of time-memory tradeoffs; Given 3×2^{69} bytes of memory, the attack requires 2^{113} DES encryptions, and given 3×2^{45} bytes of memory, the attack requires 2^{137} DES encryptions. We conclude with some questions raised by the analysis.

1 Introduction

In June 1998 the National Institute of Standards and Technology (NIST) received fifteen candidate algorithms for the Advanced Encryption Standard (AES). The AES would eventually replace DES as a federal encryption standard, and hopefully would become a world-wide encryption standard as well.

One of the hardest aspects of cipher design is the key schedule. Numerous AES submissions have been attacked through their key schedule: SAFER+ [CMK+98] in [KSW99], Crypton [Lim98] in [Bor99], DFC [GGH+98] in [Cop98a] [Cop98b], Frog [GLC98] in [WFS99], HPC [Sch98] in [Wag99,DBP+99], Magenta [JH98] in [BBF+99], MARS [BCD+98] and RC6 [RRS+98] in [Saa99]. These attacks have ranged from finding equivalent keys to weak key classes to related-key differential attacks [Bih94,KSW96,KSW97], and have generally not been serious. Still, equivalent or related keys can make the cipher unusable as a hash function (for example, in Davies-Meyer feed forward mode [Win84]), and can reduce the effective keyspace of the cipher[Knu93]; related-key differential attacks can cause vulnerabilities in applications where related-key queries are legitimate [KSW96,KSW97]. Weak key classes can mean that a percentage of the keys are vulnerable to attack.

One of the submissions was DEAL (Data Encryption Algorithm with Larger blocks) [Knu98]. Intended as the conservative choice, DEAL was designed to

Howard Heys and Carlisle Adams (Eds.): SAC'99, LNCS 1758, pp. 118–134, 2000.

leverage the cryptographic confidence in DES while creating a new cipher with a 128-bit block and key lengths of 128-, 192-, and 256-bits. In this paper, we refer to DEAL with an n-bit key as DEAL-n. Thus, we have DEAL-128, DEAL-192, and DEAL-256.

In [Luc99], an attack was presented for DEAL-192, with a number of possible tradeoffs given between number of chosen-plaintext queries, and amount of work done for the attack. The best attack in terms of computational resources requires 2^{56} chosen plaintexts, about 2^{146} encryptions' worth of work, and about 2^{63} memory locations. With 2^{40} bits (2^{37} bytes) of memory, Lucks' best attack on DEAL-192 requires 2^{33} chosen plaintexts, and work equivalent to about 6×2^{189} DES encryptions (about 2^{189} DEAL encryptions).

In [Knu98], a number of impractical attacks are discussed on DEAL-192. There is a straightforward meet-in-the-middle attack on DEAL-192 requiring about 2^{168} work and 2^{173} bytes of memory, requiring only three known plaintexts. The memory requirements are totally unreasonable, and trading off time for memory does not yield an attack with reasonable memory requirements and less work than brute-forcing the key. There is also a general attack on 6-round Feistel ciphers with bijective F-functions, based on a 5-round impossible truncated differential. Applying this attack to DEAL-192 gives an attack with 2^{119} work, 2^{70} chosen plaintexts, and 2^{68} bytes of memory. The chosen-plaintext requirements make this attack totally impractical. No attacks on DEAL-256 faster than exhaustive search were discussed.

1.1 Our Results

In this paper, we present the following results against DEAL:

- Equivalent keys for DEAL-192 and DEAL-256, with an algorithm to find them. The algorithm requires about six DES encryptions to find a set of 256 equivalent DEAL-192 keys, and eight DES encryptions to find a set of 256 equivalent DEAL-256 keys.
- Equivalent keys for DEAL-128, with an algorithm to find them. The algorithm requires about 2^{64} work to find a pair of equivalent keys.
- A related-key attack on DEAL-192 and DEAL-256, requiring three plaintexts under 2^{33} keys with a certain relationship, 3×2^{45} bytes of memory, and about 2^{137} DEAL encryptions' work, to find the last two rounds' subkeys for DEAL-192 and DEAL-256. (With more memory, this can be made faster.)
- A number of possible extensions to these attacks. DEAL-192 can be peeled down to four rounds, and then Biham's attack on four-round Ladder-DES can be applied[Bih97]; DEAL-256 can be peeled down to six rounds, and then Lucks' attack on six-round DEAL-192 can be applied. Alternatively, 64 bits can be recovered from the original key, and the remainder brute-force searched.

Importance of the Results. These results have both practical and theoretical interest.

DEAL is likely to see some use in the future in real-world systems. DEAL is an AES candidate, but even if it is not accepted as an AES finalist, it will almost certainly see some use. The general idea behind DEAL is a sound one, and has been proposed several times before [Rit94,Bih97]. As pointed out by Outerbridge at the first AES conference, widespread availability of DES hardware in many different environments makes DEAL relatively easy to implement in many different environments, at very low cost. A system designer in need of a 128-bit block cipher, and in possession of lots of DES-enabled devices, might do well to choose an algorithm like DEAL. (Certainly, he would be better off doing this than trying to design his own cipher from DES.)

In real-world use, the equivalent keys of DEAL have important practical implications–they make many standard hashing modes, e.g. Davies-Meyer mode, unsafe to use[1].

The related-key attacks are probably somewhat less practical, but may still be important in some applications. These attacks have the effect of peeling off the last two rounds of DEAL at the cost of about 2^{137} DEAL encryptions of work, using about 3×2^{45} bytes of memory, and requiring the same three plaintexts be encrypted under 2^{33} related keys. There are various time-memory tradeoffs available.

In the presence of 3×2^{69} bytes of random-access storage, the attack will run with about 2^{113} work, again recovering the last two round subkeys[2]. At that point, Biham's attack on 4-round Ladder-DES [Bih97] can be mounted, requiring another 2^{33} chosen plaintexts (under only one key) and 2^{88} time. The whole attack thus takes about 2^{113} work, 3×2^{69} bytes of random-access storage, 3 known plaintexts encrypted under 2^{33} related keys, and 2^{32} chosen plaintexts under one of those keys, to be selected after the rest of the attack has run its course. This compares with the best previously known attack, which required 2^{119} work, 2^{64} memory, and 2^{70} chosen plaintexts.

On a theoretical level, our results demonstrate an important fact: It is widely assumed that a key schedule that uses strong cryptographic components will, in practice, not be vulnerable to cryptanalysis. This assumption has motivated a number of ciphers' key schedules, including those of Khufu [Mer91], Blowfish [Sch94], and SEAL [RC98]. This assumption, unfortunately, isn't always true. In DEAL, a strong cipher is used in an apparently-reasonable way to process key material. However, the method used leaves the cipher vulnerable to related-key cryptanalysis, as well as allowing the existence of equivalent keys.

1.2 Guide to the Rest of the Paper

The rest of this paper is organized as follows: We first discuss the DEAL cipher and key schedule in the level of detail required for our attacks. We then discuss

---

[1] In [Knu98], it is noted that the slow key schedule of DEAL makes it a poor choice for hashing applications.

[2] This assumes that 3×2^{69} bytes of random-access storage can be found and used efficiently–in practice, this attack is of no practical significance, though variant attacks with lower memory requirements may be.

equivalent keys in DEAL-192 and DEAL-256, both how to find them and how many there appear to be. Next, we discuss equivalent keys in DEAL-128. After that, we discuss related-key differential attacks on DEAL-192 and DEAL-256. We conclude with a summary of our results, and some questions raised by them.

2 The DEAL Cipher and Key Schedule

DEAL is a cipher designed originally by Lars Knudsen [Knu98] and submitted for the AES by Richard Outerbridge. DEAL uses the DES as the round function of a larger balanced Feistel cipher in a Luby-Rackoff construction [LR88].

DEAL works as follows:

Let A, B be the left and right 64-bit halves of the input block, respectively. Let $R_{0..N-1}$ be the round subkeys, which are 64 bit blocks that are used as 56-bit DES keys, by ignoring the parity bits. Encryption is as follows: (Here, we show 8 rounds.)

$$A = A \oplus E_{R_0}(B)$$
$$B = B \oplus E_{R_1}(A)$$
$$A = A \oplus E_{R_2}(B)$$
$$B = B \oplus E_{R_3}(A)$$
$$A = A \oplus E_{R_4}(B)$$
$$B = B \oplus E_{R_5}(A)$$
$$A = A \oplus E_{R_6}(B)$$
$$B = B \oplus E_{R_7}(A).$$

DEAL has 6 rounds for 128- and 192-bit keys, and 8 rounds for 256-bit keys. The key schedule works as follows, where $E(X)$ means X encrypted under a constant key used only for key scheduling, and $K_{0..3}$ are the four 64-bit blocks that make up a 256-bit key. (The key schedules for DEAL-192 and DEAL-128 are very similar to the key schedule shown below for DEAL-256, but with only six round keys generated, and only three or two 64-bit blocks of input key material.)

$$R_0 = E(K_0)$$
$$R_1 = E(K_1 \oplus R_0)$$
$$R_2 = E(K_2 \oplus R_1)$$
$$R_3 = E(K_3 \oplus R_2)$$
$$R_4 = E(K_0 \oplus R_3 \oplus 1)$$
$$R_5 = E(K_1 \oplus R_4 \oplus 2)$$
$$R_6 = E(K_2 \oplus R_5 \oplus 4)$$
$$R_7 = E(K_3 \oplus R_6 \oplus 8).$$

The R_i values are used only as DES keys, and so their parity bits are ignored. This turns out to be very important for our analysis.

3 Equivalent Keys in DEAL-192 and DEAL-256

An encryption algorithm has *equivalent keys* when there are two or more keys, K, K^*, such that $K \neq K^*$ but $E_K(X) = E_{K^*}(X)$ for all X. Equivalent keys can reduce the effective keyspace of an algorithm in some cases, and if pairs of keys can be efficiently found, render the encryption algorithm unsafe to use in hashing modes.

We have an algorithm for finding sets of 256 equivalent keys in DEAL. For a special class of weak keys consisting of 2^{-64} of all keys of length 192 or 256, it is always possible to find sets of 256 equivalent keys. Further, an efficient algorithm exists to find weak keys of this type. Equivalent keys also exist for DEAL-128, but a very different algorithm is needed to find these keys, and they are discussed in the next section.

3.1 The Algorithm to Find Sets of Equivalent Keys

Consider the DEAL key schedule again:

$$R_0 = E(K_0)$$
$$R_1 = E(K_1 \oplus R_0)$$
$$R_2 = E(K_2 \oplus R_1)$$
$$R_3 = E(K_3 \oplus R_2)$$
$$R_4 = E(K_0 \oplus R_3 \oplus 1)$$
$$R_5 = E(K_1 \oplus R_4 \oplus 2)$$
$$R_6 = E(K_2 \oplus R_5 \oplus 4)$$
$$R_7 = E(K_3 \oplus R_6 \oplus 8).$$

Our general strategy will be as follows:

1. Find a "weak key" such that $R_0 = R_3 \oplus 2$ for 192-bit keys, or such that $R_1 = R_5 \oplus 4$.
2. Choose Δ active only in parity bits.
3. Let:

$$K_0^* = K_0$$
$$K_1^* = K_1$$
$$K_2^* = D(R_2 \oplus \Delta) \oplus R_1$$
$$K_3^* = K_3 \oplus \Delta$$

4. The result is a sequence of round subkeys such that:

$$R_0 = R_0^*$$
$$R_1 = R_1^*$$

$$R_2 = R_2^* \oplus \Delta$$
$$R_3 = R_3^*$$
$$R_4 = R_4^*$$
$$R_5 = R_5^*$$
$$R_6 = R_6^* \oplus \Delta$$
$$R_7 = R_7^*$$

We choose K_2^*, K_3^* as:

$$K_3^* = K_3 \oplus \Delta$$
$$K_2^* = D(R_2 \oplus \Delta) \oplus R_1$$

This gives us a pair of equivalent keys:

$$(K_0, K_1, K_2, K_3)(K_0, K_1, K_2^*, K_3^*).$$

In fact, for each Δ satisfying the above-mentioned requirements, we get a key equivalent to (K_0, K_1, K_2, K_3). The result is that we get a family of 256 equivalent keys, since there are 256 Δ values (including zero) that satisfy the requirements for Δ to be active only in parity bits.)

3.2 Why It Works

Let's consider the values of subkeys between the two related keys: overflowing as the equation was long. Had to seperate them. (K_0, K_1, K_2, K_3), (K_0, K_1, K_2^*, K_3^*)

Recall that:

$$R_1 = R_5 \oplus 4$$
$$K_3^* = K_3 \oplus \Delta$$
$$K_2^* = D(R_2 \oplus \Delta) \oplus R_1$$

Also, recall that $R_i \oplus \Delta$ is equivalent to R_i, so long as Δ is active only in its parity bits.

1. There is no change in K_0, K_1, so there can be no change in R_0, R_1. That is,

We know that:
$$K_0 = K_0^*$$
$$K_1 = K_1^*$$
Therefore:
$$R_0 = R_0^*$$
$$R_1 = R_1^*$$

2. $R_2 = R_2^* \oplus \Delta$ because

We know that:
$$K_2^* = D(R_2 \oplus \Delta) \oplus R_1$$
$$R_2 = E(K_2 \oplus R_1)$$
Therefore:
$$R_2^* = E(K_2^* \oplus R_1^*)$$
$$= E(D(R_2 \oplus \Delta) \oplus R_1 \oplus R_1)$$
$$= E(D(R_2 \oplus \Delta))$$
$$= R_2 \oplus \Delta$$

3. $R_3 = R_3^*$ because:

We know that:
$$K_3^* = K_3 \oplus \Delta$$
$$R_3 = E(K_3 \oplus R_2)$$
$$R_2^* = R_2 \oplus \Delta$$
Therefore:
$$R_3^* = E(K_3^* \oplus R_2^*)$$
$$= E(K_3 \oplus \Delta \oplus R_2 \oplus \Delta)$$
$$= E(K_3 \oplus R_2)$$
$$= R_3.$$

4. R_4 and R_5 are unchanged, (that is, $R_4 = R_4^*, R_5 = R_5^*$) because R_4, R_5 are dependent only upon $K_0, K_1, and R_3$, and we have already established that those values are all unchanged.

$$R_4 = E(K_0 \oplus R_3 \oplus 1)$$
$$= R_4^*$$
$$R_5 = E(K_1 \oplus R_4 \oplus 2)$$
$$= R_5^*$$

5. $R_6 = R_6^* \oplus \Delta$, because

We know that:
$$R_5 = R_1 \oplus 4$$
$$R_1 = R_1^*$$
$$R_5 = R_5^*$$
$$R_6 = E(K_2 \oplus R_5 \oplus 4)$$

$$= E(K_2 \oplus R_1 \oplus 4 \oplus 4)$$
$$= E(K_2 \oplus R_1)$$
$$= R_2$$

Therefore:
$$R_6^* = E(K_2^* \oplus R_5 \oplus 4)$$
$$= E(K_2^* \oplus R_1)$$
$$= R_2^*$$
$$= R_2 \oplus \Delta$$

And thus:
$$R_6^* = R_6 \oplus \Delta$$

6. Finally, $R_7 = R_7^*$ because

We know that:
$$R_7 = E(K_3 \oplus R_6 \oplus 8)$$
$$R_6^* = R_6 \oplus \Delta$$
$$K_3 = K_3^* \oplus \Delta$$

Therefore:
$$R_7^* = E(K_3^* \oplus R_6^* \oplus 8)$$
$$= E(K_3 \oplus \Delta \oplus R_6 \oplus \Delta \oplus 8)$$
$$= E(K_3 \oplus R_6 \oplus 8)$$
$$= R_7$$

3.3 Effect on the DEAL Keyspace

This set of equivalent keys has essentially no effect on the size of the effective keyspace, since it applies only to such a tiny fraction (about $3 * 2^{-64}$) of special keys.

3.4 Extensions

A variant of the same algorithm works with K_1, K_2 or K_0, K_1 as the active pair of key blocks. A variant of the algorithm can be carried out against DEAL-192. Against DEAL-128, a much more complex algorithm can be used to find equivalent keys, as will be discussed later in this paper.

3.5 Efficiently Finding Equivalent Keys

The naive algorithm for finding equivalent keys would be to try about 2^{64} different keys, waiting until $R_1 = R_5 \oplus 4$. This has complexity 2^{64}, and thus is no easier than looking for a collision in a 128-bit hash function, such as might be built from DEAL in Davies-Meyer hashing mode. However, the search for a class 256 of equivalent keys can be converted to a straightforward algebra problem, as follows:

1. Choose $K_{0,1,2}$ arbitrarily.
2. Derive:

$$R_0 = E(K_0)$$
$$R_1 = E(K_1 \oplus R_0)$$
$$R_2 = E(K_2 \oplus R_1)$$

3. Use the requirement that $R_5 = R_1 \oplus 4$ to derive:

$$R_5 = R_1 \oplus 4$$
$$= E(K_1 \oplus R_4 \oplus 2)$$

Thus:

$$R_4 = D(R_5) \oplus K_1 \oplus 2$$

4. Having learned R_4, we next compute R_3, and thus K_3:

$$R_4 = E(R_3 \oplus K_0 \oplus 1)$$
$$= D(R_5) \oplus K_1 \oplus 2$$

Thus:

$$R_3 = D(D(R_5) \oplus K_1 \oplus 2) \oplus K_0 \oplus 1$$
$$= E(R_2 \oplus K_3)$$

Thus:

$$K_3 = D(R_3) \oplus R_2$$
$$= D(D(D(R_5) \oplus K_1 \oplus 2) \oplus K_0 \oplus 1) \oplus R_2$$

5. With $K_{0,1,2,3}$, we now have a "weak" key.

The process is nearly identical with DEAL-192.

4   Finding Equivalent Keys in DEAL-128

In this section[3], we discuss an algorithm for finding equivalent keys in DEAL-128. Unlike the previous algorithm, this does not find classes of 256 equivalent keys, but instead pairs of equivalent keys. Also unlike the previous algorithm, this algorithm requires about 2^{64} runs of the DEAL key schedule to find a single pair of equivalent keys.

---

[3] We are indebted to David Wagner for pointing out the possibility of finding equivalent keys in DEAL-128, and proposing another, earlier method for finding them.

4.1 An Overview of Our Method

The goal is to find a pair of keys, K, K^*, such that $R_{0..5}$ and $R_{0..5}^*$ are all either equal or equivalent (equal in all bits except their parity bits, which will be ignored by the DES key schedule).

4.2 The Algorithm

1. For each Δ active only in parity bits:
   (a) For each K_0 value from 0 to $2^{64} - 1$:
       i. Compute $K_0^* = D(E(K_0) \oplus \Delta)$
       ii. Compute $K_1 = D(1) \oplus E(K_0)$
       iii. Compute $K_1^* = K_1 \oplus \Delta$
       iv. Use $K_{0,1}$ to compute $R_{0..5}$, and $K_{0,1}^*$ to compute $R_{0..5}^*$.
       v. Note that $R_{0..3}$ and $R_{0..3}^*$ are now equivalent:

$$R_0 = R_0^* \oplus \Delta$$
$$R_1 = R_1^*$$
$$R_2 = R_2^* \oplus \Delta$$
$$R_3 = R_3^*$$

       vi. Check to see whether $R_4 \oplus R_4^* = \Delta$ This should happen with probability 2^{-64}
       vii. If so, we're done; R_5 will also equal R_5^*. If not, we must keep looking.

4.3 Why It Works

1. $R_0 = R_0^* \oplus \Delta$ because

We know that:
$$K_0^* = D(E(K_0) \oplus \Delta)$$
$$R_0 = E(K_0)$$
Therefore:
$$R_0^* = E(K_0^*)$$
$$= E(D(E(K_0) \oplus \Delta))$$
$$= E(K0) \oplus \Delta$$
$$= R_0 \oplus \Delta$$

2. $R_1^* = R_1$ because:

We know that:
$$K_1^* = K_1 \oplus \Delta$$
$$R_0^* = R_0 \oplus \Delta$$

$$R_1 = E(R_0 \oplus K_1)$$

Therefore:

$$R_1^* = E(R_0^* \oplus K_1^*)$$
$$= E(R_0 \oplus \Delta \oplus K_1 \oplus \Delta)$$
$$= E(R_0 \oplus K_1)$$
$$= R_1$$

3. $R_1 = 1$, because

We know that:

$$K_1 = D(1) \oplus E(K_0)$$
$$= D(1) \oplus R_0$$

Therefore:

$$R_1 = E(R_0 \oplus K_1)$$
$$= E(R_0 \oplus E(K_0) \oplus D(1))$$
$$= E(R_0 \oplus R_0 \oplus D(1))$$
$$= E(D(1))$$
$$= 1$$

4. $R_1 = 1$ is necessary so that $R_2^* = R_2 \oplus \Delta$:

We know that:

$$R_0^* = E(K_0^*)$$
$$= R_0^*$$
$$R_1 = 1$$
$$= R_1^*$$
$$R_2 = E(R_1 \oplus 1 \oplus K_0)$$
$$= E(K_0)$$
$$= R_0$$

Therefore:

$$R_2^* = E(R_1^* \oplus 1 \oplus K_0^*)$$
$$= E(R_1 \oplus 1 \oplus K_0^*)$$
$$= E(K_0^*)$$
$$= R_0^*$$
$$= R_0 \oplus \Delta$$
$$= R_2 \oplus \Delta$$

5. $R_3^* = R_3$ because

We know that
$$R_2^* = R_2 \oplus \Delta$$
$$K_1^* = K_1 \oplus \Delta$$

Therefore:
$$\begin{aligned} R_3^* &= E(R_2^* \oplus 2 \oplus K_1^*) \\ &= E(R_2 \oplus \Delta \oplus 2 \oplus K_1 \oplus \Delta) \\ &= E(R_2 \oplus 2 \oplus K_1) \\ &= R_3 \end{aligned}$$

6. We keep trying different values for (K_0, K_1) until we see $R_4^* = R_4 \oplus \Delta$.
7. $R_5^* = R_5$ because

We know that:
$$R_4^* = R_4 \oplus \Delta$$
$$K_1^* = K_1 \oplus \Delta$$

Therefore:
$$\begin{aligned} R_5^* &= E(R_4^* \oplus 8 \oplus K_1^*) \\ &= E(R_4 \oplus d \oplus 8 \oplus K_1 \oplus \Delta) \\ &= E(R_4 \oplus 8 \oplus K_1) \\ &= R_5 \end{aligned}$$

5 Related-Key Attacks on DEAL-256 and DEAL-192

Consider the algorithm for finding equivalent keys in DEAL-256. If we applied the algorithm without the special key property that $R_1 = R_5 \oplus 4$, we would end up with *nearly equivalent* keys: key with the same subkeys for all but the last two rounds. We could then mount an attack based on this fact, given encryptions from the two keys.

Here, we will discuss a related-key attack based on finding a pair of nearly-equivalent keys. We will discuss several issues with this attack, and then present the whole attack:

- How to detect that we have a pair of nearly-equivalent keys.
- How to use detection to learn information about the key.
- How to extract the last two rounds' subkeys when this property holds.
- How to mount the full attack.

5.1 Detecting Nearly-Equivalent Keys

Given three plaintext/ciphertext pairs from a pair of keys, (K, K^*) believed to be nearly-equivalent, we can determine whether they have this property with very high probability of being right, at the cost of about 2^{64} work and about 3×2^{56} memory locations. We mount something very similar to the meet-in-the-middle attack on double DES encryption.

Consider one text, broken into two 64-bit halves, (A_0, B_0). All but the last two rounds of encryption are identical between the keys, so after the identical rounds, we get (C_0, D_0) for this plaintext under both keys. The last two rounds are different, so we get (Y_0, Z_0) from K, and (Y_0*, Z_0*) from K^*.

Note that:

$$Z_0 = D_0 \oplus E_{R_7}(Y_0)$$
$$Z_0* = D_0 \oplus E_{R_7^*}(Y_0*).$$

We know three plaintext,ciphertext pairs, so we know three different sets of Y_0, Y_0*, and Z_0, Z_0* values. We can mount a DES keysearch effort on R_7 and R_7^*. We try all 2^{56} possible values of R_7, and for each one, we get candidate D_0 values from all three plaintexts. We do the same for all possible values of R_7^*. We get two tables of 2^{56} different 192-bit values, which must be sorted. We then find the matches between the two tables. For 192-bit keys, the keysearch would be on R_5 and R_5^*.

If we find a pair of matching values, it is overwhelmingly likely that we have found the right values for R_7, R_7^* (or R_5, R_5^*).

This shows how to determine whether a pair of keys is nearly-equivalent, but not how to find which pair in a batch of 2^{33} of them is nearly-equivalent.

Imagine a situation in which we had unlimited memory resources. We could do the same kind of meet-in-the-middle computation described above, but on all 2^{33} keys. This would take $2^{56} \times 2^{33} = 2^{89}$ encryptions, 89×2^{89} swap operations, and about 2^{95} bytes of memory. At the end, we would sweep through the 2^{89} 192-bit blocks computed from three ciphertexts under each key, and look for duplicates. We would not expect to see any duplicates (though it wouldn't be totally surprising to see them) unless there is a pair of nearly-equivalent keys. Any duplicates that came either from the same key, or from keys with the same Δ value would simply be ignored.

In practice, we have limited memory resources, and so we consider time-memory tradeoffs.

The time-memory tradeoffs available here can be summarized as follows [4]:

Memory (bytes)	Work (DES encryptions)	Updated
3×2^{69}	2^{113}	
3×2^{61}	2^{121}	
3×2^{53}	2^{129}	
3×2^{45}	2^{137}	
3×2^{37}	2^{145}	

5.2 Extracting the Rest of the Key

Once we know R_7, R_7^*, we can mount the same kind of attack to get R_6, R_6^*. We have then peeled off the last two rounds, and have a six-round cipher remaining to attack. (In the case of DEAL-192, we have a four-round cipher remaining to attack.) In the case of DEAL-256, knowing R_6 and R_7 allows us to find K_3. In the case of DEAL-192, knowing R_4 and R_5 allows us to find K_2. This leaves us with a 192-bit search to break DEAL-256, or a 128-bit search to break DEAL-192.

5.3 Selecting the Keys

Let K be the original key. Let K_i be the ith additional key requested. We request Δ keys such that:

- Start with initial targeted key, K, and Δ active in parity bits only.
- For $i = 0$ to 255, do
  - Let Δ_j = next delta active in parity bits only.
  - For $j = 0$ to 2^{25}, do

$$K[0]_i = K[0]$$
$$K[1]_i = K[1] \oplus Random\_Block_j$$
$$K[2]_i = K[2] \oplus \Delta_i$$

$$R_2[i] = R_2[j] \oplus \Delta.$$

by the birthday paradox. So, we will have Δ pairs of keys to test, of which we expect one pair to be nearly-equivalent.

---

[4] These computational cost estimates assume memory available with no additional costs for random accesses. If the attack were implemented with tape memory, for example, then the actual time taken for the attack would go up substantially.

5.4 The Full Attack

The full attack is thus carried out as follows:

1. We request 2^{33} related keys according to the pattern described above. We expect one pair of these keys to be nearly-equivalent, but we don't yet know which pair.

2. We request the same three chosen plaintexts to be encrypted under each key. (We don't have to be able to choose anything about them, but the same three plaintexts must be encrypted under each key.)

3. We apply our test to the whole set of ciphertexts from the related keys. Given 3×2^{45} bytes of memory, we will have to carry out 2^{137} DES encryptions.

4. Let K, K^* be the pair of nearly-equivalent keys, which we have now detected. In detecting the property, we have learned the last round's subkey. We now apply the same meet-in-the-middle attack to find the next-to-last round's subkey. (In DEAL-256, this is R_6; in DEAL-192, this is R_4.)

5. We may now either apply some other attack on the cipher with two fewer rounds, or we may use knowledge of the last two rounds' subkeys to learn 64 bits of the input key, and then brute-force the remaining key.

6. Assuming we just brute-force the remaining key, the attacks on DEAL-192 and DEAL-256 both require 2^{33} related-key queries, the same three chosen-plaintexts requested under each key, and 3×2^{53} bytes of memory. The attack on DEAL-192 then requires 2^{129} work, and the attack on DEAL-256 requires 2^{192} work.

7. There may be improved attacks that exploit weaknesses in four- or six-round DEAL once we have discovered the last two round keys. For example, Biham's attack against Ladder-DES can also be applied to DEAL-192, once the last two rounds have been peeled off.

6 Conclusions

In this paper, we have demonstrated a weakness in the key schedule of DEAL, leading to both equivalent keys and vulnerability to related-key attacks. While the related-key attacks are of primarily academic interest (requiring 2^{128} DEAL encryptions worth of work for the cheapest attack), the equivalent keys are of immediate interest for anyone using DEAL in certain hashing modes. The important lessons we draw from this analysis are:

1. Simply using a cryptographic primitive in a reasonable-looking way to design a key schedule does not guarantee resistance to attacks on the key schedule.

2. In the specific case of DEAL, ignoring the parity bits of the keys sent in allowed nearly-equivalent keys to be found. A special class of keys were then found for which, instead of nearly-equivalent keys, these keys would be equivalent. Had those bits been immediately used, our attacks would not work.

Unfortunately, we don't have a general design principle we can pull out of this analysis; designing key schedules is hard, and there aren't any sure-fire shortcuts. This is borne out by the long list of AES candidates cryptanalyzed based on their key schedules which appears in the introduction.

6.1 Open Questions

A number of questions are raised by this research:

1. Are there key schedules we can build from cryptographic mechanisms that are provably secure against various forms of attack?
2. In the absence of these, can we at least find some useful design principles for cryptographic key schedules?
3. Are there similar attacks on other cryptographic key schedules, e.g., those of Khufu, Blowfish, and SEAL?

Acknowledgements

Thanks to David Wagner, Stefan Lucks, Ron Rivest, Adi Shamir, Richard Outerbridge, and Eli Biham for useful questions and comments during and after the FSE '99 rump session in Rome. Thanks to the anonymous referees for useful comments on the original submission of this paper.

References

BBF+99. B. Biham, A. Biryukov, N. Ferguson, L. Knudsen, B. Schneier, and A. Shamir, "Cryptanalysis of Magenta," *Second AES Candidate Conference*, Mar 99.

BCD+98. C. Burwick, D. Coppersmith, E. D'Avignon, R. Gennaro, S. Halevi, C. Jutla, S.M. Matyas, L. O'Connor, M. Peyravian, D. Safford, and N. Zunic, "MARS — A Candidate Cipher for AES," NIST AES Proposal, Jun 98.

Bih94. E. Biham, "New Types of Cryptanalytic Attacks Using Related Keys," *Journal of Cryptology*, v. 7, n. 4, 1994, pp. 229–246.

Bih97. E. Biham, "Cryptanalysis of Ladder-DES," *Fast Software Encryption, Fourth International Workshop*, Springer-Verlag, 1997.

Bor99. J. Borst, "Weak Keys of Crypton," *Second AES Candidate Conference*, rump session presentation, Mar 99.

CMK+98. L. Chen, J.L. Massey, G.H. Khachatrian, and M.K. Kuregian, "Nomination of SAFER+ as Candidate Algorithm for the Advanced Encryption Standard (AES)," NIST AES Proposal, Jun 98.

Cop98a. D. Coppersmith, "DFC Weak Keys," Note to NIST AES Discussion Group, 10 Sep 98.

Cop98b. D. Coppersmith, "Re: DFC Weak Keys," Note to NIST AES Discussion Group, 22 Oct 98.

DBP+99. C. D'Halluin, G. Bijnens, B. Preneel, V. Rijmen, "Equivalent keys of HPC, draft paper, 1999. Available online at:
http://www.esat.kuleuven.ac.be/~cosicart/ps/VR-9900.ps.gz

GGH+98. H. Gilbert, M. Girault, P. Hoogvorst, F. Noilhan, T. Pornin, G. Poupard, J. Stern, and S. Vaudenay, "Decorrelated Fast Cipher: an AES Candidate," NIST AES Proposal, Jun 98.

GLC98. D. Georgoudis, D. Lerous, and B.S. Chaves, "The 'Frog' Encryption Algorithm," NIST AES Proposal, Jun 98.

JH98. M.J. Jacobson and K. Huber, "The MAGENTA Block Cipher Algorithm," NIST AES Proposal, Jun 98.

KSW96. J. Kelsey, B. Schneier, and D. Wagner, "Key-Schedule Cryptanalysis of IDEA, G-DES, GOST, SAFER, and Triple-DES," *Advances in Cryptology — CRYPTO '96 Proceedings*, Springer-Verlag, 1996, pp. 237–251.

KSW97. J. Kelsey, B. Schneier, and D. Wagner, "Related-Key Cryptanalysis of 3-WAY, Biham-DES, CAST, DES-X, NewDES, RC2, and TEA," *Information and Communications Security, First International Conference Proceedings*, Springer-Verlag, 1997, pp. 203–207.

KSW99. J. Kelsey, B. Schneier, and D. Wagner "Key Schedule Weaknesses in SAFER+," *Second AES Candidate Conference*, Mar 99.

Knu93. L. Knudsen, "Cryptanalysis of LOKI '91," *Advances in Cryptography — AUSCRYPT '92 Proceedings*, Springer-Verlag, 1993.

Knu98. L Knudsen, "DEAL — A 128-bit Block Cipher," NIST AES Proposal, Jun 98.

Lim98. C.H. Lim, "CRYPTON: A New 128-bit Block Cipher," NIST AES Proposal, Jun 98.

LR88. M. Luby, and C. Rackoff, "How to construct pseudorandom permutations from pseudorandom functions," SIAM Journal of Computing, 17: #2, 373-386, 1988.

Luc99. S. Lucks, "On the Security of the 128-bit Block Cipher DEAL," *Fast Software Encryption, Sixth International Workshop*, Springer-Verlag, 1999, to appear.

Mer91. R.C. Merkle, "Fast Software Encryption Functions," *Advances in Cryptology — CRYPTO '90 Proceedings*, Springer-Verlag, 1991, pp. 476–501.

RC98. P. Rogaway and D. Coppersmith, "A Software-Optimized Encryption Algorithm," *Journal of Cryptology*, v. 11, n. 4, 1998, pp. 273–287.

Rit94. T. Ritter, *Ladder-DES: A Proposed Candidate to Replace DES,* appeared in the Usenet newsgroup sci.crypt, Feb 1994.

RRS+98. R. Rivest, M. Robshaw, R. Sidney, and Y.L. Yin, "The RC6 Block Cipher," NIST AES Proposal, Jun 98.

Saa99. M. Saarinen, "A Note Regarding the Hash Function Use of MARS and RC6," available online from http://www.jyu.fi/~mjos/, 1999.

Sch94. B. Schneier, "Description of a New Variable-Length Key, 64-Bit Block Cipher (Blowfish)," *Fast Software Encryption, Cambridge Security Workshop Proceedings*, Springer-Verlag, 1994, pp. 191–204.

Sch98. R. Schroeppel "Hasty Pudding Cipher Specification," NIST AES Proposal, Jun 98.

Wag99. D. Wagner, "Equivalent keys for HPC," *Second AES Candidate Conference*, rump session presentation, Mar 99.

WFS99. D. Wagner, N. Ferguson, and B. Schneier, "Cryptanalysis of FROG," *Second AES Candidate Conference*, Mar 99.

Win84. R.S. Winternitz, "Producing One-Way Hash Functions from DES," *Advances in Cryptology: Proceedings of Crypto 83*, Plenum Press, 1984, pp. 203–207.

Efficient Evaluation of Security against Generalized Interpolation Attack

Kazumaro Aoki

NTT Laboratories
1-1 Hikarinooka, Yokosuka-shi, Kanagawa-ken, 239-0847 Japan
maro@isl.ntt.co.jp

Abstract. Interpolation attack was presented by Jakobsen and Knudsen at FSE'97. Interpolation attack is effective against ciphers that have a certain algebraic structure like the $\mathcal{PURE}$ cipher which is a prototype cipher, but it is difficult to apply the attack to real-world ciphers. This difficulty is due to the difficulty of deriving a low degree polynomial relation between ciphertexts and plaintexts. In other words, it is difficult to evaluate the security against interpolation attack. This paper generalizes the interpolation attack. The generalization makes easier to evaluate the security against interpolation attack. We call the generalized interpolation attack *linear sum attack*. We present an algorithm that efficiently evaluates the security of byte-oriented ciphers against linear sum attack. Moreover, we show the relationship between linear sum attack and higher order differential attack. In addition, we show the security of CRYPTON, E2, and RIJNDAEL against linear sum attack using the algorithm.

1 Introduction

Interpolation attack [4] was presented for attacking the $\mathcal{PURE}$ cipher [14,4], though the $\mathcal{PURE}$ cipher is provably secure [14,13] against differential cryptanalysis [1] and linear cryptanalysis [8]. The basic idea of interpolation attack is as follows: First, the attack focuses on the algebraic structure in the cipher. Next, the attack tries to express ciphertexts using a polynomial of a plaintext. The applicability of the attack is determined by the degree of the polynomial above, more precisely, by the number of the unknown coefficients of the polynomial.

It is easy to find the degree of the polynomial for the $\mathcal{PURE}$ cipher since the non-linear operation in the $\mathcal{PURE}$ cipher is only a cubic operation in $GF(2^n)$. However, it is basically difficult to find the degree for real-world ciphers. We know of only two examples of successful interpolation attacks against ciphers. One is an attack [4] on a modified version of SHARK [15]. The other is an attack [10] on SNAKE [6]. The non-linear operation of both ciphers is an inversion in $GF(2^n)$, which is also a simple operation in $GF(2^n)$. On the other hand, nobody knows a cipher which is provably secure against interpolation attack.

First, this paper introduces the concept of linear sum attack, a generalization of interpolation attack. Introducing linear sum attack leads to a clear vista on studying the security against interpolation attack. Next, the paper proposes an

Howard Heys and Carlisle Adams (Eds.): SAC'99, LNCS 1758, pp. 135–146, 2000.

effective algorithm which judges whether linear sum attack is applicable or not for a given cipher. Moreover, we show a relationship between linear sum attack and higher order differential attack [5,4]; provable security against linear sum attack implies provable security against higher order differential attack. Finally, we evaluate the security of CRYPTON [7], E2 [11], and RIJNDAEL [3] against linear sum attack using the security evaluation algorithm for linear sum attack.

2 Preliminaries

2.1 Notations and Analysis Target

This paper studies the following situation. Let p be a plaintext and c be a ciphertext. Let $c = E_k(p)$ be a block cipher whose block is n-bits long with a product structure. The encryption key k is in the set $K\ (= \{k_1, k_2, \ldots, k_L\})$. $E_k(p)$ consists of R round functions $F_{k^{(r)}}$ $(r = 1, 2, \ldots, R)$ as follows:

$$E_k(p) = (F_{k^{(R)}} \circ F_{k^{(R-1)}} \circ \cdots \circ F_{k^{(1)}})(p) \ ,$$

where $k^{(r)}$ is the rth round subkey, generated from k by a key scheduling algorithm.

We define $\tilde{c}$ as the input of the last round,

$$\tilde{c} = F^{-1}_{k^{(R)}}(c) = \tilde{E}_k(p) = (F_{k^{(R-1)}} \circ F_{k^{(R-2)}} \circ \cdots \circ F_{k^{(1)}})(p) \ .$$

Moreover, we consider the following maps used in the interpolation attack (see Fig. 1)

$$\begin{aligned} \mathsf{p} &: \mathrm{GF}(q) \to \mathrm{GF}(2)^n \\ \tilde{\mathsf{c}}' &: \mathrm{GF}(2)^n \to \mathrm{GF}(q) \ , \end{aligned}$$

where $\mathrm{GF}(q)$ is a finite field that contains q elements. This paper considers interpolation attacks using polynomials in $\mathrm{GF}(q)$. Note that we do not assume that q is a power of 2 and p and c' are bijective.

$$\begin{array}{ccccc} \text{plaintext: } \mathrm{GF}(2)^n & \xrightarrow{\tilde{E}_k} & \mathrm{GF}(2)^n & \xrightarrow{F_{k^{(R)}}} & \mathrm{GF}(2)^n\text{: ciphertext} \\ \mathsf{p} \uparrow & & \downarrow \tilde{\mathsf{c}}' & & \\ \mathrm{GF}(q) & \overset{f_k}{\rightsquigarrow} & \mathrm{GF}(q) & & \end{array}$$

Fig. 1. Attack diagram

2.2 Interpolation Attack

Although several types of interpolation attack are known, this section describes the basic interpolation attack. If the reader is not familiar with interpolation attack, please refer to [4].

An outline of the attack is as follows.

Preparation: Find p and $\tilde{c}'$ that satisfy

$$\tilde{c}'(\tilde{E}_k(\mathsf{p}(x))) = f_k(x) \in \mathrm{GF}(q)[x] \ ,$$

by analyzing the target cipher. Let N be the number of the unknown coefficients of the polynomial $f_k(x)$.

Attack:

Step 1: Obtain $N+1$ ciphertexts $c = E_k(\mathsf{p}(x))$ that are derived from the chosen plaintexts $\mathsf{p}(x)$ ($x \in \mathrm{GF}(q)$).

Step 2: Guess $k^{(R)}$ using exhaustive search.

2-1: Calculate $\tilde{c} = F_{k^{(R)}}^{-1}(c)$ from obtained c and guessed $k^{(R)}$ to decrypt 1 round.

2-2: Find $f_k(x)$ from N pairs of $(x, \tilde{c}'(\tilde{c}))$ using polynomial interpolation.

2-3: Verify the correctness of $f_k(x)$ derived in Step 2-2 using a pair of $(x, \tilde{c}'(\tilde{c}))$ not used in Step 2-2.

This interpolation attack can be applied if $N < q$ holds. However, it is very difficult to estimate N precisely for a real-world cipher. We give an answer to solve the problem in the following sections.

3 Linear Sum Attack

Consider the interpolation attack replacing the polynomial interpolation with Gaussian elimination in Step 2-2 described in Sect. 2.2. In this case, we can attack a cipher in the same way even if $f_k(x)$ is represented by a linear sum of linearly independent polynomials $b_i(x) \in \mathrm{GF}(q)[x]$ as in

$$f_k(x) = \sum_{i=1}^{q} a_i(k)b_i(x) \quad (a_i(k) \in \mathrm{GF}(q)) \ .$$

We call this attack the *linear sum attack*.

The attack succeeds if the number of unknown $a_i(k)$s is less than q. We estimate the worst case complexity. The number of chosen plaintexts is at most q. The attack requires Gaussian eliminations corresponding to all possible values of $k^{(R)}$. It is well known that Gaussian elimination requires $O(q^3)$ arithmetic operations in $\mathrm{GF}(q)$. So, the attack requires $O(Lq^3)$ arithmetic operations in $\mathrm{GF}(q)$ and L evaluations of F^{-1}.

Linear sum attack is equivalent to interpolation attack, if $b_i(x) = x^{i-1}$ holds, that is $b_i(x)$ is a monomial. Consider the case of $f_k(x) = g(k) \cdot x^1 + 2g(k) \cdot 1$, for example. If we apply interpolation attack described in Sect. 2.2, we need 3 chosen plaintexts since the number of unknown coefficients is 2, which are $g(k)$ and $2g(k)$. On the other hand, applying linear sum attack, we can factorize the polynomial to $f_k(x) = g(k) \cdot (x + 2)$. This means that we need only 2 chosen plaintexts, since the number of unknown coefficients is 1, which is $g(k)$. As shown by this example, linear sum attack requires less or equal number of chosen plaintexts than interpolation attack.

4 Search for Effective Basis

This section discusses how to find an effective basis $\{b_1(x), b_2(x), \ldots, b_q(x)\}$ for linear sum attack. Linear sum attack requires a basis while interpolation attack requires a polynomial expression of ciphertexts, where we regard a plaintext as a variable for interpolation attack. This section introduces an effective search algorithm for finding an effective basis.

We focus on the following properties of $\mathrm{GF}(q)$.

1. Any function over $\mathrm{GF}(q)$ can be expressed by a polynomial over $\mathrm{GF}(q)$.
2. The set of all functions over $\mathrm{GF}(q)$ is a q-dimensional vector space, $\mathrm{GF}(q)[x]^1$.
3. Any polynomial over $\mathrm{GF}(q)$ can be expressed by a linear sum of a basis $\{b_1(x), b_2(x), \ldots, b_q(x)\}$, where $b_i(x) \in \mathrm{GF}(q)[x]$ $(i = 1, 2, \ldots, q)$.

Using the above facts, we developed an algorithm for finding a basis $\{b_1(x), b_2(x), \ldots, b_q(x)\}$ so that $f_k(x) = \tilde{c}'(\tilde{E}_k(\mathsf{p}(x)))$ has the fewest unknown coefficients when $f_k(x)$ is expressed by a linear sum using the basis.

Assume that $f_k(x)$ is expressed as

$$f_k(x) = \sum_{i=1}^{q} a_i(k)b_i(x) \quad (a_i(k) \in \mathrm{GF}(q)) \ .$$

The smallest number of unknown coefficients we want to find is

$$N = \mathrm{rank} \begin{bmatrix} a_1(k_1) \ a_2(k_1) \ \cdots \ a_q(k_1) \\ a_1(k_2) \ a_2(k_2) \ \cdots \ a_q(k_2) \\ \ldots\ldots \ \ldots\ldots \ \ldots \ \ldots\ldots \\ a_1(k_L) \ a_2(k_L) \ \cdots \ a_q(k_L) \end{bmatrix} \ .$$

It is practically impossible to calculate the rank described above for all bases and for all keys $k_1, k_2, \ldots, k_L$, since the complexity exceeds an exhaustive search for a key. We solve the problem by the following theorems.

Theorem 1. *The expectation of d is less than $q + 2$, where d is defined as*

$$\dim_{\mathrm{GF}(q)} \langle v_1, v_2, \ldots, v_d \rangle = q \ ,$$

for randomly chosen v_i in the q-dimensional vector space over $\mathrm{GF}(q)$.

---

[1] For simple description, we use $\mathrm{GF}(q)[x]$ for $\mathrm{GF}(q)[x]/(x^q - x)$.

Proof. Since a randomly chosen element in the q-dimensional vector space over GF(q) is contained in a particular i-dimensional ($i \leq q$) subspace with probability $\dfrac{q^i}{q^q}$, we need to choose, on average, $\dfrac{1}{1 - \frac{q^i}{q^q}}$ elements in order to find one that is not in the subspace. Thus, the expectation of d can be evaluated as follows.

$$\sum_{i=0}^{q-1} \frac{1}{1 - \frac{q^i}{q^q}} = \sum_{i=0}^{q-1}\left(1 + \frac{q^i}{q^q - q^i}\right) = q + \sum_{i=1}^{q} \frac{1}{q^i - 1}$$

$$\leq q + \frac{1}{q - 1} + \sum_{i=2}^{q} \frac{1}{q^{i-1}} = q + \frac{2 - (\frac{1}{q})^{q-1}}{q - 1}$$

$$\leq q + 2$$

$\square$

Theorem 2. $q + r$ $(r \geq 0)$ *randomly chosen vectors in the q-dimensional vector space over* GF(q) *span at least the $(q - 1)$-dimensional subspace with probability at most q^{-r}.*

Proof.

$$\Pr_{v_1, v_2, \ldots, v_{q+r}} [\dim_{\mathrm{GF}(q)} \langle v_1, v_2, \ldots, v_{q+r} \rangle \leq q - 1]$$

$$= \sum_{i=0}^{q-1} \Pr_{v_1, v_2, \ldots, v_{q+r}} [\dim_{\mathrm{GF}(q)} \langle v_1, v_2, \ldots, v_{q+r} \rangle = i]$$

Since the dimension of the vector space $\langle v_1, v_2, \ldots, v_{q+r} \rangle$ is i, we can choose i vectors which span the i-dimensional vector space from $\{v_1, v_2, \ldots, v_{q+r}\}$. We assume $\dim_{\mathrm{GF}(q)} \langle v_1, v_2, \ldots, v_i \rangle = i$ without loss of generality.

$$\sum_{i=0}^{q-1} \Pr_{v_1, v_2, \ldots, v_{q+r}} [\dim_{\mathrm{GF}(q)} \langle v_1, v_2, \ldots, v_{q+r} \rangle = i]$$

$$= \sum_{i=0}^{q-1} \Pr_{v_1, v_2, \ldots, v_{q+r}} [\{v_{i+1}, v_{i+2}, \ldots, v_{q+r}\} \subseteq \langle v_1, v_2, \ldots, v_i \rangle]$$

$$= \sum_{i=0}^{q-1} \left(\frac{q^i}{q^q}\right)^{q+r-(i+1)+1}$$

$$= \sum_{i=0}^{q-1} q^{-(q-i)(q+r-i)}$$

$$\leq q \cdot q^{-(q-(q-1))(q+r-(q-1))}$$

$$= q^{-r}$$

$\square$

> **Corollary 3.** $q + r$ $(r \geq 0)$ *randomly chosen vectors in the q-dimensional vector space over* $\mathrm{GF}(q)$ *span the q-dimensional subspace with probability at least* $1 - q^{-r}$.

Assume that $f_k(x)$ is random in $\mathrm{GF}(q)[x]$ if we randomly choose k. Then, according to Theorem 1 and Corollary 3, it is sufficient to calculate N, i.e. the rank, using $q + 2$ randomly chosen keys k.

Thus, we can find the basis for the smallest number of coefficients with probability at least $1 - q^{-2}$ by calculating

$$N = \mathrm{rank} \begin{bmatrix} a_1(k_{i_1}) & a_2(k_{i_1}) & \cdots & a_q(k_{i_1}) \\ a_1(k_{i_2}) & a_2(k_{i_2}) & \cdots & a_q(k_{i_2}) \\ \cdots\cdots & \cdots\cdots & \cdots & \cdots\cdots \\ a_1(k_{i_{q+2}}) & a_2(k_{i_{q+2}}) & \cdots & a_q(k_{i_{q+2}}) \end{bmatrix},$$

where $\{k_{i_1}, k_{i_2}, \ldots, k_{i_{q+2}}\}$ is a random subset of K and $a_1(k_{i_j}), a_2(k_{i_j}), \ldots, a_q(k_{i_j})$ $(j = 1, 2, \ldots, q + 2)$ are coefficients of the polynomial basis $\{1, x, \cdots, x^{q-1}\}$ derived by some polynomial interpolation algorithm. Since a rank is an invariable with different bases, it is sufficient to consider only the polynomial basis.

We summarize the basis search algorithm.

Algorithm 4.

Step 1: *Choose appropriate parameters for the attack:*
    − a finite field $\mathrm{GF}(q)$
    − a map $\mathsf{p} : \mathrm{GF}(q) \rightarrow \mathrm{GF}(2)^n$
    − a map $\tilde{\mathsf{c}}' : \mathrm{GF}(2)^n \rightarrow \mathrm{GF}(q)$

Step 2: *Generate $q + 2$ randomly chosen keys* $k_{i_1}, k_{i_2}, \ldots, k_{i_{q+2}} \in K$.

Step 3: *Calculate all input-output pairs of* $f_{k_{i_j}}$ $(= \tilde{\mathsf{c}}' \circ \tilde{E}_{k_{i_j}} \circ \mathsf{p})$,

$$(x, f_{k_{i_j}}(x))$$

    for all $x \in \mathrm{GF}(q)$ *and* $1 \leq \forall j \leq q + 2$.

Step 4: *Using some polynomial interpolation algorithm, determine coefficients*

$$a_1(k_{i_j}), a_2(k_{i_j}), \ldots, a_q(k_{i_j})$$

of polynomial $f_{k_{i_j}}(x) = \sum_{l=1}^{q} a_l(k_{i_j}) x^{l-1}$ *for $q+2$ keys* k_{i_j} $(1 \leq j \leq q+2)$ *using the input-output pairs of* $f_{k_{i_j}}$ *calculated in Step 3.*

Step 5: *Calculate the number of effective coefficients*

$$N = \mathrm{rank} \begin{bmatrix} a_1(k_{i_1}) & a_2(k_{i_1}) & \cdots & a_q(k_{i_1}) \\ a_1(k_{i_2}) & a_2(k_{i_2}) & \cdots & a_q(k_{i_2}) \\ \cdots\cdots & \cdots\cdots & \cdots & \cdots\cdots \\ a_1(k_{i_{q+2}}) & a_2(k_{i_{q+2}}) & \cdots & a_q(k_{i_{q+2}}) \end{bmatrix}$$

using Gaussian elimination.

A proper program for Gaussian elimination to calculate the rank can also find the effective basis for an attack.

A cipher is secure against linear sum attack if N equals q. In other words, linear sum attack is effective if N is less than q.

We studied the complexity of the above algorithm. Note that in Step 4 we can interpolate polynomials for each k_{i_j} by calculating only 1 Gaussian elimination, which requires $O(q^3)$ arithmetic operations in $\mathrm{GF}(q)$. The algorithm requires $O(q^4)$ $(=(q+2) \times O(q^3) + O(q))$ arithmetic operations in $\mathrm{GF}(q)$, with the assumption that the encryption time is much less than Gaussian elimination. Thus, it is sufficient for recent computers to calculate N if $q \approx 2^8$.

5 Experimental Results

This section evaluates the security of CRYPTON, E2, and RIJNDAEL, using Algorithm 4. CRYPTON, E2, and RIJNDAEL have 12, 12, and 10 rounds, respectively, and the basic operations of these ciphers are 8 bits long.

Unfortunately, since it is infeasible to check all combinations of $\mathrm{GF}(q)$, p, $\tilde{\mathsf{c}}'$, we ran the algorithm for only the following combinations.

- $\mathrm{GF}(q) = \mathrm{GF}(2^8)$
- $\mathsf{p}_i : x \mapsto (0, \ldots, 0, \overset{ith}{\check{x}}, 0, \ldots, 0)$ $(i = 1, 2, \ldots, 16)$
- $\tilde{\mathsf{c}}'_j : (x_1, x_2, \ldots, x_{16}) \mapsto x_j$ $(j = 1, 2, \ldots, 16)$

The results are summarized in Table 1. We evaluated only the 128-bit key versions of the ciphers[2]. We count the number of rounds as 0 in the case of the cipher with only initial transformation.

Table 1. Smallest number of unknown coefficients

Number of Rounds	CRYPTON	E2	E2*	RIJNDAEL
0	1	1	—	1
1	1	1	0	1
2	252	1	1	255
3	255	1	1	255
≥ 4	256	256	256	256

*: without IT- and FT-Functions

According to Table 1, there are no long linear relation of these ciphers comparing with the number of rounds of the specification of these ciphers. It seems that these ciphers are secure against generalized interpolation attack, linear sum attack.

---

[2] We evaluated only the 128-bit block length version of RIJNDAEL.

The goal of this paper is the security evaluation of a given cipher against linear sum attack. Thus, we do not go into the details of the attacks for these ciphers, however, a rough sketch of the attacks using Table 1 are shown in the Appendix.

6 Relationship between Linear Sum Attack and Higher Order Differential Attack

This section describes the strength of linear sum attack in comparison with higher order differential attack.

Definition 5. $E_k(p)$ *is secure against linear sum attack* with respect to $\mathrm{GF}(q)$, p, *and* $\tilde{c}'n \overset{\text{def}}{\Leftrightarrow} N = q$ *holds, where N is determined by Algorithm 4.*

Definition 6. *Let $\tilde{e}_k^{(i)}(p)$ be the ith output bit of $\tilde{E}_k(p)$, i.e.,*

$$\tilde{E}_k(p) = (\tilde{e}_k^{(1)}(p), \tilde{e}_k^{(2)}(p), \ldots, \tilde{e}_k^{(n)}(p)) \ .$$

Let p be a map

$$\mathsf{p} : \mathrm{GF}(2)^t \to \mathrm{GF}(2)^n; \ (x_1, x_2, \ldots, x_t) \mapsto (p_1, p_2, \ldots, p_n) \ ,$$

where $p_i = \begin{cases} x_{\pi^{-1}(i)} & \text{if } \pi^{-1}(i) \text{ is defined} \\ \text{constant} & \text{otherwise} \end{cases}$ *and π is an injective map from* $\{1, 2, \ldots, t\}$ *to* $\{1, 2, \ldots, n\}$.
$E_k(p)$ is secure against higher order differential attack with respect to p *and* $u \overset{\text{def}}{\Leftrightarrow} \deg_{\{x_1, x_2, \ldots, x_t\}} \tilde{e}_k^{(u)}(\mathsf{p}(x_1, x_2, \ldots, x_t)) = t$ *holds.*

Note that Definition 6 does not consider improved higher order differential attacks such as proposed in [9] and the case of $t = n$, and if a cipher is not secure against higher order differential attack according to Definition 6, we cannot conclude that the cipher is insecure against an actual higher order differential attack.

The following theorem means that resistance against linear sum attack, which is a generalized interpolation attack, implies resistance against higher order differential attack.

Theorem 7. *Let* p *be a map*

$$\mathsf{p} : \mathrm{GF}(2^t) \to \mathrm{GF}(2)^n; \ (x_1, x_2, \ldots, x_t) \mapsto (p_1, p_2, \ldots, p_n) \ ,$$

where $p_i = \begin{cases} x_{\pi^{-1}(i)} & \text{if } \pi^{-1}(i) \text{ is defined} \\ \text{constant} & \text{otherwise} \end{cases}$ *and* π *is an injective map from* $\{1, 2, \ldots, t\}$ *to* $\{1, 2, \ldots, n\}$. *Let* $\tilde{c}'$ *be a map*

$$\tilde{c}' : \mathrm{GF}(2)^n \to \mathrm{GF}(2^t); \ (\tilde{c}_1, \tilde{c}_2, \ldots, \tilde{c}_n) \mapsto (y_1, y_2, \ldots, y_t) \ ,$$

where $y_i = \tilde{c}_{\tau(i)}$ *and* τ *is an injective map from* $\{1, 2, \ldots, t\}$ *to* $\{1, 2, \ldots, n\}$.
For $1 \leq \forall i \leq t$, $E_k(\mathsf{p})$ *is secure against linear sum attack with respect to* $\mathrm{GF}(2^t)$, p, *and* $\tilde{c}' \Rightarrow E_k(\mathsf{p})$ *is secure against higher order differential attack with respect to* p *and* $\tau(i)$.
Note that we regard an element $(a_1, a_2, \ldots, a_t) \in \mathrm{GF}(2)^t$ *as* $a \in \mathrm{GF}(2^t)$ *with* $\mathrm{GF}(2)$ *basis.*

Before proving Theorem 7, we show a well-known lemma. This lemma was introduced by [12, Proposition 4, p.60], for example.

Lemma 8. *Let* $y = x^d$ *in* $\mathrm{GF}(2^t)$ *and regard* $(y_1, y_2, \ldots, y_t) \in \mathrm{GF}(2)^t$ *as* y *with* $\mathrm{GF}(2)$ *basis.*

$$\deg_{\{x_1, x_2, \ldots, x_t\}} y_i = w_H(d) \quad \text{for } 1 \leq \forall i \leq t$$

holds, where x *is regarded as* $(x_1, x_2, \ldots, x_t) \in \mathrm{GF}(2)^t$ *with* $\mathrm{GF}(2)$ *basis and* $w_H(d)$ *is the Hamming weight of the binary representation of* d.

Proof (of Theorem 7). According to the assumption of the theorem and Definition 5, $\tilde{E}_k(\mathsf{p}(x))$ should be expressed as

$$\tilde{E}_k(\mathsf{p}(x)) = \sum_{i=1}^{2^t} a_i(k) x^{i-1} \ ,$$

where $a_i(k) \in \mathrm{GF}(2^t)$ is an unknown coefficient for $1 \leq \forall i \leq 2^t$. Using Lemma 8,

$$w_H(x^d) = t \text{ if } d = 2^t - 1$$
$$< t \text{ otherwise}$$

holds. Since the degree-t term of Boolean representation of $\tilde{e}_k^{(\tau(i))}(\mathsf{p}(x))$ comes only from $x^{2^t - 1}$ and never comes from x^d $(d < 2^t - 1)$,

$$\deg_{\{x_1, x_2, \ldots, x_t\}} \tilde{e}_k^{(\tau(i))}(\mathsf{p}(x)) = t$$

holds for $1 \leq \forall i \leq t$. □

7 Conclusion

This paper presented linear sum attack, which is a generalized form of interpolation attack, and presented an algorithm that efficiently evaluates the security of a cipher against linear sum attack. We applied the algorithm to 128-bit key CRYPTON, E2, and RIJNDAEL, which have 12, 12, and 10 rounds, respectively, and showed that the ciphers reduced to 3 rounds have non-trivial linear sum relations. Moreover, we showed that resistance against linear sum attack implies resistance against higher order differential attack.

There are 2 open problems remaining.

1. How to find effective $GF(q)$, p, $\tilde{c}'$?
2. How to construct a rational version of linear sum attack like interpolation attack?

Acknowledgment

We wish to thank T. Shimoyama and anonymous referees of workshops and conferences for giving us comments. Some of them conflicted, but they significantly improved the presentation of our paper.

References

1. Eli Biham and Adi Shamir. Differential cryptanalysis of DES-like cryptosystems. *Journal of Cryptology*, 4(1):3–72, 1991. (The extended abstract was presented at CRYPTO'90).
2. Joan Daemen, Lars Ramkilde Knudsen, and Vincent Rijmen. The block cipher SQUARE. In Eli Biham, editor, *Fast Software Encryption — 4th International Workshop, FSE'97*, volume 1267 of *Lecture Notes in Computer Science*, pages 54–68, Berlin, Heidelberg, New York, 1997. Springer-Verlag.
3. Joan Daemen and Vincent Rijmen. *AES Proposal: Rijndael*, 1998. (http://www.esat.kuleuven.ac.be/~rijmen/rijndael/).
4. Thomas Jakobsen and Lars Ramkilde Knudsen. The interpolation attack on block cipher. In Eli Biham, editor, *Fast Software Encryption — 4th International Workshop, FSE'97*, volume 1267 of *Lecture Notes in Computer Science*, pages 28–40, Berlin, Heidelberg, New York, 1997. Springer-Verlag.
5. Lars Ramkilde Knudsen. Truncated and higher order differentials. In Bart Preneel, editor, *Fast Software Encryption — Second International Workshop*, volume 1008 of *Lecture Notes in Computer Science*, pages 196–211. Springer-Verlag, Berlin, Heidelberg, New York, 1995.
6. Chang-Hyi Lee and Young-Tae Cha. The block cipher: SNAKE with provable resistance against DC and LC attacks. In *1997 Korea-Japan Joint Workshop on Information Security and Cryptology (JW-ISC'97)*, pages 3–17, Seoul, KOREA, 1997. KIISC (Korea) and ISEC Group of IEICE (Japan).

7. Chae Hoon Lim. *CRYPTON: A New 128-bit Block Cipher – Specification and Analysis –*. Future Systems, 1998. (urlhttp://crypt.future.co.kr/ chilim/crypton.html).

8. Mitsuru Matsui. Linear cryptanalysis method for DES cipher. In Tor Helleseth, editor, *Advances in Cryptology — EUROCRYPT'93*, volume 765 of *Lecture Notes in Computer Science*, pages 386–397. Springer-Verlag, Berlin, Heidelberg, New York, 1994. (A preliminary version written in Japanese was presented at SCIS93-3C).

9. Shiho Moriai, Takeshi Shimoyama, and Toshinobu Kaneko. Higher order differential attack using chosen higher order differences. In Stafford Tavares and Henk Meijer, editors, *Selected Areas in Cryptography — 5th Annual International Workshop, SAC'98*, volume 1556 of *Lecture Notes in Computer Science*, pages 106–117, Berlin, Heidelberg, New York, 1999. Springer-Verlag.

10. Shiho Moriai, Takeshi Shimoyama, and Toshinobu Kaneko. Interpolation attacks of the block cipher: SNAKE. In Lars Ramkilde Knudsen, editor, *Fast Software Encryption — 6th International Workshop, FSE'99*, volume 1636 of *Lecture Notes in Computer Science*, pages 275–289, Berlin, Heidelberg, New York, 1999. Springer-Verlag. (A preliminary version written in Japanese was presented at SCIS'98-7.2.C).

11. Nippon Telegraph and Telephone Corporation. *Specification of E2 — a 128-bit Block Cipher*, 1998. (http://info.isl.ntt.co.jp/e2/).

12. Kaisa Nyberg. Differentially uniform mappings for cryptography. In Tor Helleseth, editor, *Advances in Cryptology — EUROCRYPT'93*, volume 765 of *Lecture Notes in Computer Science*, pages 55–64. Springer-Verlag, Berlin, Heidelberg, New York, 1994.

13. Kaisa Nyberg. Linear approximation of block ciphers. In Alfredo De Santis, editor, *Advances in Cryptology — EUROCRYPT'94*, volume 950 of *Lecture Notes in Computer Science*, pages 439–444. Springer-Verlag, Berlin, Heidelberg, New York, 1995.

14. Kaisa Nyberg and Lars Ramkilde Knudsen. Provable security against a differential attack. *Journal of Cryptology*, 8(1):27–37, 1995. (A preliminary version was presented at CRYPTO'92 rump session).

15. Vincent Rijmen, Joan Daemen, Bart Preneel, Antoon Bosselaers, and Erik De Win. The cipher SHARK. In Dieter Gollmann, editor, *Fast Software Encryption — Third International Workshop*, volume 1039 of *Lecture Notes in Computer Science*, pages 99–111. Springer-Verlag, Berlin, Heidelberg, New York, 1996.

Appendix: Linear Sum Attack of Reduced Round Variants of CRYPTON, E2, and RIJNDAEL

We evaluate the security against linear sum attack for CRYPTON, E2, and RIJNDAEL using the results shown in Table 1. Since these linear sum attacks are not superior than the known attacks against the ciphers and the attack procedures are almost the same as the interpolation attack described in Sect. 2.2, we do not analyze and describe the details.

First, we consider CRYPTON and RIJNDAEL. Both ciphers are based on the same structure of SQUARE [2], and there are 3-round linear sum relations with $N < q$. Applying the 3-round linear sum relation from the 2nd round to the 4th round, and guessing the 1st, the 5th, and the 6th round subkeys related to the linear sum relation exhaustively, we can attack the ciphers reduced to 6 rounds faster than exhaustive search. The attack is almost the same as SQUARE attack [3, pp.28–31].

Next, we consider E2. There exists 3-round linear sum relations with $N < q$ in spite of the existence of IT- and FT-Functions. We can attack E2 with IT- and FT-Functions reduced to 3 rounds faster than exhaustive search, by applying the linear sum relation from the 1st round to the 3rd round, and guessing key bits used in FT-Function related to the linear sum relation. We can attack E2 without IT- and FT-Functions reduced to 5 rounds faster than exhaustive search, by applying the linear sum relation from the 2nd round to the 4th round, and guessing the 1st and the 5th round subkey bits related to the linear sum relation.

Efficient Implementation of Cryptosystems Based on Non-maximal Imaginary Quadratic Orders

Detlef Hühnlein

secunet Security Networks AG
Mergenthalerallee 77-81
D-65760 Eschborn, Germany
huehnlein@secunet.de

Abstract. In [14] there is proposed an ElGamal-type cryptosystem based on non-maximal imaginary quadratic orders with trapdoor decryption. The trapdoor information is the factorization of the non-fundamental discriminant $\Delta_p = \Delta_1 p^2$. The NICE-cryptosystem (**N**ew **I**deal **C**oset **En**-cryption) [24,12] is an efficient variant thereof, which uses an element $\mathfrak{g}^k \in \mathrm{Ker}(\phi_{Cl}^{-1}) \subseteq Cl(\Delta_p)$, where k is random and $\phi_{Cl}^{-1} : Cl(\Delta_p) \to Cl(\Delta_1)$ is a map between the class groups of the non-maximal and maximal order, to mask the message in the ElGamal cryptosystem. This mask simply "disappears" during decryption, which essentially consists of computing ϕ_{Cl}^{-1}. Thus NICE features quadratic decryption time and hence is very well suited for applications in which a central server has to decrypt a large number of ciphertexts in a short time. In this work we will introduce an *efficient batch decryption* method for NICE, which allows to speed up the decryption by about 30% for a batch size of 100 messages.

In [17] there is proposed a NICE-Schnorr-type signature scheme. In this scheme one uses the group $\mathrm{Ker}(\phi_{Cl}^{-1})$ instead of $\mathbb{F}_p^*$. Thus instead of modular arithmetic one would need to apply standard ideal arithmetic (multiply and reduce) using algorithms from [5] for example. Because every group operation needs the application of the Extended Euclidean Algorithm the implementation would be very inefficient. Especially the signing process, which would typically be performed on a smartcard with limited computational power would be too slow to allow practical application. In this work we will introduce an *entirely new arithmetic* for elements in $\mathrm{Ker}(\phi_{Cl}^{-1})$, which uses the generator and ring-equivalence for exponentiation. Thus the signer essentially performs the exponentiation in $(\mathcal{O}_{\Delta_1}/p\mathcal{O}_{\Delta_1})^*$, which turns out to be about *twenty* times as fast as conventional ideal arithmetic. Furthermore in [17] it is shown, how one can further speed up this exponentiation by application of the Chinese Remainder Theorem for $(\mathcal{O}_{\Delta_1}/p\mathcal{O}_{\Delta_1})^*$. With this arithmetic the signature generation is about *forty* times as fast as with conventional ideal arithmetic and *more than twice* as fast as in the original Schnorr scheme [26].

Howard Heys and Carlisle Adams (Eds.): SAC'99, LNCS 1758, pp. 147–162, 2000.
© Springer-Verlag Berlin Heidelberg 2000

1 Introduction

The utilization of imaginary quadratic class groups in cryptography is due to Buchmann and Williams [4], who proposed a key agreement protocol analogue to [7] based on class groups of imaginary quadratic fields, i.e. the class group of the *maximal order*. Since the computation of discrete logarithms in the class group of the imaginary quadratic number field is at least as difficult as factoring the corresponding discriminant (see [4,27]) these cryptosystems are very interesting from a theoretical point of view. In practice however these cryptosystems seemed to be less efficient than popular cryptosystems based on computing discrete logarithms in $\mathbb{F}_p^*$, like [7,9] or factoring integers, like [25]. Furthermore the computation of the group order, i.e. the class number, is in general almost as hard as computing discrete logarithms itself by application of the algorithm of Hafner / McCurley [10] or more practical variants like [8,19], which is subexponential with $L[\frac{1}{2}]$. Hence it seemed to be impossible to set up signature schemes analogue to [9,22] or [25]. In [14] however it was shown how the application of *non-maximal* imaginary quadratic orders may be used to construct an ElGamal-type cryptosystem with fast decryption and that it is in principle possible to set up ElGamal and RSA-type signature schemes.

In [24] there is proposed an ElGamal-type cryptosystem, later on called NICE for **N**ew **I**deal **C**oset **E**ncryption [12], with very fast decryption. It was shown that the decryption process only needs quadratic time, which makes NICE unique in this sense. First implementations show that the time for decryption is comparable to the time for RSA-*encryption* with $e = 2^{16}$. The central idea of this scheme is to use an element $\mathfrak{g}^k$ of the kernel $\mathrm{Ker}(\phi_{Cl}^{-1})$ of the surjective map $\phi_{Cl}^{-1} : Cl(\Delta_p) \to Cl(\Delta_1)$ to mask the message in the ElGamal-type cryptosystem [14]. The map ϕ_{Cl}^{-1} is induced by the isomorphic map $\varphi^{-1} : \mathcal{I}_{\Delta_p}(p) \to \mathcal{I}_{\Delta_1}(p)$ which maps $\mathcal{O}_{\Delta_p}$-ideals which are prime to the conductor p to $\mathcal{O}_{\Delta_1}$-ideals which are also prime to p. Hence this mask simply "disappears" during the trapdoor-decryption, which just consists of applying ϕ_{Cl}^{-1}, reducing the resulting ideal in the maximal order (and possibly going back to the non-maximal order using φ). The most time consuming step in the decryption is to compute the map ϕ_{Cl}^{-1}, which is essentially the computation of a modular inverse (modulo p) using the Extended Euclidean Algorithm, which needs $O(\log^2(p))$ bit operations.

It is clear that because of this feature NICE is very well suited for applications where a central server has to decrypt a large number of ciphertexts in a short time. Thus it is natural to search for an efficient batch decryption method. In Section 4 we will introduce a simple yet efficient method for batch decryption, which speeds up the system in this scenario even further. The timings in Section 4 show that it is possible to speed up the decryption process for 100 messages by about 30%.

While the main application of the novel arithmetic for $\mathrm{Ker}(\phi_{Cl}^{-1})$ to be introduced in Section 5 might be in the signing procedure of the NICE-Schnorr-type signature scheme [17], its development was actually motivated by cryptosystems based on *totally non-maximal* orders. Due to the very recent result [16] however, which reduces the DL-problem in these totally non-maximal orders to the

DL-problem in finite fields, these cryptosystems seem to have lost much of its attractiveness.

In [15] it was proposed to use totally non-maximal imaginary quadratic orders $\mathcal{O}_{\Delta_{pq}}$, where $\Delta_{pq} = \Delta_1 p^2 q^2$ to set up RSA-type cryptosystems. Because one chooses Δ_1 such that $h(\Delta_1) = 1$ it is easy to compute $h(\Delta_{pq}) = (p - (\Delta_1/p))(q - (\Delta_1/q))$. It is clear that a similar strategy may be used to set up DSA analogues based on totally non-maximal imaginary quadratic orders. First implementations however have shown that these cryptosystems using standard ideal arithmetic are far to inefficient to be used in practice [11]. This lack of efficiency was the motivation for developing a more efficient arithmetic for $Cl(\Delta_p)$, or $\mathrm{Ker}(\phi_{Cl}^{-1})$ which is the same in the case of totally non-maximal orders.

In Section 5 we will introduce this entirely new method for efficient exponentiation of elements in $\mathrm{Ker}(\phi_{Cl}^{-1})$. Instead of using the standard ideal arithmetic (multiplication and reduction of *ideals*) in the non-maximal order we multiply and "reduce" the corresponding *generators* in the maximal order and later on lift the resulting principal ideal, which corresponds to the computed generator, to the non-maximal order. Thus one essentially reduces the arithmetic in $\mathrm{Ker}(\phi_{Cl}^{-1}) \subseteq Cl(\Delta_p)$ to arithmetic in $(\mathcal{O}_{\Delta_1}/p\mathcal{O}_{\Delta_1})^*$ which turns out to be much more efficient.

The timings in Section 5 show that the naive variant of the new exponentiation technique, as proposed here, is already about *twenty* times as fast as classical ideal arithmetic. Very recently it was shown in [17] that one can even do twice as good by utilizing the Chinese Remainder Theorem for $(\mathcal{O}_{\Delta_1}/p\mathcal{O}_{\Delta_1})^*$. With this improvement the signature generation of the proposed NICE-Schnorr-variant is more than twice as efficient as in the original Schnorr-scheme [26].

This paper is organized as follows: In Section 2 we will provide the necessary basics of imaginary quadratic orders. We will concentrate on the relation between the maximal and non-maximal orders and explain the structure of $\mathrm{Ker}(\phi_{Cl}^{-1})$. In Section 3 we will briefly recall the NICE cryptosystem. In Section 4 we will introduce the new batch decryption for NICE and compare the running times of the implementation. The new exponentiation methods for elements in $\mathrm{Ker}(\phi_{Cl}^{-1})$ are explained in Section 5. We will give the initially proposed method in Section 5.1 and outline the even more efficient CRT - variant from [17] in Section 5.2. In Section 5.3 we will also provide a timing comparison between the new methods, conventional ideal- and modular arithmetic.

2 Imaginary Quadratic Orders

The basic notions of imaginary quadratic number fields may be found in [1,13] or [5]. For a more comprehensive treatment of the relationship between maximal and non-maximal orders we refer to [6] or [14].

Let $\Delta \equiv 0, 1 \pmod 4$ be a negative integer, which is not a square. The quadratic order of discriminant Δ is defined to be

$$\mathcal{O}_\Delta = \mathbb{Z} + \omega\mathbb{Z},$$

where

$$\omega = \begin{cases} \sqrt{\frac{\Delta}{4}}, & \text{if } \Delta \equiv 0 \pmod 4, \\ \frac{1+\sqrt{\Delta}}{2}, & \text{if } \Delta \equiv 1 \pmod 4. \end{cases} \tag{1}$$

The standard representation of some $\alpha \in \mathcal{O}_\Delta$ is $\alpha = x + y\omega$, where $x, y \in \mathbb{Z}$.

If Δ_1 is squarefree, then $\mathcal{O}_{\Delta_1}$ is the *maximal order* of the quadratic number field $\mathbb{Q}(\sqrt{\Delta_1})$ and Δ_1 is called a fundamental discriminant. The *non-maximal order* of conductor $f > 1$ with (non-fundamental) discriminant $\Delta_f = \Delta_1 f^2$ is denoted by $\mathcal{O}_{\Delta_f}$. In this work we will omit the subscripts to reference arbitrary (fundamental or non-fundamental) discriminants. Because $\mathbb{Q}(\sqrt{\Delta_1}) = \mathbb{Q}(\sqrt{\Delta_f})$ we also omit the subscripts to reference the number field $\mathbb{Q}(\sqrt{\Delta})$. The standard representation of an $\mathcal{O}_\Delta$-ideal is

$$\mathfrak{a} = q \left(\mathbb{Z} + \frac{b + \sqrt{\Delta}}{2a} \mathbb{Z} \right) = (a, b), \tag{2}$$

where $q \in \mathbb{Q}_{>0}, a \in \mathbb{Z}_{>0}, c = (b^2 - \Delta)/(4a) \in \mathbb{Z}, gcd(a, b, c) = 1$ and $-a < b \leq a$. The norm of this ideal is $\mathcal{N}(\mathfrak{a}) = aq^2$. An ideal is called primitive if $q = 1$. A primitive ideal is called *reduced* if $|b| \leq a \leq c$ and $b \geq 0$, if $a = c$ or $|b| = a$. It can be shown, that the norm of a reduced ideal $\mathfrak{a}$ satisfies $\mathcal{N}(\mathfrak{a}) \leq \sqrt{|\Delta|/3}$ and conversely that if $\mathcal{N}(\mathfrak{a}) \leq \sqrt{|\Delta|/4}$ then the ideal $\mathfrak{a}$ is reduced. We denote the reduction operator in the maximal order by $\rho_1()$ and write $\rho_f()$ for the reduction operator in the non-maximal order of conductor f.

The group of invertible $\mathcal{O}_\Delta$-ideals is denoted by $\mathcal{I}_\Delta$. Two ideals $\mathfrak{a}, \mathfrak{b}$ are equivalent, if there is a $\gamma \in \mathbb{Q}(\sqrt{\Delta})$, such that $\mathfrak{a} = \gamma\mathfrak{b}$. This equivalence relation is denoted by $\mathfrak{a} \sim \mathfrak{b}$. The set of principal $\mathcal{O}_\Delta$-ideals, i.e. which are equivalent to $\mathcal{O}_\Delta$, are denoted by $\mathcal{P}_\Delta$. The factor group $\mathcal{I}_\Delta/\mathcal{P}_\Delta$ is called the *class group* of $\mathcal{O}_\Delta$ denoted by $Cl(\Delta)$. $Cl(\Delta)$ is a finite abelian group with neutral element $\mathcal{O}_\Delta$. Algorithms for the group operation (multiplication and reduction of ideals) can be found in [5]. The order of the class group is called the *class number* of $\mathcal{O}_\Delta$ and is denoted by $h(\Delta)$.

Our cryptosystems make use of the relation between the maximal and non-maximal orders. Any non-maximal order may be represented as $\mathcal{O}_{\Delta_f} = \mathbb{Z} + f\mathcal{O}_{\Delta_1}$. If $h(\Delta) = 1$ then $\mathcal{O}_{\Delta_f}$ is called a *totally non-maximal* imaginary quadratic order of conductor f. An $\mathcal{O}_\Delta$-ideal $\mathfrak{a}$ is called prime to f, if $gcd(\mathcal{N}(\mathfrak{a}), f) = 1$. It is well known, that all $\mathcal{O}_{\Delta_f}$-ideals prime to the conductor are invertible. In every class there is an ideal which is prime to any given number. The algorithm FindIdealPrimeTo in [14] will compute such an ideal. If we denote the (principal) $\mathcal{O}_{\Delta_f}$-ideals, which are prime to f by $\mathcal{P}_{\Delta_f}(f)$ and $\mathcal{I}_{\Delta_f}(f)$ respectively then there is an isomorphism

$$\mathcal{I}_{\Delta_f}(f) \Big/ \mathcal{P}_{\Delta_f}(f) \simeq \mathcal{I}_{\Delta_f} \Big/ \mathcal{P}_{\Delta_f} = Cl(\Delta_f). \tag{3}$$

Thus we may 'neglect' the ideals which are not prime to the conductor, if we are only interested in the class group $Cl(\Delta_f)$. There is an isomorphism between the group of $\mathcal{O}_{\Delta_f}$-ideals which are prime to f and the group of $\mathcal{O}_{\Delta_1}$-ideals, which are prime to f, denoted by $\mathcal{I}_{\Delta_1}(f)$ respectively:

Proposition 1. *Let $\mathcal{O}_{\Delta_f}$ be an order of conductor f in an imaginary quadratic field $\mathbb{Q}(\sqrt{\Delta})$ with maximal order $\mathcal{O}_{\Delta_1}$.*

(i.) *If $\mathfrak{A} \in \mathcal{I}_{\Delta_1}(f)$, then $\mathfrak{a} = \mathfrak{A} \cap \mathcal{O}_{\Delta_f} \in \mathcal{I}_{\Delta_f}(f)$ and $\mathcal{N}(\mathfrak{A}) = \mathcal{N}(\mathfrak{a})$.*
(ii.) *If $\mathfrak{a} \in \mathcal{I}_{\Delta_f}(f)$, then $\mathfrak{A} = \mathfrak{a}\mathcal{O}_{\Delta_1} \in \mathcal{I}_{\Delta_1}(f)$ and $\mathcal{N}(\mathfrak{a}) = \mathcal{N}(\mathfrak{A})$.*
(iii.) *The map $\varphi : \mathfrak{A} \mapsto \mathfrak{A} \cap \mathcal{O}_{\Delta_f}$ induces an isomorphism $\mathcal{I}_{\Delta_1}(f) \tilde{\rightarrow} \mathcal{I}_{\Delta_f}(f)$.*
      The inverse of this map is $\varphi^{-1} : \mathfrak{a} \mapsto \mathfrak{a}\mathcal{O}_{\Delta_1}$.

Proof: See [6, Proposition 7.20, page 144] . $\qquad\square$

Thus we are able to switch to and from the maximal order. The algorithms GoToMaxOrder($\mathfrak{a}, f$) to compute φ^{-1} and GoToNonMaxOrder($\mathfrak{A}, f$) to compute φ respectively may be found in [14].

It is important to note that the isomorphism φ is between the ideal groups $\mathcal{I}_{\Delta_1}(f)$ and $\mathcal{I}_{\Delta_f}(f)$ and *not the class groups*.

If, for $\mathfrak{A}, \mathfrak{B} \in \mathcal{I}_{\Delta_1}(f)$ we have $\mathfrak{A} \sim \mathfrak{B}$, it is not necessarily true that $\varphi(\mathfrak{A}) \sim \varphi(\mathfrak{B})$.

On the other hand, equivalence *does* hold under φ^{-1}. More precisely we have the following:

Proposition 2. *The isomorphism φ^{-1} induces a surjective homomorphism $\phi_{Cl}^{-1} : Cl(\Delta_f) \to Cl(\Delta_1)$, where $\mathfrak{a} \mapsto \rho_1(\varphi^{-1}(\mathfrak{a}))$.*

Proof: This immediately follows from the short exact sequence:

$$Cl(\Delta_f) \longrightarrow Cl(\Delta_1) \longrightarrow 1$$

(see [23, Theorem 12.9, p. 82]). $\qquad\square$

In the following we will study the kernel $\text{Ker}(\phi_{Cl}^{-1})$ of the above map ϕ_{Cl}^{-1} and hence the relation between a class in the maximal order and the associated classes in the non-maximal order in more detail. We start with yet another interpretation of the class group $Cl(\Delta_f)$.

Proposition 3. *Let $\mathcal{O}_{\Delta_f}$ be an order of conductor f in a quadratic field. Then there are natural isomorphisms*

$$Cl(\Delta_f) \simeq \mathcal{I}_{\Delta_f}(f) \big/ \mathcal{P}_{\Delta_f}(f) \simeq \mathcal{I}_{\Delta_1}(f) \big/ \mathcal{P}_{\Delta_1, \mathbb{Z}}(f),$$

where $\mathcal{P}_{\Delta_1, \mathbb{Z}}(f)$ denotes the subgroup of $\mathcal{I}_{\Delta_1}(f)$ generated by the principal ideals of the form $\alpha\mathcal{O}_{\Delta_1}$ where $\alpha \in \mathcal{O}_{\Delta_1}$ satisfies $\alpha \equiv a \pmod{f\mathcal{O}_{\Delta_1}}$ for some $a \in \mathbb{Z}$ such that $\gcd(a, f) = 1$.

Proof: See [6, Proposition 7.22, page 145]. $\qquad\square$

The following corollary is an immediate consequence.

Corollary 1. *With notations as above we have the following isomorphism*

$$\mathrm{Ker}(\phi_{Cl}^{-1}) \simeq {}^{\mathcal{P}_{\Delta_1}(f)}\big/_{\mathcal{P}_{\Delta_1, \mathbb{Z}}(f)}.$$

The next result explains the relation between $\mathrm{Ker}(\phi_{Cl}^{-1})$ and $(\mathcal{O}_{\Delta_1}/f\mathcal{O}_{\Delta_1})^*$.

Lemma 1. *The map* $(\mathcal{O}_{\Delta_1}/f\mathcal{O}_{\Delta_1})^* \rightarrow \mathrm{Ker}(\phi_{Cl}^{-1})$, *where* $\alpha \mapsto \varphi(\alpha\mathcal{O}_{\Delta_1})$ *is a surjective homomorphism.*

Proof: This is shown in the more comprehensive proof of Theorem 7.24 in [6] (page 147). □

Another immediate consequence of Proposition 3 allows to decide which principal ideals in the maximal order are mapped to principal ideals in the non-maximal order by applying φ:

Corollary 2. *Let* $\alpha \in \mathcal{O}_{\Delta_1}$ *be an element of the maximal order and* $\mathcal{O}_{\Delta_f}$ *be the order of conductor* f. *Then* $\varphi(\alpha\mathcal{O}_{\Delta_1}) \sim \mathcal{O}_{\Delta_f}$ *if and only if*

$$\alpha \equiv a \pmod{f\mathcal{O}_{\Delta_1}}$$

with $a \in \mathbb{Z}$ *such that* $\gcd(a, f) = 1$

Thus we are able to "model" the equivalence relation in the non-maximal order by considering generators of principal ideals in the maximal orders. This fact is called *ring-equivalence*.

In Section 5 we will use the above results to formulate concrete algorithms for efficient exponentiation of elements in $\mathrm{Ker}(\phi_{Cl}^{-1})$.

Finally, we will give the exact relationship between the class numbers $h(\Delta_1)$ and $h(\Delta_f)$.

Theorem 1. *Let* $\mathcal{O}_{\Delta_f}$ *be the order of conductor* f *in a quadratic field* $\mathbb{Q}(\sqrt{\Delta})$ *with maximal order* $\mathcal{O}_{\Delta_1}$. *Then*

$$h(\Delta_f) = \frac{h(\Delta_1)f}{[\mathcal{O}_{\Delta_1}^* : \mathcal{O}_{\Delta_f}^*]} \prod_{p|f}\left(1 - \frac{\left(\frac{\Delta_1}{p}\right)}{p}\right) = nh(\Delta_1),$$

where $n \in \mathbb{N}$ *and* $\left(\frac{\Delta_1}{p}\right)$ *is the Kronecker-symbol.*

Proof: See [6, Theorem 7.24, page 146]. □

Because $\mathcal{O}_{\Delta_1}^* = \mathcal{O}_{\Delta_p}^* = \{\pm 1\}$, for $\Delta_p = \Delta_1 p^2$, p prime and $\Delta_1 < -4$ we have an immediate corollary of Theorem 1.

Corollary 3. *Let* $\Delta_1 < -4$, $\Delta_1 \equiv 0, 1 \pmod 4$ *and* p *prime. Then* $h(\Delta_p) = h(\Delta_1)\left(p - \left(\frac{\Delta_1}{p}\right)\right)$ *and* $|\mathrm{Ker}(\phi_{Cl}^{-1})| = \left(p - \left(\frac{\Delta_1}{p}\right)\right)$, *where* $\left(\frac{\Delta_1}{p}\right)$ *is the Kronecker-symbol.*

Thus we are able to control the order of the kernel and consequently set up a Schnorr analogue using the group $\mathrm{Ker}(\phi_{Cl}^{-1})$ instead of $\mathbb{F}_p^*$ as proposed in [17].

3 The NICE Cryptosystem

In this section we will briefly recall the setup of NICE. We refer to [24,12,18] for a more comprehensive treatment.

Choose two primes p, q, $p > 2\sqrt{q}$ and set $\Delta_1 = -q$ if $q \equiv 3 \pmod 4$, $\Delta_1 = -4q$ otherwise and $\Delta_p = \Delta_1 p^2$. Then $\mathcal{O}_{\Delta_1}$ is a maximal order and $\mathcal{O}_{\Delta_p}$ is a non-maximal order of conductor p. Note that by [14, Lemma 8] all reduced $\mathcal{O}_{\Delta_1}$-ideals are guaranteed to be prime to p, because $p > \sqrt{|\Delta_1|}$. Furthermore choose a reduced $\mathcal{O}_{\Delta_p}$-ideal $\mathfrak{g} \in \mathrm{Ker}(\phi_{Cl}^{-1})$. In [18] there is given a simple algorithm which computes such a kernel element $\mathfrak{g}$.

The *secret* key is just

- the conductor p.

The *public* key consists of

- the non-fundamental discriminant Δ_p and
- the ideal $\mathfrak{g}$.

Because the system is entirely broken if one is able to factor Δ_p one should, as explained in [14], at least choose $p, q > 2^{200}$.

To *encrypt* a message $1 \le m < \sqrt{|\Delta_1|/4}$ one proceeds as follows:

1. Choose a random $k \in \mathbb{Z}$ with $1 < k < 2^{80}$.
2. Compute the reduced $\mathcal{O}_{\Delta_p}$-ideal $\mathfrak{k} = \rho_p(\mathfrak{g}^k)$.
3. Embed the message $m \in \mathbb{Z}$ in a $\mathcal{O}_{\Delta_p}$-Ideal $\mathfrak{m}$ with $\mathcal{N}(\mathfrak{m}) < \sqrt{|\Delta_1|/4}$.
4. Compute the ciphertext $\mathfrak{c} = \rho_p(\mathfrak{m}\mathfrak{k})$.

For the message embedding one may use the algorithm given in [18]. It is clear that the ideal $\mathfrak{k}$ is simply used to "mask" the message in the ElGamal-type scheme. Furthermore note that $k < 2^{80}$ can be chosen to be "unusually small", because in contrast to the classical ElGamal cryptosystem the ciphertext consists of just *one* element and hence one would have to apply a brute force strategy to determine the message. It is just not possible to compute some discrete logarithm using more sophisticated e.g. (baby-step-giant-step) techniques if one is only given the cipher text. We refer to [18] for a detailed treatment of this issue.

To *decrypt* the ciphertext $\mathfrak{c}$ one proceeds as follows:

1. Compute $\mathfrak{C} = \varphi^{-1}(\mathfrak{c})$ using algorithm GotoMaxorder$(\mathfrak{c}, p)$ from [14].
2. Reduce $\mathfrak{C}$, i.e. compute $\mathfrak{M} = \rho_1(\mathfrak{C})$.
3. Compute $\mathfrak{m} = \varphi(\mathfrak{M})$ using algorithm GotoNonMaxorder$(\mathfrak{M}, p)$ from [14].

Note that the computation in Step 1.-2. is just the computation of ϕ_{Cl}^{-1}.

The correctness of the decryption procedure is easy to see. Because $\mathfrak{g} \in \mathrm{Ker}(\phi_{Cl}^{-1})$ we have
$$\varphi^{-1}(\mathfrak{c}) = \varphi^{-1}(\mathfrak{m}\mathfrak{k}) = \varphi^{-1}(\mathfrak{m})(\alpha)\mathcal{O}_{\Delta_1} = \mathfrak{M}(\alpha)\mathcal{O}_{\Delta_1} \sim \mathfrak{M}, \text{ where } \alpha \in \mathcal{O}_{\Delta_1}.$$
Because $\mathcal{N}(\mathfrak{m}) < \sqrt{|\Delta_1|/4}$ we know that $\mathfrak{m} = \varphi(\mathfrak{M}) = \varphi(\rho_1(\mathfrak{C}))$ is a reduced $\mathcal{O}_{\Delta_p}$-ideal - the message-ideal $\mathfrak{m}$.

Note that if the message is embedded in the norm of the ideal $\mathfrak{m}$ only, as proposed in [18], then the step back to the non-maximal order (Step 3.) may be omitted, because we have $\mathcal{N}(\mathfrak{m}) = \mathcal{N}(\mathfrak{M})$.

For the readers convenience we will recall the algorithm GotoMaxOrder from [14]:

Algorithm 2 *(GoToMaxOrder)*
   Input: *A primitive $\mathcal{O}_{\Delta_p}$-ideal $\mathfrak{a} = (a, b)$, the fundamental discriminant Δ_1 and the conductor p*
   Output: *A primitive $\mathcal{O}_{\Delta_1}$-ideal $\mathfrak{A} = \varphi^{-1}(\mathfrak{a}) = \mathfrak{a}\mathcal{O}_{\Delta_1}$*

1. $b_{\mathcal{O}} \leftarrow \Delta_1 \pmod{2}$
2. *Solve $1 = \mu p + \lambda a$ for $\mu, \lambda \in \mathbb{Z}$*
3. $B \leftarrow b\mu + ab_{\mathcal{O}}\lambda \pmod{2a}$
4. *RETURN (a, B)*

4   Efficient Batch Decryption for NICE

It is clear that because of its very fast decryption NICE is very well suited for applications in which a central server has to decrypt a large number of ciphertexts in a short time. Thus it is desireable to have an efficient batch decryption procedure at hand. In the following we will introduce a simple method which decrypts n ciphertexts $\mathfrak{c}_i$, $1 \leq i \leq n$ in one step, which turns out to be much faster than the sequential processing.

If we have a closer look at the decryption procedure above we recognize that the most time consuming operation is the computation of GotoMaxOrder. This step is essentially the computation of a modular inverse modulo the conductor. Thus we can speed up the decryption process by applying a batch-gcd-strategy, like proposed in [21][1]. The central idea is to replace all but one costly inversions with the Extended Euclidean Algorithm by a few modular multiplications.

If one is asked to compute $b_1 \equiv a_1^{-1} \pmod{p}$ and $b_2 \equiv a_2^{-1} \pmod{p}$. Then instead of performing two inversions one can compute $a \equiv a_1 a_2 \pmod{p}$, $b \equiv a^{-1} \pmod{p}$, $b_1 \equiv ba_2 \pmod{p}$ and $b_2 \equiv ba_1 \pmod{p}$. Thus one replaces one inversion by three modular multiplications, which are usually faster, because in most implementations one inversion is "about" 15 modular multiplications.

It is an easy matter to generalize this strategy to n inversions. This immediately leads to the following algorithm for batch decryption, where we assume that the message is entirely encoded in the norm of the message-ideal, like proposed in [18].

Algorithm 3 *(NICE-Batch-Decryption)*
   Input: *n ciphertexts, i.e. reduced $\mathcal{O}_{\Delta_p}$-ideals $\mathfrak{c}_i = (a_i, b_i)$, $1 \leq i \leq n$, the fundamental discriminant Δ_1 and the conductor p.*
   Output: *The n corresponding plaintexts, i.e. the norms A_i of the corresponding ideals $\mathfrak{M}_i = (A_i, B_i)$, for $1 \leq i \leq n$.*

---

[1] The author would like to thank V. Müller for pointing out the reference.

1. $b_{\mathcal{O}} \leftarrow \Delta_1 \pmod{2}$
2. $g_0 \leftarrow 1$
3. $g_1 \leftarrow a_1$
4. FOR i FROM 2 TO n DO $g_i \leftarrow g_{i-1}a_i \pmod{p}$
5. Compute $h_n \leftarrow g_n^{-1} \pmod{p}$
6. FOR i FROM n TO 1 DO
    6.1 $\lambda_i \leftarrow h_i g_{i-1} \pmod{p}$
    6.2 $h_{i-1} \leftarrow h_i a_i \pmod{p}$
    6.3 $\mu_i \leftarrow \frac{1-\lambda_i a_i}{p}$
    6.4 $B_i \leftarrow b_i \mu_i + a_i b_{\mathcal{O}} \lambda_i \pmod{2a_i}$
    6.5 $\mathfrak{M}_i = (A_i, B_i) \leftarrow \rho_1(a_i, B_i)$
7. RETURN n plaintexts A_i, $1 \le i \le n$

Thus instead of n inversions with the Extended Euclidean Algorithm we only have to perform one inversion, $3n - 3$ modular multiplications, n integer multiplications and n integer divisions. Thus in typical implementations we are able to reduce the time for n decryptions, as shown in Table 1 below.

The implementation was done using the LiDIA-package [20] on a Pentium 133 MHz choosing random primes p, q of the respective bit-length. The timings are given in microseconds, averaged over a number of 100 randomly chosen messages. The first row shows how many modular multiplications are as costly as one inversion in LiDIA. The next rows give the time for a NICE-encryption using 80bit exponents and the binary, usual BGMW-, and the signed BGMW-method [2] for exponentiation. This includes the time for the message-embedding. The last four rows give the decryption time (per message) for batch sizes of 1, 5, 10 and 100 messages respectively. This shows that for a batch size of 100 we are able to speed up the decryption by about 30%.

bitlength p, q	200		300		400		500	
mult / inv	13.9		15.4		16.2		15.6	
	ms	%	ms	%	ms	%	ms	%
NICE Enc. (binary)	1861.7	100	4065.2	100	7368.9	100	12182.1	100
NICE Enc. (BGMW)	669.7	35.97	1786.6	43.95	3556.5	48.26	6461.9	53.04
NICE Enc. ($\pm$-BGMW)	640.9	34.43	1732.6	42.62	3493.6	47.41	6315.5	51.84
NICE Dec. (1 mess.)	9.50	100	16.75	100	26.30	100	35.66	100
NICE Dec. (5 mess.)	8.20	86.32	13.16	78.57	20.00	76.05	26.93	75.52
NICE Dec. (10 mess.)	7.45	78.42	12.34	73.67	19.11	72.66	25.61	71.82
NICE Dec. (100 mess.)	6.70	70.53	11.64	69.49	18.30	69.58	24.61	69.01

Table 1. Timings for NICE with sequential and batch decryption

5 Efficient Exponentiation for Elements of $\mathrm{Ker}(\phi_{Cl}^{-1})$

In this section we will introduce a novel arithmetic for classes in $\mathrm{Ker}(\phi_{Cl}^{-1})$ which turns out to be much more efficient than standard ideal arithmetic.

Since we need to apply φ during our computation we will only consider ideals $\mathfrak{a}$ which are prime to the conductor f. Thus if we are considering principal (integral) ideals $\alpha \mathcal{O}_{\Delta_1}$, for some $\alpha \in \mathcal{O}_{\Delta_1}$, then we require $\gcd(N(\alpha), f) = 1$.

We start with providing the details of a naive generator arithmetic in Section 5.1. While an exponentiation of an ideal using this arithmetic turns out to be about *twenty* times (for the Schnorr-scheme and thirteen times for the DSA-scheme in totally non-maximal orders) as fast as conventional ideal arithmetic, we can do even twice as good by applying CRT in $(\mathcal{O}_{\Delta_1}/f\mathcal{O}_{\Delta_1})^*$ as proposed in [17]. For the readers convenience this method is briefly outlined in Section 5.2. With this arithmetic the signature generation in the Schnorr-analogue [17] is more than twice as fast as in the original scheme.

5.1 Arithmetic in $\mathrm{Ker}(\phi_{Cl}^{-1})$ Using $(\mathcal{O}_{\Delta_1}/f\mathcal{O}_{\Delta_1})^*$

While we already know from Lemma 1 that the arithmetic in $\mathrm{Ker}(\phi_{Cl}^{-1})$ can be reduced to the arithmetic in $(\mathcal{O}_{\Delta_1}/f\mathcal{O}_{\Delta_1})^*$, we will give a very elementary proof here, which ends up in a "ready to implement" algorithm.

It is clear that all integral ideals $\mathfrak{a} \in \mathrm{Ker}(\phi_{Cl}^{-1}) \subseteq Cl(\Delta_f)$ are of the form

$$\mathfrak{a} = \varphi(\alpha \mathcal{O}_{\Delta_1}), \tag{4}$$

for some $\alpha \in \mathcal{O}_{\Delta_1}$.

Now instead of multiplying and reducing the ideals in the non-maximal order we will work with the generators which are corresponding to principal ideals in the maximal order.

We will start with a simple lemma, which can easily be verified by straightforward calculation.

Lemma 2. *Let* $\alpha_i = x_i + y_i\omega \in \mathcal{O}_{\Delta_1}$, $x_i, y_i \in \mathbb{Z}, i \in \{1,2\}$ *and* ω *like given in* (1). *Then* $\beta = x + y\omega = \alpha_1\alpha_2$ *is given by*

$$x = x_1x_2 + y_1y_2\frac{\Delta_1}{4} \tag{5}$$

$$y = x_1y_2 + x_2y_1 \tag{6}$$

in the case that $\Delta_1 \equiv 0 \pmod 4$ *and*

$$x = x_1x_2 + y_1y_2\frac{\Delta_1 - 1}{4} \tag{7}$$

$$y = x_1y_2 + x_2y_1 + y_1y_2 \tag{8}$$

if $\Delta_1 \equiv 1 \pmod 4$.

Thus multiplying two generators α_i is more efficient than multiplying the two ideals $\alpha_i \mathcal{O}_{\Delta_1}$, because no application of the costly Extended Euclidean Algorithm is necessary.

It is clear however that we "somehow need to reduce" intermediate results during exponentiation to obtain a polynomial time algorithm. The central idea is to "model" reduction of ideals (in the non-maximal order) by manipulating the generator. This task will turn out to be surprisingly simple.

The following lemma is immediate.

Lemma 3. Let $\alpha = x + y\omega, \alpha' = x' + y'\omega \in \mathcal{O}_{\Delta_1}$ and $f \in \mathbb{Z}_{>1}$. Then $\alpha \equiv \alpha'$ (mod $f\mathcal{O}_{\Delta_1}$) if and only if $x' \equiv x$ (mod f) and $y' \equiv y$ (mod f).

Next we will consider the norm of an element $\alpha \in \mathcal{O}_{\Delta_1}$ under this congruence.

Lemma 4. Let $\alpha, \beta \in \mathcal{O}_{\Delta_1}$ and $f \in \mathbb{Z}_{>1}$. If $\alpha \equiv \beta$ (mod $f\mathcal{O}_{\Delta_1}$) then $\mathcal{N}(\alpha) \equiv \mathcal{N}(\beta)$ (mod f).

Proof: Let $\alpha = x + y\omega$. Then by Lemma 3 above we have $\beta = x' + y'\omega$, where $x' \equiv x$ (mod f) and $y' \equiv y$ (mod f).
Then we have

$$\begin{aligned}
\mathcal{N}(\alpha) &= x^2 - y^2\omega^2 \\
&\equiv x'^2 - y'^2\omega^2 \quad (\text{mod } f) \\
&= \mathcal{N}(\beta).
\end{aligned}$$

$\square$

The following corollary is immediate.

Corollary 4. Let $\alpha, \beta \in \mathcal{O}_{\Delta_1}$, $f \in \mathbb{Z}_{>1}$ and $\alpha \equiv \beta$ (mod $f\mathcal{O}_{\Delta_1}$). $\gcd(\mathcal{N}(\alpha), f) = 1$ if and only if $\gcd(\mathcal{N}(\beta), f) = 1$.

Lemma 5. Let $\alpha, \beta \in \mathcal{O}_{\Delta_1}$ such that $\gcd(\mathcal{N}(\alpha), f) = \gcd(\mathcal{N}(\beta), f) = 1$ and φ as defined in Proposition 1. Furthermore let $\gamma \equiv \alpha\beta$ (mod $f\mathcal{O}_{\Delta_1}$). Then $\gcd(\mathcal{N}(\gamma), f) = 1$ and if $\alpha \equiv \beta$ (mod $f\mathcal{O}_{\Delta_1}$) then $\varphi(\alpha\mathcal{O}_{\Delta_1}) \sim \varphi(\beta\mathcal{O}_{\Delta_1})$ in $Cl(\Delta_f)$.

Proof: That $\gcd(\mathcal{N}(\gamma), f) = 1$ is immediate by the multiplicativity of the norm and Corollary 4.

Because $\alpha \equiv \beta$ (mod $f\mathcal{O}_{\Delta_1}$) it follows, that $\alpha = \beta\delta$ for some $\delta \in \mathbb{Q}(\sqrt{\Delta})$, where $\delta \equiv 1$ (mod $f\mathcal{O}_{\Delta_1}$). Thus by Proposition 2 we know that $\varphi(\delta\mathcal{O}_{\Delta_1}) \sim \mathcal{O}_{\Delta_f}$ and hence the assertion follows. $\square$

Furthermore we need the following result, which is immediate because φ is an isomorphism.

Lemma 6. Let $\alpha \in \mathcal{O}_{\Delta_1}$, such that $\gcd(\mathcal{N}(\alpha), f) = 1$, $n \in \mathbb{Z}$ and φ as defined in Proposition 1. Then we have $\varphi(\alpha\mathcal{O}_{\Delta_1})^n = \varphi(\alpha^n\mathcal{O}_{\Delta_1})$.

By combining the above results we immediately obtain the following.

Lemma 7. Let $\alpha \in \mathcal{O}_{\Delta_1}$, such that $\gcd(\mathcal{N}(\alpha), f) = 1$, $n \in \mathbb{Z}$ and φ as defined in Proposition 1. Then we have $\varphi(\alpha\mathcal{O}_{\Delta_1})^n \sim \varphi(\gamma\mathcal{O}_{\Delta_1})$ for some $\gamma \equiv \alpha^n$ (mod $f\mathcal{O}_{\Delta_1}$).

The following lemma follows immediately from (5)-(8) and Lemma 3.

Lemma 8. *Let* $\alpha_i = x_i + y_i\omega \in \mathcal{O}_{\Delta_1}$, $x_i, y_i \in \mathbb{Z}, i \in \{1,2\}$, ω *like given in (1) and* $f \geq 1$. *Then* $\beta = x + y\omega \equiv \alpha_1\alpha_2 \pmod{f\mathcal{O}_{\Delta_1}}$ *is given by*

$$x \equiv x_1x_2 + y_1y_2\frac{\Delta_1}{4} \pmod{f} \tag{9}$$

$$y \equiv x_1y_2 + x_2y_1 \pmod{f} \tag{10}$$

in the case that $\Delta_1 \equiv 0 \pmod 4$ *and*

$$x \equiv x_1x_2 + y_1y_2\frac{\Delta_1 - 1}{4} \pmod{f} \tag{11}$$

$$y \equiv x_1y_2 + x_2y_1 + y_1y_2 \pmod{f} \tag{12}$$

if $\Delta_1 \equiv 1 \pmod 4$.

This result enables us to "model" the conventional ideal arithmetic (multiplication and reduction) by simple calculations modulo f. This leads to the following algorithm for exponentiation, which is based on binary method for exponentiation. We denote the binary length of n by $\lambda(n) = \lfloor \log_2(n) \rfloor + 1$.

Algorithm 4 *(Gen-Exp)*
   Input: $\alpha = x + y\omega \in \mathcal{O}_{\Delta_1}$, *the conductor* f *such that* $\gcd(\mathcal{N}(\alpha), f) = 1$ *and the exponent* $n \in \mathbb{Z}$.
   Output: $\mathfrak{a} = (a, b) = \rho_f(\varphi((\alpha\mathcal{O}_{\Delta_1})^n))$.

1. *IF* $n = 0$ *THEN OUTPUT*$(1, \Delta_1 \pmod 2)$
2. *IF* $n < 0$ *THEN* $n \leftarrow -n$, $y \leftarrow -y$
3. $l \leftarrow \lambda(n) - 1$, $(n_l \ldots n_0)_2 \leftarrow$ *binary expansion of* n, *i.e.* $n_l = 1$
4. $x_h \leftarrow x \pmod f$
5. $y_h \leftarrow y \pmod f$
6. *IF* $\Delta_1 \equiv 0 \pmod 4$ *THEN* $D \leftarrow \Delta_1/4$ *ELSE* $D \leftarrow (\Delta_1 - 1)/4$
7. *FOR* $i = l - 1$ *DOWNTO* 0 *DO*
   7.1 $h \leftarrow x_h$
   7.2 $x_h \leftarrow h^2 + y_h^2 D \pmod f$
   7.3 *IF* $\Delta_1 \equiv 0 \pmod 4$ *THEN* $y_h \leftarrow 2hy_h \pmod f$ *ELSE* $y_h \leftarrow 2hy_h + y_h^2$ $\pmod f$
   7.4 *IF* $n_i = 1$ *THEN*
      7.4.1 $h \leftarrow x_h$
      7.4.2 $x_h \leftarrow hx + y_h yD \pmod f$
      7.4.3 *IF* $\Delta_1 \equiv 0 \pmod 4$ *THEN* $y_h \leftarrow hy + xy_h \pmod f$
            ELSE $y_h \leftarrow hy + xy_h + y_h y \pmod f$
8. /* *Compute the standard representation* $\mathfrak{A} = d(a, b) = \alpha_h\mathcal{O}_{\Delta_1}$ */
   8.1 /* *Use* $\frac{x+y\sqrt{\Delta_1}}{2}$-*form* */
      $x_h \leftarrow 2x_h$
      IF $\Delta_1 \equiv 1 \pmod 4$ *THEN* $x_h \leftarrow x_h + y_h$
   8.2 *Compute* $d \leftarrow \gcd(y_h, (x_h + y_h\Delta_1)/2) = \lambda y_h + \mu(x_h + y_h\Delta_1)/2$, *for* $\lambda, \mu \in \mathbb{Z}$
   8.3 $A \leftarrow |x_h^2 - \Delta_1 y_h^2|/(4d^2)$
   8.4 $B \leftarrow (\lambda x_h + \mu(x_h + y_h)\Delta_1/2)/d \pmod{2A}$

9. /* Lift $\mathfrak{A}' = (1/d)\mathfrak{A}$ to the non-maximal order and reduce it */
   $b \leftarrow Bf \pmod{2A}$
   $(a, b) \leftarrow \rho_f(A, b)$
10. $OUTPUT(a, b)$

Proof: By Lemma 7 we only have to compute $\gamma \equiv \alpha^n \pmod{f\mathcal{O}_{\Delta_1}}$. The correctness of the exponentiation algorithm is immediate because it is the well known binary method with the operation given in Lemma 8 as group operation.

In step 8 we simply compute the standard representation of the ideal $\mathfrak{A} = \alpha_h\mathcal{O}_{\Delta_1} = d(a\mathbb{Z} + (b + \sqrt{\Delta_1})/2\mathbb{Z})$. By Corollary 4 we know that $N(\alpha_h\mathcal{O}_{\Delta_1}) = ad^2$ is prime to f. This clearly implies that $\gcd(d, f) = 1$. Because $\mathfrak{A} = (d)\mathfrak{A}'$ for $d \in \mathbb{Z}$, $\mathfrak{A}' = a\mathbb{Z} + (b + \sqrt{\Delta_1})/2\mathbb{Z}$ we know from Proposition 2 that $\varphi(\mathfrak{A}) \sim \varphi(\mathfrak{A}')$. Finally it is clear that we can apply φ from Proposition 1, because $\gcd(a, f) = 1$ □

5.2 Even More Efficient Arithmetic in $\mathrm{Ker}(\phi_{Cl}^{-1})$ Using CRT in $(\mathcal{O}_{\Delta_1}/p\mathcal{O}_{\Delta_1})^*$

In the previous section we saw that the arithmetic in $\mathrm{Ker}(\phi_{Cl}^{-1})$ can be reduced to arithmetic in $(\mathcal{O}_{\Delta_1}/f\mathcal{O}_{\Delta_1})^*$, which turns out to be much more efficient. In this section we *outline* yet another method for a further speed up. We refer to [17,16] for the details.

We will only concentrate on a special case which seems to be most important for practical application, as it is used in the Schnorr-analogue from [17]. That is we assume that the conductor is a prime p, where $\left(\frac{\Delta_1}{p}\right) = 1$.

Lemma 9. *Let $\mathcal{O}_{\Delta_1}$ be the maximal order and p be prime. Then there is an isomorphism*

$$(\mathcal{O}_{\Delta_1}/p\mathcal{O}_{\Delta_1})^* \simeq \mathbb{F}_p[X]\big/(f(X)),$$

where $(f(X))$ is the ideal generated by $f(X) \in \mathbb{F}_p[X]$ and

$$f(X) = \begin{cases} X^2 - \frac{\Delta_1}{4}, & \text{if } \Delta_1 \equiv 0 \pmod{4}, \\ X^2 - X + \frac{1-\Delta_1}{4}, & \text{if } \Delta_1 \equiv 1 \pmod{4}. \end{cases} \tag{13}$$

Proof: See [16, Proposition 5].   □

Theorem 5. *Assume that $\left(\frac{\Delta_1}{p}\right) = 1$ and the roots $\rho, \bar{\rho} \in \mathbb{F}_p$ of $f(X) \in \mathbb{F}_p[X]$ as given in (13) are known. Then the following isomorphism can be computed in time $O((\log p)^2)$:*

$$(\mathcal{O}_{\Delta_1}/p\mathcal{O}_{\Delta_1})^* \simeq \mathbb{F}_p^* \otimes \mathbb{F}_p^*$$

Proof: From Lemma 9 we know that there is an isomorphic map $(\mathcal{O}_{\Delta_1}/p\mathcal{O}_{\Delta_1})^* \to \mathbb{F}_p[X]/(f(X))$, where $f(X) \in \mathbb{F}_p[X]$ is given in (13). And that this isomorphism is trivial to compute.

Because $\left(\frac{\Delta_1}{p}\right) = 1$ the polynomial $f(X)$ is not irreducible, but can be decomposed as $f(X) = (X - \rho)(X - \bar{\rho}) \in \mathbb{F}_p[X]$ where $\rho, \bar{\rho} \in \mathbb{F}_p$ are the roots of $f(X)$. Thus if $\Delta_1 \equiv 0 \pmod 4$ and $D = \Delta_1/4$ we have $\rho \in \mathbb{F}_p$ such that $\rho^2 \equiv D \pmod p$ and $\bar{\rho} = -\rho$. In the other case $\Delta_1 \equiv 1 \pmod 4$ we have $\rho = (1+b)/2$, where $b^2 \equiv \Delta_1 \pmod p$ and $\bar{\rho} = (1-b)/2 \in \mathbb{F}_p$. Thus we have the isomorphisms

$$(\mathcal{O}_{\Delta_1}/p\mathcal{O}_{\Delta_1})^* \simeq \left(\mathbb{F}_p[X]\Big/(X-\rho)\right)^* \otimes \left(\mathbb{F}_p[X]\Big/(X-\bar{\rho})\right)^* \simeq \mathbb{F}_p^* \otimes \mathbb{F}_p^*.$$

Let $\alpha = a + b\omega \in (\mathcal{O}_{\Delta_1}/p\mathcal{O}_{\Delta_1})^*$ then the mapping $\psi : (\mathcal{O}_{\Delta_1}/p\mathcal{O}_{\Delta_1})^* \to \mathbb{F}_p^* \otimes \mathbb{F}_p^*$ is given as $x_1 = \psi_1(\alpha) = a + b\rho \in \mathbb{F}_p^*$ and $x_2 = \psi_2(\alpha) = a + b\bar{\rho} \in \mathbb{F}_p^*$. The inverse map ψ^{-1} is computed by solving the small system of linear equations. I.e. one will recover $a, b \in \mathbb{F}_p^*$ by computing $b = \frac{x_2 - x_1}{\bar{\rho} - \rho}$ and $a = x_1 - b\rho$. Thus both transformations ψ and ψ^{-1} need time $O((\log p)^2)$. $\qquad\square$

With this result we immediately obtain the of the following algorithm.

Algorithm 6 *(Gen-CRT)*
    Input: $\alpha = x + y\omega \in \mathcal{O}_{\Delta_1}$, the conductor p, such that $\gcd(\mathcal{N}(\alpha), p) = 1$, $\left(\frac{\Delta_1}{p}\right) = 1$, the roots $\rho, \bar{\rho} \in \mathbb{F}_p^*$ of $f(X)$ as given in (13) and the exponent $n \in \mathbb{Z}$.
    Output: $\mathfrak{a} = (a, b) = \rho_p(\varphi((\alpha\mathcal{O}_{\Delta_1})^n))$.

1. IF $n = 0$ THEN OUTPUT$(1, \Delta_1 \pmod 2)$
2. IF $n < 0$ THEN $n \leftarrow -n$, $y \leftarrow -y$
3. $x_1 \leftarrow (x + \rho y)^n \pmod p$
4. $x_2 \leftarrow (x + \bar{\rho}y)^n \pmod p$
5. $r \leftarrow (\bar{\rho} - \rho)^{-1} \pmod p$
6. $y_h \leftarrow (x_2 - x_1)r \pmod p$
7. $x_h \leftarrow x_1 - y_h\rho \pmod p$
8. Compute standard representation, lift and reduce as in Algorithm 4 Step 8.-9.
9. OUTPUT(a, b)

Note that the computation of r in Step 5 can be done in a precomputation phase, as is it independent of the current α.

5.3 Timings for Different Arithmetics

In this section we will give the timinings of a first implementation of the novel arithmetics for $\mathrm{Ker}(\phi_{Cl}^{-1})$. We will also include timings for standard-ideal arithmetic and modular arithmetic to allow comparison.

For the RSA analogues in totally non-maximal orders [15] we fixed $\Delta_1 = -163$ and chose a random exponent $k < n = pq$. For all DL-based systems (DSA and Schnorr) we chose a random $k < 2^{160}$. For the DSA-analogue based on *totally non-maximal* orders we also fixed $\Delta_1 = -163$. Note that due to the recent result [16] this analogue with Δ_p is only as secure as the original scheme with p. Thus one needs to compare the lines for the 1200 bit DSA-analogue in $Cl(\Delta_p)$ with the time for 600 bit modular arithmetic.

For the NICE-Schnorr-analogue [17] we also chose a random $k < 2^{160}$ and $\Delta_p = \Delta_1 p^2$ where $\Delta_1 = -q$ (or $\Delta_1 = -4q$ if $q \equiv 1 \pmod 4$ respectively) and p, q with equal bitlength. Because factoring integers is about as hard as the computation of discrete logarithms (modulo p) one needs to compare the timings where Δ_p and the prime modulus have the same bitlength.

The timings are given in microseconds on a pentium 133 MHz using the LiDIA - package [20]. One should note that the implementation of neither variant is optimized. This is no problem, because we are interested in the comparison, rather than the absolute timings.

cryptosystem		Schnorr / DSA				RSA		
arithmetic	mod.	ideal	Gen-exp	Gen-exp	Gen-CRT	mod.	ideal	Gen-exp
bitlength of	p	Δ_p	$\Delta_p = -163p^2$	$\Delta_p = -qp^2$	$\Delta_p = -qp^2$	$n = pq$	$n = pq$	$n = pq$
600	188	3182	240	159	83	258	10490	994
800	302	4978	368	234	123	583	22381	2053
1000	447	7349	542	340	183	886	35231	3110
1200	644	9984	724	465	249	1771	68150	6087
1600	1063	15751	1156	748	409	3146	125330	10864
2000	1454	22868	1694	1018	563	5284	224799	18067

Table 2. Timings for exponentiation with different arithmetics

The timings in Table 2 show the impressive improvement. One can see that the exponentiation using Algorithm 4 is already about *thirteen* times as fast as an exponentiation using conventional ideal arithmetic, if $\Delta_p = -163p^2$ and *more than twenty* times as fast for the Schnorr-analogue.

If we apply Algorithm 6 as proposed in [17] and outlined in Section 5.2, we are about *forty times* as fast as conventional ideal arithmetic. Using this arithmetic the signature generation in the NICE-Schnorr-analogue is *more than twice* as fast as in the original scheme in $\mathbb{F}_p^*$.

On the other side we see that the RSA-analogue [15] in totally non-maximal orders is still far less efficient than the original scheme and although immune against low exponent and chosen ciphertext attack not preferable for practice.

Finally one should note that for the signature verification in the NICE-Schnorr-scheme one has to use standard ideal arithmetic, which is very inefficient. Thus an important task for the future will be to speed up the standard-ideal arithmetic as well, to enable practical application of the proposed Schnorr-analogue [17].

References

1. Z.I. Borevich and I.R. Shafarevich: *Number Theory* Academic Press: New York, 1966
2. E. Brickell, D. Gordon, K. McCurley, D. Wilson: *Fast Exponentiation with Precomputation*, Proceedings of Eurocrypt 1992, LNCS **658**, Springer, 1993, pp. 200-207
3. J. Buchmann, S. Düllmann: *On the computation of discrete logarithms in class groups*, Advances in Cryptology - CRYPTO '90, LNCS **773**, Springer, 1991, pp. 134-139

4. J. Buchmann and H.C. Williams: *A key-exchange system based on imaginary quadratic fields.* Journal of Cryptology, **1**, 1988, pp. 107-118
5. H. Cohen: *A Course in Computational Algebraic Number Theory.* Graduate Texts in Mathematics **138**. Springer: Berlin, 1993.
6. D.A. Cox: *Primes of the form $x^2 + ny^2$*, John Wiley & Sons, New York, 1989
7. W. Diffie and M. Hellman: *New directions in cryptography*, IEEE Transactions on Information Theory **22**, 1976, pp. 472-492
8. S. Düllmann: *Ein Algorithmus zur Bestimmung der Klassenzahl positiv definiter binrer quadratischer Formen*, PHD-thesis (in german), University of Saarbrücken: 1991
9. T. ElGamal: *A public key cryptosystem and a signature schem based on discrete logarithms*, IEEE Transactions on Information Theory **31**, 1985, pp. 469-472
10. J.L. Hafner, K.S. McCurley: *A rigorous subexponential algorithm for computation of class groups*, Journal of the American Mathematical Society, **2**, 1989, 837-850
11. S. Hamdy, A. Meyer: *personal communication*, 1999
12. M. Hartmann, S. Paulus and T. Takagi: *NICE - New Ideal Coset Encryption*, to appear in the proceedings of CHES, 1999
13. L.K. Hua: *Introduction to Number Theory.* Springer-Verlag, New York, 1982.
14. D. Hühnlein, M.J. Jacobson, S. Paulus and T. Takagi: *A cryptosystem based on non-maximal imaginary quadratic orders with fast decryption*, Advances in Cryptology - EUROCRYPT '98, LNCS **1403**, Springer, 1998, pp. 294-307
15. D. Hühnlein, A. Meyer, T. Takagi: *Rabin and RSA analogues based on non-maximal imaginary quadratic orders*, Proceedings of ICICS '98, ISBN 89-85305-14-X, 1998, pp. 221-240
16. D. Hühnlein, T. Takagi: *Reducing logarithms in totally non-maximal imaginary quadratic orders to logarithms in finite fields*, Advances in Cryptology - Asiacrypt'99, LNCS **1716**, Springer, 1999, pp. 219-231
17. D. Hühnlein, J. Merkle: *An efficient NICE-Schnorr-type cryptosystem*, to appear at PKC2000, Melbourne, January 2000 and Springer LNCS, preprint via `http://www.informatik.tu-darmstadt.de/TI/Veroeffentlichung/TR/Welcome.html#1999`
18. D. Hühnlein: *NICE - Ein neues Public Key Kryptosystem mit sehr schneller Entschlüsselung und seine potentiellen Anwendungen*, (in german) manuscript, 1999
19. M.J. Jacobson Jr.: *Subexponential Class Group Computation in Quadratic Orders*, Berichte aus der Informatik, Shaker, ISBN 3-8265-6374-3, 1999
20. LiDIA: *A c++ library for algorithmic number theory*, via `http://www.informatik.tu-darmstadt.de/TI/LiDIA`
21. P.L. Montgomery: *Speeding the Pollard and Elliptic Curve Methods for Factorization*, Mathematics of Computation, vol. **48**, nr. **177**, Jan. 1987, pp. 243-264
22. National Institute of Standards and Technology (NIST): *Digital Signature Standard (DSS).* Federal Information Processing Standards Publication 186, **FIPS-186**, 19th May, 1994
23. J. Neukirch, *Algebraische Zahlentheorie*, Springer, Berlin, 1992
24. S. Paulus, T. Takagi: *A new public-key cryptosystem over the quadratic order with quadratic decryption time*, to appear in Journal of Cryptology, 1998, preprint via `http://www.informatik.tu-darmstadt.de/TI/Mitarbeiter/sachar.html`
25. R. Rivest, A. Shamir, L. Adleman: *A method for obtaining digital signatures and public key-cryptosystems*, Communications of the ACM,**21**, 1978, pp. 120-126
26. C.P. Schnorr: *Efficient identification and signatures for smart cards*, Advances in Cryptology - CRYPTO '89, LNCS **435**, Springer, 1990, pp. 239-252
27. R.J. Schoof: *Quadratic Fields and Factorization.* In: H.W. Lenstra, R. Tijdeman, (eds.): *Computational Methods in Number Theory.* Math. Centrum Tracts **155**. Part II. Amsterdam, 1983. pp. 235-286.

Improving and Extending the Lim/Lee Exponentiation Algorithm

Biljana Cubaleska[1], Andreas Rieke[2], and Thomas Hermann[3]

[1] FernUniversität Hagen, Department of communication systems
Feithstr. 142, 58084 Hagen, Germany
biljana.cubaleska@fernuni-hagen.de
http://ks.fernuni-hagen.de/mitarbeiter/cubalesk/
[2] ISL Internet Sicherheitslösungen GmbH
Feithstr. 142, 58097 Hagen, Germany
andreas.rieke@isl-online.de
http://ks.fernuni-hagen.de/~rieke/
[3] MMK GmbH, Feithstr. 142
58097 Hagen, Germany
thomas.hermann@mmk-hagen.de
http://www.mmk-hagen.de/

Abstract. In [5] Lim and Lee present an algorithm for fast exponentiation in a given group which is optimized for a limited amount of storage. The algorithm uses one precomputation for several computations in order to minimize the average time needed for one exponentiation. This paper generalizes the previous work proposing several improvements and a method for fast precomputation. The basic Lim/Lee algorithm is improved by determining the optimal segmentation of the exponent. Finally, it is shown that the improved Lim/Lee algorithm is faster than the previous one in average case.

1 Introduction

Modular exponentiation is a basic operation widely used in cryptography. In many cryptographic protocols users must perform one or more exponentiations in a given group. Well known examples are encryption, decryption and signatures with RSA [8], signature generation and identification as in Digital Signature Standard (DSS) [7], Brickell/McCurley [2], Schnorr [10], and many other schemes. The exponentiation can be decomposed into a large number of multiplications, so it is an operation which is heavily computational, consumes a lot of time and constitutes a computational bottleneck in many protocols. The efficiency of most public-key crypto systems mainly depends on the speed of the exponentiation algorithm.

Classical algorithms for exponentiation are the binary algorithm (known as the square-and-multiply method, [4]) and the signed binary algorithm [3]. Other algorithms use some amount of storage for intermediate values in order to improve the performance. Examples are the windowing method [4,6] and algorithms based on addition chains [1,9]. In [5] Lim and Lee present a new exponentiation

Howard Heys and Carlisle Adams (Eds.): SAC'99, LNCS 1758, pp. 163–174, 2000.
© Springer-Verlag Berlin Heidelberg 2000

algorithm based on precomputations. The goal of this algorithm is to achieve a minimal number of operations (squarings and multiplications) for an exponentiation under the condition of limited amount of storage. The required number of operations for the precomputation has thereby not been considered.

The Lim/Lee algorithm optimizes the evaluation of the exponentiation g^e in a given group (usually Z_N, N being a large prime or a product of two large primes) in a case when the base g is fixed and the exponent e is randomly chosen. The fixed base g allows the usage of a precomputation table in order to reduce the number of computations required, but the algorithm has an additional cost of storage for the precomputed values. Such an algorithm that is independent of e, but depends on g is suitable for use in most discrete logarithm based protocols for signature generation and identification (e.g. [7,2,10]).

In this paper we present a generalization and several improvements of the exponentiation algorithm of Lim/Lee. We focus our observations on the speed of the algorithm without concerning the storage costs for the precomputed elements, and then compare it's behaviour for limited storage. Furthermore, we present an efficient algorithm for precomputation and therewith optimize the total number of operations for a given exponentiation, i.e. the number of operations for the precomputation and for several computations based on it. Finally, both algorithms are compared for variable length of the exponent.

The Lim/Lee algorithm is described in section 2 and our improvements are presented in section 3. A new precomputation algorithm is proposed in section 4. Some comparisons of the variants of the Lim/Lee algorithm in a case when unlimited storage is available with the windowing method are given in section 5 and the behaviour of the algorithm under the condition of limited storage is presented in section 6. Finally, section 7 concludes the paper.

2   The Lim/Lee Algorithm

In this section the Lim/Lee exponentiation algorithm is briefly presented with a slightly changed terminology. In the next section we present and discuss the improved and extended algorithm.

In order to compute the exponentiation g^e with the Lim/Lee algorithm, the l-bit exponent e is divided into h blocks e_i, each with length $a = \lceil \frac{l}{h} \rceil$. The exponent e can be written as

$$e = e_{h-1}e_{h-2}\ldots e_1 e_0 = \sum_{i=0}^{h-1} e_i 2^{ia}. \tag{1}$$

Each of the blocks e_i is further subdivided into v smaller blocks of size $b = \lceil \frac{a}{v} \rceil$ and each block e_i can be represented as

$$e_i = e_{i,v-1}e_{i,v-2}\ldots e_{i,1}e_{i,0} = \sum_{j=0}^{v-1} e_{i,j} 2^{jb}. \tag{2}$$

Each block $e_{i,j}$ consists of b bits $e_{i,j,k}$ and can be represented as

$$e_{i,j} = e_{i,j,b-1}e_{i,j,b-2}\ldots e_{i,j,1}e_{i,j,0} = \sum_{k=0}^{b-1} e_{i,j,k}2^k. \qquad (3)$$

It is further assumed that the number of blocks h and v are chosen in a way that e_{h-1} and $e_{i,v-1}, 0 \le i < h - 1$ are not equal to zero. The segmentation of the exponent e is shown in figure 1. Based on the length l of the exponent and on the parameters h and v, the precomputation leads to the array $G[j][u]$ with $0 \le j < v$ and $1 \le u < 2^h$. Employing the binary representation $u_{h-1}u_{h-2}\ldots u_1 u_0$ of u and $r_i = g^{2^{ia}}$, the array $G[j][u]$ is defined by the following equations:

$$G[0][u] = \quad r_{h-1}^{u_{h-1}} r_{h-2}^{u_{h-2}} \ldots r_1^{u_1} r_0^{u_0} \qquad (4)$$

$$G[j][u] = (G[j-1][u])^{2^b} = G[0][u]^{2^{jb}} \quad \forall \quad 1 \le j < v \qquad (5)$$

Using the definition

$$I_{j,k} = \sum_{i=0}^{h-1} e_{i,j,k}2^i, \qquad (6)$$

the exponentiation can be described with the following algorithm:

1. SET $R = 1$.
2. FOR $k = b - 1$ DOWNTO 0
    (a) SET $R = R^2$.
    (b) FOR $j = v - 1$ DOWNTO 0
        i. SET $R = R \cdot G[j][I_{j,k}]$.
3. RETURN R.

We denote the considered algorithm as 1. Lim/Lee algorithm. This algorithm needs $b - 1$ squarings[1] and $\frac{2^h-1}{2^h}a - 1$ multiplications in average, but $a - 1$ multiplications in the worst case. Thus, the average number of operations needed to perform a single exponentiation with this algorithm is

$$C_{Lim/Lee,1} = a(b-1) + \frac{2^h - 1}{2^h}a - 1. \qquad (7)$$

In [5] the exponent is represented either as in figure 1 – in several rows each of v blocks – or as shown in figure 2 – with a shortened last row. The length of the blocks by partitioning as in figure 2 (we denote it as 2. Lim/Lee algorithm) is

$$b_2 = \left\lceil \frac{l}{(h-1)v + v_{last}} \right\rceil \qquad (8)$$

$$b_1 = \left\lceil \frac{l - b_2 \cdot h \cdot v_{last}}{(h-1)(v - v_{last})} \right\rceil. \qquad (9)$$

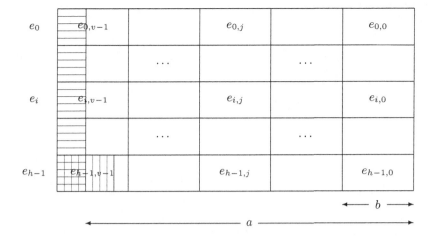

Fig. 1. Partitioning an l-bit exponent e in h rows with the same length according to the 1. Lim/Lee algorithm

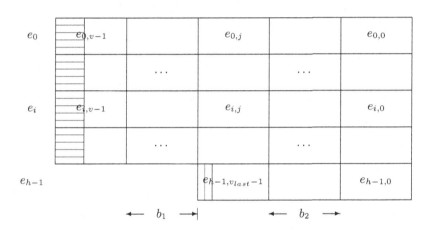

Fig. 2. Partitioning of a l-bit-exponent e with shortened last row according to the 2. Lim/Lee algorithm

The computational cost in this case consists of $b_2 - 1$ squarings, $b_1(v - v_{last}) + b_2 \cdot v_{last} - 1$ multiplications in the maximum and $\frac{2^{h-1}-1}{2^{h-1}}b_1(v - v_{last}) + \frac{2^h-1}{2^h}b_2 \cdot v_{last} - 1$ multiplications in the average. Thus, the average number of operation

---

[1] Many squaring algorithms are faster than an ordinary multiplication, by making use of the fact that both multiplicands are equal. On the other hand, multiplication is performed with a constant multiplicand and – after performing some precomputations – may also be faster than a squaring. Here α denotes the ratio of the computational complexity of the algorithms for squaring and multiplying.

needed for one exponentiation is

$$C_{Lim/Lee,2} = \alpha\,(b_2 - 1) + \frac{2^{h-1} - 1}{2^{h-1}}b_1\,(v - v_{last}) + \frac{2^h - 1}{2^h}b_2 \cdot v_{last} - 1. \quad (10)$$

3 The Improved Algorithm

When using the algorithms described in the last section, the following problems arise:

- Two algorithms are presented by Lim and Lee without a statement which algorithm should be preferred in a given case.
- It is not examined how to find the optimal choice of the parameters h and v resp. h, v and v_{last}; exhaustive search with three parameters is very expensive.

In order to find appropriate solutions for this problem we examine the algorithms described in the previous section in some detail. If we allow the partitioning of the exponent with $v_{last} \geq 0$ in a rectangular form as a special case of the second algorithm, the result in case of same partitioning ($h_1 = h_2 - 1$ and $v_1 = v_2$) is $b_1 = b = b_2$ and thus $C_{Lim/Lee,1} \geq C_{Lim/Lee,2}$. It is obvious that in case of $v_{last} = 0$ the second algorithm can not be better than the first one.

It is also shown in section 5 that the second algorithm is not worse than the first one in any point. This can also be seen from the results of the numerical tests for all lengths of the exponent l in the range up to 512 bit.

Since the second algorithm has been identified to be the better one, we further try to decrease the number of basic parameters in this algorithm. The existence of three basic parameters (h, v and v_{last}) makes the exhaustive search expendable and slow. A fundamental advantage can be achieved in the case if a and b are used as basic parameters instead of h and v. We derive the parameters $h = \lceil \frac{l}{a} \rceil$ and $v = \lceil \frac{a}{b} \rceil$ from the basic parameters a and b, and the partitioning of the exponent that results from this determination of the basic parametar is given in figure 3. We denote the partitioning the exponent in this way as 3. Lim/Lee algorithm. The number of bits in the last row is now only $a_{last} = l - a(h - 1)$, and they are divided into $v_{last} = \lceil \frac{a_{last}}{b} \rceil$ blocks. The number of bits in the last block is $b_{last} = a_{last} - b(v_{last} - 1)$. With this new way of partitioning of the exponent we can achieve computational cost of

$$C_{Lim/Lee,3} = \alpha\,(b - 1) + \frac{2^h - 1}{2^h}a - 1 \quad (11)$$

as the average number of operations for one exponentiation. Although this formula is the same as (7), the parameters a, b, and h can have values different from those in (7) due to the different segmentation. It is shown in section 5 that the computational cost for this algorithm is never higher than the computational cost for each of both basic algorithms.

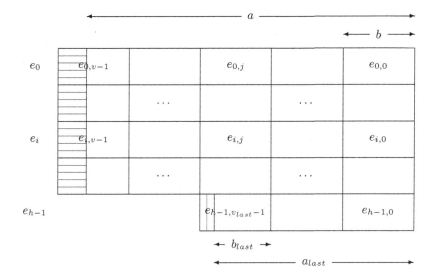

Fig. 3. Partitioning of a l-bit exponent e according to the extended, 3. Lim/Lee algorithm

A further improvement results from the observation of the last row in figure 3: The term $\frac{2^h-1}{2^h}a - 1$ in equation 11 results from the fact that the multiplication in line 2.b.i in the algorithm description in section 2 is trivial with probability 2^{-h}. Concerning the fact that the last row must not be filled completely we can use the term $\frac{2^{h-1}-1}{2^{h-1}}(a - a_{last}) + \frac{2^h-1}{2^h}a_{last} - 1$ instead (we denote it as 4. Lim/Lee algorithm). This improvement does not concern the algorithm itself, but only the specification of its average number of operation, and leads to

$$C_{Lim/Lee,4} = \alpha(b-1) + \frac{2^{h-1}-1}{2^{h-1}}(a - a_{last}) + \frac{2^h-1}{2^h}a_{last} - 1 \qquad (12)$$

as the average number of operations for one exponentiaton.

4 Precomputation

In all variations of the Lim/Lee algorithm analyzed above only the number of operations for the computation is concerned, assuming that the precomputation has already been performed. The computational cost for the precomputation of the array $G[j][u]$ has not been considered at all and an algorithm for the precomputation of the array $G[j][u]$ is not given in [5]. Proposals for the precomputation algorithm can be found in other works (e.g. [6, p. 626]), but they are not efficient. Since the precomputation makes a considerable fraction of the total number of operations, we present an efficient algorithm for the precomputation consisting of two steps:

1. Since we have the array $G[j][u]$ for $u = 2^i$, $0 \le i < h$ and $0 \le j < v$ in form r^{2^x}, the appropriate values can be computed with repeated squarings beginning with r. Always when the exponent matches to the exponent in (4) and/or (5), the corresponding value is assigned to the array element. The number of squarings needed for this step is

$$a(h-1) + b(v_{last} - 1).\tag{13}$$

2. The remaining elements can be computed directly from the last step with one multiplication for each case. From $2^{h-1} - 1$ rows in the upper half, $h - 1$ rows have already been computed in the first step, whereas only one from the 2^{h-1} rows from the lower half is already finished. The number of multiplications needed for this step is

$$v\left(2^{h-1} - h\right) + v_{last}\left(2^{h-1} - 1\right).\tag{14}$$

Thus, the total number of operations needed for the precomputation is

$$P = \alpha\left(a(h-1) + b\left(v_{last} - 1\right)\right) + v\left(2^{h-1} - h\right) + v_{last}\left(2^{h-1} - 1\right).\tag{15}$$

An example for precomputation with partitioning of the exponent with $h = 3$, $v = 3$, $v_{last} = 2$ is given in figure 4. The values computed with squarings in the first step are marked with S, and the multiplications in the second step are marked with M. The results of the precomputations and computations with

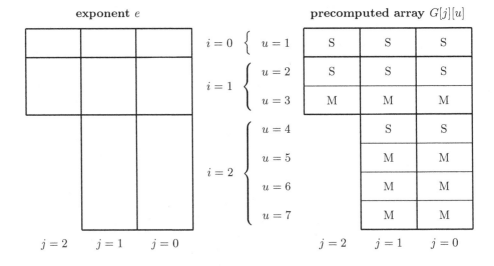

Fig. 4. Precomputation of the array $G[j][u]$ in the Lim/Lee algorithm ($h = 3$, $v = 3$ and $v_{last} = 2$)
M: Multiplication
S: Squaring

various parameters and partitioning for one exponent with length $l = 15$ are shown in table 1. Using exhaustive search, the parameters shown in the table have been found out as optimal for this case. The computational cost is

$$O_{Lim/Lee,x} = P + z \cdot C_{Lim/Lee,x} \tag{16}$$

where z denotes the number of computations based on a single precomputation, and $x = 1, 2, 3, 4$.

Table 1. Comparison of the Lim/Lee algorithms using the example $l = 15, \alpha = 1$ and $z = 1$
C: Number of operations needed for the computation
P: Number of operations needed for the precomputation
O: Total number of operations (precomputation and computation)

	Algorithm 1	Algorithm 2	Algorithm 3	Algorithm 4
h	1	2	2	2
v	1	2	2	2
v_{last}		1	1	1
a	15		8	8
b_1		5		
b resp. b_2	15	5	7	7
C	20.5	9.25	11	10.75
P	0	11	9	9
O	20.5	20.25	20	19.75

5   Optimization of Precomputation and Computation for (Nearly) Unlimited Memory

The variations of the Lim/Lee algorithm described in the sections 2 and 3 are analyzed and compared in this section for exponents up to 512 bit length. A comparison with the windowing exponentiation algorithm is also given. The efficiency of the algorithms is measured by the average number of operations, where the multiplications and the squarings are treated equally ($\alpha = 1$).

The optimal parameters for each algorithm have been determined with exhaustive search. The results for the range $l \leq 192$ are shown in figure 5. The improvements compared to the first Lim/Lee algorithm are shown in per cents.

An exact comparison of the required number of operations in one exponentiation (precomputation and computation) shows that for all exponent lengths l and a single exponentiation ($z = 1$) the following inequality

$$O_{Lim/Lee,1} \geq O_{Lim/Lee,2} \geq O_{Lim/Lee,3} \geq O_{Lim/Lee,4} \tag{17}$$

is satisfied. This means that the fourth Lim/Lee algorithm has the lowest computational cost, and we set

$$O_{Lim/Lee} = O_{Lim/Lee,4}. \tag{18}$$

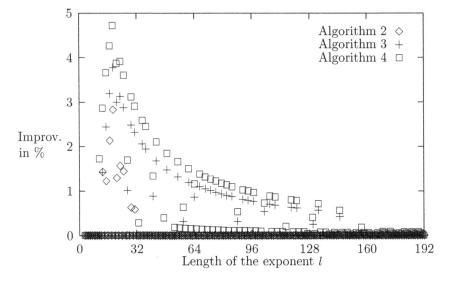

Fig. 5. Comparison of the variants of the Lim/Lee algorithm

In the range of $l > 192$ that is not presented, the algorithms 1-3 behave in the same way and only the fourth algorithm has small improvements.

We now compare the windowing exponentiation algorithm with the Lim/Lee algorithm. In figure 6 we can see the average number of operations, whereby the average number of operations needed for one exponentiation consist of one precomputation and z computations.

First, for a given length of the exponent l and given number of exponentiations z, the optimal values of the parameters (k for the windowing algorithm, a and b for the Lim/Lee algorithm) are determined with exhaustive search. Then the total number of operations is determined as a sum of the number of operations for the precomputation and number of operations for z computations. We get the average number of operations dividing the total number of operations by z, in order to get comparable results.

If only a single exponentiation is performed, the windowing algorithm leads to the lowest number of operations. In a case when several exponentiations which base on the same precomputation need to be performed, and the exponents have the same length l, the Lim/Lee algorithm has the best performance.

6   Optimization of the Computation for Limited Memory

The results presented in the last section concern the case when the amount of storage needed for the intermediate results of the precomputation is practically unlimited. This condition is satisfied when the exponentiation is performed on a PC or workstation. But the case when only limited storage and processing power are available must also be concerned, since many of the cryptographic protocols

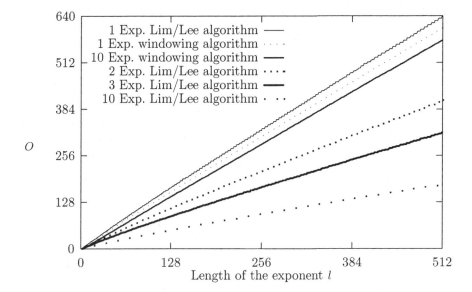

Fig. 6. Comparison of the exponentiation algorithms
O: Average number of operations needed for a single exponentiation

using exponentiation (signature generation and verification schemes) are performed on smart cards. The precomputation table in the Lim/Lee algorithm can reduce the number of multiplications required at the expense of storage for the precomputed values.

The numerical results for the time-memory tradeoffs for exponent lengths of 160 and 512 bit are summarized in the tables 2 and 3 for various variants of the Lim/Lee algorithm and optimal partitioning of the exponent in each case. The same examples as in [5] are considered and it is assumed that the squarings and the multiplications have the same computational cost ($\alpha = 1$). The improved Lim/Lee algorithm is usually faster and never slower than the others in average case. We can see that if more storage is available, the algorithm becomes faster by the decreasing number of multiplications required. The compromise by limited storage is a slower algorithm due to the increasing number of operations required. An exponentiation with 160 bit exponent can be performed with only 19.96 multiplications in average if 2299 intermediate values from the precomputation are stored. If only 10 values can be stored, the same exponentiation requires 82 multiplications. So, by known storage capacity of a smart card, we can estimate how fast the given exponentiation can be and vice versa.

Table 2. Exponentiations with 160 bit (*AC*: Average case, *WC*: Worst case)

Sto-rage	Algorithm 1 Conf. h/v	AC	WC	Algorithm 2 Conf. $h/v/v_{last}$	AC	WC	Algorithm 3 Conf. a/b	AC	WC	Algorithm 4 Conf. a/b	AC	WC
6	2/2	98	118	3/2/0	98	118	80/40	98	118	80/40	98	118
10	2/3	85	105	3/2/1	82	94	80/27	85	105	64/32	82	94
14	3/2	72.25	79	4/2/0	72.25	79	54/27	72.25	79	54/27	72	79
22	3/3	63.25	70	4/2/1	62.69	67	54/18	63.25	70	46/23	62.63	67
30	4/2	55.5	58	5/2/0	55.5	58	40/20	55.5	58	40/20	55.5	58
45	4/3	49.5	52	5/3/0	51.38	54	40/14	49.5	52	40/14	49.5	52
62	5/2	45	46	6/2/0	45	46	32/16	45	46	32/16	45	46
77	4/5	43.5	46	5/3/2	42.63	44	34/12	42.94	44	34/12	42.63	44
93	5/3	40	41	6/3/0	40.97	42	32/11	40	41	32/11	40	41
124	5/4	37	38	6/4/0	37	38	32/8	37	38	32/8	37	38
157	5/5	36	37	6/3/2	35.44	36	28/10	35.56	36	28/10	35.44	36
189	6/3	33.58	34	7/3/0	33.58	34	27/9	33.58	34	27/9	33.55	34
252	6/4	31.58	32	6/6/2	32.22	33	27/7	31.58	32	27/7	31.55	32
317	6/5	30.58	31	7/3/2	29.75	30	24/8	29.81	30	24/8	29.75	30
381	7/3	28.82	29	6/7/5	29.44	30	23/8	28.82	29	23/8	28.81	29
508	7/4	26.82	27	7/5/2	27.69	28	23/6	26.82	27	23/6	26.81	27
762	7/6	24.82	25	7/6/4	25.75	26	23/4	24.82	25	23/4	24.81	25
1020	8/4	22.92	23	9/4/0	22.92	23	20/5	22.92	23	20/5	22.92	23
1785	8/7	20.92	21	8/11/3	21.85	22	20/3	20.92	21	20/3	20.92	21
2299	8/7	20.92	21	9/5/4	19.96	20	18/4	19.96	20	18/4	19.96	20

Table 3. Exponentiations with 512 bit (*AC*: Average case, *WC*: Worst case)

Sto-rage	Algorithm 1 Conf. h/v	AC	WC	Algorithm 2 Conf. $h/v/v_{last}$	AC	WC	Algorithm 3 Conf. a/b	AC	WC	Algorithm 4 Conf. a/b	AC	WC
6	2/2	318	382	3/2/0	318	382	256/128	318	382	256/128	318	382
10	2/3	276	340	3/2/1	267.6	306	257/85	275.8	340	205/103	267.5	306
14	3/2	233.6	255	4/2/0	234.5	256	171/86	233.6	255	171/86	233.5	255
22	3/3	204.6	226	4/2/1	204.4	218	171/57	204.6	226	146/74	204.4	218
30	4/2	182	190	5/2/0	182	190	128/64	182	190	128/64	182	190
45	4/3	161	169	5/3/0	161.9	170	128/43	161	169	128/43	161	169
62	5/2	149.8	153	5/3/1	149.9	156	103/52	149.8	153	103/52	149.7	153
93	5/3	132.8	136	6/3/0	134.7	138	103/35	132.8	136	103/35	132.7	136
125	5/4	123.8	127	6/3/1	123.5	126	103/26	123.8	127	96/32	123.5	126
157	5/5	118.8	122	6/3/2	117.2	119	90/31	117.6	119	90/31	117.2	119
189	6/3	111.7	113	7/3/0	112.6	114	86/29	111.7	113	86/29	111.6	113
252	6/4	104.7	106	6/5/3	106.1	108	86/22	104.7	106	86/22	104.6	106
317	6/5	100.7	102	7/3/2	100.2	101	82/21	100.4	101	82/21	99.88	101
381	7/3	96.42	97	7/4/2	97.06	98	79/20	96.38	97	79/20	96.06	97
508	7/4	90.42	91	7/5/3	91.16	92	74/19	90.42	91	74/19	90.38	91
635	7/5	86.42	87	8/5/0	87.41	88	74/15	86.42	87	74/15	86.38	87
892	7/7	82.42	83	8/4/3	80.68	81	66/17	80.74	81	66/17	80.68	81
1020	8/4	77.75	78	9/4/0	77.75	78	64/16	77.75	78	64/16	77.75	78
1275	8/5	74.75	75	9/5/0	75.75	76	64/13	74.75	75	64/13	74.75	75
1530	8/6	72.75	73	8/7/5	73.68	74	64/11	72.75	73	64/11	72.75	73
2040	8/8	69.75	70	9/8/0	69.75	70	64/8	69.75	70	64/8	69.75	70
2555	9/5	66.89	67	9/6/4	67.84	68	59/10	66.88	67	59/10	66.85	67
3066	9/6	64.89	65	9/8/4	65.83	66	57/10	64.89	65	57/10	64.89	65
4089	9/8	62.89	63	10/7/1	61.90	62	56/8	61.95	62	56/8	61.90	62
5626	9/10	60.89	61	10/6/5	58.94	59	52/9	58.95	59	52/9	58.94	59
7672	10/7	57.95	58	10/8/7	56.95	57	53/6	56.95	57	53/6	56.93	57
10234	10/9	55.95	56	11/6/4	53.97	54	48/8	53.98	54	48/8	53.97	54
13305	11/6	52.98	53	11/7/6	51.97	52	47/7	51.98	52	47/7	51.97	52

7 Conclusions

We generalize the exponentiation algorithm [5] by making several improvements in the computations and in the precomputation achieving a decrease of the computational cost for a single exponentiation (precomputation and computation). For the computations, the partitioning of the exponent is modified in a way which reduces the number of multiplications. Furthermore, we propose a new efficient method of precomputation for the Lim/Lee algorithm, minimizing the total time needed for a single exponentiation. We compare the exponentiation algorithms, showing that if several exponentiations based on the same precomputation are performed, the Lim/Lee algorithm has the best performance. The fact that time consuming precomputations have to be done limits the applicability of the algorithm to those cryptosystems where the same base is used often, which holds for most discrete logarithm based systems. Although only slight improvements are made, these are quite remarkable because of the importance of exponentiation. The exponentiation can be additionally speeded up by applying parallel processing and is applicable to various computing environments due to its wide range of time-storage trade-offs.

References

1. J. Bos and M. Coster. *Addition Chain Heuristics*. In G. Brassard, editor, *Advances in Cryptology - CRYPTO '89*. LNCS 435, pp. 400-407. Springer-Verlag, 1990.
2. E. F. Brickell and K. S. McCurley. *An Interactive Identification Scheme Based on Discrete Logarithms and Factoring*. In *Journal of Cryptology 5* (1992), no. 1, pp. 29-39.
3. J. Jedwab and C. J. Mitchell. *Minimum Weight Modified Signed-Digit Representations and Fast Exponentiation*. Elect. Let. 25 (17), pp. 1171-1172 (1989).
4. D. E. Knuth. *The Art of Computer Programming, Vol.2: Seminumerical algorithms*. Third edition, Addison-Wesley, 1997.
5. C. H. Lim and P. J. Lee. *More Flexible Exponentiation with Precomputation*. In Yvo G. Desmedt, editor, *Advances in Cryptology - CRYPTO '94*. LNCS 839, pp. 95-107. Springer-Verlag, 1994.
6. A. J. Menezes, P. C. van Oorschot, and Scott A. Vanstone. *Handbook of Applied Cryptography*. CRC Press series on discrete mathematics and its applications. CRC Press, Boca Raton, 1997.
7. National Institute of Technology and Standards. *Specifications for the Digital Signature Standard (DSS)*. Federal Information Processing Standards Publication XX, US Department of Commerce, February 1 1993.
8. R. L. Rivest, A. Shamir, and L. Adleman. *A Method for Obtaining Digital Signatures and Public Key Cryptosystems*. Communications of ACM 21 (1978), pp 120-126.
9. P. de Rooij. *Efficient Exponentiation Using Precomputation and Vector Addition Chains*. In de Santis, editor, *Advances in Cryptology - EUROCRYPT '94*. LNCS 950, pp. 389-399. Springer-Verlag, 1994.
10. C. P. Schnorr. *Efficient Signature Generation by Smart Cards*. In *Journal of Cryptology 4 (1991), no. 3, pp. 161-174*.

Software Optimization of Decorrelation Module

Fabrice Noilhan

Université Paris-Sud, LRI
Bât. 490, 91405 Orsay, Cedex, France
Fabrice.Noilhan@lri.fr

Abstract. This paper investigates software optimization of special multiplication. In particular we concentrate on $ax + b \bmod 2^{64} + 13 \bmod 2^{64}$ which is the bottleneck operation in the DFC cipher. We show that we can take advantage of the language and architecture properties in order to get efficient implementations.

In this paper we use the ANSI C and the Java languages. We also investigate assembly code, and data structure alternatives. Finally, we show that we can also use floating point arithmetic.

1 Introduction

Several cryptographic algorithms require that some particular multiplication is optimized. In particular, the DFC AES candidate [1] was believed to be substantially slower than the others because its main operation $ax + b \bmod 2^{64} + 13 \bmod 2^{64}$ was believed to be necessarily slow. In this paper we concentrate on optimization techniques for this operation. The results are of course not restricted to DFC since other cryptographic algorithms use this kind of primitive. For instance, the MMH MAC algorithm [3] uses the $\sum_{i=1}^{k} m_i x_i \bmod (2^{32} + 15) \bmod 2^{32}$ function, the Shazam [5] algorithm uses the $(x + k)^2 \bmod p \bmod n$ operation.

We will first introduce how to do a division-less modular reduction. Then, we will see what are the choices to implement the multiplication and this modular reduction. We will point out some security issues about the implementation itself since there are many ways to implement it and see that most concerns can be solved using proper operations. We finally will show what are the best choices to get optimal performances with generic ANSI C, 64-bit C, assembly language and Java on Alpha, Pentium II, UltraSparc processors and on IA64 architecture.

2 Calculation of $ax + b \bmod 2^{64} + 13 \bmod 2^{64}$

The multi-precision multiplication is best implemented in a straightforward manner since optimizations such as Karatsuba do not seem worthwhile for such small operands.

As a division is rather slow, we must have another method to do modular reduction. We will use the following method:

Howard Heys and Carlisle Adams (Eds.): SAC'99, LNCS 1758, pp. 175–183, 2000.

Let $P = ax + b$. Note that since a, x and b are 64-bit numbers, P is a 128-bit number $(ax + b \leq 2^{128} - 2^{64})$. We first write

$$P = Q2^{64} + R$$

where R is the remainder of the Euclidean division of P by 2^{64}. It follows that

$$P = Q(2^{64} + 13) + R - 13Q$$

and this is equal to $R - 13Q$ modulo $2^{64} + 13$.

The subtraction is a problem since it can lead to two different cases: $R - 13Q \geq 0$ and $R - 13Q < 0$. Dealing with negative values is tedious since we have to take care about timing attacks and use sometimes back and forth conversions between signed and unsigned integers (we want to use all register bits for multiplication). This can be avoided while splitting the value into smaller words but, usually, it is not effective.

As we are doing arithmetic modulo $2^{64} + 13$, we can use the bitwise complement to do subtraction:

$$\begin{aligned} P' = R - 13Q &= R + 13(2^{64} - 1 - Q) - 13(2^{64} - 1) \mod 2^{64} + 13 \\ &= R + 13(2^{64} - 1 - Q) + 182 \qquad \mod 2^{64} + 13. \end{aligned}$$

$2^{64} - 1 - Q$ is the 64-bit bitwise complement of Q. The result is always positive and is most of the time greater than $2^{64} + 13$. Thus, we can perform a similar reduction for P': $P' = Q'2^{64} + R'$, and $Q' \leq 14$. Then, we can use a small table to compute the final values.

3 Some Possibilities

3.1 Multiplication

Implementations should use arithmetic on numbers of the largest size that is efficiently available on the target processor.

The key factor for speed is the multiplication of two 64-bit quantities yielding a 128-bit result. We have to do a number of multiplications which depends on the multiplier of the processor as shown in the table 1.

Table 1. Number of multiplications required

operands(bits)	result(bits)	# multiplications
64	128	1
32 or 64	64	4
16 or 32	32	16
8 or 16	16	64

We also have to add the resulting values and the number of additions depends on the size of the registers used (cf table 2).

cf table 2

Table 2. Number of additions required

registers(bits)	# additions
64	4
32	18
16	88

The total cost of additions is typically less than the cost of the multiplications but is not negligible. Thus, optimizations of this part of the algorithm are of prime importance, especially when dealing with carries.

It is sometimes worth doing more operations on smaller operands, since they may be faster. Tables 1 and 2 should give a fair estimation of the cycle counts.

3.2 Modular Reduction

Before the modular reduction, we need to add the constant b. This can be done either before or after the multiplication. The choice is generally made by the language used: a low-level language with "add with carry" implies usually a straightforward implementation of the multiplication. Otherwise, adding the constant in the same time as we multiply can save some cycles.

Then, we can implement the modular reduction in many different ways. First, we have to split the 128-bit result of the multiplication into many words. On the one hand, if we use words of the maximum size available, then we will not have any room left to store carries so that we will need to propagate them. On the other hand, using words of smaller size will imply more operations. Depending on the processor and its parallelization level, one solution is faster than the other.

In the reduction itself, the multiplication by the constant 13, as explained in the previous section is usually optimized by the compiler. This is not the case on UltraSparc (Sun WC 5.0 compiler) or in Java; we have to do it manually with shifts and adds. The second step of the reduction implies another multiplication of a low operand. On most processors, this operation is faster using a small lookup table. Not only it is faster but it avoids some problems of timings attacks with such small operands.

4 Security Issues

Since the implementation of the algorithm can be done in many distinct ways, one has to take care about security issues of the implementation itself.

First of all, the multipliers on some chips can compute the product of small operands in fewer cycles than for large operands. This feature may make timing attacks possible, as is the case with most algorithms using integer multiplications (e.g. RC6, Mars).

Recently, Harvey [2] has noticed that an attack of DFC can be made on careless implementations. He supposes a different approach than the one we present here. Our implementations can be easily made resistant to timings attacks (except on the multiplier itself), and rare code paths are easy to test.

Care must be taken with the propagation of carries. On some chips, the fastest implementation uses branches and thus is vulnerable to timing attacks. On low end processors, the cost of such a protection is noticeable since there are many carries to propagate. But on Pentium Pro for instance, the cost is only about 40 cycles.

5 Dedicated Optimizations

5.1 ANSI C

Writing portable ANSI C code entails that you do not know anything about the representation of the objects. When you need a 32-bit unsigned integer, you have to use an **unsigned long**.

So, using 32-bit integers for both multiplication and additions, an implementation of the round function requires at least 16 multiplications and 18 additions.

On most processors, this implementation will not have a high speed compared to an assembly coded function: the processor may be able to deal with larger registers or the processor may have some particular properties (e.g. a larger multiplier, or an add-with-carry opcode). Those characteristics can not be used in a portable ANSI C code.

Still, an ANSI code should compile and produce the same results whichever system and (ANSI) compiler you use. The tradeoff between portability and efficiency is generally costly.

As regards to the modular reduction, since we do not know anything about the processor, it does not make much sense to choose between alternatives. The addition of b can be made within the multiplication. We should use 32-bit words to do the modular reduction, since it would otherwise require too many operations.

5.2 C with 64-Bit Integers

A new norm, called C9X, will allow to use 64-bit integers (such as in JAVA for instance). Indeed, it will not only help 64-bit processors to give their full power, but also it will be helpful for 32-bit processors (such as Pentium II) which have a larger multiplier.

Using 64-bit **unsigned long long**, one can use only 4 multiplications to compute the 128-bit multiplication of the round function. One should switch back to the 32-bit integers next, since other operations on 64-bit integers are emulated by the compiler. Thus they yield to poor performance.

For native 64-bit processors, not only does the use of 64-bit types reduce the number of operations, but these operations are faster: 32-bit operations are often emulated by the processor (using integer masks for example) and are slower than 64-bit opcodes.

In this code, we can use 32-bit words, even on 64-bit processors, to do the modular reduction. With 32-bit processors, it is obvious. With 64-bit processors, many instructions are executed each cycle. So you may group into 32-bit words for free if it helps parallelization. The main advantage is that the propagation of carries is eased since we do them only once at the end of the computing (they are stored in the 32 most significant bits of the registers during the calculation).

5.3 Alpha

The Alpha 21164 has a multiplier which takes two 64-bit inputs and provides the least significant or most significant half of the 128-bit result after 12 or 14 cycles respectively. Also, the multiplications can overlap and can run in parallel with other operations.

If we use portable ANSI C code, which only guarantees arithmetic up to 32 bits, then performance is relatively poor on 64-bit chips. We have to break numbers into 32-bit pieces and cannot use any 64-bit capabilities, in particular fast multipliers such as that on the 21164.

ANSI C permits implementations to provide 64-bit arithmetic however, and by taking advantage of this we gain a lot of speed. We still cannot get the most significant half of a 64×64-bit product however. On Alpha we use the assembly language instruction, umulh from C (by implementation-dependent methods) to attain the best performance on this architecture.

Since the multiplication is atomic, the addition of $b + 182$ is made after it. We use 64-bit words, the first multiplication by 13 is done via shifts and the second one is left to the compiler (which implements it correctly). This can be done efficiently in C.

More extensive use of assembly language does not appear to yield any significant improvement.

5.4 Pentium II

The Pentium II is a 32-bit processor with a multiplier which takes two 32-bit inputs and returns the 64-bit result. The multiplication instruction is fast: it only takes 4 cycles. So, the entire multiplication and the modular reduction should be fast as well.

However, the expected speed is not achievable in C. Using only ANSI C, we are not able to use the multiplication with 64-bit result. Even if we do use 64-bit integers via the **long long** type (which will be part of C9X), compiled code does not use addition with carry instruction and it does a lot of unnecessary data movement between registers and memory.

To implement the integer multiplication in assembly, we take advantage of two operations: addition with carry and 32-by-32 multiplication.

The modular reduction is done with 32-bit words, and use a table lookup. Once again, we need the addition with carry, so that it is also done in assembly language.

When the whole computation is done in registers using assembly language, we get the expected speed of the function.

5.5 UltraSparc

The UltraSparc is a 64-bit processor. Until recently, it could not be used as such in C since there was no compiler for 64-bit mode. Sun's new C compiler 5.0 handles 64-bit integers and performs well on 64-bit C code.

The multiplier takes two 64-bit inputs and computes the least significant half of their product. Unlike the situation on Alpha, there is no method to get the most significant half. Thus, we have to do four multiplications to get the full result. These multiplications are rather slow: each of them takes about 20 cycles so that the time for the entire multiplication is large. The time for modular reduction is insignificant in comparison.

In order to achieve better results, we can use the Floating Point Unit. The FPU has a double precision multiplier which we will use in a slightly unusual way. Since the FPU uses the IEEE 754 [1] representation of numbers, we can use 52 significant bits with double precision floating-point numbers. This means that we can multiply 24-bit values and add several of the results without any round-off error occurring. Thus, we can do a 64×64-bit product using nine 24×24-bit multiplications (and some additions). Alternatively we can do eight 16×32-bit multiplications. These methods are faster than using four integer multiplications.

The only problem is to convert from integers to floats. When done with casts in C, it uses a function of the C library and is very slow. When done in assembler using the FiTOd instruction, it is not much better. For reasonable speed we have to do it manually via a bit mask and an addition. Similar tricks are used to convert from floating-point numbers back to integers in order to do the modular reduction.

This enables us to achieve better performances for the multiplication than the standard 64-bit C code.

The modular reduction is implemented with 32 bit words and carries are stored into high order bits of the registers. Multiplications by 13 are all made using shifts and additions.

5.6 IA64 Architecture

Intel has recently unveiled specifications of its next architecture, called IA64. This enables us to estimate the cycle counts of the Merced processor.

The Merced is a 64-bit processor. We have no idea at the moment whether compilers will be able to deal with the full set of instructions so that we will

---

[1] ANSI/IEEE Standard 754-1985: Standard for Binary Floating Point Arithmetic

only consider assembly language. The key point is that IA64 has a full 64-bit to 128-bit unsigned integer multiply so it will end up in the fast category. The instruction xma is an integer $a * x + b$ (which can never overflow 128 bits).

Terje Mathisen has written an IA64 implementation of the round function and gets a round timing of 30 cycles with some more or less obvious possibilities to save a few more cycles. Of these 30 cycles, 10 are taken by a pair of sequential xma operation, but the second can be handled with integer code instead, since the multiplier is small and known (13).

The one possible problem is that integer multiplication uses the floating point registers, so the (currently unknown but believed to be 1 cycle) time to convert back and forth between integers and floating point mantisses is in addition to the two xma.u operations needed for the low and high halves of the result. For best performance, all the integers and floating point constants need to be placed in registers before starting the inner loop.

As predication replaces branches in the carry propagation, there should be no possibility for a timing attack based on key or data values.

Thus, the 240 cycles count compares well to the 231 cycles on a 21264 Alpha. This answers to the criticism that the decorrelation module should be slow on Merced and shows that some non-trivial optimizations of the code can give a huge improvement of speed. We also note that the numerous registers and the multiplier should enable a fast RSA implementation.

5.7   Java

There is a very simple way to implement the multiplication and the modular reduction in JAVA, using BigIntegers. Unfortunately, this slows down the speed dramatically. It has the advantage of only taking two or three lines of code and can provide a reference but not an optimized implementation.

Java provides a 64-bit integer data type, which is always signed. Anyway, the signed-ness can just be ignored in the arithmetic operations we need: additions, subtractions and multiplications are defined in the standard as if they were modulo 2^{64} and bitwise logical operations use the sign bit as in normal twos-complement representation. There is an unsigned right shift operator, as well as a signed one. The only restriction is that we can neither use comparisons (which could have been useful to propagate carries) nor use signed divisions (which we do not need anyway). These characteristics are described in the Java Virtual Machine specifications [4].

Thus, the implementation is essentially the same as a 64-bit C version. Since we cannot do casts (even using "assembly" Java bytecode) and since we cannot use comparisons, the implementation is naturally resistant to endianess issues and to most timing attacks (except for the multiplications).

Even if one could produce specific Java code for a processor, it does not gain very much. Optimized versions for Pentium II and UltraSparc uses the same tricks as optimized C codes. Most of the optimizations dedicated to the processors are done in JIT compilers. Even hand-written bytecode, which should produce faster code, does not have a noticeable speedup. The reason why we can not do optimizations is that the set of opcodes is very small and the whole job is given to the JIT compiler which optimizes the code for the given processor. Since 64-bit operations are part of the language, they are well optimized by the compiler, which reorders and expands some instructions.

Some errors should be avoided to help the compiler: splitting into functions as we can do in C, using a multiplication by 13 on UltraSparc processor. But the Java compilers are relatively new and improve quickly.

With the development of Web services and online payment, these JAVA implementations become all the more important and huge improvements of speed have been done during the past year: JIT compilers and now HotSpot technology should give a speed equivalent to C++ according to Sun Microsystems (that is roughly the speed of C in cryptography).

6 Conclusion

When going to results, there are two facts to outline: one should use the largest integers available and the round function is not always well optimized by compilers.

On Alpha, on account of the lack of a C instruction to get the most significant half of the multiplication, 200 cycles are lost. The same problem may exist on IA64. On Pentium II, compilers do not achieve the expected speed because there are too few registers. Results on the UltraSparc are disappointing as a result of the slow multiplier.

In the following table 3, we compare ANSI C portable code and 64-bit C code to the best implementation available in order to show the importance of the optimizations.

Table 3. Number of cycles for DFC

Processor	JAVA	ANSI C	64-bit C	Best
Alpha 21164	n/a	2562	526	310 (ASM)
Pentium II	1481	2592	1262	392 (ASM)
UltraSparc	4087	4160	875	775 (C with floats)
Alpha 21264	n/a	n/a	335	231 (ASM)
IA64	n/a	n/a	n/a	240 (estimated)

With generic ANSI C code, DFC is one of the slowest AES candidates on all platforms. Using assembly language, it becomes the fastest on Alpha processors and among the fastest on Intel Pentium II and Merced processors.

We have seen what are the best solutions on various microprocessors and languages. Harvey [2] thought that "correct implementations may be difficult to achieve". We have shown that correct and fast implementations can be easily made.

As the cost of this decorrelation module is nearly the same as the cost of the multiplication, it could be used as a plug-in in many other algorithm without significant decrease of the performances. The drawback is that its optimization requires access to some low-level instructions (add with carry, most significant bits of the multiplication) which are generally not available in a high-level language such as C.

Acknowledgments

We thank Serge Vaudenay, Robert Harley and Terje Mathisen for comments and suggestions on this work. We also thank Dominik Behr, Robert Harley, Danjel McCougan, Terje Mathisen and David Seal for their implementations of DFC from which most of the work is derived.

Java is a trademark of Sun Microsystems, Inc. in the United States and other countries.

References

1. H. Gilbert, M. Girault, P. Hoogvorst, F. Noilhan, T. Pornin, G. Poupard, J. Stern, S. Vaudenay. Decorrelated Fast Cipher: an AES Candidate. (Extended Abstract.) In *Proceedings from the First Advanced Encryption Standard Candidate Conference*, National Institute of Standards and Technology (NIST), August 1998.
2. Harvey. The DFC Cipher: an attack on careless implementations In *Proceedings of the second AES Workshop*, 1999
3. Haveli, Krawczyk MMH: Message authentication in software in the Gbit/sec rates In *Proceedings of the 4th Workshop on Fast Software Encryption*, 1997
4. Lindholm, Yellin The Java[tm] Virtual Machine Specification, Second Edition Sun Microsystems, ISBN: 0-201-43294-3
5. Patel, Ramzan, Sundaram. Towards Making Luby-Rackoff Ciphers Optimal and Practical To appear in *Proceedings of the 6th Workshop on Fast Software Encryption*, 1999

Pseudonym Systems

(Extended Abstract)

Anna Lysyanskaya[1], Ronald L. Rivest[1], Amit Sahai[1], and Stefan Wolf[2]

[1] MIT LCS, 545 Technology Square, Cambridge, MA 02139 USA
{anna,rivest,amits}@theory.lcs.mit.edu
[2] Computer Science Department, ETH Zürich, CH-8092 Zürich, Switzerland
wolf@inf.ethz.ch

Abstract. Pseudonym systems allow users to interact with multiple organizations anonymously, using pseudonyms. The pseudonyms cannot be linked, but are formed in such a way that a user can prove to one organization a statement about his relationship with another. Such a statement is called a credential. Previous work in this area did not protect the system against dishonest users who collectively use their pseudonyms and credentials, i.e., share an identity. Previous practical schemes also relied very heavily on the involvement of a trusted center. In the present paper we give a formal definition of pseudonym systems where users are motivated not to share their identity, and in which the trusted center's involvement is minimal. We give theoretical constructions for such systems based on any one-way function. We also suggest an efficient and easy-to-implement practical scheme.

Keywords: Anonymity, pseudonyms, nyms, credentials, unlinkability, credential transfer.

1 Introduction

Pseudonym systems were introduced by Chaum [8] in 1985, as a way of allowing a user to work effectively, but anonymously, with multiple organizations. He suggests that each organization may know a user by a different pseudonym, or *nym*. These nyms are *unlinkable*: two organizations cannot combine their databases to build up a dossier on the user. Nonetheless, a user can obtain a credential from one organization using one of his nyms, and demonstrate possession of the credential to another organization, without revealing his first nym to the second organization. For example, Bob may get a credential asserting his good health from his doctor (who knows him by one nym), and show this to his insurance company (who knows him by another nym).

Anonymity and pseudonymity are fascinating and challenging, both technically —can we achieve them?—and socially—do we want them? We focus on technical feasibility, referring the reader in the social question to excellent recent treatments by Brin [4] and Dyson [17].

Chaum and Evertse [10] develop a model for pseudonym systems, and present an RSA-based implementation. While pseudonyms are information-theoretically unlinkable, the scheme relies on a trusted center who must sign all credentials.

Howard Heys and Carlisle Adams (Eds.): SAC'99, LNCS 1758, pp. 184–199, 2000.

Damgård [14] constructs a scheme based on multi-party computations and bit commitments that provably protects organizations from credential forgery by malicious users and the central authority, and protects the secrecy of the users' identities information-theoretically. The central authority's role is limited to ensuring that each pseudonym belongs to some valid user.

Chen [12] presents a discrete-logarithm-based scheme, where a trusted center has to validate all the pseudonyms, but does not participate in the credential transfer. Chen's scheme relies very heavily on the honest behavior of the trusted center, because a malicious trusted center can also transfer credentials between users.

These schemes have a common weakness: there is little to motivate or prevent a user from sharing his pseudonyms or credentials with other users. For example, a user may buy an on-line subscription, obtaining a credential asserting his subscription's validity, and then share that credential with all of his friends. More serious examples (e.g. driver's licenses) are easy to imagine.

We base our proposed scheme on the presumption that each user has a *master public key* whose corresponding secret key the user is highly motivated to keep secret. This master key might be registered as his legal digital signature key, so that disclosure of his master secret key would allow others to forge signatures on important legal or financial documents in his name. Our proposed scheme then has the property that a user can not share a credential with a friend without sharing his master secret key with the friend, that is, without *identity sharing*. Tamper-resistant devices such as smartcards are not considered in this work.

Basing security on the user's motivation to preserve a high-value secret key has been proposed before, such as in Dwork *et al.*'s work on protecting digital content [16] and Goldreich *et al.*'s study of controlled self-delegation [21]. In recent work, Canetti *et al.* [6] incorporated this notion into anonymous credential-granting schemes to prevent credential sharing among users. However, the model considered in their work differs considerably from our own: while we explore a whole system of organizations interacting with pseudonymous users, [6] assume that organizations only grant credentials to users who reveal their identity to them, though the credentials can then be used anonymously. The practical constructions they give, while based on weaker assumptions than ours, are not applicable to our situation since they take crucial advantage of the fact that the credential granting organization knows the identity of the user it grants a credential to.

In our model, a certification authority is needed only to enable a user to prove to an organization that his pseudonym actually corresponds to a master public key of a real user with some stake in the secrecy of the corresponding master secret key, such that the user can only share a credential issued to that pseudonym by sharing his master secret key. As long as the CA does not refuse service, a cheating CA can do no harm other than introduce invalid users into the system, i.e. users who have nothing to lose in the outside world.

In our model, each user must first register with the CA, revealing his true identity and his master public key, and demonstrating possession of the corresponding master secret key. (Sometimes it is not required that a user should be motivated not to share his identity. In those cases, the CA is not needed altogether.) After registration, the user may open accounts with many different organizations using different, unlinkable pseudonyms. However, all pseudonyms are related to each other—there exists an identity extractor that can compute a user's public and secret master keys given a rewindable user who can authenticate himself as the holder of the pseudonym.

An organization may issue a credential to a user known by a pseudonym. A credential may be *single-use* (such as a prescription) or *multiple-use* (such as a driver's license), and may also have an expiration date. Single-use credentials are similar to electronic coins, since they can only be used once in an anonymous transaction. Some electronic coin protocols protect against double-spending by violating the anonymity of double-spenders, but generally do not protect against transfer of the coin. A credential should be usable only by the user to whom it was issued.

In section 2 we formally define our model of a pseudonym system. In section 3 we extend Damgård's result [14], and prove that a pseudonym system can be constructed from any one-way function. In section 4 we give a practical construction of a pseudonym system based on standard number-theoretic assumptions and the hardness of a new Diffie-Hellman-like problem [15,3] which we prove hard with respect to generic group algorithms. Our construction is easily implementable. Moreover, the secret key that motivates the user not to share his identity is usable in many existing practical encryption and signature schemes [13,15,18,31]. As a result, our system integrates well with existing technology. Finally, we close by discussing some open problems.

2 The Pseudonym Model

2.1 Overview

Informal Definitions. In a pseudonym system, users and organizations interact using procedures. We begin the discussion of the model by introducing the procedures.

- *Master key generation.* This procedure generates master key pairs for users and organizations. A crucial assumption we make is that users are motivated to keep their master secret key secret. This assumption is justified, because master public/secret key pairs can correspond to those that the users form for signing legal documents or receiving encrypted data. A user, then, is an entity (a person, a group of people, a business, etc.) that holds a master secret key that corresponds to a master public key.
- *Registration with the certification authority.* The certification authority (CA) is a special organization that knows each user's identity, i.e. the master public key of the user. Its role is to guarantee that users have master public/secret key pairs that will be compromised if they cheat. The user's nym with the CA is his master public key. The CA issues a credential to him that states that he is a valid user.

- *Registration with an organization.* A user contacts the organization and together they compute a nym for the user. There exists an identity extractor which, given a rewindable user that can authenticate himself as the nym holder, extracts this user's master public/secret key pair. Then the user demonstrates to the organization that he possesses a credential from the CA.
- *Issue of credentials.* The user and the organization engage in an interactive protocol by which the user obtains a credential.
- *Transfer of credentials.* A user who has a credential can prove this fact to any organization, without revealing any other information about himself. We call this operation "transfer" of a credential, because a credential is transferred from the user's pseudonym with one organization, to his pseudonym with the other.

We want to protect the system from two main types of attacks:

- *Credential forgery:* Malicious users, possibly in coalition with other organizations including the CA, try to forge a credential for some user.
- *User identity compromise or pseudonym linking:* Malicious organizations form a coalition to try to obtain information about a user's identity, either by getting information about the user's master public/secret key pair, or by identifying a pair of pseudonyms that belong to the same user.

The main difference between our model of a pseudonym system and the previous models is that in our model the notion of a user is well-defined. In the treatment of Damgård, a user is an entity who happens to be able to demonstrate the validity of a credential with the certification authority. Whether this credential was originally issued to the same entity, or to a different one who subsequently shared it, remains unclear and therefore such systems are liable to a credential forgery attack, namely credential forgery by sharing.

2.2 The General Definitions

Preliminaries.
Let k be the security parameter, and let 1^k denote the unary string of length k. We use the terms such as Turing machine, interactive Turing machine, probabilistic Turing machine, polynomial-time Turing machine, secure interactive procedure, and rewindable access in a standard way defined in the literature [19] and in the full version of the present paper [26].

Procedures.
Master Key Generation:

Definition 1. *Asymmetric key generation G is a probabilistic polynomial-time procedure which, on input 1^k, generates master public/secret key pair (P, S) (notation $(P, S) \in G(1^k)$ means that (P, S) were generated by running G) such that*

1. The public key P that is produced contains a description (possibly implicit) of a Turing machine V which accepts input S.
2. For any family of polynomial-time Turing machines $\{M_i\}$, for all sufficiently large k, for $(P, S) \in G(1^k)$,

$$\Pr_{P,S}[M_k(P) = s \text{ such that } V(s) = ACCEPT] = neg(k)$$

Each user U generates a master key pair $(P_U, S_U) \in G(1^k)$ and each organization O generates a master public/secret key pair $(P_O, S_O) \in G_U(1^k)$ using asymmetric key generation procedure G_U.

Organization's Key Generation: For each type C of credential issued by organization O, O generates a key pair $(P_O^C, S_O^C) \in G_O(1^k)$ using asymmetric key generation procedure G_O. In this paper, we assume that each organization only issues one type of credential; our results generalize straightforwardly to handle multiple credential types per organization.

Nym Generation: The user U generates a nym N for interacting with organization O by engaging in a secure interactive procedure NG between himself and the organization.

Definition 2. *Nym generation NG is a secure interactive procedure between two parties, a user with master key pair (P_U, S_U), and an organization with master key pair (P_O, S_O). The common input to NG is (P_O), U has private input (P_U, S_U), and O has private input (S_O). We assume that nym generation is done through a secure anonymous communication channel that conceals all information about the user. The common output of the protocol is a nym N for user U with the organization. The private output for the user is some secret information $SI_{U,O}^U$, and for the organization some secret information $SI_{N,O}^O$.*

We let $N(U, O)$ denote the set of nyms that user U has established with organization O. In this paper we assume that there is at most one such nym, although our results can be easily generalized. Similarly, we let $N(U)$ denote the set of nyms the user U has established with any organization, and let $N(O)$ denote the set of nyms that the organization O has established for any user.

Communication between a User and an Organization: After a nym is established, the user can use it to communicate with the organization, using secure nym authentication defined as follows:

Definition 3. *Secure nym authentication is a secure interactive procedure between user U and organization O. Their common input to the procedure is $N \in N(U, O)$. The organization accepts with probability $1 - neg(k)$ if the user can prove that he knows $(P_U, S_U, SI_{U,O}^U)$ such that S_U corresponds to P_U and N was formed by running NG with user's private input (P_U, S_U) and private output $SI_{N,O}^O$. Otherwise, the organization rejects with probability $1 - neg(k)$.*

Single-Use Credentials: A single-use credential is a credential that a user may use safely once, but if used more than once may allow organizations to link different nyms of the user. A user who wishes to use such a credential more than once should request instead multiple copies of the credential from the organization.

Multiple-Use Credentials: A multiple-use credential may be safely transferred to as many organizations as the user wishes without having to interact further with the issuing organization.

Credential Issue: To issue a credential to nym $N \in N(U, O)$, the organization first requires that the user proves that he is the owner of N by running nym authentication, and then the organization O and the user U run interactive procedure CI.

Definition 4. *Credential issue procedure CI is a secure interactive procedure between the user with master public/secret key pair (P_U, S_U) and secret nym generation information $SI_{U,O}^U$, and the organization with master public/secret key pair (P_O, S_O) and secret nym generation information $SI_{N,O}^O$, with the following properties:*

1. *The common input to CI is (N, P_O).*
2. *The user's private input to CI is $(P_U, S_U, SI_{U,O}^U)$*
3. *The organization's private input to CI is $(S_O, SI_{N,O}^O)$.*
4. *The user's private output is the credential, $C_{U,O}$.*
5. *The organization's private output is secret information, $CSI_{N,O}^O$.*

Note that the output of CI, namely $C_{U,O}$, is not necessarily known to the organization.

Credential transfer: To verify that a user with nym $N \in N(U, O')$ has a credential from organization O, organization O' runs a secure interactive procedure CT with the user U.

Definition 5. *Credential transfer procedure CT is a secure interactive procedure between user U with master public/secret key pair (P_U, S_U), nyms $N \in N(U, O)$ and $N' \in N(U, O')$, corresponding secret nym generation information $SI_{U,O}^U$ and $SI_{U,O'}^U$), and credential $C_{U,O}$; and organization O' that has master public/secret key pair $(P_{O'}, S_{O'})$ and secret nym generation information $SI_{N',O'}^O$. Their common input to CT is (N', P_O). U's private input to CT is $(P_U, S_U, C_{U,O}, N, SI_{U,O}^U, SI_{U,O'}^U)$ (where N is U's pseudonym with O). O' has private input to CT $SI_{N',O'}^O$. If the inputs to CT are valid, i.e. formed by running the appropriate protocols above, then O' accepts, otherwise O' rejects with probability $1 - neg(k)$.*

Note that if the credential is single-use, CT does not need to be an interactive procedure. The user needs only reveal $C_{U,O}$ to O', and then O' will perform the necessary computation.

If the credential is multiple-use, this procedure need not be interactive either. The user might only need to compute a function on $C_{U,O}$, P_U and S_U and hand the result over to O' to convince O' that he is a credential holder.

Requirements.

All the procedures described above constitute a secure pseudonym system if and only if they satisfy the requirements outlined below. The reader is referred to the full version of the present paper for a more rigorous treatment of these requirements.

Each Authenticated Pseudonym Corresponds to a Unique User: Even though the identity of a user who owns a nym must remain unknown, we require that there exists a canonical Turing machine called the *identity extractor ID*, such that for any valid nym N, given rewindable access to a Turing machine M that can successfully authenticate itself as the holder of N with non-negligible probability, $ID(N, M)$ outputs valid master public key/secret key pair with high probability. Moreover, we require that for each nym, this pair be unique.

Security of the User's Master Secret Key: We want to make sure that user U's master secret key S_U is not revealed by his public key P_U or by the user's interaction with the pseudonym system. We require that whatever can be computed about the user's secret key as a result of the user's interaction with the system, can be computed from his public key alone.

Credential Sharing Implies Master Secret Sharing: User Alice who has a valid credential might want to help her friend Bob to improperly obtain whatever privileges the credential brings. She could do so by revealing her master secret key to Bob, so that Bob could successfully impersonate her in all regards. We cannot prevent this attack, but we do require of a scheme that whenever Alice discloses some information that allows Bob to use her credentials or nyms, she thereby is effectively disclosing her master secret key to him. That is to say that there exists an extractor such that if Bob succeeds in using a credential that was not issued to his pseudonym, then the secret key of another user who does possess a valid credential, can be extracted by having rewindable access to Bob.

Unlinkability of Pseudonyms: We don't want the nyms of a user to be linkable at any time better than by random guessing.

Unforgeability of Credentials: We require that a credential may not be issued to a user without the organization's cooperation.

Pseudonym as a Public Key for Signatures and Encryption: Additionally, there is an optional but desirable feature of a nym system: the ability to sign with one's nym, as well as encrypt and decrypt messages.

2.3 Building a Pseudonym System from these Procedures

If we are given procedures with the properties as above, we can use them as building blocks for nym systems with various specifications. To ensure that each user uses only one master public/secret key pair, and one that is indeed external to the pseudonym system, we need the certification authority. The certification authority is just an organization that gives out the credential of validity. The user establishes a nym N with the CA, reveals his true identity and then authenticates himself as the valid holder of N. He then proves that $ID(N) = (P_U, S_U)$, where P_U is U's master public key, as the CA may verify. Then the CA issues a credential of validity for N, which the user may subsequently transfer to other organizations, to prove to them that he is a valid user.

In some systems there is no need for a certification authority, because there is no need for a digital identity to correspond to a physical identity. For example, in a banking system it is not a problem if users have more than one account or if groups of individuals open accounts with banks and merchants.

We refer the reader to the full version of the paper for a comprehensive treatment of other useful features a pseudonym system might have.

3 Constructions of Pseudonym Systems Based on Any One-Way Function

This section focuses on demonstrating that the model that we presented in Section 2 is feasible under the assumption that one-way functions exist. Our theoretical constructions use zero-knowledge proofs, and therefore they do not suggest a practical way of implementing a pseudonym system. Rather, their significance is mostly in demonstrating the feasibility of pseudonym systems of various flavors. It is also in demonstrating that the existence of one-way functions is a necessary and sufficient condition for the existence of pseudonym systems as we define them.

3.1 Preliminaries

The definitions for the terms such as one-way functions, zero-knowledge proofs and knowledge extractors, bit commitment schemes [28], and signature schemes [24,30] can be found in standard treatments [22].

Theorem 1. *The existence of one-way functions is a necessary condition for the existence of pseudonym systems.*

This theorem follows from the way we defined asymmetric key generation. See the final version of this paper [26] for the proof.

In the constructions of a pseudonym systems presented below, we will need to use the fact that existence of one-way functions implies the existence of secure bit commitment schemes [28] and signature schemes [24,30]; and also of zero-knowledge protocols with knowledge extractors [19].

3.2 Construction of a System with Multiple-Use Credentials

Our theoretical construction of a system with multiple-use credentials is a straightforward extension of the construction by Damgård [14].

Suppose we are given a signature scheme $(G, Sign, Verify)$, where G is the key generation algorithm; $Sign(PK, SK, m)$ is the procedure that, on input key pair $(PK, SK) \in G(1^k)$ and message m produces a signature s, denoted as $s \in \sigma_{PK}(m)$; and $Verify(PK, m, s)$ is the verification algorithm.

Also suppose we are given a bit commitment scheme $(Commit, Check)$ where $Commit(a, r)$ is the commitment algorithm that produces a commitment to a with randomness r; if $c = Commit(a, r)$ then $Check(c, a, r)$ verifies that c is a commitment to a.

A user U runs $G(1^k)$ to create his master public key/secret key pair (P_U, S_U); an organization O creates its master public key pair (P_O, S_O) similarly.

To register with the CA, the user reveals his public key P_U to the CA. The CA outputs $C_{U,CA} \in \sigma_{CA}(P_U)$.

To establish a pseudonym with an organization O, the user U computes $N_{U,O} = Commit((P_U, S_U), R_{U,O})$ where $R_{U,O}$ is a random string that the user has generated for the purposes of computing this pseudonym and which corresponds to his private output $SI_{U,O}^U$.

To prove that his pseudonym $N_{U,O}$ is valid and that he has registered with the CA, the user proves knowledge of P_U, S_U, $R_{U,O}$ and $C_{U,CA}$ such that

1. S_U corresponds to P_U.
2. $N_{U,O} = Commit((P_U, S_U), R_{U,O})$,
3. $Verify_{CA}(P_U, C_{U,CA}) = ACCEPT$.

The identity extractor ID is the knowledge extractor for the above zero-knowledge proof of knowledge that outputs P_U and S_U components.

To issue a credential to a user known to the organization O as N, the organization O outputs a signature $C_{U,O} \in \sigma_O(N)$.

Let the user's nym with organization O' be N'. To prove to O' that he has a credential from O, the user executes a zero-knowledge proof of knowledge of P_U, S_U, R, R', N and $C_{U,O} \in \sigma_O(N)$ such that

1. S_U corresponds to P_U.
2. $N = Commit((P_U, S_U), R)$,
3. $N' = Commit((P_U, S_U), R')$,
4. $Verify_O(N, C_{U,O}) = ACCEPT$.

Theorem 2. *The system described above is a pseudonym system.*

The proof can be found in the full version of the paper.

3.3 Construction of a System with Single-Use Credentials

This is essentially the same construction. The master key and pseudonym generation procedures are identical. The difference is that each credential has a serial number, which is an additional input in the credential issue and transfer procedures.

4 Practical Constructions

We will begin this section by describing some well-known constructions based on the discrete logarithm problem. We then show how, using the constructions, to build a scheme that implements our model of a pseudonym system with one-time credentials.

4.1 Preliminaries

Setting We assume that we are working in a group G_q of prime order q, in which the discrete logarithm problem and the Diffie-Hellman problems (computational, decisional, etc.) are believed to be hard. We also rely on the random oracle model.

4.2 Building Blocks

Proving Equality of Discrete Logarithms First, we review protocol Π, the protocol of Chaum and Pedersen [11] that is assumed to be a zero knowledge proof of equality of discrete logarithms.

Protocol Π for Proving Equality of Discrete Logarithms:

Common inputs: $g, h, \tilde{g}, \tilde{h} \in G_q$
Prover knows: $x \in \mathbb{Z}_q^*$ such that $h = g^x$ and $\tilde{h} = \tilde{g}^x$

$\quad P \longrightarrow V :$ Choose $r \in_R \mathbb{Z}_q^*$; Send $(A = g^r, B = \tilde{g}^r)$.
$\quad V \longrightarrow P :$ Choose $c \in_R \mathbb{Z}_q^*$; Send c.
$\quad P \longrightarrow V :$ Send $y = r + cx \bmod q$.
$\quad V :$ $\qquad$ Check that $g^y = Ah^c$ and $\tilde{g}^y = B\tilde{h}^c$.
Note that to obtain Π_{NI}, the non-interactive version of Π,
$\quad$ set $c = \mathcal{H}(A, B)$, where $\mathcal{H}$ is the hash function.

This protocol proves both knowledge of the discrete logarithm x, and the fact that it is the same for (g, h) and $(\tilde{g}, \tilde{h})$. The following summarizes what is known about such a protocol:

Theorem 3. *If, as a result of executing protocol Π, the verifier accepts, then with probability $1 - neg(k)$, the prover knows x such that $g^x = h \bmod p$.*

Theorem 4. *If, as a result of executing protocol Π, the verifier accepts, then with probability $1 - neg(k)$, $x_1 = x_2$, where x_1 is such that $g^{x_1} = h \bmod p$ and x_2 is such that $\tilde{g}^{x_1} = \tilde{h} \bmod p$.*

Conjecture 1. Protocol Π is a secure interactive procedure [11,31].

We note that the knowledge extractor E for protocol Π just needs to ask the prover two different challenges on the same commitment, and then solve the corresponding system of linear equations $y_1 = r + c_1 x$ and $y_2 = r + c_2 x$ to compute the secret x.

Non-interactive Proof of Equality of DL. We note that Π can be made non-interactive (we denote it by Π_{NI}) by using a sufficiently strong hash function $\mathcal{H}$ (for example a random oracle [2]) to select the verifier's challenge based on the prover's first message.

Blind Non-interactive Proof of Equality of DL. Clearly, we can obtain a transcript of this non-interactive protocol by executing the interactive protocol. In addition, we can execute the interactive protocol in such a way that the prover's view of it cannot be linked with the resulting transcript. In protocol Γ, if γ is selected at random, the transcript produced by Γ is equally likely to have come from any $\tilde{g}$ and any choice of r and c.

Protocol Γ: Producing a Blinded Transcript of Protocol Π_{NI}:

Common inputs and prover knowledge: same as in protocol Π
Verifier input: $\gamma \in \mathbb{Z}_q^*$.
Verifier wants: use prover of Π to produce valid transcript of protocol Π_{NI} on input $g, h, \tilde{G} = \tilde{g}^\gamma, \tilde{H} = \tilde{h}^\gamma$.
Note: Prover behavior is identical to protocol Π.

$P \longrightarrow V$: Choose $r \in_R \mathbb{Z}_q^*$; Send $(A = g^r, B = \tilde{g}^r)$.
$V \longrightarrow P$: Choose $\alpha, \beta, \in_R \mathbb{Z}_q^*$. Let $A' = A g^\alpha h^\beta$, $B' = (B \tilde{g}^\alpha \tilde{h}^\beta)^\gamma$.
         Send $c = \mathcal{H}(A', B') + \beta \bmod q$.
$P \longrightarrow V$: Send $y = r + cx \bmod q$.
V :   Check that $g^y = Ah^c$ and $\tilde{g}^y = B\tilde{h}^c$.
         Note: $g^{(y+\alpha)} = A' h^{(c-\beta)}$ and $\tilde{G}^{(y+\alpha)} = B'\tilde{h}^{(c-\beta)}$.
V :   Output transcript: $((A', B'), \mathcal{H}(A', B'), y + \alpha)$.

The above protocol is blind, that is, if the verifier runs it with the prover several times and then shows one of the outputs to the prover, the prover will not be able to guess correctly which conversation the output refers to, any better than by random guessing. The following theorem is well-known; we refer the reader to the final version of this paper for a proof:

Theorem 5. *The verifier's output in protocol Γ is independent of the prover's view of the conversation.*

4.3 The Construction

We are now ready to present our construction based on the building blocks introduced above. Our construction is similar in flavour to that given by Chen [12].

High-Level Description. A user's master public key is g^x, and the corresponding master secret key is x. A user's nym is formed by taking a random base a, such that the user does not know $\log_g a$, and raising it to the power x. As a result, all of the user's nyms are tied to his secret x. When a credential is issued, we want to make sure that it will not be valid for any secret other than x.

A credential in our construction is a non-interactive proof of knowledge of the organization's secret. If the user uses it twice, it can be linked, since he cannot produce another such credential on his own.

Detailed Description. The pseudonym system protocols are implemented as follows:

User Master Key Generation: The user picks his master secret $x \in \mathbb{Z}_q^*$ and publishes $g^x \bmod p$.

Organization Credential Key Generation: The organization picks two secret exponents, $s_1 \in \mathbb{Z}_q^*$ and $s_2 \in \mathbb{Z}_q^*$, and publishes $g^{s_1} \bmod p$ and $g^{s_2} \bmod p$.

Nym Generation: We describe this protocol in the figure below.

Pseudonym Generation:

User U's master public key: g^x
User U's master secret key: x

$\quad U:$ Choose $\gamma \in_R \mathbb{Z}_q^*$. Set $\tilde{a} = g^\gamma$ and $\tilde{b} = \tilde{a}^x$.
$\quad U \longrightarrow O:$ Send $(\tilde{a}, \tilde{b})$.
$\quad O:$ Choose $r \in_R \mathbb{Z}_q^*$. Set $a = \tilde{a}^r$.
$\quad O \longrightarrow U:$ Send a.
$\quad U:$ Compute $b = a^x$.
$\quad U \longleftrightarrow O:$ Execute protocol Π to show $\log_a b = \log_{\tilde{a}} \tilde{b}$
$\quad U, O:$ Remember U's nym $N = (a, b)$.
Note that in the special case that O is the CA, the user should
    send (g, g^x) instead of $(\tilde{a}, \tilde{b})$.

Communication between a User and an Organization: To authenticate nym (a, b), the user and the organization execute a standard secure protocol that proves user's knowledge of $\log_a b$. (E.g. they can run Π to prove that $\log_a b = \log_a b$.)

Credential Issue and Transfer: These protocols are described in the figure below.

Issuing a Credential:

User's nym with organization O: (a, b) where $b = a^x$

Organization O's public credential key: (g, h_1, h_2) where $h_1 = g^{s_1}, h_2 = g^{s_2}$
Organization O's secret credential key: (s_1, s_2)

$\quad O \longrightarrow U:$ Send $(A = b^{s_2}, B = (ab^{s_2})^{s_1})$.
$\quad U:$ Choose $\gamma \in_R \mathbb{Z}_q^*$.
$\quad O \longleftrightarrow U:$ Run Γ to show $\log_b A = \log_g h_2$ with Verifier input γ.
         Obtain transcript T_1.
$\quad O \longleftrightarrow U:$ Run Γ to show $\log_{(aA)} B = \log_g h_1$ with Verifier input γ.
         Obtain transcript T_2.
$\quad U:$ Remember credential $C_{U,O} = (a^\gamma, b^\gamma, A^\gamma, B^\gamma, T_1, T_2)$.

Transferring a Credential to Another Organization:

Organization O's public credential key: (g, h_1, h_2) *where* $h_1 = g^{s_1}, h_2 = g^{s_2}$
User's nym with organization O': $(\tilde{a}, \tilde{b})$ *where* $\tilde{b} = \tilde{a}^x$
User's credential from organization O: $C_{U,O} = (a', b', A', B', T_1, T_2)$

O' :	Verify correctness of T_1 and T_2 as transcripts for Π_{NI}
	for showing $\log_{b'} A' = \log_g h_2$ and $\log_{(a'A')} B' = \log_g h_1$.
$U \longleftrightarrow O'$:	Execute Protocol Π to show $\log_{\tilde{a}} \tilde{b} = \log_{a'} b'$.

The Nym as Public Key for Signatures and Encryption: There are many encryption and signature schemes based on the discrete logarithm problem that can be used, such as the ElGamal [18] or Schnorr [31] schemes.

Security of the Scheme. We prove that the scheme presented above satisfies the definition of a pseudonym system given in section 2 in the full version of the present paper [26]. Below we outline the assumptions under which this follows.

Recall the setting – a group G_q of order q; access to a random oracle. The following assumptions are necessary:

1. We rely on the Decisional Diffie-Hellman assumption.
2. We assume that Protocol Π for proving equality of discrete logarithms is secure.
3. We assume that the following problem is hard:

   Problem 1. Let G be a cyclic group with generator g and of order $|G|$. Let g^x and g^y be given. Furthermore, assume that an oracle can be called that answers a query s by a triple (a, a^{sy}, a^{x+sxy}), where $a = g^z$ is a random group element of G. Let this oracle be called for $s_1, s_2, \ldots$. Then, the problem is to generate a quadruple $(t, b, b^{ty}, b^{x+txy})$, where $t \notin \{0, s_1, s_2, \ldots\}$, and where $b \neq e$.

   Theorem 6 shows the hardness of Problem 1 with respect to generic algorithms (as defined by Shoup [32]) unless the group order is divisible by a small prime factor.

   Theorem 6. *Let p be the smallest prime factor of n. The running time of a probabilistic generic algorithm solving Problem 1 for groups of order n is of order $\Omega(\sqrt{p}/(\log n)^{O(1)})$.*

   Proof Idea. The proof is based on the fact that the event $\mathcal{E}$ that two of the computed group elements are equal ($\mathcal{E}$ is called the *collision event*), has the following two properties. First, the event has probability of order $O(T^2/p)$, where T is the number of steps performed by the generic algorithm. Second, given that the event $\mathcal{E}$ does not occur, the algorithm produces a correct 4-tuple only with probability $O(1/p)$. $\qquad\qquad\qquad\square$

Although for any particular group used, there can exist specific (non-generic) algorithms solving Problem 1, the generic hardness of the problem is strong evidence for the existence of groups for which the problem is hard.

4.4 Multiple-Use Credentials

We have not been able to construct a system with multiple-use credentials which would completely conform to the specifications of our model. However, with a slight variation on the model and a straightforward modification of the scheme described above, we can get a scheme with multiple-use credentials. Moreover, in this setting we will no longer require the random oracle.

To implement this, our pseudonym generation and credential issue procedure will remain the same. As a result, the user will possess $C_{U,O} = (a, b, A, B)$, where $A = b^{s_2}$, $B = (ab^{s_2})^{s_1}$, and $(a, b) = (a, a^x)$ is the user's nym with the issuing organization. The user can therefore sample, for any γ, the 4-tuples $f_\gamma(C_{U,O}) = (a^\gamma, b^\gamma, A^\gamma, B^\gamma)$. For any 4-tuple formed that way, for any correctly formed pseudonym (a', b'), the user will be able to prove that $\log_a b = \log_{a'} b'$. If the issuing organization is required to cooperate with the receiving organization, it can confirm that $f_\gamma(C_{U,O})$ is a valid credential that corresponds to nym (a^γ, b^γ), or disprove that statement if it is not true. This is as secure as the scheme with one-time credentials.

5   Conclusions and Open Questions

The present work's contributions are in defining a model for pseudonym systems and proving it feasible, as well as proposing a practical scheme which is a significant improvement over its predecessors. Open problems lie in the area of identifying useful features for a pseudonym system (some features not mentioned in this extended abstract have been introduced and discussed in the full version of the present paper [26]); in removing interactiveness in the theoretical constructions; and in coming up with good practical constructions that conform to our specifications.

Acknowledgements

The first author would like to acknowledge the support of an NSF Graduate Fellowship and the Lucent Technologies GRPW; the third author would like to acknowledge the support of a DOD NDSEG fellowship; the first, second, and third authors would also like to acknowledge DARPA grant DABT63-96-C-0018. The fourth author acknowledges the Swiss National Science Foundation (SNF), grant No. 20-42105.94.

References

1. M. Bellare, A. Desai, D. Pointcheval, and P. Rogaway. Relations among notions of security for public-key encryption schemes. In *Advances in Cryptology—CRYPTO 98*, pages 26–40. Springer-Verlag, 1998.

2. Mihir Bellare and Phillip Rogaway. Random oracles are practical: A paradigm for designing efficient protocols. In *First ACM Conference on Computer and Communications Security*, pages 62–73, 1993.

3. Dan Boneh. The decision Diffie-Hellman problem. In *Proceedings of the Third Algorithmic Number Theory Symposium*, pages 48–63. Springer-Verlag, 1998.

4. David Brin. *The Transparent Society: Will Technology Force Us to Choose between Privacy and Freedom?* Perseus Press, 1998.

5. Jan Camenisch and Markus Stadler. Efficient group signature schemes for large groups (extended abstract). In *Advances in Cryptology—CRYPTO '97*, pages 410–424. Springer-Verlag, 1997.

6. Ran Canetti, Moses Charikar, Ravi Kumar, Sridhar Rajagopalan, Amit Sahai, and Andrew Tomkins. Non-transferable anonymous credentials. *Manuscript, 1998. Revision in submission*, 1999.

7. Ran Canetti, Oded Goldreich, and Shai Halevi. Random oracle methodology, revisited. In *Proceedings of the Thirtieth Annual ACM Symposium on Theory of Computing*, pages 209–218, 1998.

8. David Chaum. Security without identification: transaction systems to make Big Brother obsolete. *Communications of the ACM*, 28(10), 1985.

9. David Chaum. Designated confirmer signatures. In *Advances in Cryptology—EUROCRYPT 94*, pages 86–91. Springer-Verlag, 1994.

10. David Chaum and Jan-Hendrik Evertse. A secure and privacy-protecting protocol for transmitting personal information between organizations. In *Advances in Cryptology—CRYPTO '86*, pages 118–167. Springer-Verlag, 1986.

11. David Chaum and Torben Pryds Pedersen. Wallet databases with observers (extended abstract). In *Advances in Cryptology—CRYPTO '92*, pages 89–105. Springer-Verlag, 1992.

12. Lidong Chen. Access with pseudonyms. In Ed Dawson and Jovan Golić, editors, *Cryptography: Policy and Algorithms*, pages 232–243. Springer-Verlag, 1995. Lecture Notes in Computer Science No. 1029.

13. R. Cramer and V. Shoup. A practical public-key cryptosystem provably secure against adaptive chosen ciphertext attack. In *Advances in Cryptology—CRYPTO 98*. Springer-Verlag, 1998.

14. Ivan Bjerre Damgård. Payment systems and credential mechanisms with provable security against abuse by individuals (extended abstract). In *Advances in Cryptology—CRYPTO '88*, pages 328–335. Springer-Verlag, 1988.

15. W. Diffie and M. Hellman. New directions in cryptography. *IEEE Transactions on Information Theory*, 22(6):644–654, 1976.

16. C. Dwork, J. Lotspiech, and M. Naor. Digital signets: Self-enforcing protection of digital information. In *Proceedings of the 28th STOC*, pages 489–498, 1996.

17. E. Dyson. *Release 2.1: A design for living in the digital age*. Broadway, 1998.

18. T. ElGamal. A public-key cryptosystem and a signature scheme based on discrete logarithms. *IEEE Transactions on Information Theory*, 31(4):469–472, 1985.

19. Oded Goldreich. Secure multi-party computation. *http://theory.lcs.mit.edu/~oded*, 1998.

20. Oded Goldreich, Silvio Micali, and Avi Wigderson. How to play any mental game or a completeness theorem for protocols with honest majority. In *Proceedings of the Nineteenth Annual ACM Symposium on Theory of Computing*, pages 218–229, 1987.

21. Oded Goldreich, Birgit Pfitzmann, and Ronald L. Rivest. Self-delegation with controlled propagation - or - what if you lose your laptop. In *Advances in Cryptology—CRYPTO 98*, pages 153–168. Springer-Verlag, 1998.

22. Shafi Goldwasser and Mihir Bellare. Lecture notes in cryptography. *ftp://theory.lcs.mit.edu/pub/classes/6.875/crypto-notes.ps*, 1996.

23. Shafi Goldwasser and Silvio Micali. Probabilistic encryption. *Journal of Computer and System Sciences*, 28(2):270–299, April 1984.

24. Shafi Goldwasser, Silvio Micali, and Ronald L. Rivest. A digital signature scheme secure against adaptive chosen-message attacks. *SIAM Journal on Computing*, 17(2):281–308, April 1988.

25. Joe Kilian and Erez Petrank. Identity escrow. In *Advances in Cryptology—CRYPTO '98*, pages 169–185. Springer-Verlag, 1998.

26. Anna Lysyanskaya, Ronald L. Rivest, Amit Sahai, and Stefan Wolf. Pseudonym systems. *http://theory.lcs.mit.edu/˜anna/lrsw99.ps*, 1999.

27. David Mazières and M. Frans Kaashoek. The design, implementation and operation of an email pseudonym server. In *Proceedings of the 5th ACM Conference on Computer and Communications Security*, 1998.

28. Moni Naor. Bit commitment using pseudorandomness. *Journal of Cryptology*, 4(2):151–158, 1991.

29. Tatsuaki Okamoto. Designated confirmer signatures and public-key encryption are equivalent. In *Advances in Cryptology—CRYPTO '94*, pages 61–74. Springer-Verlag, 1994.

30. John Rompel. One-way functions are necessary and sufficient for secure signatures. In *Proceedings of the Twenty Second Annual ACM Symposium on Theory of Computing*, pages 387–394, 1990.

31. C. P. Schnorr. Efficient signature generation by smart cards. *Journal of Cryptology*, 4(3):161–174, 1991.

32. V. Shoup. Lower bounds on discrete logarithms and related problems. In *Advances in Cryptology—EUROCRYPT '97*, pages 256–266. Springer-Verlag, 1997.

33. Michael Sipser. *Introduction to the Theory of Computation*. PWS Publishing Company, 1997.

Unconditionally Secure Proactive Secret Sharing Scheme with Combinatorial Structures

Douglas R. Stinson and R. Wei

Department of Combinatorics and Optimization
University of Waterloo
Waterloo, Ontario N2L 3G1, Canada
{dstinson,rwei}@cacr.math.uwaterloo.ca

Abstract. Verifiable secret sharing schemes (VSS) are secret sharing schemes dealing with possible cheating by the participants. In this paper, we propose a new unconditionally secure VSS. Then we construct a new proactive secret sharing scheme based on that VSS. In a proactive scheme, the shares are periodically renewed so that an adversary cannot get any information about the secret unless he is able to access a specified number of shares in a short time period. Furthermore, we introduce some combinatorial structure into the proactive scheme to make the scheme more efficient. The combinatorial method might also be used to improve some of the previously constructed proactive schemes.

1   Introduction

One important topic in cryptography is how to securely share a secret among a group of people. In some cases, many people need to share the power to use a cryptosystem. Thus some secret information should be shared by a group so that the cryptosystem can be used only if it is permitted by a specified subset of the group. The study of how to keep a secure backup of a secret key and how to recover it securely has been first studied by Blakley [4] and Shamir [23] independently. Shamir proposed a polynomial threshold scheme. In a (t, n)-threshold scheme, a secret value is shared by n participants such that any t of the participants can reconstruct the secret value by putting their shares together, but any $t - 1$ participants cannot get any information about the secret value. In such a scheme, an adversary needs to compromise at least t locations in order to learn the secret, and corrupt at least $n - t - 1$ locations to destroy the secret.

In many situations, such as cryptographic master keys, data files, legal documents, etc., a secret value needs to be stored for a long time. In these situations, an adversary may attack the locations one by one and eventually get the secret or destroy it. To prevent such an attack, proactive secret sharing schemes are proposed. Proactive security for secret sharing was first suggested by Ostrovsky and Yung in [18]. In [18] they presented, among other things, a proactive polynomial secret sharing scheme. Proactive security refers to security and availability in the the presence of a mobile adversary. Herzberg et al. [15] specialized this notion to robust secret sharing schemes and gave a detailed efficient proactive

Howard Heys and Carlisle Adams (Eds.): SAC'99, LNCS 1758, pp. 200–214, 2000.

secret sharing scheme. In their scheme, a secret value is shared by n servers. The mobile adversary is able to attack all the servers during a long period of time. However, since the corrupted servers can be rebooted, in any time period there are only a subset of servers that are corrupted. "Robust" means that in any time period, the servers can reconstruct the secret value correctly.

The scheme in [15] is based on Shamir's polynomial threshold scheme, thus most aspects of the scheme are unconditionally secure. However, their scheme depends on verifiable secret sharing schemes based on [9,19] which depend on some cryptographic assumptions. The security of the scheme in [9] is based on the hardness of solving discrete logarithm. In the scheme of [19], the privacy of the secret is unconditionally secure, but the correctness of the shares depends on a computational assumption. In a sense, these two schemes complement each other.

The purpose of this paper is to provide a new proactive secret sharing scheme which is unconditionally secure, i.e., the security of any part of the scheme is not based on any cryptographic assumption. Let S be the set of possible secret values, where $|S| = q$. Then unconditional security of the scheme means that at any time the adversary cannot guess the shared secret $s \in S$ with probability better than $\frac{1}{q}$.

We first propose an unconditionally secure verifiable secret sharing scheme. This scheme has some similar features to the absolute VSS in [3]. Then we propose several protocols to make it proactive. Following from the method of [15], the lifetime of the secret is divided into periods of time in the proactive scheme. In each time period, the n shares will be renewed while the secret remains the same. In this way, a mobile adversary who is able to attack (learn or corrupt) at most b shares in a time period cannot learn any information about the secret in the long lifetime. This scheme is also robust, i.e., the secret can be reconstructed at any time.

Furthermore, we introduce some combinatorial structures in the scheme so that the scheme will be more efficient. With the combinatorial structure, most of the computation of the system will depend on the parameter b. Thus there is a "trade-off" between the computation and the value of b: when b is smaller (the ability of the adversary is more limited), the computation takes less time. Thus our scheme is more efficient in the situation when the number of the possible corrupted servers are much smaller as compared to the total number of the servers in the system. On the other hand, our combinatorial method might be easily adapted to the scheme of [15] to make the scheme more efficient.

The rest of this paper is arranged as follows. In Section 2 we give some preliminaries and the main settings of the system. Section 3 describes our new verifiable secret sharing scheme. We also propose an anonymous VSS in a subsection. Section 4 describes the proactive scheme without combinatorial structure. Section 5 introduces the combinatorial structure and describes how to apply it to the proactive scheme.

2 Preliminaries

2.1 Previous Work

Proactive refers to the security of the scheme in the presence of a mobile adversary who may corrupt all participants of the scheme throughout the lifetime of the system but cannot corrupt too many participants during any short period of time. Such a mobile adversary was first considered by Ostrovsky and Yung in [18].

The motivation of [18] is to combat mobile viruses. The scheme requires the participants to constantly exchange messages and to be able to erase parts of its memory. A polynomial secret sharing proactive scheme is proposed which uses the verifiable secret sharing scheme of [22].

Herzberg et al. [15] further discussed proactive secret sharing schemes and gave a detailed practical scheme. In their scheme the lifetime is divided into periods of time. At the beginning of each time period, the share holders engage in an interactive update protocol which includes a share recovery protocol and a share renewal protocol. At the end of the period, each shareholder holds completely new shares of the same secret. The secret will not be computed during the update phase while it can be reconstructed at any time. They used the polynomial-based method from [18] for the renewal protocol. They also proposed a polynomial-based method for share recovery protocol. The verifiable secret sharing schemes they used are from [9,19].

There are also many papers that discuss proactive security, see e.g., [6,14,11,21] and their references. Our discussion will mainly follow the papers [15,18].

2.2 The Setting

We will follow the setting of the scheme in [15,18]. We assume that there is a system of n servers $P_1, P_2, \cdots, P_n$, which are connected to a common broadcast channel such that messages sent through this channel instantly reach every server. We also assume that the system is synchronized, i.e., the servers can access a common global clock, and that each server has a local source of randomness. To make things simpler, we assume that there are private channels between each pair of servers and that messages sent by broadcast are safely authenticated. With these assumptions, we are able to focus on the proactive scheme itself.

There is an adversary which can corrupt b servers during any time period. Corrupting a server means learning the secret information in the server, modifying its data, sending out wrong message, changing the intended behavior of the server, disconnecting it, and so on. Since the server can be rebooted, the adversary is a mobile one.

A secret value $s \in GF(q)$ will be shared by the servers through the scheme. The value of s needs to be maintained for a long period of time. The life time is divided into time periods which are determined by the global clock. At the beginning of each time period the servers engage in an interactive update protocol. The update protocol will not reveal the value of s. At the end of the period the servers hold new shares of s. The mobile adversary who corrupts b servers in a time period cannot get any information about the secret value s. The system can reproduce s in the presence of the mobile adversary at any time.

We consider unconditional security in this paper, which means that the adversary cannot guess the secret with probability better than $\frac{1}{q}$ if the secret $s \in GF(q)$.

3   Verifiable Secret Sharing

Since secret sharing schemes were proposed initially by Shamir [23] and Blakley [4], research on this topic has been extensive. In the "classic" secret sharing schemes, there are assumed to be no faults in the system. Tompa and Woll [26], and McEliece and Sarwate [17] first considered schemes with faulty participants and gave partial solutions for that problem. In their schemes, the dealer is always assumed honest. Chor et al. [8] first defined the complete notion of Verifiable Secret Sharing (VSS), and gave a solution which is based on some cryptographic assumption. In a VSS, each holder of a share can verify that the share is consistent with the other shares. Thus both the dealer and other participants can be verified in such a scheme. There are two aspects of the security in a VSS. One is the security of the secret and the other is the security of the verification.

There are many papers which have discussed VSS recently. Most schemes use zero-knowledge proofs, e.g., [3,7,10,13,20,22]. Others use cryptographic assumptions such as the hardness of discrete logarithm, see [9,19]. [12] proposed a simple and efficient VSS, but it based on some "collision resistance" assumption. On the other hand, many known VSS are not easy to adapt for proactive property.

The VSS in [22,19,9] are used in proactive schemes in [18,15]. [18] used the VSS from [22] which used some zero-knowledge proofs. [15] used the VSS of Feldman [9] and Pedersen [19]. The security of the scheme in [9] is based on the hardness of solving discrete logarithm. In the scheme of [19], the privacy of the secret is unconditionally secure, but the verification depends on a computational assumption.

In [3] it was shown that in any unconditionally secure VSS, $b < \frac{n}{3}$. Thus the VSS with $b \geq \frac{n}{3}$ will either depend on some cryptographic assumption or have small probability of errors. In this section, we will propose an unconditionally secure VSS with $b \leq \frac{n}{4} - 1$, which is simpler and more efficient than the scheme in [3]. Moreover, our scheme has the threshold property that any coalition of $t - 1$ participants cannot get any information about the secret value (regardless of whether the coalition consists of good or bad participants), a property which the scheme of [3] does not have, since secret information may be revealed during the "share" protocol. Another feature of our scheme is that it requires less secret information to be communicated by the dealer, and the dealer is not required to take part in the protocol after the initial distribution of secret information.

3.1 Definition

Now we give a formal definition of VSS, as follows.

Suppose there are a dealer D and n other participants $P_1, P_2, \cdots, P_n$ all connected by private communication channels. They also have access to a broadcast channel. There is a static adversary A that can corrupt up to b of the participants including the D. Here static means that the b participants controlled by the adversary are fixed.

Let π be a protocol consisting of two phases *Share* and *Reconstruct*. Let S be the set of possible secret values. At the beginning of *Share*, the dealer inputs a secret $s \in S$. At the end of *Share* each participant P_i is instructed to output a Boolean value ver_i. At the end of *Reconstruct* each participant is instructed to output a value in S.

The protocol π is an unconditionally secure *Verifiable Secret Sharing* protocol if the following properties are hold:

1. If a good player P_i outputs $ver_i = 0$ at the end of *Share* then every good player outputs $ver_i = 0$;
2. If the dealer is good, then $ver_i = 1$ for every good P_i.
3. If at least $n - b$ players P_i output $ver_i = 1$ at the end of *Share*, then there exists an $s' \in S$ such that the event that all good P_i output s' at the end of *Reconstruct* is fixed at the end of *Share* and $s' = s$ if the dealer is good;
4. If $|S| = q$ and s is chosen randomly from S, and the dealer is good, then any coalition of at most $t - 1$ participants cannot guess at the end of *Share* the value s with probability better than $\frac{1}{q}$.

3.2 The New VSS

In this subsection we provide a new unconditionally secure VSS which will be used in our proactive scheme later.

Suppose there is a dealer D and n participants P_i, $1 \le i \le n$, where $n \ge t + 3b$ and $t > b$. Let $S = GF(q)$ be a finite field and let ω be a primitive element in $GF(q)$. In the following protocol, all the computations are in the field $GF(q)$. We first state the share phase as follows.

Share

1. When D wants to share a secret value $s \in S$, he chooses a random symmetric polynomial

$$f(x, y) = \sum_{i=0}^{t-1} \sum_{j=0}^{t-1} a_{ij} x^i y^j,$$

where $a_{00} = s$ and $a_{ij} = a_{ji}$ for all i, j. Then, for each k, D sends $h_k(x) = f(x, \omega^k)$ to P_k through a private channel.
2. After receiving $h_k(x)$, each P_k sends $h_k(\omega^l)$ to P_l for $1 \le l \le n, (l \ne k)$ through a private channel.

3. Each P_l checks whether $h_k(\omega^l) = h_l(\omega^k)$ for $1 \le k \le n$, $(l \ne k)$. If P_l finds that $h_k(\omega^l) \ne h_l(\omega^k)$, then P_l broadcasts (l, k).
4. Each P_i computes the maximum subset $G \subseteq \{1, \cdots, n\}$ such that any ordered pair $(l, k) \in G \times G$ is not broadcasted. If $|G| \ge n - b$, then P_i outputs $ver_i = 1$. Otherwise, P_i outputs $ver_i = 0$.

It is obvious that every good participant computes the same subset G in the end of *Share*. Next we consider the reconstruct phase. Note that although the adversary is static, he could provide correct information in *Share* phase but wrong information in *Reconstruct* phase.

Reconstruct

1. Each P_i sends $h_i(0)$ to P_k, where $i \in G$.
2. After receiving $h_i(0)$, P_k computes a polynomial $f_k(0, y)$ such that $f_k(0, \omega^i) = h_i(0)$ for at least $n - 2b$ of the data he received. This can be done efficiently using methods of [24].
3. P_k computes and output $s' = f_k(0, 0)$.

In order to prove that the protocol is an unconditionally secure VSS, we need the following lemma.

Lemma 1 *Suppose there are T polynomials $h_1(x), h_2(x), \cdots, h_T(x)$ with degree at most $t - 1$, where $T \ge t$, such that $h_i(\omega^j) = h_j(\omega^i)$ for all i, j. Then there exists a polynomial $h(x)$ of degree at most $t - 1$ such that $h(\omega^i) = h_i(0)$ for all $i, 1 \le i \le T$. Equivalently, any t of the shares $h_i(0), 1 \le i \le T$, determine the same secret $K = h(0)$.*

Proof First we note that for any t-subset $I = \{i_1, i_2, \cdots, i_t\} \subseteq \{1, 2, \cdots, T\}$ and any $h_j(x)$, where $1 \le j \le T$, we can use the Lagrange interpolation formula (see [25]) to compute

$$h_j(0) = \sum_{i \in I} h_j(\omega^i) b_i = \sum_{i \in I} h_i(\omega^j) b_i,$$

where

$$b_i = \prod_{k \in I, k \ne j} \frac{\omega^k}{\omega^k - \omega^j},$$

$1 \le i \le t$. This comes from the condition $h_i(\omega^j) = h_j(\omega^i)$ for any $i, j \in \{1, 2, \cdots, T\}$.

Now suppose that I and J are two different t-subsets of $\{1, 2, \cdots, T\}$. Then we can compute a polynomial $h_I(x)$ such that $h_I(\omega^i) = h_i(0)$ for all $i \in I$, and then $h_I(0)$ can be obtained by the Lagrange interpolation:

$$h_I(0) = \sum_{i \in I} h_i(0) b_i.$$

By the above discussion we have

$$h_I(0) = \sum_{i \in I} b_i h_i(0)$$

$$= \sum_{i \in I} b_i \sum_{j \in J} h_i(\omega^j) b_j$$

$$= \sum_{j \in J} b_j \sum_{i \in I} h_i(\omega^j) b_i$$

$$= \sum_{j \in J} b_j h_j(0)$$

$$= h_J(0).$$

$\square$

We are now in a position to prove the following theorem.

Theorem 2 *The scheme of this section is an unconditionally secure verifiable secret sharing scheme.*

Proof We prove that the above scheme satisfies the conditions of the VSS as follows.

1. If a good player P_i outputs $ver_i = 0$, then the size of the maximum subset G is at most $n - b - 1$. Thus every good player will output "0".

2. If the dealer is good, then the good player receives $f(x, \omega^i)$. Since $f(x, y)$ is symmetric, $f(\omega^l, \omega^i) = f(\omega^i, \omega^l)$ for all good players P_l. Thus all good players are in the subset G. Therefore $ver_i = 1$ for each good player P_i.

3. Suppose at least $n - b$ players output "1" at the end of the *Share*. Then there is a subset G of size $n - b$ such that no one in the subset complained the others. Since we assume that there are at most b bad players, there are at least $n - 2b$ good players in G, who all have consistent shares. By Lemma 1, any t-subset of the good players can compute the same value K. It is easy to check that if the dealer is good, then we have $K = s$, the secret value. Further at most b out of the $n - b$ shares in G are not consistent with the secret K. Since $n - b \geq t + 2b$, the algorithms in [24] can be used to find the maximum consistent set of shares and thus determine K.

4. Without loss of generality, we assume that the coalition knows the values of $h_1(x), h_2(x), \cdots, h_{t-1}(x)$. It is easy to show (see, e.g., [5]) that for any value $s' \in GF(q)$, we can find $b_{ij} \in GF(q)$, where $b_{00} = s', b_{ij} = b_{ji}, 0 \leq i, j \leq t - 1$ such that if

$$f'(x, y) = \sum_{i=0}^{t-1} \sum_{j=0}^{t-1} b_{ij} x^i y^j,$$

then $f'(x, \omega^k) = h_k(x)$ for $k = 1, 2, \cdots, b$. $\square$

Remark. This scheme is modified from Blom's key predistribution scheme (see [5] for the details). For simplicity, our description used a Reed-Solomon code instead of general MDS codes. It is straightforward to generalize our scheme by using MDS codes.

3.3 An Example

We display a toy example in this subsection. Let $q = 13, \omega = 2, n = 9, t = 3$ and $b = 2$. First suppose the dealer D is good. First D selects a polynomial as follows:

$$f(x, y) = 3 + 9x + 2x^2 + 9y + 2y^2 + 8xy + 11xy^2 + 11x^2y + 4x^2y^2.$$

Then D sends the vector (v_1, v_2, v_3) to the players as follows, each of which determines a polynomial $v_1 + v_2x + v_3x^2$:

$$h_1 \longleftarrow (3, 4, 1)$$
$$h_2 \longleftarrow (6, 9, 6)$$
$$h_3 \longleftarrow (8, 10, 8)$$
$$h_4 \longleftarrow (9, 2, 6)$$
$$h_5 \longleftarrow (12, 11, 4)$$
$$h_6 \longleftarrow (9, 12, 8)$$
$$h_7 \longleftarrow (6, 11, 9)$$
$$h_8 \longleftarrow (12, 10, 10)$$
$$h_9 \longleftarrow (7, 12, 1)$$

Suppose that only P_1 and P_2 are bad and send wrong data to the other players. Then the pairs broadcasted are of the form $(1, i), (2, i), (i, 1)$ or $(i, 2)$. So the good players will find $G = \{3, 4, 5, 6, 7, 8, 9\}$ and output "1". Since we assume that there are at most 2 bad players, all the good players will output "1" if the dealer is good. On the other hand, the player P_i chooses "0" or "1" only depending on the broadcasted pairs, so all good players will output the same value of ver_i.

Now suppose that there are at least 7 players who output "1". Since there are at most 2 bad players, it is true that the subset G is found. Suppose, for example, $G = \{1, 2, 3, 4, 5, 6, 7\}$. Then all the good players in G possess consistent shares regardless of whether D is good or bad. However up to two of these players may be bad, and send incorrect shares during *Reconstruction*. Thus in the *Reconstruction* phase, there are at least 5 consistent shares held by each of the players. Thus each good player will compute the same polynomial $f(x, 0)$ using the methods of [24].

3.4 VSS without Dealer

Secret sharing without dealer means that there is no dealer in the scheme, who knows and distributes the secret. Secret sharing without dealer is first considered in [16]. One such secret sharing scheme is considered in [19].

We can remove the dealer from our scheme as follows. The other properties of the scheme are the same as in the previous subsection.

Share

1. Each P_k chooses an independent random symmetric polynomial

$$f^{(k)}(x, y) = \sum_{i=0}^{t-1} \sum_{j=0}^{t-1} a_{ij} x^i y^j,$$

where $a_{00} = s_k$ and $a_{ij} = a_{ji}$ for all i, j. Then P_k sends $h_l^{(k)}(x) = f^{(k)}(x, \omega^l)$ to P_l through a private channel.
2. After receiving $h_l^{(k)}(x)$, each P_l sends $h_l^{(k)}(\omega^m)$ to P_m for $1 \leq m \leq n$ through a private channel.
3. P_m checks whether $h_m^{(k)}(\omega^l) = h_l^{(k)}(\omega^m)$ for $1 \leq l \leq n$. If P_m finds that $h_m^{(k)}(\omega^l) \neq h_l^{(k)}(\omega^m)$, then P_m broadcasts $(k; m, l)$.
4. For every $k \neq m$, each player P_m computes the maximum subset G_k such that for any pair $(m, l) \in G_k \times G_k$, $(k; m, l)$ is not broadcasted. If $|G_k| \geq n-b$, then P_m puts the value k in a list $\mathcal{L}$.
5. If $|\mathcal{L}| \geq n - b$, then P_m outputs $ver_m = 1$ and computes his share as

$$h_m = \sum_{l \in \mathcal{L}} h_m^{(l)}(x).$$

Otherwise, P_m refuses the shares and outputs $ver_m = 0$.

The reconstruct phase is the same as the previous scheme. Note that in this scheme the shared secret is

$$s = \sum_{i \in \mathcal{L}} s_i.$$

In this scheme, each player in turn plays the part of the dealer. Thus the security of scheme follows from Theorem 2. We need only to show that each good player has the same list $\mathcal{L}$, which is obvious.

Remark. As we indicated before, our VSS is modified from Blom's key predistribution scheme. In the original scheme, there is a dealer to construct the schemes. Using the methods of this section, we obtain a key predistribution scheme without dealer.

4 New Proactive Scheme

In this section, we describe our proactive secret sharing scheme without combinatorial structure. We will add combinatorial structures in this scheme to improve the efficiency of the scheme in next section.

4.1 Initialization

In the initial step, we assume that there is a dealer to set up the scheme. After the initialization phase, the dealer will no longer be needed.

In the initialization, we use the *share* phase of the VSS described in the Section 3, but we assume that $t > b+1$. The first four steps are the same. Then we do the following.

5. If at least $n - b$ of the servers output $ver_i = 1$, then the dealer erases all the information about the scheme on his end. Otherwise, the dealer reboots the whole system and initializes the system again.

4.2 Share Renewal

In the share renewal phase, all good servers do the following:

1. Each server P_l selects a random symmetric polynomial

$$r^{(l)}(x, y) = \sum_{i=0}^{t-1} \sum_{j=0}^{t-1} r_{ij} x^i y^j,$$

where $r_{00} = 0$ and $r_{ij} = r_{ji}$ for all i, j.

2. P_l sends $h_k^{(l)}(x) = r^{(l)}(x, \omega^k)$ to P_k for $k = 1, 2, \cdots, n$ by a private channel and broadcasts $h_0^{(l)}(x) = r^{(l)}(x, 0)$.

3. P_k checks whether $h_0^{(l)}(0) = 0$ and $h_k^{(l)}(0) = h_0^{(l)}(\omega^k)$. If the conditions are satisfied, then P_k computes and sends P_m the value $h_k^{(l)}(\omega^m)$. Otherwise P_k broadcasts an accusation of P_l.

4. P_m checks whether $h_m^{(l)}(\omega^k) = h_k^{(l)}(\omega^m)$ for the values of l not accused by $n - b$ servers of the system. If the equation is not true for more than b values of k, then P_m broadcasts an accusation of P_l.

5. If P_l is accused by at most b servers, then he can defend himself as follows. For those P_i that P_l is accused by, P_l broadcasts $h_i^{(l)}(x)$. Then server P_k checks whether $h_i^{(l)}(\omega^k) = h_k^{(l)}(\omega^i)$ and broadcasts "yes" or "no". If there are at least $n - b - 2$ servers broadcasting yes, then P_l is not a bad server.

6. P_m updates the list of bad servers $\mathcal{L}$ by including all values l for which P_l is accused by at least $b + 1$ servers, or found bad in the previous step. Then P_m updates its shares as

$$h_m(x) \longleftarrow h_m(x) + h_m^{(k)}(x)$$

for all $k \notin \mathcal{L}$.

Remark. We can remove the private channels in step 2, since our scheme is also a key predistribution scheme and the server P_i and P_j can use $h_i(j) = h_j(i)$ as a key to communicate securely.

To check the security of the renewal phase, first we note that any coalition of at most b servers cannot get any information about any shares except their own. In fact, a server P_i only knows $h_i^{(l)}(x)$ and $h_0^{(l)}(x)$. Since $b < t - 1$, the coalition of b servers knows at most $t - 1$ polynomials which cannot reveal $r^{(l)}(x, y)$ (see, e.g., [5]). Secondly, from the protocol we know that every good server should have the same list $\mathcal{L}$. Therefore, the good servers will keep consistent shares after renewal.

Note that a good server P_l can be accused by at most b servers. In this case, P_l will broadcast b polynomials in its defense. Thus P_l will broadcasts total $b+1$ polynomials. Since $t > b + 1$, these information will not reveal $r^{(l)}(x, y)$. On the other hand, suppose P_l gives P_i a wrong share, i.e., the share P_i received is not consistent with at least $\frac{n-b}{2}$ other servers (the majority of good servers). Then P_i will accuse P_l in step 4, since $\frac{n-b}{2} > b$. If P_l broadcasts a correct share in the defense, then P_i can correct his share. Otherwise, P_l will be found to be bad.

4.3 Recover a Share

When a server is corrupted or replaced, it needs to be rebooted and thus it needs to recover the secret shares.

We first provide a protocol, to detect the corrupted servers, which we call detection.

Detection

1. P_l computes and sends $h_l(\omega^k)$ to P_k for $k = 1, 2, \cdots, n$ by private channels.
2. P_k checks whether $h_l(\omega^k) = h_k(\omega^l)$. P_k then broadcasts an accusation $list_k$ which contains those l such that $h_l(\omega^k) \neq h_k(\omega^l)$ or $h_l(\omega^k)$ was not received.
3. Each good server updates the list $\mathcal{L}$ so that it contains those l accused by at least $b + 1$ servers of the system.

After running *Detection*, the system will recover the shares for all server P_l, where $l \in \mathcal{L}$. The recovery protocol is as follows.

1. For each $l \in \mathcal{L}$, every good server P_i computes and sends $h_i(\omega^l)$ to P_l.
2. Upon receiving the data, P_l computes a polynomial $h_l(x)$ such that $h_l(\omega^k) = h_k(\omega^l)$ for the majority of k it received, using the algorithms of [24]. P_l sets $h_l(x)$ as its shares.

4.4 Reconstruct the Secret

The reconstruction protocol is similar to the *Reconstruction* of VSS introduced in Section 3. We need only to change the first two steps as follows.

1' For each good server P_i, P_i sends $h_i(0)$ to P_k, where k is not in the list $\mathcal{L}$.
2' After receiving $h_i(0)$, P_k computes a polynomial $f_k(0, y)$ such that $f_k(0, \omega^i) = h_i(0)$ for at least $n - 2b$ of the data he received.

5 Combinatorial Structure

In this section, we will introduce some combinatorial structure into our scheme. The combinatorial structure provides a predetermined arrangement of the servers which permits the possibility of reducing the computation of the scheme.

5.1 Set Systems

A set system is a pair $(X, \mathcal{B})$, where X is a set of n points and $\mathcal{B}$ is a collection of subsets of X called blocks.

We will use a set system with the following properties, where $t \leq \frac{n}{4} - 1$:

1. $|B| \geq t$ for any $B \in \mathcal{B}$.
2. For any subset $F \subset X$ with $|F| \leq b$, there exists a $B \in \mathcal{B}$ such that $F \cap B = \emptyset$.

It is easy to see that such a set system exists. For example, we can choose $\mathcal{B}$ to be all the t-subsets of X. However, there are often better set systems (i.e., set systems containing fewer blocks). The following definition is well-known (see, e.g., [24]).

Definition 3 *A collection $\mathcal{T}$ of k-subsets of $\{1, \ldots, n\}$ (called blocks) is an (n, k, b)-covering if every b-subset of $\{1, \ldots, n\}$ is contained in at least one block.*

It is easy to see that if $(X, \mathcal{T})$ is an $(n, n-t, b)$-covering, then the set system

$$\{\{1, \ldots, n\} \setminus T : T \in \mathcal{T}\}$$

is a set system satisfying our purpose. There are several efficient constructions of $(n, n-t, b)$-coverings in [24] which can be easily implemented by a computer.

5.2 Applying Set System to the Proactive VSS

The idea of using the set system is to reduce the computations for the share renewal and share recover protocols. In the scheme of Section 4, share renewal and share recover used the data from all the participants. However, these operations can be carried out using the data from t good servers. For example, in share renewal protocol, any t good servers can renew the shares, since the shares are polynomials of degree at most $t - 1$. In protocol of Section 4, every good server provides information to renew shares. So there are redundant computations. If the system can determine t good servers, then the protocol will be more efficient. Note that there are at least $3t + 1$ good servers in the system. Thus we can save at least one third of the computations. On the other hand, we should be very careful when the t good servers are selected, since the adversary is mobile. The good server could turn to bad at any time. Thus in the scheme of this section, we will actually select correct information instead of good servers, although we will still use "good server " for convenience.

Now let us use the set system to improve our proactive scheme. Suppose $(X, \mathcal{B})$ is a set system satisfying the conditions of subsection 5.1, where $X = \{1, 2, \cdots, n\}$, and $\mathcal{B} = \{B_1, B_2, \cdots, B_s\}$. The set system is published so that each participant can consult it.

Note that in our scheme, in any phase there is a list $\mathcal{L}$ containing all the bad servers. By the property of the set system, there is a block B which contains only good servers. If the system can determine one of the "good" blocks, then the system can renew the shares or recover the shares only using the data from these servers. We will call these servers the members of an *executive committee*.

For a list $\mathcal{L}$ of bad servers, the system can decide following list of blocks: $B_{i_1}, B_{i_2}, \cdots, B_{i_e}$, such that $B_{i_j} \cap \mathcal{L} = \emptyset, j = 1, 2, \cdots, e$, and $1 \leq i_1 < i_2 < \cdots < i_e \leq s$. These blocks are called *executive committee candidates*. Note that the adversary is mobile, therefore we cannot guarantee that these candidates contain only good servers in the next time period.

The proactive secret sharing scheme with combinatorial structure works as follows. The initialization is the same as that in Section 4. In each time period the system does the following.

1. Run *Detection* to obtain the list $\mathcal{L}$ of bad servers and the executive committee candidates: $B_{i_1}, B_{i_2}, \cdots, B_{i_e}$.
2. If an executive committee has not been found, then for next executive committee candidate B, each $P_g \in B$ does the following:
   (a) Selects a random symmetric polynomial

$$r^{(g)}(x, y) = \sum_{i=0}^{t-1} \sum_{j=0}^{t-1} r_{ij} x^i y^j,$$

   where $r_{00} = 0$ and $r_{ij} = r_{ji}$ for all i, j, and sends $h_k^{(g)}(x) = r^{(g)}(x, \omega^k)$ to P_k for $k = 1, 2, \cdots, n, k \neq g$ by private channel and broadcasts $h_0^{(g)}(x) = r^{(g)}(x, 0)$.
   (b) P_k checks whether $h_0^{(g)}(0) = 0$ and $h_k^{(g)}(0) = h_0^{(g)}(\omega^k)$ for $g \in B$. If the conditions are satisfied, then P_k computes and sends P_m the value $h_k^{(g)}(\omega^m)$. Otherwise P_k broadcasts an accusation of P_g.
   (c) P_m checks whether $h_m^{(g)}(\omega^k) = h_k^{(g)}(\omega^m)$ for $g \in B$. If the equation is not true, then P_m broadcasts an accusation of P_g.
   (d) A member in B is accused by at least $b+1$ servers is bad. If a member in B is accused by at most b servers, then it can defend itself. If no member in B is bad, then B is found to be the executive committee.
3. The system runs the recovery protocol to recover the shares for the servers in $\mathcal{L}$.
4. Each server P_m updates its shares as

$$h_m(x) \longleftarrow h_m(x) + h_m^{(g)}(x)$$

for all $g \in B$.

The reconstruction protocol is the same as that in Section 4.

5.3 Applying Combinatorial Structures to Other Schemes

The proactive secret sharing scheme proposed by Herzberg et al. in [15] is similar to our scheme in Section 4. Thus it is straightforward to modify our method with combinatorial structures to their scheme. In general, suppose a proactive secret sharing scheme has the following properties:

1. Information from any t good servers can be used to renew shares and recover shares.
2. A VSS exists in which any server can use this VSS to send data which can be verified by the system.
3. There is a detection protocol to find the bad servers.
4. There is a defense protocol so that an accused server can be determined bad or good by the system.
5. There are renewal and share recovery protocols.
6. There is set system $(X, \mathcal{B})$ satisfying the conditions of Subsection 5.1.

Then we can use the following scheme for renewal and share recovery protocols.

1. Run the detection protocol to obtain a list $\mathcal{L}$ of bad servers and the executive committee candidates: $B_{i_1}, B_{i_2}, \cdots, B_{i_e}$.
2. If executive committee has not been found, then for next executive committee candidate B, each $P_g \in B$ does:
   (a) Send recovery information rc_k^g to P_k for each $k \in \mathcal{L}$ in the system and send renewal information rn_l^g to P_l for each l in the system by VSS.
   (b) The system checks the correctness of rc_k^g and rn_l^g. If some mistake is found, then P_g is accused.
   (c) A member in B is accused, then it can defend itself and the system can decide whether it is bad. If no member in B is bad, then B is defined to be the executive committee.
3. The $P_k \in \mathcal{L}$ recovers its share using $\{rc_k^g : g \in B\}$.
4. Each server P_l renews its share using $\{rn_l^g : g \in B\}$.

It is readily checked that the proactive secret sharing scheme of [15] satisfies all the properties we needed. Thus we can use the combinatorial method to improve their scheme. The details are omitted here.

Acknowledgment

The authors thank K. Kurosawa for his valuable comments.

References

1. N. Alon, Z. Galil and M. Yung, Efficient dynamic-resharing "verifiable secret sharing" against mobile adversary, European Symposium on Algorithms (ESA) 95, LNCS 979, 523-537.
2. J. C. Benaloh, Secret sharing homomorphisms: keeping shares of a secret secret, Advances in Cryptology-Crypto'86, LNCS 263, 1987, 251-260.
3. M. Ben-Or, S. Goldwasser and A. Wigderson, Completeness Theorems for Non-cryptographic Fault-Tolerant Distributed Computations, Proc. 20th Annual Symp. on the Theory of Computing, ACM, 1988, 1-10.
4. G.R. Blackley, Safeguarding cryptographic keys. Proc. Nat. Computer Conf. AFIPS Conf. Proc., 1979, 313-317.

5. R. Blom, An optimal class of symmetric key generation systems, Eurocrypt'84, LNCS 209, (1985), 335-338.

6. R. Canetti and A. Herzberg, Maintaining security in the presence of transient faults, Crypto'94, LNCS 839, 1994.

7. D. Chaum, C. Crepeau and I. Damgard, Multiparty Unconditionally Secure Protocols, Proc. 20th Annual Symp. on the Theory of Computing, ACM, 1988, 11-19.

8. B. Chor, S. Goldwasser, S. Micali and B. Awerbuch, Verifiable Secret Sharing and Achieving Simultaneity in Presence of Faults, Proc. 26th Annual Symp. on the Foundations of Computing Science, IEEE, 1985, 383-395.

9. P. Feldman, A Practical Scheme for Non-Interactive Verifiable Secret sharing, Proc. 28th Annual Symp. on the Foundations of Computing Science, IEEE, 1987, 427-437.

10. P. Feldman and S. Micali, An Optimal Algorithm for Synchronous Byzantine Agreement, Proc. 20th Annual Symp. on Theory of Computing, ACM, 1988, 148-161.

11. Y. Frankel, P. Gemmel, P. D. MacKenzie and M. Yung, Proactive RSA, Crypto'97, LNCS 1294, 440-452.

12. R. Gennaro, M. O. Rabin and T. Rabin, Simplified VSS and fast-track multiparty computations with applications to threshold cryptography, Proc. of 17th ACM Symp. on Principles of Distributed Computing, (1998), 101-111.

13. O. Goldreich, S. Micali and A. Wigderson, Proofs that Yield Nothing But Their Validity or All Languages in NP Have Zero-Knowledge Proof Systems, Journal of the ACM, 38(1991), 691-729.

14. A. Herzberg, M. Jakobsson, S. Jarecki, H. Krawczyk and M. Yung, Proactive public key and signature systems, The 4th ACM Symp. on Comp. and Comm. Security, April 1997.

15. A. Herzberg, S. Jarecki, H. Krawczyk and M. Yung, Proactive secret sharing or: How to cope with perpetual leakage, Crypto'95, LNCS 963339-352.

16. I. Ingemarsson and G. J. Simmons, A protocol to set up shared secret schemes without the assistance of a mutually trusted party, Eurocrypt'90, LNCS 473, 1990, 266-282.

17. R. J. McEliece and D. V. Sarwate, On Sharing Secrets and Reed-Solomon Codes, Communications of the ACM, 24(1981), 583-584.

18. R. Ostrovsky and M. Yung, How to withstand mobile virus attacks, ACM Symposium on principles of distributed computing, 1991, 51-59.

19. T. P. Pedersen, Non-interactive and information-theoretic secret sharing, Advances in Cryptology - Crypto'91, LNCS 576, 1991, 129-140.

20. T. Rabin, Robust sharing of secrets when the dealer is honest or faulty, Journal of the ACM, 41(1994), 1089-1109.

21. T. Rabin, A simplified approach to threshold and proactive RSA, Crypto'98, LNCS 1462, 1998, 89-104.

22. T. Rabin and M. Ben-Or, Verifiable secret sharing and multiparty protocols with honest majority, Proc. 21st Annual Sympo. on the Theory of Computing, ACM, 1989, 73-85.

23. A. Shamir, How to share a secret, Commun. ACM, 22(1979), 612-613.

24. R. S. Rees, D. R. Stinson, R. Wei and G. H. J. van Rees, An application of covering designs: determining the maximum consistent set of shares in a threshold scheme, Ars Combin., to appear.

25. D. R. Stinson, Cryptography Theory and Practice, CRC Press, 1995.

26. M. Tompa and H. Woll, How to share a secret with cheaters, Journal of Cryptology, 1(1988), 133-138.

Protecting a Mobile Agent's Route against Collusions

Dirk Westhoff[1], Markus Schneider[2], Claus Unger[1], and Firoz Kaderali[2]

[1] FernUniversität Hagen, D-58084
Fachgebiet Praktische Informatik II
[2] FernUniversität Hagen, D-58084
Fachgebiet Kommunikationssysteme
{dirk.westhoff,mark.schneider,claus.unger,firoz.kaderali}@fernuni-hagen.de

Abstract. In the world of mobile agents, security aspects are extensively being discussed, with strong emphasis on how agents can be protected against malicious hosts and vice versa. This paper discusses a method for concealing an agent's route information from being misused by sites en route to collect profile information of the agent's owner. Furthermore, it is shown that the protected route resists attacks from a single malicious host and from colluding malicious hosts as well.

1 Introduction

Mobile agents are becoming more and more important for Internet based electronic markets. In many scenarios, mobile agents represent customers, salesmen or mediators for information, goods and services [1]. Agents are autonomous programs, which, following a route, migrate through a network of sites to accomplish tasks or take orders on behalf of their owners. Without any protection scheme, a visited site may read an agent's data and thus collect information about the agent's owner, e.g. its services, customers, service strategies, collected data, etc. To avoid such a situation, the amount of data accessible to a visited site has to be restricted as much as possible [2].

In this paper, we concentrate on an agent's route information, i.e. the address list of sites to be visited during a trip. The owner provides its agent with an initial route. On its travel, the agent works through the route stage by stage. Protecting the route guarantees that none of the visited stations can manipulate the route in a malicious way or can get an overview of other sites the agent's owner is contacting. To repulse malicious programs like Trojan horses, the identity of an agent becomes known to all visited sites [3], anonymous agents [4] are not dealt with in this paper. In the following we use the concept and terminology of the ALOHA[1]-software package [5].

---

[1] The ALOHA (Agent Local Help Application) environment allows its users to easily define, send, receive and evaluate agents.

Howard Heys and Carlisle Adams (Eds.): SAC'99, LNCS 1758, pp. 215–225, 2000.

2 Related Work

Methods that protect an agent against attacks can be categorized into those which prevent attacks and those which detect attacks.

Cryptographic traces [6] detect illegal modifications of an agent by a post-mortem analysis of data the agent collected during its journey. *State appraisal* [7] mechanisms protect an agent's dynamical components, especially its execution state, against modifications. When an agent reaches a new site, the appraisal function is evaluated passing as a parameter the agent's current state.

Tamper-proof devices [8] are hardware based and therefore not suitable in open systems. Software based approaches include the *computation of encrypted functions* [9] and *code scrambling* [10]. Unfortunately the first approach can only be applied to polynominal and rational functions. In [10] the code of an agent is re-arranged to disguise the agent's functionality.

Although *onion routing* [11] is not an agent specific approach, it uses partial encryption similar to our method. Onion routing allows anonymous connections and is used to protect a variety of Internet services against eavesdropping and traffic analysis attacks. In contrast, beside concealing the route, our solution detects attacks that modify an agent's route but allows legal route changes.

3 Framework

An agent is an autonomous program which acts on behalf of its owner. According to its route, it visits sites linked together via a communication network. An agent is created, sent, finally received and evaluated in its owner's *home context*. At a visited site, the agent is executed in a *working context*. To save costs, an agent usually does not return to its home context before it has worked off its route; thus during the agent's journey its home site has not to be connected to the communication network all the time. To forward an agent to its next site or to extend an agent's route, each visited site needs access to a certain part of the route. A site is not allowed to remove a not yet visited site from the initial route and thus, e.g., exclude sites from offering their services to the agent. When a visited site extends a route, all added sites must become aware of the fact that they have not been on the initial route, and thus may, e.g., restrict the agent's access rights and functions, e.g. for electronic cashing. When a site changes a route, the change must be uniquely be associated with the site. To avoid arousing suspicion, as soon as a site detects an attack against an agent, it has to send the agent back to its home context.

In the following, we present a concept which reduces the route information, that becomes visible to a visited site, to a minimum, and which protects the route against malicious changes. In addition the concept is flexible enough to handle route extensions during the agent's journey. Our concept carefully considers efficiency aspects like computational complexity, additional network traffic, etc. Because of the latter, the concept of a trustworthy center to be visited between each two consecutive sites, is not taken up. Each site is only given access to the address of its predecessor and its successor site.[2]

Additionally to the route, the agent includes other components like *profile*, *binary code*, *mobile data* and a *trip marker* per journey. Agents have to be protected against passive, reading attacks, and active attacks that modify an agent's functionality or even fully destroy it. This paper concentrates on the route and its protection against attacks performed by one single context as well as on attacks performed by collusions of cooperating malicious contexts.

4 Protecting the Initial Route

When an agent migrates from working context c_i to working context c_{i+1}, all its objects are encrypted and thus protected against passive attacks. Before starting an agent, (except in very special cases [9]) a working context has to decrypt parts of the agent and thus make the agent vulnerable against active or passive attacks. Thus, the agent's route should be protected as much as possible.

An unprotected route $r = ip(c_1) \ || \ \ldots \ || \ ip(c_n)$ is a concatenated list of Internet addresses $ip(c_i)$. To abort an agent's journey, each site has to know the Internet address $ip(h)$ of the home context h, which therefore is stored in plaintext separate from the protected route.

The home context h signs data relevant for each working context to be visited by means of a signature S and encrypts the agent's route using an asymmetrical encryption method E and the i-th working context's public key e_i for $i = 1, \ldots, n$.[3] Applying encryption in a manner as it is known from onion routing network [11] for achieving untraceable communication h composes

$$
\begin{aligned}
r = \ E_{e_1}\Big[& h, ip(c_2), S_h\big(h, ip(c_1), ip(c_2), t, E_{e_2}[\ldots]\big), \\
& E_{e_2}\Big[ip(c_1), ip(c_3), S_h\big(ip(c_1), ip(c_2), ip(c_3), t, E_{e_3}[\ldots]\big), \\
& \quad \vdots \\
& \quad \vdots \\
& E_{e_{n-1}}\Big[ip(c_{n-2}), ip(c_n), S_h\big(ip(c_{n-2}), ip(c_{n-1}), ip(c_n), t, E_{e_n}[\ldots]\big), \\
& E_{e_n}\big[ip(c_{n-1}), EoR, S_h\big(ip(c_{n-1}), ip(c_n), EoR, t)\big)\big]\Big] \ldots \Big]\Big]
\end{aligned}
\tag{1}
$$

---

[2] In general the communication protocol itself automatically provides a receiver with the address of the sender.

[3] The ALOHA-software package uses RSA as asymmetrical encryption E. The signature S is based on a combination of SHA and RSA. We suppose that problems according to generation of asymmetrical key-pairs, certification and distribution of public keys are solved.

Thereby, t denotes a trip marker which is unique for each agent's journey and the EoR entry indicates the end of the route. Thus, the route contains the encrypted addresses of all working contexts that shall be visited and the signatures to prove the integrity of the route.

During the agent's journey, a working context c_i decrypts the Internet address $ip(c_{i+1})$ of its successor and $ip(c_{i-1})$ of its predecessor, its relevant signature and all the remaining ciphertext by using its private key d_i that corresponds to the public key e_i. Then, each site removes the decrypted address and signature from the agent's route. All other route entries are hidden from the actual working context.

With the help of digital signatures, active attacks can be detected. The signature of the address which is signed by the agent's home context h and presented to the actual working context c_i, proves that the route entry for c_i has not been modified. The influence of Internet address $ip(c_i)$ and trip marker t on the signature guarantees the actual working context that itself is part of the initial route. The predecessor's address $ip(c_{i-1})$ is taken into account for the signature's computation in order to avoid a special collusion attack to be explained later.

The uniqueness of the trip marker t is necessary to prevent replay attacks. Otherwise, a malicious working context could replace the complete route of the actual agent with a copied route of an agent's earlier journey.

With the help of the EoR entry, working context c_n realizes that it itself is the final entry of the agent's route. Via EoR and t in the signature, working context c_n is able to check whether these data have been generated by h and whether it itself was really included into the initial route.

Signatures must be encrypted by the home context as well, otherwise, if the agent carried the signatures in plaintext, under certain circumstances an attacker, who knows t, would be able to reconstruct the complete route by arranging and testing combinations of possible addresses. Such an attack would be feasible if the number of relevant sites is small.

In the following, we discuss methods with regard to active attacks which modify the functionality of an agent's route. Such attacks can be classified into those where the attacker solely tries to cheat without the help of any other working context and those where the attacker are acting in collusion with other dishonest working contexts.

The onion-like signature of the route ensures that all the desired working contexts have to be visited in order that the further route information can be decrypted. The signatures which depend on all instantaneously existing route data allow the detection of attacks as early as possible.

If context c_i receives an agent, then c_i is the only one that can reveal the successor's address; if the signature check is positive, c_i can be sure that

- it was included in the initial route,
- it received the agent from the correct predecessor,
- the successor's address is correct,
- all further data contained in the route are not compromised.

The home context knows the last entry c_n of the agent's route, i.e. the context from which it finally expects the agent. This prevents any other working context in the initial route from returning the agent too early.

If a malicious working context c_i intends to cheat without the help of any other working context, e.g. by deleting entries from the route, by replacing entries in the route or by adding new entries to the route, the next honest working context will detect such an attack immediately.

If c_i deletes ciphertext whose corresponding plaintext refers to a working context c_j with $j > i + 1$, working context c_{i+1} will detect immediately by signature check that the route was compromised. If c_i tries to skip c_{i+1}, it would not be able to reveal the address $ip(c_{i+2})$. So the malicious context c_i is only able to forward the agent to a randomly chosen address.

If c_i adds new addresses or if c_i replaces entries either in plaintext or in ciphertext, it would never be able to use the right signature key, and so the attack would become obvious as early as possible.

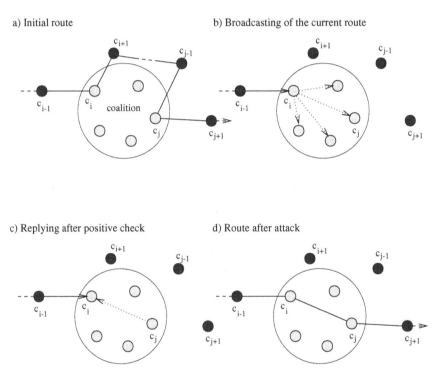

Fig. 1. Attack on an atomic encrypted route under collusion.

In all previous attacks, it was assumed that a malicious working context does not exploit the help of another dishonest working context. In general, a home context does not know if there exist collusions, and which working contexts are acting in collusions.

The performance of the secured route, presented in expression (1), becomes clear when considering collusions. If the route entries are encrypted in an atomic way instead of an onion-like structure and if the initial route contains at least two members c_i, c_j of a colluding group, which are not adjacent $(j > i + 1)$, the first visited dishonest context c_i could act in the following way: having obtained the agent, c_i broadcasts copies of the current route to its accomplices. Afterwards, the accomplices try to reveal by sequential decryption if they are members of the initial route. If accomplice c_j obtains a reasonable result after decryption of the presented ciphertexts, c_j found itself as a valid member of the initial route. Now, c_j informs c_i that it is also member of the agent's route and c_i forwards the agent to c_j by skipping all those route entries in the initial route lying in between c_i and c_j [see fig. 1]. No other honest working context c_k, $j < k < n$, would ever be able to detect this attack.

Skipping honest contexts exploiting the power of collusions can be avoided if the route is secured like in expression (1). In an onion-like protection scheme, a malicious working context c_i is only able to reveal more than one succeeding route entries $c_{i+1}, \ldots, c_m$ if all these adjacent contexts belong to the colluding group. In this case, a copy of the route can be forwarded context by context as long as the succeeding context is member of the colluding group.[4] Then, the last member of the colluding group c_m found in that way is able to order the agent from c_i and can forward it to the honest context c_{m+1} which is not able to detect that contexts $c_{i+1}, \ldots, c_{m-1}$ have been skipped.

Even if such an attack is possible, accomplices $c_i, \ldots, c_{m-1}$ are not motivated to act in the described way. In contrast to the atomic encrypted approach, no honest context can become the victim of such an attack.

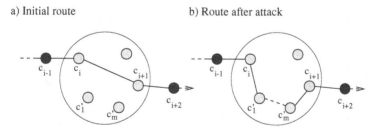

Fig. 2. Attack on onion-like protected route under collusion.

---

[4] The probability for a malicious context to find one of its accomplices as successor in the initial route depends on the number of members in the colluding group, the total number of contexts in the whole agent system and, when using the atomic encrypting approach, the current length of the route. In most cases, with an onion-like protected route, this probability is significantly smaller than in case of atomic encryption.

Instead of skipping dishonest contexts, malicious contexts may try to add new dishonest contexts to the initial route. If there are two adjacent malicious contexts c_i and c_{i+1} in the initial route, c_i can forward the agent via new dishonest contexts $c'_1, \ldots, c'_m$ to c_{i+1} [see fig. 2]. This attack can not be detected by the following honest context c_{i+2}. But again, no honest context can become the victim of such an attack.

The influence of the predecessor's address becomes obvious if one considers a similar attack. Because of the dependence of the signature from the predecessor's address, a malicious context c_i is not able to forward the agent via accomplices $c'_1, \ldots, c'_m$ to an honest context c_{i+1} [see fig. 3].

a) Initial route   b) Route after attack

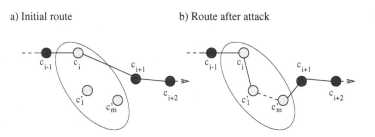

Fig. 3. Detectable attack on onion-like protected route under collusion.

To sum it up and to illustrate the strength of the protection scheme, neither

- skipping of honest working contexts, nor
- replacing honest working contexts by new contexts, nor
- adding honest contexts

is feasible without being detected afterwards, either by an honest working context or by the home context.

Of course, visited working contexts are able to exchange information about agents (predecessors, successors) *a posteriori* to perform route analysis and to obtain information about the visited contexts. For example, a malicious working context c_i can broadcast to all its accomplices that it was visited by a concrete agent with predecessor c_{i-1} and successor c_{i+1}. If the agent later visits a collaborating context c_j, this context can reply its predecessor c_{j-1} and successor c_{j+1} to context c_i. The larger the number of members in the colluding group, the higher the probability becomes that at least one accomplice is member of the initial route. But with growing probability this attack becomes more and more costly, because of the increasing number of candidates to which the agent information has to be forwarded. Without hiding the agent's identity such an attack can never be prevented by means of cryptography.

To summarize the properties of the presented scheme; onion-like encryption provides concealment of route entries at a maximum degree. Without collusions, every attack can be detected as early as possible by the next visited working context. But even under collusions, no honest context can be skipped and no maliciously added or replaced honest working contexts can be visited without being noticed. If the home context receives its agent without an error message, it can be sure that its agent visited all honest contexts in the initial route, and as many addresses as possible are kept secret. Furthermore, every visited honest working context can verify if it is a member of the initial route.

In the following we will examine cases in which routes are legally extended during an agent's journey.

5 Extending the Initial Route

If for providing its service a context c_i on the agent's initial route needs the cooperation with other contexts $c_1^X, \ldots, c_m^X$, then working context c_i should be allowed to extend the initial route in a legal way. Of course c_i should not be allowed to delete unvisited entries from the initial route.

To protect the home context's interests, the new entries do not include any confidential information.[5] On the other hand, c_i may be interested in protecting its new entries. Let $c_1^X, \ldots, c_m^X$ be these new entries. Like a home context, c_i encrypts the new route extension and includes the route extension as a prefix to the current route r:

$$
\begin{aligned}
r^X = \; & E_{e_{X1}}\Big[ip(c_i), ip(c_2^X), S_i\big(ip(c_i), ip(c_1^X), ip(c_2^X)\big), t, E_{e_{X2}}[\ldots], r\big), \\[4pt]
& E_{e_{X2}}\Big[ip(c_1^X), ip(c_3^X), S_i\big(ip(c_1^X), ip(c_2^X), ip(c_3^X)\big), t, E_{e_{X3}}[\ldots], r\big), \\
& \qquad \vdots \\
& \qquad \vdots \\
& E_{e_{Xm-1}}\Big[ip(c_{m-2}^X), ip(c_m^X), S_i\big(ip(c_{m-2}^X), ip(c_{m-1}^X), ip(c_m^X)\big), t, E_{e_{Xm}}[\ldots], r\big), \\[4pt]
& E_{e_{Xm}}\Big[ip(c_{m-1}^X), EoX, S_i\big(ip(c_{m-1}^X), ip(c_m^X), EoX, t, r\big)\Big] \ldots \Big]\Big] \parallel r \qquad (2)
\end{aligned}
$$

In contrast to the protection scheme of the initial route, the signature in the extension of the route depends on the extension and on the current initial route r. The new parameter EoX indicates the end of extension. If c_i extends a route it must not delete its successor and the corresponding signature from the current initial route.

Having visited all sites $c_1^X, \ldots, c_m^X$ of a route extension, the presented concept provides that the agent returns to c_i [see fig. 4].

---

[5] The new contexts get just informed that c_i is on the initial route.

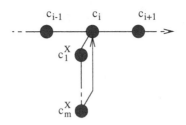

Fig. 4. Extending a route.

When the agent returns to c_i, the context obtains its original part of the initial route and can now decrypt its successor's address and check the signature. If it does not receive the agent from the expected context c_m^X, then it knows that something illegal happened during the agent's journey at the extended route.

The route extension inherits the protection properties of the scheme described in section 4. All signatures in the route extension stem from c_i and the route extension ends with an EoX entry. If a context receives such an EoX entry it sends the agent back to c_i. To detect attacks as early as possible, the remaining ciphertexts of the initial route are included into c_i's signature. Thus, when the agent returns from c_m^X to c_i, working context c_i can be sure, that all honest sites of the route extension have been visited.

The concept of route extension may be extended: each context of a route extension may be allowed to extend the route extension itself as well. In all these cases the presented scheme guarantees that either all honest sites in the initial route as well as all allowed route extensions are visited, or the journey is explicitly aborted because of an attack or a not accessible site.

6   Unreachable Working Contexts

In many systems, the gain of technical data protection conforms with a loss of functionality and flexibility. If a working context c_{i+1} is unavailable, because it terminated regularly/irregularly or the network connection was interrupted, then context c_i, that can decrypt only the Internet address $ip(c_{i+1})$, may not just skip over context c_{i+1}. In such a case, context c_i has to choose one of the following strategies:

- As long as c_{i+1} is unreachable, the agent waits in c_i.
- The agent aborts its journey and migrates back to its home context.
- Having tried to reach c_{i+1} for a certain time, the agent migrates back to its home context.

When an agent aborts its journey, the reason should become obvious to its home context. When the probability to reach a context falls below a certain level, the route protection mechanism should be changed to become more flexible, though from the data protection point of view this may be disadvantageous.

7 Conclusions

In this paper we presented a method for the concealment of an agent's route information. Furthermore, we showed that our method resists all presented attacks performed by a single malicious context. But even under attacks of malicious contexts acting in collusion no honest working context can become a victim. Thus, when receiving its agent without an error message the home context can be sure that all honest contexts have been visited. All working contexts, and naturally also the honest ones, can detect if the home context intended its agent to visit them.

Additionally, in cases a working context needs the cooperation of other contexts for providing a service, the method allows legal route extensions. If a context extends an agent's initial route, having visited all sites of the route extension the agent returns to the context that has extended the route, and proceeds on its initial route. Following this pattern, one can develop several levels of route extension and use the described method for protecting the agent's route against attacks.

8 Future Work

To precisely identify that contexts which ran the attack, more in-depth research is needed. We are also extending our route protection mechanisms to other agent components. Mobile data can be handled similar to routes: at least parts of them must only become accessible to specific contexts. In contrast, the agent's binary code has fully to be decrypted at each site. By using checksums and a kind of third party protocol [13],[14], attacks can be detected and afterwards malicious contexts can be forced to forward correct binary code. Nevertheless such a protocol can not verify if a working context really started an agent. Maybe detection objects [15] ensure this.

References

1. F. Mattern: 'Mobile Agenten', it + ti - Oldenbourg Verlag, 1998, 4, pp.12-17.
2. W. Ernestus, D. Ermer, M. Hube, M. Köhntopp, M. Knorr, G. Quiring-Kock, U. Schläger, G. Schulz: 'Datenschutzfreundliche Technologien', DuD 21, 1997, 12, pp.709-715.
3. S. Berkovits, J. Guttman, V. Swarup: 'Authentication for Mobile Agents', in 'Mobile Agents and Security', Proceedings, Springer Verlag, LNCS 1419, 1998, pp.114-136.
4. D. Chess: 'Security Issues in Mobile Code Systems', in 'Mobile Agents and Security', Proceedings, Springer Verlag, LNCS 1419, 1998, pp.1-14.
5. D. Westhoff: 'AAPI: an Agent Application Programming Interface', Informatikbericht 247-12/1998, FernUniversität Gesamthochschule in Hagen 1998.
6. G. Vigna: 'Cryptographic Traces for Mobile Agents', in 'Mobile Agents and Security', Proceedings, Springer Verlag, LNCS 1419, 1998, pp.138-153.

7. W.M. Farmer, J. Guttman, V. Swarup: 'Security for Mobile Agents: Authentication and State Appraisal', in 'Proc. of the 4th European Symp. on Research in Computer Security', Springer Verlag, LNCS 1146, 1996, pp.118-130.

8. U.G. Wilhelm: 'Cryptographically protected Objects'. Technical report, Ecole Polytechnique Federale de Lausanne, Switzerland, 1997.

9. T. Sander, C. Tschudin: 'Protecting Mobile Agents Against Malicious Hosts', in 'Mobile Agents and Security', Proceedings, Springer Verlag, LNCS 1419, 1998, pp.44-60.

10. F. Hohl: 'Time Limited Blackbox Security: Protecting Mobile Agents from Malicious Hosts', in 'Mobile Agents and Security', Proceedings, Springer Verlag, LNCS 1419, 1998, pp.92-113.

11. M.G. Reed, P.F. Syverson, D.M. Goldschlag : 'Anonymous Connections and Onion Routing', in 'IEEE Journal on Selected Areas in Communication - Special Issue on Copyright and Privacy Protection', Vol. 16, No. 4, 1998, pp.482-494.

12. R. Rivest, A. Shamir, L. Adleman: 'A Method for Obtaining Digital Signatures and Public-Key Cryptosystems' in 'Communication of ACM', Volume 21, Number 2, February 1978, pp.120-126.

13. N. Asokan, V. Shoup, M. Waidner: 'Asynchronous Protocols for Optimistical Fair Exchange', 1998 IEEE Symposium on Research in Security and Privacy, IEEE Computer Society Press, Los Alamitos 1998, pp.86-99.

14. Y. Han: 'Investigation of Non-repudiation Protocols', in 'Information Security and Privacy', Proceedings of ACISP'96, Springer Verlag, LNCS 1172, 1996, pp.38-47.

15. C. Meadows: 'Detecting Attacks on Mobile Agents', Center for High Assurance Computing Systems, Naval Research Laboratory, Washington DC, 1997.

Photuris: Design Criteria

William Allen Simpson

DayDreamer
Computer Systems Consulting Services
1384 Fontaine
Madison Heights, Michigan 48071
wsimpson@umich.edu
wsimpson@greendragon.com (preferred)

Abstract. Historic look at design principles and requirements for a
practical key management communication protocol. Refinement of terms,
threat environment and limitations, and necessary features. Dynamic
computational time and network round-trip time are well integrated with
protocol specification. First use of anti-clogging tokens to defend against
resource attacks.

1 Motivation

Photuris[1] is a session-key management protocol featuring authenticated key
agreement with confirmation, defense against resource clogging, forward secrecy
of the session-keys, and privacy protection for the parties.

Photuris [KS99] was based on currently available tools, by experienced network protocol designers with an interest in cryptography, rather than by cryptographers with an interest in network protocols. Designing and implementing
protocols for an open public network requires consideration of a distributed
threat environment that includes bandwidth limitations and propagation latency, ubiquitous casual packet snooping and malicious interference, as well as
faulty hardware and software implementation errors.

The definitions of protocol features and threats are more stringent than found
in recent survey publications [MvOV97]. Distinctions are made between similar
failure modes that have different causes to assist in analysis and specifying cor-
rective measures. Other distinguishing terminology is used, with the usual de-
notative interpretation, conveying concepts that have more colorful terms (such
as "spam" and "smurf") in the network operations community.

---

[1] "Photuris" is the latin name for the firefly. "Firefly" is in turn the name for the
USA National Security Administration's (classified) key exchange protocol for the
STU-III secure telephone.

Howard Heys and Carlisle Adams (Eds.): SAC'99, LNCS 1758, pp. 226–241, 2000.
© Springer-Verlag Berlin Heidelberg 2000

2 Fundamental Principles

2.1 End-to-End

The ultimate objective of Internet Security is to facilitate direct Internet Protocol (IP) end-to-end connectivity between sensitive hosts and users over the Internet. Users will rely on Internet Security to protect the confidentiality of the traffic they send across the Internet and depend on it to block unauthorized external access to their internal hosts and networks.

Users must have confidence in every Internet Security component, including key management. Without this confidence, users may erect barriers ("firewalls") that impede legitimate use of the Internet, or forego the Internet entirely.

2.2 Keys

Internet Security must not place any significance on the easily forged IP Source field. It relies instead on proof of possession of secret knowledge: that is, a cryptographic key.

However, secure manual distribution and maintenance of these keys is often cumbersome and problematic. User distribution often leads to long-lived keys, with concommitant opportunity for compromise of the keys.

2.3 Decentralized

Widespread deployment and use of Internet Security is possible through the use of a key management protocol. For example, Kerberos [KN93] can generate host-pair keys for use in Internet Security, much as it now generates session-keys for use by encrypted telnet and other "kerberized" applications.

The Kerberos model has some widely recognized drawbacks. Foremost is the requirement for a highly available on-line Key Distribution Center (KDC), with a database containing every principal's secret-key. This entails significant security risk.

Public-key cryptography [DH76] enables decentralization. Communicating entities can generate session-keys without real-time communication with any third party.

3 Threat Environment

Photuris establishes short-lived session-keys for Internet nodes that frequently access or are accessed by a large and unpredictable number of other nodes. In addition to stationary wired land-line installations, Photuris is intended to support mobile, wireless and satellite environments. Common activities include creating virtual private networks over the common public Internet, transient connections for mobile users and networks operating over bandwidth-limited links, and commercial transactions between numerous clients and servers.

3.1 Delivery of Messages

The Internet Protocol [Pos81] implements best-effort datagram delivery. Datagrams can be damaged, discarded, or duplicated. Successive datagrams may take different paths through the internetwork, resulting in differences in round trip timing, and re-ordering of the datagrams.

3.2 Eavesdropping

The Internet model of operation [Pos81] assumes that nodes listen to each other on their local network, and that intermediate nodes carry traffic between such networks. Every message will be passively monitored by many other parties.

3.3 Interdiction

An interceptor might selectively prevent the transmission of a correct message from one party to another.

3.4 Modification

An interceptor might selectively prevent the transmission of a correct message from one party to another, and modify the message, before sending it to the latter party. This is sometimes called a "Monkey In The Middle" (MITM).

3.5 Races

An interloper can observe the passage of a message from one party to another, and quickly send a bogus message (to either party), before the next correct message arrives (from the other party). When the transmission path of successive datagrams can vary, this race condition is unpredictable.

3.6 Reflection

An interloper can observe the passage of a message from one party to another, extract important fields, and send another message with those fields to that originating party.

3.7 Replay

An interloper can observe the passage of a message from one party to another, extract important fields, and send another message with those fields to the latter party.

3.8   Resource Clogging

The easiest and most common attack experienced in the Internet is an excessive number of datagrams sent to a target network or node. Processing these datagrams can exhaust the computing resources of a target node. This form of attack often has a randomized, forged IP Source.

3.9   Resource Flooding

A large number of datagrams might exceed the available bandwidth of a link, preventing the passage of legitimate datagrams. This form of attack usually has a sub-network broadcast IP Source. These are difficult to distinguish without knowledge of the specific topology of the (distant) sub-network.

4   Threat Limitations

Internet Security is not a panacea. It is not intended to prevent or recover from all possible security threats. Rather, it is designed to protect against most probable and feasible attacks.

In particular, non-cryptographic attacks are outside the scope of this document. For example, cutting a link, jamming a radio signal, or tampering with a computer device might be important security threats, but are not within the province of a key management protocol.

By the very nature of a key management protocol, the threat of *Interdiction* (3.3) can be reduced to a non-cryptographic attack. Prevention of key management traffic is no more harmful than prevention of normal data traffic. In a secure environment, no normal traffic will flow without successful key agreement.

The *Resource Flooding* (3.9) denial of service attack (exceeding the bandwidth of a link) is another non-cryptographic attack. These infrastructure attacks are best dealt with through other means, such as [BCC+98]. However, the use of Internet Security firewalls around vulnerable links (between links of significantly different bandwidth) can change the effect of the attack to *Resource Clogging* (3.8), where Internet Security provides a tractable solution.

4.1   Anonymity

Internet Security is not expected to function in an environment where the identities of the principals are concealed from each other. Authenticated key agreement is antithetical to promiscuously accepting "anonymous" null and/or unverifiable identities.

The effectiveness of any provision of anonymity is unknown. Some folks have asserted that traffic analysis is sufficiently thorough to determine the parties to any transaction. Unfortunately, thus far these analysts have refused to give concrete details.

4.2   Multicast

Key management is more difficult in a multicast environment. The IP Destination indicates a potentially large and disparate group, rather than a single node.

Senders to a multicast group may share common a Security Parameters Index (SPI), when all communications are using the same security configuration parameters. In this case, the receiver only knows that the message came from a node knowing the SPI for the group, and cannot authenticate which member of the group sent the datagram.

Multicast groups may also use a separate SPI value for each IP Source. As each sender is keyed separately, data origin authentication is also provided.

A participating node is not necessarily in control of the SPI selection process. A single node or cooperating subset of the multicast group may work on behalf of the entire group to set up a Security Association.

It is anticipated that Photuris would be used first to establish a distribution SPI and session-key, and that another orthogonal key distribution mechanism will use that SPI to send the group keys. This is a matter for future research. Such mechanisms are outside the scope of this document.

4.3   Multi-user Hostility

Internet Security protects against threats that come from the external network, not from mutually suspicious users of the nodes themselves. In essence, this is another non-cryptographic mode of attack that warrants further elaboration:

- A secure multi-user operating system is able to protect its resources from hostile users, and prevent one hostile user from damaging the resources controlled by another user.
- A secure multi-user operating system incorporates strong support for user-oriented discretionary access controls.
- If the operating system has any security vulnerability, such that internal information may be revealed or the information of one user may be inadvertently disclosed to another user, then there is no basis for separate user-oriented key management.

It has been suggested that the Photuris exchange could also be established between particular application or transport processes associated with a user of a node. This is a matter for future research. Such mechanisms are outside the scope of this document.

Successful use of application, transport or user-oriented keying requires a significant level of operating system support. Use of multi-user segregated exchanges likely requires added functionality in the transport API of the implementation operating system. Such mechanisms are emphatically outside the scope of this document.

5 Design Requirements

The fundamental role of this key management protocol is to verify the values exchanged, while ensuring that the resulting keys are not known by another party.

5.1 Strength

It is required that it be computationally infeasible for any unintended party to discover the mutually computed shared-secret during the lifetime of the key management exchange.

While it might seem obvious that a computer security protocol must be computationally secure, this requirement defines the extent of its cryptographic strength. That is, the minimal requirement is related to the lifetime of the ephemeral exchange itself, although other goals might extend the desired lifetime. There is no requirement that the strength be effectively infinite. Typical exchange lifetimes are measured in minutes or hours.

When coupled with the features described later, this minimal requirement imposes conservative design limitations on the exchange messages and key derivation techniques. While it is preferable that the strongest available method be used, a light-weight requirement allows the protocol to be securely deployed in cellular telephones, and other low computational power devices.

In practice, the estimated strength of the computed shared-secret is chosen to match the cryptographic strength of the session-keys for the chosen security parameters. These relative strengths are measured in time rather than entropy. The protocol must transparently support increasing amounts of entropy corresponding to adversary improvements in computational power.

5.2 Confirmation

Explicit confirmation is required for completion of each phase of the protocol.

While it might seem obvious (to an experienced network protocol designer) that the protocol run is not complete until the parties agree it has completed, there abound numerous examples of theoretical key agreement protocols without this important property. Typical network protocols execute a three-way handshake for both initiation and termination of a communication session.

This requirement ensures that the protocol is robust against duplication, loss and re-ordering of messages, and effectively prevents many reflection and replay attacks.

5.3 Authentication and Authorization

Each party must successfully verify the exchanged protocol values before using any resulting keys.

It has been shown [DvOW92] that secure key agreement must be coupled to authentication. Each party needs assurance that an exchanged key is not shared with an imposter.

In addition to ensuring protocol correctness, this requirement allows the resulting keys to be associated with access permissions and authorization policies. When using asymmetric (public/private key-pair) identities, it is possible that an active interception and modification attack will use entirely valid certificates. Operators should be suspicious when the peer identities are all certified by a single entity, such as the regional security agency equivalent. This attack can only be prevented through rigorous authorization policy enforcement.

6   Design Features

Photuris establishes short-lived session-keys between two parties, without passing the session-keys across the Internet. These session-keys directly replace the long-lived secret-keys (such as passwords and passphrases) historically configured for security purposes.

The basic Photuris protocol [KS99] utilizes these existing previously configured secret-keys for identification of the parties. This is intended to speed deployment and reduce administrative configuration changes.

Photuris is independent of any particular party identification method or certificate format. Support for symmetric key party identification is required to be implemented, and asymmetric key party identification is optionally supported by extensions [Sim99].

In addition to establishing session-keys, Photuris is easily capable of generating high quality unpredictable secrets. This facility can be useful to augment or expand lower quality user symmetric secret-keys, and to substitute for computationally expensive asymmetric public/private-key operations.

Photuris has been designed:

− for frequent exchange of limited lifetime session-keys between parties.
− for associating security parameters with these session-keys.
− to thwart certain types of denial of service attacks on node resources.
− to maximize computational efficiency.
− to scale to a large number of networks and nodes.
− to support the use of a variety of authentication methods, and facilitate the exchange of many identification types.
− to protect the privacy of the parties and the associated security parameters.
− to provide these services with minimal administrative configuration and user effort.

6.1   Forward Secrecy

Many security breaches in cryptographic systems have been facilitated by designs that generate traffic session-keys (or their equivalents) well before they are needed, and then keep them around longer than necessary. This creates many opportunities for compromise, especially by insiders. A carefully designed key management system can avoid this problem.

The rule is to avoid using any long-lived keys (such as a public/private key-pair) to encrypt session-keys or actual traffic. Such keys should be used solely for identification (entity authentication) purposes. Theft of the key used to authenticate key management exchanges might allow the thief to impersonate the party in future exchanges, but itself would not decode any past traffic that might have been recorded.

Session-keys for traffic authentication and encryption should be generated immediately before use, and then destroyed immediately after use, so that they cannot be recovered. Key generation values should not be directly derived from the values of any previous session-keys.

Photuris utilizes cryptographic hashing algorithms for its key generation pseudo-random functions. The initializing data values are carefully arranged to avoid related key analysis.

Session-keys are derived from large, unpredictable data values. At least two of these values are secret:

1. the computed shared-secret. This is based on short-term secret values. In theory, it is possible that the shared-secret could be recovered (computationally) from the publically exchanged values.
2. authentication key(s) associated with the parties. These involve medium to long-term secret values. In practice, it is more likely that the authentication key(s) would be recovered (by theft or coercion) from the parties.

This combination of multiple disparate secret values ensures that computational discovery of session-keys through cryptanalysis of the key management system requires the solution of multiple "hard" problems.

6.2   Perfect Forward Secrecy

Photuris goes to considerable lengths to achieve perfect forward secrecy [Dif90]. When the authentication key(s) are periodically destroyed, and the destruction is sooner than the feasible recovery of the shared-secret, the derived session-keys are not recoverable from the exchange.

This goal raises the desirable strength for the computed shared-secret, to the expected lifetime of the authentication key(s).

6.3   Privacy Masking

Concealing the correspondents from other parties is often desirable for confidential traffic, especially where this would reveal the location of a mobile user. Although each IP datagram carries a cleartext IP Destination, the ultimate destination can be hidden by "laundering" it through an encrypted tunnel. The IP Source could be hidden in the same manner. If the tunnel IP Source has been dynamically allocated, it provides no useful information to an eavesdropper.

Hiding Identities. This leaves the identifying information that the parties send for authentication. The identities can be easily protected using a privacy-key based on the established shared-secret. Message padding conceals variations in identity lengths. This prevents an eavesdropper from learning the identities of the parties, either directly from names in certificates or by checking against a known database of public keys.

> *Nota Bene:* The terminology is a play on words. Masking in computational algorithms is often applied to the hiding or extraction of field values. Masking in social venues is a physical device to hide identity and protect privacy.

This privacy masking is distinguished from party *anonymity* (4.1), where one of the parties refuses to identify itself to the other. Mutual verification of authentication and authorization is fundamental to the security of this protocol.

> *Caveats:* The scheme is not foolproof. By posing as the Responder, an adversary could trick the Initiator into revealing its identity.

The attack requires the adversary to (1) gain access to a physical transmission link and race the Responder, or (2) subvert Internet routing for the same purpose. These attacks are considerably more difficult than passive vacuum-cleaner monitoring. Moreover, unless the adversary can steal the authentication key belonging to the Responder, the Initiator will discover the deception when verifying the exchanged values.

It is not possible for an Initiator to similarly trick the Responder. The Responder will verify the Initiator Identification before returning its own identity.

Inhibiting Cryptanalysis. In addition to more obvious benefits, hiding the message fields inhibits cryptanalysis of session-key generation by reducing the number of known fields.

Also, privacy masking conceals the attributes associated with the visible traffic Security Parameters Index (SPI). Message padding conceals variations in attribute lengths. When multiple transform algorithms are implemented, hiding attribute choices may inhibit traffic cryptanalysis.

Preventing Forgery. In real time transaction environments, such as banking, it can be even more critical that protection be provided against forgery. The confidentiality of the transaction might only be needed for a short period of time, yet protection against forgery will be needed for a relatively long period of time. Hiding the message verification fields prevents an adversary from direct verification of forgery attacks on the authentication function.

However, unlike the Station-To-Station authentication protocol [DvOW92], the security of the message exchange is not dependent on hiding of the verification fields. Instead of unilateral signatures over public values, Photuris uses keying material contributed by both parties. In effect, the derived verification-keys are session-keys for the exchange, and share the property of multiple "hard" problems.

6.4 Resource Defenses

Protecting sensitive data against compromise while in transit over the Internet is necessary, but not sufficient. The network and computing resources themselves must also be protected against unauthorized access, malicious attack or sabotage.

To grant access to authorized users regardless of location, it must be possible to cheaply detect and discard bogus datagrams. Otherwise, an adversary intent on sabotage might rapidly send datagrams to exhaust the node's CPU or memory resources.

Using Internet Security authentication facilities, when a datagram does not pass an authentication check, it can be discarded without further processing. This is easily done with manual (null) session-key management between trusted nodes at relatively little cost, given the speed of cryptographic hashing functions compared to public-key algorithms.

Unfortunately, such a trusted node will have only a fixed number of keys available. These keys will tend to have long lifetimes. This entails significant security risk.

Automatic key management is necessary to generate short-lived session-keys between parties. But, there is a potential Achilles heel in the key management protocol.

Because of the use of CPU-intensive operations such as modular exponentiation, key management schemes based on public-key cryptography are vulnerable to *Resource Clogging* (3.8). Although a complete defense against such attacks is impossible, Photuris features make them much more difficult. Resistance is accomplished with multiple, successive, inter-dependent layers.

Anti-clogging Tokens. Path validation is achieved through the exchange of unique "cookies" in the first phase. These tokens are included as an exchange identifier (M_{IR}) in every subsequent message.

This *Cookie Exchange* (A.1) provides a weak form of message origin authentication and verifies the presence of network communications between the parties, thwarting the saboteur from using random IP Source addresses. The simple validation of these cookies uses the same level of resources as other Internet Security authentication mechanisms.

This forces the adversary to (1) use its own valid IP address, or (2) gain access to a physical transmission link and appropriate a range of IP addresses, or (3) subvert Internet routing for the same purpose. The first option allows the target to detect and filter out such attacks, and significantly increases the likelihood of identifying the adversary. The latter two attacks are considerably more difficult than merely sending large numbers of datagrams with randomly chosen IP Source addresses from an arbitrary point on the Internet.

Caveats: The cookie exchange does not protect against an interloper that can race to substitute another cookie (3.5), or an interceptor that can modify and replace a cookie (3.4). As noted earlier, these attacks are considerably more difficult than passive vacuum-cleaner monitoring. Moreover, unless the adversary can steal the authentication key belonging to the Responder, the Initiator will discover the deception when verifying the exchanged values.

Exchange Identifier. The message exchange identifier (M_{IR}) consists of an ordered pair (both cookies). The Responder cookie (c_R) is dependent on a time-variant secret (Kc_R), the Initiator cookie (c_I), an anti-replay exchange counter (C'), and other implementation specific factors. It should not be possible to successfully *Reflect* (3.6) or *Replay* (3.7) an earlier cookie from either party.

Exchange State. In addition to the obvious benefits, path validation inhibits exhaustion of memory and storage resources. No storage state is created in the Responder until after a successful three-way handshake.

Validating Messages. Initial integrity checking of every message is provided by the UDP [Pos80] length and checksum, inhibiting casual message *Modification* (3.4). In the later phases of the exchange (A.3, A.4, A.5), the combination of the privacy mask with checking of the message padding values prevents appending modification. Chaining of successive verification values in calculation of message validation and resulting session keys aids in preventing *Reflection* (3.6) and *Replay* (3.7).

6.5 Scalability

A common predilection in the theoretical cryptological community is an expressed desire to eliminate "interactiveness", and otherwise minimize the number of messages between parties. That appears to arise from the unwarranted assumption this would reduce the opportunity for interference.

However, in the Internet Security environment, an adversary that can interfere with any message can probably interfere with all of the messages. The key management protocol can only protect against late comers through verification of the whole message exchange.

Pacing Messages. Interactivity can distribute computations over time, utilizing inherent latency associated with geographic network topology. For a local network, there are few nodes with low latency between them. As the network environment expands, so does the round-trip time of the message exchanges, affording an opportunity to employ larger computational effort between passes, or to support a larger number of nodes with the same effort.

In Photuris, each computationally expensive operation involves a separate message. As computational or network resources are available, the message pacing naturally varies, and prevents synchronization between multiple Photuris exchanges.

Reduced Computation. In addition to the obvious benefits, this arrangement grants an opportunity for pre-computation of a public-value to be used in multiple closely spaced Photuris exchanges. The pre-computed value can be sent immediately, allowing parallel computation of the resulting shared-secret during the round-trip time.

6.6 Simplicity

The hallmark of successful Internet protocols is that they are relatively simple. This aids in analysis of the protocol design, improves implementation interoperability, and reduces operational considerations.

In Photuris, each message has a single purpose. Message fields are organized in the order that they are processed. Similar message fields appear in the same order in each message.

No more than one optional feature is included in any message, and such options are listed at the end of the message. The format of options is the same as in other Internet protocols, so that implementation code is familiar and can be re-used from other projects.

Although abundant combinations of algorithms offer great flexibility, only a few have been selected for inclusion in the underlying protocol. Choosing these selected schemes in advance allows intensive review of characteristics and potential interactions. This analysis can promote confidence in the security of the implementations.

7 Conclusion

Photuris provides a scalable solution for session-key management. Comprehensive resource defenses ensure that deployment is robust. Provision of privacy masking and forward secrecy raise a strong barrier against cryptanalysis of the key management system.

The distinguishing terminology developed here is used to clarify *"Photuris: Design Rationale"*. Elaboration on the design of the messages will be found there.

A Message Summary

In Photuris, the traditional Alice (A) and Bob (B) are called the Initiator (I) and Responder (R) instead. The following sections describe an exchange where both parties have asymmetric keys, resulting in a pair of secret identities and associated symmetric secret-keys.

When the parties already have existing secret keys (pre-configured or generated by an earlier exchange), the *Secret Exchange* may be omitted.

The *Secret Exchange* and *SPI Messages* may also flow in the other direction (from Responder to Initiator). Only the Initiator to Responder form is illustrated. See [KS99] and [Sim99] for further details.

A.1 Cookie Exchange

The Initiator begins the exchange. The Responder provides an exchange counter (C'), a list of available exchange schemes (So), and a unique exchange identifier (M_{IR}).

$$(1) \qquad I \rightarrow R : c_I, 0, C$$
$$(2) \qquad I \leftarrow R : M_{IR}, 1, C', So$$

C = previous counter (or zero)
C' = assigned counter (usually $C' = C + 1$)
c_I = Initiator Cookie
$c_R = H(Kc_R, c_I, C', So, Initiator IP Source, \ldots)$
Kc_R = Responder cookie secret
$M_{IR} = c_I \| c_R$
So = list of offered schemes

A.2 Value Exchange

The Initiator selects a scheme (Ss), and completes the initial three-way handshake by returning the correct counter (C') and exchange identifier (M_{IR}). The parties also exchange their public values (g^x, g^y) and lists of available attributes (Ao_I, Ao_R). A shared-secret (g^{xy}) is calculated.

$$(3) \qquad I \rightarrow R : M_{IR}, 2, TBV_I, g^x, Ao_I$$
$$(4) \qquad I \leftarrow R : M_{IR}, 3, TBV_R, g^y, Ao_R$$

Ao_I = Initiator list of offered attributes
Ao_R = Responder list of offered attributes
Ss = scheme selected from So
$TBV_I = C' \| Ss$ Initiator three byte value
TBV_R = zero (reserved)   Responder three byte value

$$VV_I = TBV_I \| g^x \| Ao_I \| TBV_R \| g^y \| Ao_R \| So$$
$$VV_R = TBV_R \| g^y \| Ao_R \| TBV_I \| g^x \| Ao_I \| So$$

A.3 Secret Exchange (Optional)

The parties exchange public keys (K_I, K_R), and secret nonces ($k_{I \leftarrow R}, k_{R \leftarrow I}$) encrypted in those keys. These nonces are combined with the current shared-secret to make high quality symmetric secret keys (Ku_I, Ku_R) to be used in current and future *Identity Exchanges*.

$$(5) \qquad I \rightarrow R : M_{IR}, 6, PSILT_I, PSI_I, E_{Kp''_I}(v''_I, K_I, Mp''_I)$$
$$(6) \qquad I \leftarrow R : M_{IR}, 5, PSILT_R, PSI_R, E_{Kp''_R}(v''_R, X_I, K_R, Mp''_R)$$

$Mp_I'' = $ Initiator message padding
$Mp_R'' = $ Responder message padding
$PSI_I = $ Initiator Party Secret Index
$PSI_R = $ Responder Party Secret Index
$PSILT_I = $ Initiator PSI LifeTime
$PSILT_R = $ Responder PSI LifeTime
$v_I'' = MAC_{Kv_I''}(M_{IR}, 6, PSILT_I, PSI_I, K_I, Mp_I'', VV_I)$
$v_R'' = MAC_{Kv_R''}(M_{IR}, 5, PSILT_R, PSI_R, X_I, K_R, Mp_R'', VV_R)$

$Kp_I'' = H(g^x, g^y, M_{IR}, 6, PSILT_I, PSI_I, [g^{xy}])$ Initiator privacy key
$Kp_R'' = H(g^y, g^x, M_{IR}, 5, PSILT_R, PSI_R, [g^{xy}])$ Responder privacy key
$Kv_I'' = H(g^{xy})$ Initiator verification key
$Kv_R'' = H(v_I'', g^{xy})$ Responder verification key

$K_I = $ Initiator public key
$K_R = $ Responder public key
$U_I = PSI_I \| v_R''$ Initiator party symmetric identity
$U_R = PSI_R \| v_R'' \| PSI_I$ Responder party symmetric identity
$X_I = E_{K_I}(k_{I \leftarrow R})$
$X_R = E_{K_R}(k_{R \leftarrow I})$

$Ku_I = H(M_{IR}, 6, PSILT_I, PSI_I, 5, PSILT_R, PSI_R, k_{I \leftarrow R}, k_{R \leftarrow I}, g^{xy})$
$Ku_R = H(M_{IR}, 5, PSILT_R, PSI_R, 6, PSILT_I, PSI_I, k_{R \leftarrow I}, k_{I \leftarrow R}, g^{xy})$

A.4   Identity Exchange

The parties verify their identities by proving knowledge of the symmetric secrets, and select attributes (As_I, As_R) for the generated session-keys (Ks_I, Ks_R).

(7) $I \rightarrow R : M_{IR}, 4, SPILT_I, SPI_I, E_{Kp_I'}(X_R, v_I', As_I, Mp_I')$

(8) $I \leftarrow R : M_{IR}, 7, SPILT_R, SPI_R, E_{Kp_R'}(U_R, v_R', As_R, Mp_R')$

$As_I = $ Initiator list of attributes selected from Ao_R
$As_R = $ Responder list of attributes selected from Ao_I
$Mp_I' = $ Initiator message padding
$Mp_R' = $ Responder message padding
$SPI_I = $ Initiator Security Parameters Index
$SPI_R = $ Responder Security Parameters Index
$SPILT_I = $ Initiator SPI LifeTime
$SPILT_R = $ Responder SPI LifeTime
$v_I' = MAC_{Kv_I'}(M_{IR}, 4, SPILT_I, SPI_I, U_I, As_I, Mp_I', VV_I)$
$v_R' = MAC_{Kv_R'}(M_{IR}, 7, SPILT_R, SPI_R, U_R, v_I', As_R, Mp_R', VV_R)$

$Kp_I' = H(g^x, g^y, M_{IR}, 4, SPILT_I, SPI_I, [g^{xy}])$ Initiator privacy key
$Kp_R' = H(g^y, g^x, M_{IR}, 7, SPILT_R, SPI_R, [g^{xy}])$ Responder privacy key
$Kv_I' = H(Ku_I, g^{xy})$ Initiator verification key
$Kv_R' = H(Ku_R, g^{xy})$ Responder verification key

$$Ks_I = H(M_{IR}, Ku_I, Ku_R, v'_I, [g^{xy}]) \qquad \text{Initiator session key}$$
$$Ks_R = H(M_{IR}, Ku_R, Ku_I, v'_R, [g^{xy}]) \qquad \text{Responder session key}$$

A.5 SPI Messages (Optional)

Either party may request another set of attributes at a later time, or provide another session-key (Ks_u) to quickly replace one that is expiring.

$$(9) \qquad I \to R : M_{IR}, 8, SPILT_n, SPI_n, E_{Kp_n}(v_n, As_n, Mp_n)$$
$$(10) \qquad I \leftarrow R : M_{IR}, 9, SPILT_u, SPI_u, E_{Kp_u}(v_u, As_u, Mp_u)$$

As_n = Needed list of attributes
As_u = Update list of attributes
Mp_n = Needed message padding
Mp_u = Update message padding
SPI_n = zero (reserved)
SPI_u = Update Security Parameters Index
$SPILT_n$ = non-zero random
$SPILT_u$ = Update SPI LifeTime
$v_n = MAC_{Kv'_I}(M_{IR}, 8, SPILT_n, SPI_n, v'_I, v'_R, As_n, Mp_n)$
$v_u = MAC_{Kv'_R}(M_{IR}, 9, SPILT_u, SPI_u, v'_R, v'_I, As_u, Mp_u)$

$$Kp_n = H(g^x, g^y, M_{IR}, 8, SPILT_n, SPI_n, [g^{xy}]) \qquad \text{Needed privacy key}$$
$$Kp_u = H(g^y, g^x, M_{IR}, 9, SPILT_u, SPI_u, [g^{xy}]) \qquad \text{Update privacy key}$$

$$Ks_u = H(M_{IR}, Ku_R, Ku_I, v_u, [g^{xy}]) \qquad \text{Update session key}$$

Acknowledgments

Phil Karn was principally responsible for the design of the protocol phases, particularly the "cookie" anti-clogging defense, based on network security protocol implementation experience spanning more than 4 years. In 1994, he provided much of the basic design philosophy text, and developed the initial testing implementation.

In 1995, some months after the first working drafts were distributed, this protocol was discovered to have several elements in common with the Station-To-Station authentication protocol [DvOW92]. Private messages with the authors refined the design criteria, although significant differences in emphasis remain.

This paper was originally part of a larger work. For reasons of space limitation, the more detailed latter two-thirds will be forthcoming in *"Photuris: Design Rationale"*.

References

BCC+98.   B. Braden, D. Clark, J. Crowcroft, G. Minshall, C. Partridge, L. Peterson, K. Ramakrishnan, S. Shenker, J. Wroclawski, and L. Zhang. Recommendations on Queue Management and Congestion Avoidance in the Internet. Internet RFC–2309, April 1998.

DH76.   W. Diffie and H.E. Hellman. New Directions in Cryptography. *IEEE Transactions on Information Theory*, IT–22(6):644–654, November 1976.

Dif90.   Whitfield Diffie. Authenticated Key Exchange and Secure Interactive Communication. In *Proceedings of Securicom '90*, March 1990.

DvOW92.   Whitfield Diffie, Paul C. van Oorshot, and Michael J. Wiener. Authentication and Authenticated Key Exchanges. *Designs, Codes and Cryptography*, 2:107–125, 1992.

KN93.   J. Kohl and B. Neuman. The Kerberos Network Authentication Service (V5). Internet RFC–1510, September 1993.

KS99.   Philip R. Karn and William Allen Simpson. Photuris: Session-Key Management Protocol. Internet RFC–2522, March 1999.

MvOV97.   Alfred J. Menezes, Paul C. van Oorshot, and Scott A. Vanstone. *Handbook of Applied Cryptography*. CRC Press, 1997.

Pos80.   Jon Postel. User Datagram Protocol. Internet RFC–768, August 1980. STD–6.

Pos81.   Jon Postel. Internet Protocol. Internet RFC–791, September 1981. STD–5.

Sim99.   William Allen Simpson. Photuris: Secret Exchange. Work In Progress, March 1999. draft-simpson-photuris-secret-01.txt.

Author Index